Daily TRANSFORMATION

By

John Fredericksen

Author of:
Growing in God's Grace
God's Meaning in Matthew

BEREAN BIBLE SOCIETY
N112 W17761 Mequon Road
PO Box 756
Germantown, WI 53022
(Metro Milwaukee)

Copyright, 2017

by

BEREAN BIBLE SOCIETY
N112 W17761 Mequon Road
PO Box 756
Germantown, WI 53022-0756

First Printing 2017

Library of Congress Catalog in Publication Data

    Fredericksen, John
    Daily Transformation
    ISBN 978-1-893874-44-2
    1. Bible. 2. Devotional. 3. Bible Teaching. 4. Title.

Cover art: ©iStockphoto.com/Mkeith813

Printed in the United States of America

TOTAL PRINTING SYSTEMS
NEWTON, ILLINOIS

Introduction to DAILY TRANSFORMATION

We believe the Bible, and believe it is God's will for us to study all of it. The Old Testament records the creation of the world by God, mankind's fall into sin, the depths to which man falls when rejecting God, and divine judgment. It continues to document the Lord singling out one nation through whom He would demonstrate Himself to the world, and provide a Savior who would come to redeem the world. The prophetical books specify divine promises of judgments, a Millennial Kingdom, and God's ultimate victory. Psalms and Proverbs contain exhortations about praise to the Lord and timeless wisdom for man. While written exclusively to and about Israel, the Apostle Paul tells us, "Now all these things happened unto them for ensamples: and they are written for our admonition, upon whom the ends of the world (or ages) are come" (I Corinthians 10:11).

The Gospel Accounts record the coming of Israel's Messiah, the Savior of the world. In these books, a new gospel message, many new higher standards, spiritual opportunities, and promises were given to the Jews. The book of Acts documents Israel's continued rejection of the Lord Jesus Christ. It also reveals a transition away from divine ministry to Israel, and a new ministry to the Gentiles through a new apostle, Paul. Romans 15:4 tells us these are also intended "for our learning" today.

The Jewish epistles, including the book of Revelation, were written exclusively to Jewish saints with a Millennial Kingdom hope, who were promised eternal life, literally inheriting the earth. While written to believing Jews during the Acts era, they will have special information and application to believers during the prophesied seven years of Tribulation. As part of Scripture, these books are also "profitable" for believers in the Dispensation of Grace (II Timothy 3:16-17). Therefore, it would be unwise for us to neglect any of these Jewish books.

As C.I. Scofield wrote in his notes in the book of Ephesians, it is "in Paul's epistles alone we find the doctrine, walk, and destiny of the church, which is the Body of Christ." The truths in these books were written to believers in our present Dispensation of the Grace of God and should therefore be a special focus of study and application.

We believe God intends for us to study the entire Bible and, as we do, He intends us to "rightly divide the Word of truth" (II Timothy 2:15). This means to distinguish what was written specifically to Israel, and what was written to the Body of Christ. However, **we are also to intentionally look throughout all of God's Word to find divine truth that we purposely, yet appropriately, apply to our lives so that we are constantly allowing God to transform us into His image**. Second Timothy 3:16-17 puts it this way, "All Scripture is given by inspiration of God, and is profitable for doctrine, for reproof, for correction, for instruction in righteousness, that the man of God might be perfect (meaning mature or complete) throughly furnished unto all good works." Notice these verses do not stop when telling us all of God's Word is profitable for doctrine. It goes on to say **God intends the student of Scripture to also find reproof, correction, and instruction in righteousness, in all of God's Word**. We might say, God intends His Word to be used in our lives for daily transformation (Romans 12:1-3). We welcome you, as you journey with us through the pages of this book, to not only learn information, but to benefit from examples of faith and failure, and seek to apply God's Word to every day life. Together, let's transition from only studying theories of doctrine, to applying God's truths in a practical way every day. May God use these studies to help you find daily transformation.

—Pastor John Fredericksen

Winter Garden, Florida
June, 2017

DEDICATION

There are many people who have helped to make the pages of this devotional a reality. The writings of C.R. Stam were used of God to help me see the importance of the Apostle Paul's unique ministry and distinctions between Israel and the Body of Christ. The churches where I have ministered through the years have enabled me to spend time in God's Word and slowly develop a writing ministry. My wife, Terri, shared many insights and helped to proofread the rough drafts. Our proofreaders: Charlie Fouche, Roger Massey, Dannette Bradford, and Christine Mulholland provided an invaluable ministry in helping to make needed corrections. Jessica Sadler did a wonderful job of typesetting the final product and designing the front cover and inside pages.

While acknowledging all of the above, I am particularly thankful the men of the *Berean Bible Society* Board of Directors, led by Pastor Paul Sadler. These men saw need for a daily devotional to encourage God's people with daily input from God's Word. When I shared my burden for this project, the men of the board embraced my vision that the content of this book should NOT merely be about producing more information that might merely swell the head with pride over gaining more knowledge. Instead, while seeking to provide meaty content, the thrust of this devotional is to intentionally find daily application that every reader can apply to their life and therein allow God to produce a daily transformation. I thank God for the men on the *Berean Bible Society* Board of Directors for commissioning this book therein making it possible.

May God the Father use the content in these pages to glorify the Lord Jesus Christ therein helping each of us better reflect His image and represent His name. May you see Him each day on our journey together in *Daily Transformation*.

In Christian Love,

Pastor John Fredericksen

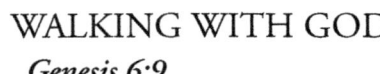

WALKING WITH GOD
Genesis 6:9

It has been this writer's blessed privilege to know a number of very godly people. Among these was Lois, the mother of my best friend in college. She epitomized the "holy women" of old (I Peter 3:1-6) who had a consistent, close walk with the Lord while cultivating genuine godliness from "the hidden man of the heart" (vs. 4). She provided a gentle, godly example to her husband and children. Lois read her Bible daily, prayed often, alluded to the Scriptures, submitted to her husband, gave wise biblical counsel, and was simply faithful.

God intentionally leaves us a written record in Scripture of a number of believers who, likewise, had a consistently close relationship with Him. Genesis 6:9 tells us, "…and Noah walked with God." While the world around him had become so vile that they no longer wanted to "retain God in their knowledge," "changed the truth of God into a lie," and "worshipped…the creature more than the Creator" (Romans 1:28,25), Noah walked with God. His relationship was demonstrated in his obedience to build the ark over 120 years, while likely ridiculed by the lost. Likewise, "Enoch walked with God…three hundred sixty and five years" (Genesis 5:22-24). There must have also been something very close, unique, and consistent about his daily walk with the Lord because "God took him" into His presence (vs. 24), sparing him the pangs of physical death. Levi was "the messenger of the Lord of hosts" through whom Israel was to learn "the [Mosaic] law of truth [that] was in his mouth" (Malachi 2:6-7). He was worthy to be God's instrument of spiritual ministry because "iniquity was not found in his lips, he walked with Me in peace and equity, and did turn many away from iniquity" (vs. 6). Moreover, it appears this "…priest's lips should [or did] keep knowledge [of God's written Word], and [influenced others to]…seek the law at his mouth" (vs. 7). During the early Acts era, Revelation 3:4 refers to "a few names even in Sardis which have not defiled their garments [with sinful conduct], and they shall walk with Me in white [in an eternal state], for they are worthy."

May these examples encourage us likewise to make it our top priority to practice a consistent walk with God. Beginning today, let's purpose to begin each day with prayer, time in God's Word, a practice apart from sin, and consistency–regardless of any hindrances.

AN UNBLEMISHED RECORD
Genesis 6:9

Among the most important places to have an unblemished record is in the American political arena. Over recent decades, winning an election has become less about the issues in one's political platform than it is about the amount of mudslinging hurled at a rival. Consequently, candidates have had to drop out of primary races for the Senate or President of the United States, and many have lost the election when their personal or political conduct has been exposed.

In a Christian's daily walk with the Lord, the need for an unblemished record is just as important. The Lord's description of Noah was that he "... was a just man and perfect in his generations" (Genesis 6:9). The word "just" means lawful or righteous;[1] and the word "perfect" means without blemish, complete, full, sincere, without spot, or undefiled.[2] The Lord was not saying Noah was completely sinless. No one other than the Lord Jesus Christ lived entirely apart from sin. The Lord was saying Noah had an unblemished record of devotion to Him, apart from heinous sins, as he consistently "walked with God." In every dispensation, those who had "the righteousness of faith" (Romans 4:13) were given a positional standing of perfection. Hebrews 10:14 describes it this way: "For by one offering He hath perfected for ever them that are sanctified." Likewise, I Corinthians 2:6 refers to believers when it says, "Howbeit we speak wisdom among them that are perfect..." While we are thankful for this secure standing with God, the Lord also urges believers to maintain a practice of righteous conduct. The "Almighty God" told Abram, "...walk before Me and be thou perfect" (Genesis 17:1). Recognizing this divine expectation, the Apostle Paul's testimony was: "Not as though I had already attained, either were already perfect: but I follow after, if that... for which I am apprehended of Christ Jesus" (Philippians 3:12). In other words, Abram was being urged to genuinely consecrate himself in devotion to the Lord apart from unrighteousness; and Paul was saying he was sincerely pursuing a consistent, godly walk with the Lord.

But how can anyone realistically achieve a life that the Lord would characterize as "perfect"? A perfect walk before the Lord is not sinlessness. It is a mature spiritual walk in genuine devotion and obedience to the Lord. It is rooted in a daily walk with God that chooses to be transformed by His Word, having regular time in prayer, and surrounding ourselves with fellowship that encourages godliness. Make the decision today to intentionally pursue perfection.

7

January 3

CHOOSING A LEADER

Genesis 12:1-4

"In a speech to West Point cadets following the Persian Gulf War, General H. Norman Schwarzkopf put into perspective not only our strength in the military but also our strength in business, church, and family. Addressing the young men and women who will play a leading role in our country's military future, Schwarzkopf said: "In the final analysis, you should never forget that the airplanes don't fly, the tanks don't run, the ships don't sail, the missiles don't fire, unless the sons and daughters of America make them do it. It's just that simple."[1]

Good leaders are hard to find, particularly when one does not know what specific qualities to look for. However, the Lord knows what He is looking for. In the early history of man, our ancestors became so vile that they no longer wanted to retain the knowledge of God in their minds (Romans 1:28). Rather than allow the entire race of man to plummet into eternal punishment, the Lord intervened. He chose one man, Abraham, through whom He would create a nation, Israel, who would be His undeniable testimony to the world, and through whom He would send our Savior, the Lord Jesus Christ. *But why did the Lord choose Abraham?* The prophet Nehemiah gives us the answer saying, "Thou art the Lord God, who didst choose Abram, and broughtest him forth out of Ur...And foundest his heart faithful before thee..." (Nehemiah 9:7-8). Abraham had a faithful heart to believe whatever God told him and to act in immediate obedience. When God promised to make from his seed a great nation through whom He could bring blessing to the entire world, Abram took God at His Word. He obediently "departed" from the heathen in his family to journey to a promised land yet unspecified (Genesis 12:1-4). After years of Sarah bearing no children, he enquired of the Lord how and when God would fulfill His previous promise. In response, the Lord confirmed that Abraham's seed with Sarah would become as the stars without number. "And he believed the Lord; and He counted it to him for righteousness" (Genesis 15:6).

Proper candidates to be used as God's servants must cultivate a similar faithful heart to believe whatever God says, hold His Word as their final authority in all matters, and proceed in obedience. God is looking for a few good men and women. *Will you choose to be one of them?*

8

THE SERIOUSNESS OF SIN
Leviticus 4-5

One only has to listen to the local or national news to realize we are living in a sin-sick world. In America, those who are caught in major crimes usually face serious jail time. Other countries impose far more severe consequences for sinful behavior. For instance, in Saudi Arabia, the death penalty is imposed for "...murder...adultery, drug smuggling, and...under certain conditions [for] rape and armed robbery."[1] Executions are carried out by beheading, firing squad, or stoning, in order to deter these serious sins.

We agree with A. W. Tozer who once wrote, "No one has ever overstated the seriousness of the sin question."[2] Throughout Scripture, the Lord continually seeks to impress upon His children how grievously heinous all sin is in the sight of God. After Adam and Eve sinned, they were cast out of the Garden of Eden with the consequences of pain in childbirth, sustenance through the sweat of the brow, and eventual physical death. Later, Israel was given an intricate system of animal sacrifice to temporarily cover sins (Leviticus 4:27-31; 5:7-15). The guilty party laid their hands on the head of an innocent animal-therein symbolically transferring one's guilt in sin upon the bullock, goat, or turtledove that was to be sacrificed. Its throat was slit, or it's neck wrung, suffering as it died. Some of the blood of this innocent animal was smeared on the horns of the altar; and the remainder of the blood was poured out at the base of the altar. Then the animal was burnt on an altar with the aroma permeating the area. The animal paid the ultimate price; bearing the consequence of the guilty party's sin. Only then would the guilty one have his sins "forgiven him." All of this pictured the Lord Jesus Christ who came to earth for sinful mankind that He might become "the Lamb of God, which taketh way the sin of the world" (John 1:29). As His flesh was torn and His lifeblood was shed for our sins, He became what Isaiah 53:10 describes as "...an offering for [our] sin."

GREAT IN THE EYES OF GOD
Numbers 12:1-13

The gifted athletes of our time have come to be heroes. Mohammad Ali proclaimed himself as the greatest boxer. Jim Brown declares himself to be the greatest running back in football history. Many consider Michael Jordan to be the greatest basketball player of his era. Michael Phelps is widely considered the greatest swimmer of all time. But these sports figures will eventually be largely forgotten. They also pale in comparison to one who is still remembered as the individual the Lord considered to be one of the greatest of His human servants.

Deuteronomy 34:10 pays tribute to Moses by saying, "And there arose not a prophet since in Israel like unto Moses, whom the Lord knew face to face." *But what made Moses such a great man in the eyes of God?* Hebrews 11:24-26 tells us that as a man of faith in Jehovah, when Moses "was come to years" in Pharoah's house, he refused the "pleasures of sin for a season." Instead, he chose to align himself with God's people, the nation of Israel. When the Lord called Moses to be His instrument through whom He would deliver Israel from the bondage of Egypt, Moses thought himself unworthy. This was primarily because "Moses was very meek [or humble], above all the men which were upon the face of the earth" (Numbers 12:3). This attitude of inadequacy was, in large part, what qualified him for service because it helped him rely on the Lord and gave Jehovah all the glory. As God's representative to Israel, whenever instructed by the Lord, he consistently "called for the elders of the people, and laid before their faces all these words which the Lord commanded him" (Exodus 19:7). He did not refuse the opportunity to be God's spokesman, nor did he add to, or take away from, the words of the Lord. Therefore, God described Moses as, "My servant...who is faithful in all Mine house" (Numbers 12:7). Indeed, Moses was faithful, not just for a time, but also for decades, and under many adverse circumstances. Finally, "...the Lord spake unto Moses face to face, as a man speaketh unto his friend" (Exodus 33:11). Moses had a regular and intimate relationship with the Lord.

While we today are not to follow the Law of Moses, we should seek to emulate the qualities that made Moses great. May we purpose to cultivate genuine humility, an intimate interaction with God in prayer, willingness to serve Him, carefulness with His Word, and faithfulness over many years.

FAITHFUL CALEB
Numbers 13-14

Trainer Felicia Foy has an amazing dog, Super Nova, who performs a large array of tricks. On command, Super Nova will walk backward or in a circle, only on his back feet, only on his front feet, or in between her legs as she walks. When Felicia bends over and issues a command, her dog will jump up, balance on her back, and then sit up. When Felicia lies down and raises either one or two feet, at the moment she is instructed, Super Nova jumps onto the soles of her feet, balances, and sits up. Whatever Super Nova is instructed to do, he does without hesitation.[1]

After being successfully brought out of Egypt, the nation of Israel was poised to enter their promised land. At the instruction of the Lord, Moses sent twelve men to spy out the land. When these spies returned, they reported that it was a rich land, flowing with milk and honey. However, ten of the twelve men said, "We be not able to go up against the people; for they are stronger than we…men of great stature…" (Numbers 13:31-32). Undeterred, two of the men, in faith, believed God would give them the land as He promised. "And Caleb stilled the people before Moses, and said, Let us go up at once, and possess it; for we are well able to overcome it" (Numbers 13:30). Unfortunately, the congregation of Israel chose to believe the "evil report." They openly wept, murmured against Moses, complained that it would have been better to remain in Egypt, and began to choose a new leader to take them back into that bondage. When Joshua and Caleb sought again to convince the people that God would give them the land, they would have been stoned to death had the Lord not intervened. This entire generation died in the wilderness for their lack of faith, but not Caleb. God said, "But my servant Caleb, because he had another spirit with him, and hath followed Me fully, him will I bring into the land…and his seed shall possess it" (Numbers 14:24).

God sees and honors those who choose to have a godly spirit of faith, and walk in obedience to whatever the Lord instructs them to do. Even today, these kind of saints inherit the blessing of God in joy and often see Him do great things simply because they choose to fully follow the Lord. Choose to be a Caleb!

WHAT ABOUT THE HEATHEN?

Deuteronomy 4:29

As an unsaved seventeen-year-old, God began to draw the heart of this writer to Himself. A pastor was patient enough to spend several hours answering directly from Scripture a number of spiritual questions I had. Two of these questions were *"What about the heathen in remote parts of the world who may never have the opportunity to hear this simple plan of salvation?"* and *"Will God have mercy on them, or send them into eternal punishment?"* Basically, I was asking if the God who was offering me eternal life as a free gift of His grace was just to every soul.

There are two principles from God's Word that sufficiently answer these questions. Genesis 18:25 asks, "Shall not the Judge [or God] of all the earth do right?" The answer is, "Yes!" God always does what is right. There is never any unrighteousness with God. Whether we understand every circumstance or not, we can trust that this principle is always true. Secondly, God will always sovereignly enable any soul who genuinely seeks the Lord and eternal life to find both. Deuteronomy 4:29 says it this way: "But if from thence thou shalt seek the Lord thy God, thou shalt find Him, if thou seek Him with all thy heart and with all thy soul." Jeremiah 29:13 promises "...ye shall seek Me, and find Me, when ye shall search for Me with all your heart." Similarly, while these promises were directly given only to Israel, we believe it is also a broad principle that has always been true for all people in every dispensation (Ruth, Rahab, and the Ethiopian Eunuch are examples). We believe this because "The Lord is...not willing that any should perish, but that all should come to repentance" (II Peter 3:9). God "...will have all men to be saved, and come unto the knowledge of the truth" (I Timothy 2:4). We believe any lost soul genuinely seeking eternal life will be divinely enabled to find salvation through faith in the Lord Jesus Christ. It may be through a missionary, radio broadcast, or a child of God placed in one's path.

The Apostle Paul assured the Gentiles on Mars' Hill that God "...hath made of one blood all nations of men...that they should seek the Lord, if haply they might...find Him, though He be not far from every one of us" (Acts 17:26-27). You can believe God is just and that He will mercifully save all who genuinely seek Him.

A LOST GENERATION
Judges 2:10-11

This author once read a testimonial from a father who lamented being so consumed with his career that he did not share his faith with his children. The result was that one of his sons plunged himself into a lifestyle of atheism, drug addiction, immorality, and other destructive behaviors. Multitudes of books and websites confirm statistics that people are abandoning church attendance in droves. Some estimate that six out of ten who were raised in sound fundamental churches become 100% spiritually disengaged once they become adults. Clearly, Christianity is in a serious spiritual crisis.

It is amazing that only one generation after the nation of Israel was miraculously given their prosperous "promised land" the next generation was spiritually lost. Judges 2:10-11 describes it this way: "…and there arose another generation after them, which knew not the Lord, nor yet the works which He had done for Israel. And the children of Israel did evil in the sight of the Lord, and served Baalim." Instead of following the Lord and His Word, "every man did that which was right in his own eyes" (Judges 17:6). *How could this have happened after so many blessings and dynamic miracles?* The answer is the older generation, and the men in particular, failed this generation spiritually. Their history was to be life changing and was to be instilled in their young people. God told them, "Only take heed to thyself, and keep thy soul diligently, lest thou forget the things which thine eyes have seen, and lest they depart from thy heart all the days of thy life; but **teach them thy sons; and thy sons' sons;**" (Deuteronomy 4:9). They were to make their absolute top priority spiritual things and teach their children God's Word, including their spiritual history. When they sat in their houses with their families, walked or worked together, retired for the night, or rose for the day, they were to "teach them diligently" the things of the Lord (Deuteronomy 6:7-9). Unfortunately, Israel became spiritually lazy and neglectful in these spiritual responsibilities. The result was that an entire generation was spiritually lost and plunged toward eternal destruction. It did not have to be this way, either.

We who know the Lord must awake to our spiritual responsibilities to bring up our children, and grandchildren, in the nurture and admonition of the Lord. With no excuses, we men need to "man up," making this our top priority. *Will you join the rank of the faithful who pass on their faith to the next generation?*

A WASTED LIFE

Judges 13-16

A rt Schlichter was a star quarterback for Ohio State and the fourth pick in the 1982 NFL draft. He was considered a "can't miss" prospect, but his gambling addiction spiraled out of control. Within a year, he was nearly one million dollars in debt to his bookies who threatened to expose him to the NFL, or worse. He went to the FBI who arrested those who threatened him; however, he ended up being permanently banned from the NFL. His is only one of many stories about gifted athletes who failed to reach their potential due to a series of bad choices.[1]

Samson was also a man who had great potential and opportunities. God chose him to be a judge of Israel in order to deliver his people and lead them into greater godliness. But Samson lived most of his public life in pursuit of self-serving gratifications. God had forbidden Israelites from intermarrying with heathen people. However, when he saw a daughter of the Philistines, he instructed his parents to make arrangements to marry her. They protested, but Samson insisted saying, "…she pleaseth me well" (Judges 14:3). The ordeal ended in disaster when this woman exposed the secret of a riddle Samson presented to her people. Samson left in disgust, and his fiancée was given in marriage to his companion. In anger, Samson slew a great number of the Philistines, who in turn sought to take his life. Samson then violated his Nazarite vow by using the jawbone of a dead donkey to slay his attackers (Judges 15). Later, Samson immorally went in to a harlot (16:1), then again chose a heathen woman, Delilah, as the object of his love. This again ended in disaster. Delilah revealed the secret of Samson's physical strength (16:4-21), and had his head shaved. His strength, unbeknown to Samson, left him. His enemies put out his eyes then imprisoned him while they demanded physical labor from him. Sadly, Samson is an example of spending much of life in self-centered pursuits, and making bad choices, with only intermittent service to the Lord. Samson invested much of his time in things with no eternal value that resulted in unfulfilled potential and wasted opportunities.

Are you like Samson in largely pursuing self-serving goals, making bad decisions in companions, only occasionally serving the Lord, and investing too little in things of eternal value? If so, right now is the time to reverse that trend. By God's strength, start making good spiritual decisions today.

MINE EBENEZER

I Samuel 7

In 1758, Robert Robinson wrote the hymn "Come Thou Fount of Every Blessing." In the second verse, he begins with these words: "Here I raise my Ebenezer." *But what does that mean?* It's meaning is drawn from First Samuel, Chapter Seven. The nation of Israel had just rededicated themselves to "serve" the Lord only; and they were bringing the Ark of the Lord, the symbol of God's blessing, back to Mizpeh. As a result, their enemies, the Philistines, went up to battle against them. After the prophet Samuel sincerely prayed for the help of Jehovah, Israel was given a supernatural victory.

Thereafter, "Samuel took a stone, and set it between Mizpeh and Shen, and called the name of it Ebenezer, saying, Hitherto hath the Lord helped us" (I Samuel 7:12). The word "Ebenezer" comes from the Hebrew words "Eben haezer (eh'-benhaw-e'-zer), which simply means "stone of help." An Ebenezer, then, is a memorial stone that is set up to remind believers that Jehovah has helped and blessed, in the past, and, by implication, that God will help them in the future. Samuel raised up a memorial stone, or an Ebenezer, for the purpose of reminding himself, and all in Israel, of this principle. Hymn writer Robert Robinson wrote that he had done so symbolically. As we sing about raising up our Ebenezer in the hymn "Come Thou Fount of Every Blessing," we are acknowledging that God has also helped us.

We still use memorials quite commonly today. Every gravestone is a memorial to a loved one that reminds us of their love and impact. The exterior of the Washington monument in Washington D.C. is largely made up of stone. It reminds us of the Father of our Country, his astute leadership as General, then his service as our humble first President. Likewise, the Vietnam War Memorial wall is a reminder of the brave men and women whose lives were taken as they fought on behalf of our country. This writer once had a huge ornamental stone in the front yard as a reminder of God's previous blessings and provisions. Today would be a good time to stop and raise your Ebenezer to the Lord by prayerfully thanking God for His divine blessings and intervention in your life. You might enhance this reminder by listing personal answers to prayer, with their dates, in the front of your Bible. Doing so can a reminder that God can still intervene in your life in the days ahead.

IMITATION
I Samuel 8

In a 2016 episode of the television comedy *Last Man Standing*, all the characters dressed up as another family member for a party. They were also to act and talk like the character they were imitating. What ensued was an exaggeration of mannerisms and philosophies to the point where one insult after another was hurled. What began as a fun activity quickly degenerated into hurt feelings, damaged relationships, and a derailed party.

When the sons of Samuel were appointed as judges over Israel, they became corrupt, perverted in judgment, and they "walked not in his ways" (I Samuel 8:3). In response, the people over-reacted by demanding Samuel anoint a king to reign over them. There were, however, several problems with this request. First, they did not try to fix the issues with the corrupt priests. They could have properly addressed their wrongdoings, given them an opportunity to correct their wretched behavior, or simply asked for new godly judges to replace them. Second, they did not inquire of the Lord for wisdom, nor did they consult God's written Word about how to best handle this situation. Instead, they willfully moved forward in human wisdom alone. Predictably, what followed was a disaster. Third, their motive in demanding a king was wrong. Twice they told Samuel they wanted a king to reign over them so that they could be "like all the nations" around them (I Samuel 8:5, 20). It is never wise for believers to seek to imitate the lost. It will lead to unwise standards, practices, priorities, attitudes, actions, and worship. It may help one to "fit in" with the crowd, but God has always intended for His children to be distinctly different from the lost. We are not to be conformed to this world, but to be transformed by the Lord into greater godliness (Romans 12:1-2). We are not to walk as Gentiles (or heathen) walk (Ephesians 4:17), but to be a peculiar people in godliness and service for Him (Titus 2:14). What ensued for Israel was the bondage of servitude to the world, an inept impact on the lost, and a derailed relationship with the Lord.

Who are you seeking to imitate? The primary lesson to learn from this example is to be careful not to imitate the unregenerate world. The Savior would have us imitate Him and those who pattern their lives after Him in godliness. We encourage you to make a conscious decision today to abandon imitating worldly people and standards. Then embrace imitating godliness.

A WORTHY CAUSE
I Samuel 17:29

When America was attacked on 9/11, it shook our nation to its core. Almost immediately, there was a patriotic surge of people voluntarily joining the armed services to defend our country. Among these brave men and women was Pat Tillman, who was making big money as a professional football player. He joined the Army Rangers in 2002 and served honorably until he was killed in Afghanistan. Why did Tillman leave home, family, and a lucrative career? He might have asked, "Is there not a cause?"

Sometimes the more important things in a story become lost in familiarity or voluminous detail. We ask you to see something new and exciting from the old record of David challenging and defeating Goliath. When the Philistines gathered their armies to assault Israel, their champion, Goliath, struck paralyzing fear into the heart of Israel and King Saul. No one would challenge him until young David arrived. Quickly assessing the situation, he was willing to fight Goliath, declaring to all, "Is there not a cause?" (I Samuel 17:29). The answer was, "Yes." God's people, God's promised land, and God's name were being assaulted. Therefore, David volunteered to go to battle against Goliath (vs. 32), and he did so in the right way and for the right reasons. He was willing to fight because this Philistine was willing to "defy the armies of the living God" (vs. 26). In other words, the testimony of Jehovah was at stake, and His integrity had to be defended. David went to battle, not in his own name, but "in the name of the Lord of hosts" (vs. 45). Upholding God's name is always a worthy cause. David was willing to go to battle because he did so, not in the confidence of his own flesh, but confident that God would give him the victory (vss. 37,47). In other words, it would be God's doing, and God would get the glory. Because David had a noble cause, he believed God would bless his efforts. David went to battle with the purpose that a God-given victory would show "all the earth...that there is a God in Israel" (vs. 46). To bring a powerful testimony of the Lord before lost souls was a cause worth fighting for.

We would ask every Christian, "Is there not a cause?" Lost souls need to hear the gospel, people of all ages need to be taught God's Word, and churches need faithful people to advance the cause of Christ. Will you report for duty?

INTERPRETING CIRCUMSTANCES
I Samuel 24

When soldiers are behind enemy lines during war, communication with commanding officers and artillery are critical. During World War II, the U.S. Army directed Privates Ben Yahzee and Charlie Whitehorse to communicate with superiors on the radio using "The Navajo Code." It was based on the Navajo language, containing a code embedded within each message. Even other native Navajo soldiers could not decipher its meaning. Only these two men could properly interpret each transmission and in turn enable their counter parts to act accordingly.[1]

When King Saul saw David as a threat to his reign, he pursued David with an army of trained soldiers, intending to put David to death. David had done nothing to deserve such treatment. He had been a loyal and valuable subject. While David and his men hid in a cave, Saul came in alone. This was David's opportunity slay the one seeking his life and ascend to the throne. His men even urged him to do so, interpreting this circumstance as God fulfilling a promise to David to "...deliver thine enemy into thine hand..." (I Samuel 24:4). However, David was very careful not to haphazardly interpret his circumstances by the counsel of other men, nor by his emotions, which surely would have drawn him into revenge out of self-preservation. Instead, he told his men it would be wrong for him to slay the Lord's anointed king (vss. 6,10). David was wise to choose not to interpret God's will merely by his circumstances. He believed principles in God's Word essentially "forbid that I should do this thing unto my master" (vs. 6). He believed God had already revealed His will in Deuteronomy 32:35-36, when the Lord explained, "To Me belongeth vengeance and recompense... For the Lord shall judge His people..." This meant it would be wrong for David to "get even" with this wrongdoer from within his nation. Instead, David turned Saul over to the Lord and trusted the Lord to take care of his present needs.

In Christian circles today it has become common for believers to almost flippantly interpret God's will by their emotions, the counsel of others, or by circumstances which are often manipulated to one's preferences. There is a better way! Like David, we need to develop a pattern of interpreting God's will by God's Word. We are behind enemy lines in Satan's territory, where interpreting God's will accurately, through Paul's letters, is essential. Trust God's Word to give you clear direction, and then act accordingly.

GREAT MEN
II Samuel 9:1-7

Some leaders of nations are feared, while others are revered (meaning to feel deep respect or admiration). Among the most respected American politicians in recent American history is Ronald Reagan. Thousands stood in line all night to touch his casket; others lined parade routes to express gratitude, affection, and love. Under President Reagan's leadership, the Berlin wall came down, interest rates were drastically reduced, the economy soared, and America was more unified. From a secular viewpoint, even many of his opponents acknowledged he demonstrated qualities of greatness.

When "the Lord preserved David whithersoever he went" (II Samuel 8:6, 14-15), he did something very unusual. "And David said, Is there yet any that is left of the house of Saul, that I may shew him kindness for Jonathan's sake?" (II Samuel 9:1). In those days, it was rare to have a peaceful transition of power. Typically, when a new king ascended the throne, he slaughtered all the family of his predecessor to eliminate divided loyalties and prevent a coup (to regain power). You might say that life insurance for them would have been a "bad risk." But in this case, David went out of his way to show kindness to Mephibosheth, the son of Jonathan, because Jonathan had shown love and kindness to him. Great men will show mercy when they have the upper hand. David also showed mercy because he had promised his friend Jonathan that he would deal kindly with his descendants (I Samuel 20: 11-17). Seeking out Jonathan's family members to show them kindness was a matter of David keeping his word. Great men always keep their word, even when it is to "…his own hurt…(he) changeth not" (Psalm 15:4). David promised Mephibosheth the honor of eating "…bread at my table continually" (II Samuel 9:7). This was more than what his pledge to Jonathan required, but great men will do more than what is required. When David's son Absalom sought to overthrow him, David and many loyal to him had to flee Jerusalem. However, Mephibosheth remained, hoping Israel would anoint him as king (II Samuel 16:3; 19:24-25). Despite his treason and ingratitude, even then David showed him mercy, because great men choose to have compassion.

Is there someone in your life who needs your kindness, mercy, and compassion? We encourage you to give your word to the Lord that you will take action today to demonstrate these qualities to an undeserving soul. Then, show greatness by keeping your word.

GOD'S REFINING PROCESS
Job 23:10

In 1978, doctors discovered cancer in the left eye of Ron Hamilton and determined his eye needed to be removed. Just before going into surgery, a comforting verse came to Ron's mind that later became the theme for a song he wrote, "Rejoice in the Lord." It states, "God never moves without purpose or plan when trying His servant and molding a man. Give thanks to the Lord, though your testing seems long. In darkness He giveth a song. Rejoice in the Lord. He makes no mistake; He knoweth the end of each path that I take. For when I am tried and purified, I shall come forth as gold."[1]

Many of us have wondered why a path of trial, heartache, or physical hardship has entered our lives. Part of the answer is found in the life of Job. In a brutal attack from Satan, faithful and godly Job lost his children, wealth, and his health. With agonizing boils from the crown of his head to the soles of his feet, he sat in misery, scraping his sores with a broken clay pot. His wife urged him to curse God and die. His friends who came to comfort him accused him of being punished by God for some hidden sin, which was not the case. For a time, in his discouragement and despair, he "felt" as if God had abandoned him. He said, "Oh that I knew where I might find Him...Behold, I go forward, but He is not there, and backward, but I cannot perceive Him" (Job 23:3-8). Thankfully, he eventually realized God had made no mistake in allowing his overwhelming circumstances. Like Ron Hamilton, he concluded that God was allowing these painful circumstances to mold him into an even stronger, more godly man. In Job 23:10 he says, "But He knoweth the way that I take: [and] when He hath tried me, I shall come forth as gold." In faith, Job chose to see His painful circumstances as a refining process to remove the dross of imperfections in his life.

God allows trials, not to ruin us, but to refine us. Just as raw materials are transformed into steel by intense fire, God seeks to transform us into His image by allowing trials. Don't despair or distance yourself from God. Allow your trial to draw you closer to Him and remove whatever is unworthy of His name.

COMPLETELY FORGIVEN

Ephesians 1:7

In Iran, it is standard practice for families to oversee the execution of one who murders a family member. They are also given the choice to pardon the offender. On April 15, 2014, Samereh Alinejad watched as a noose was slipped around the neck of Bilal Gheisari, her son's killer. This was her chance to have the vengeance she'd waited seven years to have. Instead, she and her husband stepped forward at the last minute and removed the noose from his neck. It was an act of mercy and forgiveness.[1]

Our family once had a bumper sticker that said, "Jesus paid a debt He did not owe, because we owed a debt we could not pay." That aptly describes the hopeless plight of every human since Adam. We were all born guilty sinners who commit sin every day. Because God is holy, just, and righteous, He cannot allow sin in His presence, nor can He allow sin to go unpunished. This means that our debt of sin set each of us on a path toward eternal punishment in the Lake of Fire. But God intervened. God the Father loved us so much that He sent His only Son, the Lord Jesus Christ, to bear our sin and punishment on the cross of Calvary. Doing so enabled the Lord Jesus to offer forgiveness and eternal life to all who will trust in His payment for sin, apart from anything else. Ephesians 1:7 explain it this way: "In whom we have redemption through His blood, the forgiveness of sins, according to the riches of His grace." The word "redemption" means to ransom in full, or deliver, and "forgiveness" means freedom, pardon, or deliverance. The basis of our pardon and ransom is the blood of the Lord Jesus Christ. Only the lifeblood of an innocent victim can atone for sin. The Savior is the spotless Lamb of God, slain for our sins. In effect, we all stood guilty and condemned with the noose of eternal judgment on our necks, and Christ stepped forward to grant us forgiveness. So full is our forgiveness that we are released from eternal punishment, made acceptable to the Father, given access to His throne, given new abundant life, and showered with "all spiritual blessings" (Ephesians 1:2-12).

With a sense of deep gratitude, we should praise God continually for the complete forgiveness He has given us. *Why not start right now in prayer and song?*

SEEING THE BIG PICTURE
Ephesians 1:8-11

Our grandson is a good learner, but he's not always a willing participant. He'd rather play with his brothers, watch TV, or play video games. When he is called to the table to resume schoolwork, he sometimes complains and asks why he has to do so. At this point, he can't see that what he is learning now is key to him becoming a happy, productive, fully functioning adult. But one day he'll see the big picture and realize how important his early education has been.

In Ephesians, Chapter One, God revealed the big picture of His plan for an eternal state. Previously, "the mystery of His will" (1:9) had been kept secret, but now God pulls back the curtain to reveal His ultimate plan. It is "that in the dispensation of the fullness of times He might gather together in one all things in Christ, both which are in heaven, and which are on earth; even in Him" (1:10). God will fulfill His promise to rapture believers from the Dispensation of Grace into heaven, and then bring seven years of tribulation. This will be followed by the millennial reign of Christ upon the earth. Then the heavens and earth will be renovated by fire to prepare for an eternal state (II Peter 3:10-14). Ephesians 1:8-11 reveals the events that follow. "All things," both in heaven and earth, will be "gathered together," or united, "in Christ." Satan and his forces, now occupying the atmospheric heavens and attempting to thwart the cause of Christ, will have already been banished to the Lake of Fire. The Body of Christ will forever occupy these heavenly realms (Ephesians 2:6-7). All lost souls, and remnants of sin, will be removed, and the redeemed of Israel will occupy the new earth. Both we in heaven and redeemed Israel on earth will happily serve God the Father and God the Son, who will dwell in the New Jerusalem on Earth. Occupants of both heaven and Earth will be united in harmony, joy, service to God, and in willing obedience. This is the big picture of God's plan for eternity; and God's Word declares we who believe have "an inheritance" in this future (1:11).

Do you see the big picture? God would have us realize that the things of this life are not as important as our eternal existence. Those who are saved must prioritize "laying up in store for themselves a good foundation against the time to come…" (I Timothy 6:19). Be faithful!

A CLEAR GOSPEL
Ephesians 1:13

Clear and accurate instructions are vital. After a plane hit the World Trade Center on 9/11, an employee of Aon Insurance Company on the 93rd floor had begun his escape. But he returned to his office because security officers made the announcement that the building was safe, and everyone should stay inside until they were told to leave. Before he died, he spoke to his father on the phone saying, "Why did I listen to them – I shouldn't have."[1]

A disaster took place once Adam and Eve sinned in the Garden of Eden. They plunged the entire human race into the guilt of sin, condemning each one of us to eternal punishment in the Lake of Fire. Our only hope is to be rescued. Unfortunately, there are many voices that send errant instructions, resulting in many who remain confused as to how to find escape from eternal destruction. Some voices say there is no hell. Other voices say you can only escape if you perform certain religious works, or if you are a member of their church. Tragically, some voices garble the message that points to the cross of Calvary as our only hope by saying things like, "Give your heart to Jesus," or "Make Jesus the Lord of your life." It is imperative that we who know Christ as Savior use clear, accurate, biblical words when we persuade others to flee from eternal destruction. Ephesians 1:13 tells us it is a matter of choosing to trust in Christ alone. This verse says, "<u>In whom ye also trusted</u>, after that ye heard the Word of truth, the gospel of your salvation…" We must place our entire **trust** in the Lord Jesus Christ as our only hope for forgiveness and eternal life. "Christ died for our sins according to the Scriptures; and that He was buried, and that He rose again the third day, according to the Scriptures" (I Corinthians 15:3-4). We must **trust** in His death as the payment for our sins and accept eternal life as a "free gift" (Romans 5:15-16,18). We must not trust in our merit, because "…by grace are ye saved through faith; and that not of yourselves: it is the gift of God: not of works lest any man should boast" (Ephesians 2:8-9).

Make sure your presentation of the gospel is clear and accurate. Emphasize that lost souls need to **trust** in the finished work of Christ alone.

MAXIMUM SECURITY
Ephesians 1:13

Abraham Lincoln created the Secret Service on April 14, 1865, the day he was assassinated. Although it was originally designed to discover counterfeit currencies, its agents began watching over president's full time following the 1901 assassination of President William McKinley. In addition to tracking nearly 1,500 presidential death threats each year, and coordinating their efforts with various government agencies, Secret Service agents act as bodyguards. Like the police and military soldiers, Secret Service agents also take an oath to fulfill their duty, knowing one's life may be lost. They are expected to provide maximum security to United States presidents, regardless of personal cost.

We need maximum security in the spiritual realm also. Our Savior did not "take a bullet" for us, but He willingly suffered three nails and a spear, as He laid down His life to ransom lost sinners from eternal punishment. Thankfully, once we trust in the finished work of the Lord Jesus Christ as our only hope for eternal life, we are given complete forgiveness and eternal security. Ephesians 1:13 tell us that at the moment we trust in Christ alone, we are "sealed with that Holy Spirit of promise." It is interesting that God chose to use the word "sealed" to describe how secure we are in our salvation. We are sealed like a vault so that no one, not even Satan, can break in to steal us, God's valued possession. We are sealed like a can of precious fruit so that the outside air cannot damage what is inside, nor can the purchased product spill or be lost. Romans 8:35 confirms this principle, explaining that nothing can "separate us from the love of Christ" —nothing we can do, nor anything that happens to us. We are also sealed like a legal document, identified by a mark made in wax, or by an official signature. The indwelling Holy Spirit is the special agent of God designated with the duty of keeping our salvation secure. From the moment we trust in Christ, His indwelling presence (II Corinthians 1:22; I Corinthians 6:19) is like an authoritative stamp guaranteeing that we are "sealed unto the day of redemption" (Ephesians 4:30).

Don't trust your feelings, your track record of sinful behavior, or what others say about losing your salvation. Trust in what God says in His Word. Scripture states that we are sealed by the Holy Spirit, and promised that we are eternally secure. Rejoice in this truth and share it with someone today.

INTERCESSORY PRAYER
Ephesians 1:16-19

When O.J. Simpson was charged with murdering his wife, Nicole Brown Simpson, and Ron Goldman, he hired a high-profile defense team, often referred to as the "Dream Team." Robert Shapiro and Johnnie Cochran led it. It also included F. Lee Baily, Alan Dershowitz, Robert Kardashian, Shawn Holley, Carl E. Douglas, and Gerald Uelman, with two more attorneys specializing in DNA evidence: Barry Scheck and Peter Neufeld. Their job was to plead the case of their client skillfully before a judge and jury for the purpose of obtaining a favorable verdict.

In many ways, every Christian has a similar duty to become a skilled advocate for other believers, representing them before the Judge of all mankind, Almighty God, and therein seeking to obtain a favorable outcome. In fact, it is our sacred duty. The prophet Samuel told his fellow Jews, "...God forbid that I should sin against the Lord in ceasing to pray for you..." (I Samuel 12:23). We should note that God often answers the prayers of His saints for other believers also. While Peter was imprisoned for preaching Christ, "...prayer was made without ceasing of the church unto God for him" (Acts 12:5). The Lord intervened by sending an angel to release Peter (vss. 6-11). Likewise, the Apostle Paul said that he had been delivered from death when he was persecuted intensely (II Corinthians 1:10), because his fellow saints had been "helping together by prayer for us" (vs. 11). When later imprisoned for proclaiming Christ, he assured the believers at Philippi, "For I know that this shall turn to my salvation (meaning deliverance) through your prayer..." (Philippians 1:19). Also, the Apostle Paul personally and regularly prayed for the needs of others. He told the saints at Ephesus that after he heard of their faith in Christ, he "cease[d] not to give thanks for you, making mention of you in my prayers" (Ephesians 1:16). While Philippians 4:6 assures us we can pray about anything, it is noteworthy that when Paul prayed for others, he primarily prayed for their spiritual growth (Ephesians 1:17-20). We should also follow this pattern when praying for others.

It has been a rich blessing that this writer has had a "dream team" of faithful prayer warriors representing him before the throne of grace in his times of need. I attribute divine protection, provision, and enablement to their intercessory prayer. Today, begin making it a daily habit to pray for the needs of others. Your prayers make a difference!

GOD'S GREAT LOVE
Ephesians 2:1-5

On March 2nd, 2012, as a strong tornado roared through Henryville, Indiana, Stephanie Decker raced down to the basement of her home with her two children. She quickly tied them up in a sleeping bag, and then laid over them to shield them with her body. Seconds later, the house exploded around them. A steel beam crashed down on top of Stephanie's legs, crushing them. The next day, both legs had to be amputated. Stephanie said it was a "small price to pay" because "…my children needed me, so I had to figure out what to do."[1]

Love can motivate people to accomplish extraordinary things. The greatest example of all is the love that God the Father and God the Son had for a world of guilty sinners. Ephesians 2:1 describes all of us in our natural state as spiritually "…dead in trespasses and sins." In ourselves, there is nothing lovable about us. Paul described it this way: "For I know that in me…dwelleth no good thing…(and) how to perform that which is good I find not" (Romans 7:18). By nature, we all walked "according to the course of this world, according to the prince of the power of the air (Satan)…and were by nature the children of wrath" (Ephesians 2:2-3). We all gravitate naturally toward conduct designed by the devil to harden our hearts. Like the tornado that threatened the family of Stephanie Decker, the impending clouds of eternal judgment and God's just wrath were looming over us. Our only hope is the Lord Jesus Christ, and He knew what to do. He bore our punishment on Calvary that we could have eternal life through faith in Him alone. As we read these verses and look at ourselves in the mirror of God's Word, we see that it was indeed God's "great love" (Ephesians 2:4) that saved us from eternal destruction. "For when we were yet without strength…" (Romans 5:6) and "…when we were enemies…" of the Lord (Romans 5:10), "…God commended His love toward us, in that, while we were yet sinners, Christ died for us" (5:8).

We're touched by the love and affection of others. The Lord would have us to be moved by His great love also; and He would have us love Him in return. If you truly love the Lord, tell Him today, and then demonstrate your love by walking faithfully with Him each day.

WHAT WILL HEAVEN BE LIKE?
Ephesians 2:6-7

Here is a glimpse into what to expect in your 40's: Just when the kids are able to cope with life on their own, you are likely to become a caregiver again to your parents. Age will start to manifest itself in your own body. You are likely to develop stubborn belly fat. Your back will ache if you exert it. Your knees will begin to creek, and your feet hurt. Just when you think you can afford to eat out, your doctor will put you on a restrictive diet. About this time, it will dawn on you that you are far from financially prepared for retirement.[1] Now that you are discouraged by these realities, let's take an encouraging glimpse into what your future in heaven will be like.

The Apostle Paul tells us when we trusted Christ as Savior, He effectively "...raised us up together, and made us sit together in heavenly places in Christ Jesus" (Ephesians 2:6). Positionally, our home is already in heaven, and one day we will occupy heaven as our eternal residence. *But what will that experience be like?* By comparing a number of passages, including some relating to Israel's eternal future, we have a glimpse of what heaven will be like for us. First Corinthians 15:52-53 explains we "...shall be raised incorruptible...and must put on immortality." God will give us a new spiritual body that is capable of living in the heavens. "...We shall be like Him (the Lord Jesus)..." (I John 3:2) able to eat, walk, and converse with others. Revelation 21:4 promises that in our eternal bodies, "neither shall there be any more pain." Our existence in heaven will be joyous because we will "ever be with the Lord" (I Thessalonians 4:17). "God shall wipe away all tears...and there shall be no more death, neither sorrow, nor crying..." (Revelation 21:4). Since the disciples instantly recognized Moses and Elijah on the Mount of Transfiguration (Matthew 17:4), it is reasonable to anticipate we will recognize saved friends and loved ones in heaven. The promise in I Corinthians 3:14 is a rich "reward" for serving Christ now. We will also be active in our eternal state. Paul explains that we "...shall judge the world...(and) judge angels" (I Corinthians 6:1-3). This means we will be given a position of authority over these realms, and we will be busy.

Set your affections on these things above, and allow yourself to become homesick for heaven. It will be great!

LIFE WITH PURPOSE
Ephesians 2:10

Testimonies abound online from people who lived life with only self-centered goals and then later realized it was a big mistake. They say things like, "Enough is never enough," "I sold my soul," and "There has to be more to life."[1] Paula Span wrote about Manny, a friend of her father, who made the rounds every day to check on the welfare of his aged friends in his community.[2] A purpose in life higher than himself gave him satisfaction, and it gave him joy. Those without a purpose higher than themselves tend to drift through life aimlessly, often ending up feeling empty and unfulfilled.

The world needs people, like Manny, who work in social causes, such a Meals on Wheels, as volunteer firemen or hostesses at the hospital, as school board members, and as leaders in Boy Scouts or Girl Scouts. However, the plain truth is that unsaved people can fill these positions, and there are usually plenty available. But only the Lord's people can fill the roles of ministry to further the cause of Christ. God's will for all Christians is to fulfill a far higher, nobler, and more urgently needed, Christ-centered purpose in life. Paul puts it this way: "For we are His workmanship, created in Christ Jesus unto good works (relating to serving the Lord), which God hath before ordained that we should walk in them" (Ephesians 2:10). In the local church, there is a constant need for those who know Christ to serve as greeters, nursery workers, and teachers. We can serve meals related to ministry, visit and send letters to visitors, provide transportation, type the bulletin, and canvas neighborhoods inviting people to church. There is a need to give the gospel to lost souls at work, in our neighborhoods, at restaurants, when guests visit our homes, and in every opportunity that comes our way. Our opportunities to minister for the Lord are only limited by our imagination. Willingly serving the Lord needs to become our primary purpose in life.

Even the secular writer Mark Twain wrote, "The two most important days of your life are the day you are born, and the day you figure out why."[3] Beginning today, embrace a Christ-centered purpose in life that will make an eternal difference, and then report for duty to your local church.

BOLDNESS BEFORE GOD
Ephesians 3:12

Even in our permissive and casual world, there are strict protocols for conduct when one meets Queen Elizabeth, the Queen of England. British subjects are expected to bow, or curtsy, as the Queen approaches. One is never to initiate physical contact, a kiss, hug, or even a vigorous handshake. Only if the Queen extends her hand may a subject gently place their hand in her hand. She is also to be addressed as "Your Majesty;" and she is never to be engaged in long dialogue unless the Queen prompts the conversation.[1]

In biblical days, being in the presence of a king was far more restrictive and fearful. When Nehemiah was a servant to King Artaxerxes, and sorrowful after hearing that Jerusalem had been destroyed, the king noticed and enquired why he was sad. Nehemiah wrote, "Then I was very sore afraid" (Nehemiah 2:2). Subjects were expected to be perfectly content in the presence of their Persian king. To do otherwise could be fatal. Similarly, Queen Esther knew, as did all in the realm of the King of Babylon, that if one entered the presence of the king without being summoned, the law of the land required an immediate death sentence, unless the king held out his scepter to extend mercy (Esther 4:11). Thankfully, the King of kings, the Lord Jesus Christ, and God the Father, rule over their subjects today far differently than ancient human kings. Love and grace are the standard of God. The Apostle Paul described it this way: "In whom we have boldness and access with confidence by the faith of Him (Ephesians 3:12). Believers do not have to wait to be summoned into the presence of God. We are free to "…come boldly unto the throne of grace (at any time), that we may obtain mercy, and find grace to help in time of need" (Hebrews 4:16). Believers today do not have to fear wrath, nor retribution, when we enter the presence of God in prayer. We are to come with *boldness* and *confidence*, knowing we have been both invited and instructed to do so. The basis of our confidence is solely in the merits of the Lord Jesus Christ. Therefore, the Almighty God, the Creator and Sustainer of the universe, welcomes us to come to Him continually with unfettered access.

Every believer should be extremely thankful for this kind of liberty and use it continuously. Thank God today for His loving availability, and go to Him frequently for sweet communion. He's waiting for you.

GROW UP
Ephesians 4:15

A January 24th, 2005, *Time Magazine* article entitled, "Twixters," is an investigative analysis of a troubling trend in America. Author Lev Grossman explains that many, aged twenty to twenty-nine, are not kids anymore, but they're not adults either. By looking at a host of statistics, he concludes that "twixters" just resist responsibility and maturity. They party several nights a week, take five or six years to graduate from college, then often don't use their degree in the marketplace, they change jobs frequently, are not married, nor do they have children; and they live in a state of perpetual adolescence. Grossman concludes that this lack of maturity is having profound negative sociological and economic implications.[1]

Similarly, Christians today often do not grow up spiritually. Many have matured very little years after trusting in Christ as their Savior. Paul addressed this problem when he urged the believers in the church at Ephesus to cultivate the practice of "...speaking the truth in love, (that you) may grow up into Him in all things, which is the Head, even Christ" (Ephesians 4:15). Just as parents yearn for their child to grow into full adulthood, character, and responsibility, our Heavenly Father yearns to have His children mature spiritually. Paul's testimony in I Corinthians 13:11 was this, "When I was a child, I spake as a child, I understood as a child, I thought as a child: but when I became a man, I put away childish things." In order for us to grow up spiritually, we must first make the decision to get rid of worldly philosophies, habits, and practices, and then we must replace them with standards that are consistent with God's Word. *But how can I do this successfully so that I might grow in Christ?* It can be summed up by the acronym G-R-O-W. We must **G**et on our knees in prayer, asking for His enablement; **R**ead God's Word daily; embrace that **O**thers need our service for Christ; and **W**ork selflessly to further the cause of Christ.[2] Each of these will help us to grow up in our Savior.

Let me ask you several important questions. *Are you growing spiritually? Do you read your Bible, pray, and work for the cause of Christ more in recent weeks than you did a year or two ago? If not, then ask yourself why not? It is time to "awake out of sleep" and begin to grow into a lifestyle that truly pleases the Lord? Will you make a decision to do so right now?*

SCARED STRAIGHT
Ephesians 4:17-20

A 1978 television documentary narrated by Peter Falk showed juvenile delinquents on a three-hour tour of Rahway State Prison in Georgia. These teens were brought face to face with hardened criminals who screamed, berated, and cursed at these young people as they described what prison life was really like. This program was initiated, as a last-ditch effort, with hardened youth, who were already engaged in criminal behavior, attempting to "scare them straight."[1]

It has always been the will of God for His children to live in a godly way that becomes a testimony to the lost. Israel was told she was "…the salt of the earth…" and to "…let your light shine before men…" (Matthew 5:13,16). Similarly, Paul told believers to "…walk in newness of life" (Romans 6:4), and to "…shine as lights in the world" (Philippians 2:15). Sadly, the pull of the world, the flesh, and the devil is so strong that it often pulls many blood-bought Christians into the path of a very sinful lifestyle. The words of Ephesians 4:17-32 are, in effect, God's effort to "scare them straight." We are told we are to "walk not as other Gentiles (or the unsaved) walk, in the vanity of their mind" (vs. 17). We are to be different, godly, and tenderhearted toward the Lord. Therefore, we are told to "put off…the old man (or nature)…and be renewed in the spirit of your mind" (vss. 22-23). That means to put away lying, anger, stealing, immorality, and filthy language from us. Such things "grieve…the Holy Spirit of God…" (vss. 25-30). The scary thing to realize is that refusing to implement these instructions will gradually harden our hearts and bring dire consequences while we are here on Earth. For those who willfully choose to live as sinfully as the unsaved, Paul explains that their spiritual "understanding (becomes) darkened," they become "alienated from the life of God" as they drift further away from the Lord; and, worst of all, they can become "past feeling" (vss. 18-19). There can come a point were a Christian becomes so hardened that they no longer feel any sensitivity toward the Lord, nor have any interest in the things of God. One can become a self-exiled, spiritual castaway while still possessing eternal life.

Believer, don't let this happen to you! If you're flirting with an ungodly path, allow these verses to scare you straight back into the path of a close, daily walk with the Lord Jesus Christ. If you wait too long, it may be too late.

GIVE NO PLACE TO SATAN
Ephesians 4:27

The ancient city of Babylon was considered impregnable because it had a mighty wall so broad that three chariots could ride abreast. From these walls, archers could decimate invaders. However, Babylon had an Achilles' heel. The Euphrates River ran under the wall providing drinking water and irrigation for crops. Nonetheless, God pronounced the destruction of Babylon due to the sinfulness of the King. Some historians believe that the invading Medes diverted the Euphrates. However, God promised He would intervene by creating "a drought...upon her waters; and they shall be dried up" (Jeremiah 50:38), "...and I will dry up her sea" (51:36). This could describe the invading Medes entering the city under the wall where the water previously flowed, and subsequently conquering the city.

The Apostle Paul warns believers in Ephesians 4:27, "Neither give place to the devil." By this he means we are to leave no open place in our defenses where Satan can gain an easy entry into our lives and destroy our walk with the Lord. Once within the inner walls of our lives, Satan can begin to erect walls, or patterns of behavior, that can readily enslave us. Some of his strongholds include the chains of errant doctrines inflicted by "the sleight of men" (vs. 14) upon those not grounded in God's Word. It includes luring believers into imitating the lost (vs. 17), habits of anger (vs. 26), thievery (vs. 28), filthy language (vs. 29), bitterness and malice (vs. 31). It can include outright immorality, or simply neglecting the things of the Lord. The point Paul is making about not giving place to Satan is that we have a choice. We can either fortify our spiritual defenses against the devil, or leave ourselves vulnerable to his attack.

If you have allowed Satan an open door where he can easily defeat you, there is still hope. But victory can't be achieved in the power of the flesh. "For the weapons of our warfare are not carnal, but mighty through God to the pulling down of strong holds: Casting down...every high thing that exalteth itself against the knowledge of God, and bringing into captivity every thought to the obedience of Christ" (II Corinthians 10:4-5). This simply means the walls of our defenses against Satan will have to be repaired with the mortar of God's Word in our minds, the bricks of continual prayer, and built on the foundation of reliance on the power of the indwelling Holy Spirit. If your defenses have been compromised, begin a diligent rebuilding project today.

TIME MANAGEMENT
Ephesians 5:16

Most of us feel like we're in a real-life Pac-Man game. Our responsibilities are constantly chasing us, threatening to gobble us. While engaged in many things, we know that we must carefully manage our time and then quickly scurry off in another direction. The real trick is knowing where to place our energies and for how long.

The Lord knows we are often conflicted with multiple responsibilities that vie for our time: work, parenting, extended family, house or yard work, paying bills, grocery shopping, schooling, laundry, cooking and exercising for health reasons. These are only the beginning. Then, we also add optional interests such as sports, social outings, volunteer organizations, hobbies, and leisure activities. The Lord knows that managing our time and responsibilities can become difficult to balance. To help us put everything into perspective, He gives us one prominent principle to remember in Ephesians 5:16. We must be continually "redeeming the time, because the days are evil." The word "redeeming" means "to buy." In other words, we must be wisely buying, or using, the time God has given us for things that will matter in eternity. This must be among our very top priorities! There is a very limited amount of time to reach our children with the truths of God's Word, including salvation, while their hearts are tender. We must buy back, or seize, this opportunity. We may have only a small window of opportunity to speak to a lost soul at work before we, or they, are suddenly gone. We must buy the opportunity. If our local church is to survive, it needs our regular commitment to be involved in ministry however we can. We must buy the time to serve in our church while our health still permits us to do so. The truth is that our life will near its end, even in old age, in what seems like a flash. We must buy the opportunities to leave a spiritual impact and earn eternal reward. How tragic that, for many, life will be squandered in selfish, temporal, forgettable things that are of no eternal value. At the Bema Seat we will wish we had chosen to redeem our time with spiritual priorities.

Like sands in an hourglass, our time is running out and may end soon. A wise believer once said, "Only one life, 'Twill soon be past, only what's done for Christ will last." Look at your life carefully. Starting today, *what can you do to better redeem the time?*

UNDERSTANDING GOD'S WILL
Ephesians 5:17

Does this sound familiar? You can't find your keys, so you're sure someone must have moved or hidden them somewhere. Then, your wife finds them immediately, because they were literally right in front of you. Your brain just didn't process it.

Sadly, many view the will of God as a dark, hidden secret or a riddle we must solve. But it is neither. God wants you to know, understand, and follow His will with great certainty. Moreover, His will is in plain sight, right in front of us. That's why Paul tells us two important things about the will of God in Ephesians Chapter Five. First, Paul writes, "Wherefore be ye not unwise, but understanding what the will of the Lord is" (Ephesians 5:17). In other words, *any saint can absolutely understand the will of God with certainty!* Secondly, ***God's will is provable!*** Paul's instructions to the saints at Ephesus were to continually prove "what is acceptable unto the Lord" (Ephesians 5:10). That means that finding God's will is NOT a subjective "feeling" or potentially errant advice; nor is it interpreting our circumstances as His will. No one can "prove" such things to be God's will, even though many make such claims. The only genuine, reliable, undeniable way to prove God's will is to find His clear and unmistakable instructions in His Word.

Here's a worthwhile project to consider: accumulate a list of verses from Paul's epistles that clearly identify God's will for every believer. For instance, it is His will for us to constantly "rejoice," "pray without ceasing," "in everything give thanks," "quench not the Spirit," and "abstain from all appearance of evil," (I Thessalonians 5:16-22). From Titus we know God wants us to deny ourselves "worldly lusts," live "righteously" (2:12), and "be careful to maintain good works" (3:8). We know from Ephesians it is God's will for us to endeavor to maintain unity with other believers (4:3) and forgive their wrongs (4:32). We are never to allow ourselves any kind of immorality (5:3); but we are to live "circumspectly", use our time wisely, and be controlled by the Spirit (Ephesians 5:15-18). You can make your own, more complete, list.

The knowledge of God's will is right in front of us. By remembering unmistakable biblical principles from the Apostle Paul, we can readily understand what God's will is for our lives, prove it to be so, and then go forward in genuine confidence. Whatever decisions you may consider, put it to the test of God's Word.

MEMBERS OF HIS FLESH
Ephesians 5:30

On September 25th, 2016, golfer Arnold Palmer passed away. Reaction poured in from those who knew him personally, and from those who admired him from a distance. It is generally accepted that Palmer did more to popularize the sport of golf than anyone else in history. Someone said, "He's the defining figure in golf." His identity was so intertwined with golf that one could scarcely think of the game without also thinking of Arnold Palmer.

On a much higher and nobler plain, all who have trusted in the finished work of Christ alone for eternal life have become indelibly linked with the Savior. The Apostle Paul described it this way: "For we are members of His body, of His flesh, and of His bones" (Ephesians 5:30). Becoming spiritually part of His flesh and bones speaks to several things. *It is associated with our forgiveness of sins.* When God the Father see us now, even in our present imperfections, He sees only His Son and our righteous standing in Christ. Second Corinthians 5:21 explains, we have been "…made the righteousness of God in Him." Our spiritual union with the flesh and bones of Christ is *associated with our eternal security.* None us can hardly imagine losing an eye, a leg, an arm, fingers, or an ear. We might say, "I'm attached to those things and plan to keep them." Similarly, our connection with the Lord Jesus Christ is so purely close and intimate that He will not sever us from His body. He is attached to us and we to Him in an eternal oneness. Thank God nothing can separate us from Him. No matter what we say, do, think or even if we neglect Christ, we are still part of Him. Being members of His flesh and bones *implies a close identification.* It's like a child being adopted into a family. That child is given a home, love, daily provisions, security, and a name that completely identifies him with the ones who gave him so much. Christians were given these many things in the spiritual realm because we are so closely identified with Christ. There is no closer, purer, or more valuable relationship than the connection that Christians have with their Savior.

Beyond rejoicing in this truth, there is a practical application to remember. Wherever we go, and whatever we do, Christ is with us always. Therefore, we must purpose today to abstain from sinful behavior and walk worthy of Him.

BE STRONG
Ephesians 6:10

There was once a young man who stood in the shadow of a great leader. When that leader passed away, it fell to his young apprentice to pick up the reins of leadership. As he did so, he understandably faced his circumstances with a certain amount of doubts and fears. Then, someone encouraged him to be strong and exhibit courage because God would enable him. The leader was Moses, his apprentice was Joshua, and the encourager was the Lord Himself (Joshua 1:1-9).

Likewise, God challenges believers in the Dispensation of Grace to be strong. Paul told grace believers, "...quit (or act manly) you like men, be strong" (I Corinthians 16:13) and to "...be strong in the Lord, and in the power of His might" (Ephesians 6:10). We must not cower in fear of, nor surrender to, Satan who is waging spiritual warfare against us. We must be strong! *We can do so by remembering God's power is available to us.* Paul prayed that the saints would comprehend "...the exceeding greatness of His power (that is available) to us-ward who believe..." (Ephesians 1:19). The Lord offers us His power, and He wants us to have it. Believe it! Access *God's power "...by His Spirit in the inner man"* (Ephesians 3:16). We can never triumph over Satan in our own strength, but we can find victory when we allow God's power to flow in our lives, in our inner man. Nourish your inner "new man" in Christ! *Our inner man is empowered by equipping ourselves with "the whole armour of God"* (Ephesians 6:11). This can be summarized by choosing to have a consistent daily walk in: truthfulness and righteous behavior as our standard (vs. 14), always being prepared to give the gospel (vs. 15), protecting our minds through an unmovable faith in God's Word (vs. 16), living in the confidence of our eternal victory (vs. 17), using the Scriptures to slice through Satan's lies (vs. 17), and being constant in prayer (vs. 18). Be vigilant in clothing yourself with apparel that enables you to have victory in your daily life!

Paul's admonition is this: "...and having done all to stand, stand therefore..." (Ephesians 6:13-14). *Have you done all you need to do to stand victorious today? Are you remembering that God's power is available to you? Have you been spiritually strengthening your inner man? Will you consistently equip your soul with the whole armor of God?* Be strong, believer! God will enable you if you look to Him for His power to overcome whatever you face today.

CAN'T SLEEP?
Psalm 4:8

After the annual 2014 Cincinnati Thanksgiving Day 10 kilometers race, Julie Isphording, simply couldn't sleep. She'd been the organizer of this race for 12 years. Money raised by this event went to local charities so, to her, it was important this race continued to be successful. Throughout the race, water stops were provided and participants were given free samples of protein bars. But this year, many of the participants didn't just take one protein bar. Many took as many as they could hold in both arms; others filled bags they brought and a surprising number even jumped into dumpsters to get boxes they subsequently filled with the protein bars. This degree of greed greatly upset Julie.[1]

We've all probably not been able to sleep after an upsetting situation. Such a problem isn't new. Even King David implied he struggled with this too. But he found a solution. He concluded it was unproductive and contrary to God's will for us to lose sleep to worry. In Psalm 127:2, David writes: "It is vain for you to rise up early, to sit up late, to eat the bread of sorrows: for so He [the Lord] giveth His beloved [ones] sleep." He found victory over insomnia through applying several biblical principles. David found comfort in his relationship with the Lord, writing: "...know that the Lord hath set apart him that is godly for Himself; the Lord will hear when I call..." (Psalm 4:3). When sleep was fleeting, practicing Psalm 4:4 helped: "Stand in awe, and sin not: commune with your own heart upon your bed, and be still. Selah." The word "selah" means "to pause." Since the psalms were meant to be sung, musicians were to pause at this point in the song. However, we who are reading this Psalm should pause and soak in the truth of verse four. When we can't sleep, the Lord would have us spend time with Him in prayer. *Have you ever considered that one reason why sleep is elusive is that the Lord wants you to communicate with Him in prayer?*

Psalm 4:8 tells us David found victory over sleeplessness. "I will both lay me down in peace, and sleep: for Thou, Lord, only makest me dwell in safety." When you, too, struggle with sleeplessness, don't worry. Spend time in prayer, concentrate on God's greatness, and trust Him to work through your needs.

EXUBERANT REJOICING
Psalm 5:11

My wife and I are blessed with five grandchildren. The oldest, Connor, who is nearly five, was recently told his twin cousins would soon be arriving at our house. As soon as he heard that, he got excited and went to wait at the door. After over a half hour of watching, he was still there. When their car pulled up and Alexis and Sophie got out, Connor threw the door open and ran, squealing loudly with delight, to greet them. The feeling was mutual too, because both the girls ran to him, and they exuberantly hugged one another. Then they walked hand in hand back into the house to play nicely together, at least for a while, if you know what I mean.

Watching this experience got me to thinking about a principle repeated over and over in Scripture. Psalm 5:11 tells us: "But let all those that put their trust in Thee [the Lord] rejoice: let them ever shout for joy…let them also that love Thy name be joyful in Thee." Most believers take joy in family, daily provisions, material things, even their salvation. *But do we rejoice with exuberance and such excitement that we ever shout for joy?* Again we are told in Psalm 32:11: "Be glad in the Lord, and rejoice, ye righteous: and shout for joy, all ye that are upright in heart." Oh, that all of us so loved the Lord and were so excited about Him that, with joyful hearts, we shouted His praises. Lest we dismiss such a practice as a cultural thing intended only for Israel, consider the instructions of the Apostle Paul to the Body of Christ. In Philippians 4:4, he tells us: "Rejoice in the Lord always: and again I say, rejoice." Notice here the instruction is also to rejoice in God Himself. Yes, we can rejoice in His blessings, provisions and promises, but clearly the Lord wants us to rejoice, or find joy, in Him. Just as a parent or grandparent is thrilled to the core when their little one shows great joy in seeing and being with them, God Himself instructs us to love Him enough to be excited and joyful about our relationship with Him. Such a response on our part is desired from the Holy One, not just when things are going well or when we are in a place of worship, but all the time.

How about starting today? Meditate on His love, mercy, longsuffering, and grace, and then praise Him. Now, purposely, "rejoice in the Lord."

HAVE YOU EVER FELT LIKE THE LONE RANGER

Psalm 12:1

It was as a senior in high school that I heard, or at least understood, the gospel for the first time. God's grace not only changed my eternal destiny, it gave me a desire to do right, and totally embrace every truth in Scripture. Grace also gave me a burden to see others saved. But the truth is that, as I attended a secular high school, I often felt like the Lone Ranger. I was the only real Christian in a host of hostile lost people. One experience epitomized such a feeling. In a class discussion about evolution, I was the only one in the room who believed in, and stood up for, biblical creation as explained in the Bible. Of course, student and teacher alike ridiculed me. In that, and other instances, I was the Lone Ranger.

If you've ever felt like you were the Lone Ranger too, you and I are not alone. In Psalm 12:1, David wrote, "Help, Lord; for the godly man ceaseth; for the faithful fail from among the children of men." In verses two through four, he goes on to describe the ungodly speaking words of "vanity" with arrogance because they believed they would always prevail without consequence. Chapter Fourteen goes on to explain there were many who were fools in their hearts and said, "there is no God" (14:1). It seemed to David, when God "looked down from heaven...to see if there were any that did... seek God, (His conclusion was); They are all gone aside...there is none that doeth good, no, not one" (14:2-3). It was enough for even a godly man, like David, to get discouraged.

How was David to get through these conditions without succumbing to utter defeat? There is a simple threefold answer. David continued to look into the "pure words" of Scripture for comfort and strength (Psalm 12:6-7). All of Psalm 73 describes David's struggle with envy over the wicked that prospered. But then he remembered that the end of the wicked would eventually be divine judgment "in a moment" (Psalm 73:19). Finally, David realized: "...in Thy [the Lord's] presence is fullness of joy" (Psalm 16:11). These simple but profound truths comforted and strengthened David, and remembering them can do the same for you.

The next time you get discouraged by the overwhelming ungodliness of our day, remember these things that enabled David to continue on the right path.

"LOVEST THOU ME?"

Psalm 18:1

My wife was teaching in a Christian school when, one day, two brothers came to her class utterly devastated. They were from what appeared to be a solid Christian home. Tragically, they had just learned their father had left his family to live with another woman. The wife and mother could have chosen to be angry, bitter, and hostile. Instead, she made a conscious decision to continue to love her husband and urge him to return home. When divorce papers came, she resisted by again confirming her love and asking him to come home. She and others prayed that God would turn the heart of this man back to his wife and children. After nearly a year, largely because of a decision to love, the husband returned to his family and a walk with the Lord.

Dictionaries and modern media mistakenly define love as a strong affection or emotion. But, at its core, love is a decision. Emotions usually follow later. In Psalm 18:1 David wrote, "I will love Thee, O Lord, my strength." David made this decision because often in the Scriptures the Lord instructed Israel to love Him. The very first of the Ten Commandments is, "And thou shalt love the Lord thy God with all thine heart, and with all thy soul, and with all thy might" (Deuteronomy 6:5). The Lord Jesus explained this was the greatest of all God's commandments (Matthew 22:36-38). Therefore, as God's spokesman, Moses told Israel, "...I command thee this day to love the Lord thy God, to walk in His ways, and to keep His commandments..." (Deuteronomy 30:16). David also implored others to make this decision, saying: "O love the Lord, all ye His saints..." (Psalm 31:23). Today still, it is the will of the Lord for us to decide consciously to love Him. In II Thessalonians 3:5, the Apostle Paul writes, "And the Lord direct your hearts into the love of God, and into the patient waiting for Christ." If love for God were only an uncontrolled emotion, these instructions would be meaningless. But all of these clear commands imply that loving the Lord is a decision, an act of our will.

If the Lord Jesus were physically standing beside you right now, perhaps He would ask the same question He asked Peter three times, "...Lovest thou Me?" (John 21:15-17). If your love for the Savior has waned, make the decision this moment to love Him as before and fervently follow Him.

THE POWER OF GOD'S WORD
Psalm 19

Every time we see a truck hauling products on the high-way, we should be reminded of an important spiritual truth. Each rig, when loaded, contains tons of cargo. Once in a state of movement, it is a powerful force being propelled down the road. But, as big as a truck is, and as much weight as it carries, it is powered by one relatively small thing: a battery. Without this, the truck is virtually useless and isn't going very far. In the spiritual realm, our battery that supplies us with the power to go forward in victory every day is the written Word of God, applied to a willing heart, through the ministry of the indwelling Holy Spirit.

In Psalm 19, David describes the Scriptures in a number of ways. He wrote: "the law of the Lord is perfect" (verse 7a). David realized God's Word is without blemish, spot, or flaw. Therefore, it has the power to work in sinners to produce a "converting [of] the soul" (verse 7). "The testimony of the Lord is sure (certain and true), making wise the simple" (verse 7b). Better than experience or humanistic education, God's Word produces a godly wisdom even to souls with more limited capabilities. David knew: "the statutes of the Lord are right (correct in everything they say, therefore, in a receptive believer, they produce a) rejoicing of the heart, (an) enlightening [meaning to give life] to the eyes" (verse 8). Many times we have seen the light of understanding and joy come on when a believer begins to comprehend great truths from God's Word. It is caused by a deep sense of joy and fulfillment. David continues by saying, "...the judgments of the Lord are true and righteous altogether" (verse 9). Men may scoff in disbelief at the Scriptures, but they are indeed eternal truth and always right. For David, God's Word was "more to be desired...than gold...sweeter also than honey and the honeycomb" (verse 10). He allowed his soul to hanker for time in the Scripture because he valued it so highly.

We need the daily "washing of water by the Word" (Ephesians 5:26) to cleanse our thinking. Time in God's Word, applying it to our lives, is the only way to be "transformed" (Romans 12:2) into a better "image of [God's] Son" (Romans 8:29). May we remember today, and share with another believer, that the source of our power is reading the Scriptures daily.

IN GOD WE TRUST
Psalm 20:7

It is believed the motto "In God We Trust" originated during the Civil War when Reverend M.R. Watkinson urged the Treasury Department to place on its currency a statement acknowledging the Almighty. On March 3, 1865, Act of Congress allowed the birth of our motto. But this motto was inconsistent from 1883 through 1938. "In 1956, the nation was at a particularly tense time in the Cold War, and the United States wanted to distinguish itself from the Soviet Union, which promoted state atheism. As a result, the 84th Congress passed a joint resolution 'declaring IN GOD WE TRUST the national motto of the United States.' The law was signed by President Eisenhower on July 30, 1956, and the motto was progressively added to paper money over a period from 1957 to 1966."[1]

Based on sheer repetition, "trust" is one of the key recurring themes in the Book of Psalms. David often repeated: "In Thee do I put my trust..." (Psalm 31:1;16:1). But, as today, many were not trusting in the Lord. David said, "Some trust in chariots, and some in horses [symbols of military might]: but we will remember the name of the Lord our God" (20:7). Many trusted in mere men. But David wrote: "It is better to trust in the Lord than to put confidence in man" (118:8). Likewise, the Apostle Paul warned against putting "...trust in uncertain riches," urging instead to trust "...in the living God..." (I Timothy 6:17).

The word "trust" means to be confident, carefree, or secure. David's testimony was: "They that trust in the Lord shall be as mount Zion, which cannot be removed, but abideth forever" (Psalm 125:1). His testimony was that his trust in the Lord gave him victory in any situation. He wrote: "...I will not be afraid what man can do unto me" (Psalm 56:11), "He [or I] shall not be afraid of evil tidings [gossip, lies, or threats]..." (Psalm 112:7). His trust in the Lord had banished fear of these things. His confidence in the Lord produced calmness in his spirit. Therefore, he could proclaim in Psalm 5:11: "But let all those that put their trust in Thee [the Lord] rejoice; let them ever shout for joy...."

Today, instead of worrying when troubling circumstances arise, let's choose to trust and rest in the Lord. Let's say with David: "The Lord is my strength and my shield; my heart trusted in Him" (Psalm 28:7).

LOVING CHURCH
Psalm 27:4

It gives my wife and me great joy when the grandkids get excited about coming to our house, when they ask to come and don't want to leave after getting here. It must do the same for the heart of God when His children want to be in His house, or place of worship, and when they stay excited about being there.

When David writes unto the Lord in Palm 26:8, with a joyful heart, he says, "Lord, I have loved the habitation of Thy house, and the place where Thine honor dwelleth." There were ample reasons for David, or any sincere child of God at this time, to be excited about being in the house of God. As we learn from the verse above, he met the Lord there. While the Lord is omnipresent, this was a special place of dedication and identification with the Lord. When David went to the temple, he met his God there. He was excited because it was a time to pray and worship in earnest. Psalm 27:4 puts it this way, "...I desired of the Lord...that I may dwell in the house of the Lord...to behold the beauty of the Lord, and to enquire in His temple." Attendance in a place of true worship was always intended by the Lord to be a time of divine instruction and strengthening. Micah 4:2 describes the future Millennial Kingdom when he writes, "And many nations shall come... to the house of the God of Jacob...and He will teach us of His ways, and we will walk in His paths." Being in the house of God was also a time and place to sing the praises of the Lord with heartfelt joy. David knew this and said, "...therefore will I offer in His tabernacle sacrifices of joy: I will sing, yea, I will sing praises unto the Lord" (Psalm 27:6). We realize the above passages refer to the people of Israel, the program of the law, and a divinely designed temple. Nonetheless, the principles are the same for us even today.

David considered a day in God's courts "better than a thousand" he would spend anywhere else (Psalm 84:10). We should feel the same way too. With David, let's say, "I was glad when they said unto me, Let us go into the house of the Lord" (Psalm 122:1). Let's choose to be excited about our place of worship and be extremely faithful in attending.

WHERE DO YOU RUN?
Psalm 27:5

My wife and I see it almost every day. We have three grandchildren who are toddlers. Whenever one of them falls, bumps their head, or gets a toy taken away, they immediately run crying, with outstretched arms, to mommy or grandma. They know where to find comfort, protection, and healing from what hurts. The truth is, it gives us great pleasure to take them in our arms, kiss their hurts, and sooth their aching hearts. *Where do you run in times of trouble?*

David made it his habit of life to frequently run to the Lord God Almighty when his heart was hurting and life was troubled. He told the Lord, "Thou art my hiding place and my shield..." (Psalm 119:114). In Psalm 27:5 he writes, "For in time of trouble He (the Lord) shall hide me in His pavilion, in the secret of His tabernacle shall He hide me...." He believed His God would care for those who were godly. He wrote, "Thou shalt hide them in the secret of Thy presence from the pride of man..." (Psalm 31:20). His testimony was, "The Lord is my rock, and my fortress, and my deliverer; my God, my strength, in whom I will trust; my buckler, and the horn of my salvation [being delivered], and my high tower" (Psalm 18:2). Every word in this description resonates with deep meaning as David explained why he ran to the Lord often with his problems. Yes, David believed that God would often intervene in his behalf when trials came his way. But he also knew, through experience, that the Lord does not always choose to do so. When this was the case, he realized it was an occasion to find great comfort, strength, refuge, and emotional healing in a deepening relationship with the Great Almighty.

Perhaps David summarizes it best in Psalm 31:23-24 when he writes, "O love the Lord, all ye His saints: for the Lord preserveth the faithful, and plentifully rewardeth the proud doer. Be of good courage, and He shall strengthen your heart, all ye that hope in the Lord." *Where do you run when your heart is hurting?* The next time your heart is troubled, don't try to carry your burden alone or turn to the failing help of man. Instead, run to the Lord! He will comfort and strengthen your soul. He may also choose to intervene in response to your coming to him in prayer.

DON'T GIVE UP
Psalm 27:13

Being in the pastorate can be discouraging. After all, you are an obvious target for criticism. The messages are always too long or too short. You use too many illustrations or not enough. The content is too deep or too shallow. You stand too strongly on biblical truth or not strongly enough, and so it goes. On one occasion, I had a Christian leader harshly dress me down in public for 45 minutes and accuse me of a variety of things I had simply not done. He only thought I had. I left that meeting so discouraged; I just wanted to give up ministry. Thankfully, the Lord sent me encouragement when I needed it most. But being discouraged spiritually isn't exclusive to pastors. All believers encounter this at one time or another.

You can almost feel the sorrow of heart when you read the testimonies of God's men of the past. David wrote: "I had fainted..." (Psalm 27:13). Jeremiah said, "When I would comfort myself against sorrow, my heart is faint in me" (Jeremiah 8:18). And Jonah said, "...my soul fainted within me" (Jonah 2:7). They were so discouraged and spiritually weakened that they simply felt like giving up. Thankfully, these servants of God did not give up, and there is much to learn from what carried them through. Jonah relates he was strengthened when "I remembered the Lord; and my prayer came in unto Thee, into Thine holy temple" (Jonah 2:7). Coupled with obedience to God's will, his discouragement turned when he stayed his mind on the Lord in prayer. Similarly, Isaiah proclaims, "But they that wait upon the Lord shall renew their strength...they shall run, and not be weary; and they shall walk, and not faint" (Isaiah 40: 31). So Isaiah also found it helpful to focus his thoughts on the Lord through prayer. The Apostle Paul had opposition from without and within the company of believers and much to be discouraged about. But, he didn't quit. His testimony was: "seeing we have this ministry...we faint not" (II Corinthians 4:1). He kept his heart focused on serving the Savior. He did so with Galatians 6:9 in mind, "And let us not be weary in well doing; for in due season we shall reap, if we faint not." Simply put, the promise of eternal reward from the Savior strengthened the resolve of this servant. It can for us too.

Are you discouraged spiritually? Don't quit! Pray, focus on the importance of serving Christ, and rejoice in future reward.

CHOOSE TO BE JOYFUL
Psalm 32:1

Abraham Lincoln had a very difficult life. He was born into poverty, and his mother died when he was nine years old. He ran for congress twice but was defeated by Stephan Douglas over the issue of abolition. He married Mary Todd who frequently suffered from great bouts of depression. Three of their children died before adulthood. As president of the United States, he presided over America's awful Civil War. Some observers believed he carried the weight of the nation on his shoulders. Nonetheless, an astounding statement is often attributed to Lincoln: "…folks will be about as happy as they make up their minds to be."

Have you made up your mind to be happy? Believers in every dispensation have been implored by the Lord to choose to be joyful. Old Testament saints were told, "…be glad and rejoice with all the heart…" (Zephaniah 3:14), "Be glad in the Lord, and rejoice, ye righteous: and shout for joy, all ye that are upright in heart" (Psalm 32:11). When Christ taught Kingdom saints who would undergo severe persecution, He said, "These things have I spoken unto you, that my joy might remain in you, and that your joy might be full" (John 15:11). Paul reminds the Body of Christ, "For the kingdom of God is…righteousness, and peace, and joy in the Holy Ghost" (Romans 14:17). Quite simply, it is the will of God for believers to live in a consistent state of joy. *What do we have to be joyful about?* David said, "And my soul shall be joyful in the Lord; it shall rejoice in His salvation" (Psalm 35:9). He also said, "…in Thy presence is fullness of joy…" (Psalm 16:11). Isaiah looked ahead, with focus on a time of future victory from God's hand saying, "…the ransomed…shall return, and come to Zion with songs and everlasting joy…they shall obtain joy and gladness, and sorrow and sighing shall flee away" (Isaiah 35:10). Jeremiah said, "…Thy word was unto me the joy and rejoicing of mine heart…" (Jeremiah 15:16). When teaching His disciples on prayer, Christ said, "…ask, and ye shall receive, that your joy may be full" (John 16:24). If you have eternal salvation, the presence of God within, past and future victories from the Lord, the availability of God's Word, and answered prayer, then you too have much for which to be joyful.

Remember, "…the joy of the Lord is your strength" (Nehemiah 8:10). Today, choose to be joyful and demonstrate it to others.

SEEKING THE LORD
Psalm 105:4

Presently, our oldest grandson, Connor, is obsessed with his red backpack. He stuffs everything imaginable into that thing: toys, clothing, car keys, phones, food, flashlights, eyeglasses, and more. He loves that backpack and vehemently insists on carrying it everywhere. To Connor, it doesn't matter if he's walking, sitting on the couch, riding his bike, or going in the car, his backpack is going with him. Recently, however, when ready to leave our house, he couldn't find it. But he wasn't going anywhere without it. In a frantic panic, he was asking everyone to help him find his precious backpack.

I was reminded of this incident while reading Psalm 14:2, which says, "The Lord looked down from heaven upon the children of men, to see if there were any that did understand, and seek God." From this verse we understand the Lord wants us to continually seek His face in daily fellowship. After all, this was one of the reasons why man was created and placed into the Garden of Eden. Realizing this is one of our primary purposes as designed by the Lord, David urged his fellow Jews, "Seek the Lord, and His strength: seek His face evermore" (Psalm 105:4). He practiced what he preached too. His testimony was, "In the day of my trouble I sought the Lord..." (Psalm 77:2), "I sought the Lord, and He heard me..." (Psalm 34:4). But David didn't just seek the Lord during trying times, nor did he seek the Lord in an on-again then an off-again fashion. He chose to seek Him every day. His testimony was, "One thing have I desired of the Lord, that will I seek after; that I may dwell in the house of the Lord all the days of my life, to behold the beauty of the Lord, and to enquire in His temple" (Psalm 27:4). *What does it mean to seek the Lord?* It begins with a decision. David urged in I Chronicles 22:19, "Now set your heart and your soul to seek the Lord your God...." Then we strengthen this decision when we daily "Seek ye out the book of the Lord, and read..." (Isaiah 34:16) and do as Daniel did, "I set my face unto the Lord God, to seek (Him) by prayer and supplication..." (Daniel 9:3).

Let's choose today to become as obsessed with our relationship with the Lord as Connor is about his backpack. Refuse to go anywhere without making Him your close companion.

A PORTRAIT OF A WISE MAN
Psalm 111:10

In an article entitled "Incompetence," author Stephen Greenspan, Ph.D. recounts an exchange he had with Milton Eisenhower, who was the brother of Dwight Eisenhower, then president of the United States. At the time, Mr. Greenspan considered "Ike" to be a man of only ordinary intelligence because he considered his press conferences to be "inelegant and characterized by tortured syntax." But his brother Milton defended Ike, saying he demonstrated more "common sense" than was common to men or other politicians. After considering several pointed examples, Mr. Greenspan was won over to the conclusion that Ike was indeed wiser than most.[1]

Many of us may have the concept in our minds that in order to be wise we need to be an aged man or woman. But, as far as the Lord is concerned, nearly anyone, including those with more limited years and experiences, can become truly wise. The Books of Psalms and Proverbs give us a vivid picture of a wise individual. "The fear of the Lord is the beginning of wisdom" (Psalm 111:10), so the pursuit of wisdom must be built on the foundation of a genuine reverence of the Lord. A wise individual then "will hear...wise counsels" (Proverbs 1:5), whether it be his "father's instruction" (13:1), or wise "counsel" from others (12:15; 8:33). A wise individual will be one who "departeth from evil" (14:16), and receives "reproof" when warranted (15:31; 17:10). In fact, a wise man will even "love" one who rebukes him so that he might get back on the right track. A wise individual "gathereth [wealth] in [the] summer [of his life, while health and strength remain]" (10:5). A wise individual "refraineth his lips" (10:19; 29:11) rather than saying whatever is on his mind. Finally, "he that winneth souls is wise"(11:30). Therefore, a wise individual seeks to lead many to eternal salvation by faith in Christ apart from all works.

If a portrait were being painted of you using only these positive points describing wisdom, would it be a vivid picture with many detailed lines? What quality, outlined in Psalms or Proverbs, would the Savior have you draw into your character today? Pick one of the above and put it into practice right away and share that goal with another believer.

DOES GOD FEEL DISTANT?
Psalm 145:18

Have you ever felt like God was far away, hiding His face or unwilling to answer your prayers? We have probably all felt that way at times. Even David, the man after God's own heart, sometimes felt that way. He says so in Psalm 13:1. He asks, "How long wilt Thou forget me, O Lord? Forever? How long wilt Thou hide Thy face from me?" Again in Psalm 10:1, David writes, "Why standest Thou afar off, O Lord...?" In the Old Testament era, God had a unique relationship with the nation of Israel. They were to be His special people who would represent Him to a world who did not want to even retain the knowledge of God in their minds (Romans 1:19-32). To be God's effective witness, they were to be a holy people who walked consistently close to Jehovah. When they, too, rebelled in unbelief, God's judgment fell on them to draw them back to the Lord. In this context, God's prophet told them, "...your iniquities have separated between you and your God, and your sins have hid His face from you, that He will not hear" (Isaiah 59:2). But, when God was distant from Israel, it wasn't the Lord who had moved, it was Israel.

We need to learn the lesson that David eventually learned: *not* to trust our feelings, but to trust the promises of God. The Book of Psalms echoes an amazing truth: "The Lord is nigh unto them that are of a broken heart..." (34:18). "The Lord is nigh unto all them that call upon Him, to all that call upon Him in truth" (145:18). Jeremiah 23:23 confirm the same principle: "Am I a God at hand, saith the Lord, and not a God afar off?" So, regardless of what our feelings are telling us, we need to believe God's promise that He is always near and ready to commune with us. Even to the lost, the Apostle Paul told them, "...seek the Lord...though He be not far from every one of us" (Acts 17:27).

Dear believer, God is not far from you. We sometimes drift away from Him. But in His unconditional love, He is always near and ready for close fellowship with those who have trusted Christ alone for eternal life. Believe He is near. Reach out to Him in prayer and read His Word. If you do, eventually your emotions will confirm how close the Lord is. But don't trust emotions—trust God's promises!

GOD SEES IT ALL
Proverbs 5:21

In my sophomore year of high school, my favorite teacher was Mr. Wilcox, who taught biology. During tests or exams, he always had students spread out with empty seats between them. On one occasion, he put a star basketball player, Barry, and me, on the front row. Oddly, he placed the answer key within our view. It was a real temptation. At the end of the hour, the tests were gathered and graded before we left. To our surprise, only the first three questions were correct on the answer key. In effect, Mr. Wilcox was watching to see who would cheat. I was so glad I had resisted the temptation to look on the answer key, and Barry wished he hadn't looked.

Over and over in Scripture, the Lord reminds us that He sees all we do in this life. He tells us in Proverbs 5:21, "For the ways of man are before the eyes of the Lord, and He pondereth all his goings." One of Job's friends, Elihu, grasped this principle. He said, "For His (God's) eyes are upon the ways of man, and He seeth all his goings" (Job 34:21). Through the pen of the prophet Jeremiah, the Lord told Israel, "For Mine eyes are upon all their ways: they are not hid from My face, neither is their iniquity hid from Mine eyes" (Jeremiah 16:17). Jeremiah 32:18-19 explains why God is watching the conduct of all men, "...the Great, the Mighty God, the Lord of hosts, is His name...for Thine eyes are open upon all the ways of the sons of men: to give every one according to his ways, and according to the fruit of his doings." Revelation 20:12 implies God keeps an accurate written record of every individual. When John saw the lost, small and great, gathered before the future Great White Throne of Judgment, he wrote, "the books were opened...and the dead were judged out of those things which were written in the books, according to their works." There must be a similar record for the Body of Christ because each of us will "receive the things done in his body...whether it be good or bad" (II Corinthians 5:10). The issue here is NOT punishment but accountability. "So then every one of us shall give account of himself to God" (Romans 14:12).

Knowing God sees all we do is intended to be a deterrent from doing wrong and a motivation to do right. Live today knowing God is watching.

DO YOU HATE WHAT GOD HATES?
Proverbs 6:16-19

In Mayo Clinic's website article, "Addiction: Social Commentary, I Hate Drugs," is a heartrending testimony from the husband of an addict. He writes, "I HATE DRUGS…Soma is destroying the woman I love, it is affecting our relationship…It is taking the light, the life, the joy out of my woman…I can't do any more to help her see what it is doing to her…I am so deeply in love with her, but I hate this drug." As we read these words, we can understand why he has such a hatred of drugs.

Did you know there are things Christians should hate? In fact, truly loving God necessitates hating what He hates. In Proverbs 6:16-19 the Lord tells us, "These six things doth the Lord hate: yea, seven are an abomination unto Him." "A proud look" is first on the list. Pride was at the root of Satan's fall (Isaiah 14:13) and it will likewise lead to our rebellion. God hates "a lying tongue." Just as the lies of Satan ensnared Adam and Eve with grievous woes, lies still wreak havoc on those who are victimized by lies. "Hands that shed innocent blood" is next. God hates it when greed or power leads to violence or the death of another. "A heart that deviseth wicked imaginations" makes God's list because it leads others into the path of sin and hardness against the Lord. "Feet that be swift in running to mischief" are also hated by God. It is one thing to be overtaken by sin but quite another to intentionally run into the arms of sin. "A false witness" was such a detestable sin under the Law that the Lord instituted divine penalties as a strong deterrent (Deuteronomy 19:16-21; Proverbs 19:5). Perhaps the most heinous of the sins on this list today is: "he that soweth discord among brethren." This surfaces in the form of gossip, character assassination, false accusations, half-truths, attempts to make others discontent, and negativity. Because unity among believers is so precious, yet so fragile, God says He hates this horrible sin, and we should too.

Do the sins in this list sound familiar? If you are practicing any of these, we urge you to stop immediately. If you are tempted to go down this path, don't. When someone seeks to draw you into one of these sins, let them know that God hates this kind of activity. Let's choose to hate what God hates.

A PICTURE OF A FOOL
Proverbs 10:18

For decades, our family has put a large puzzle together over the Christmas season. For us, it is an enjoyable project. It encourages us to take time out of busy schedules to simply spend time together and visit. But there is also a sense of satisfaction as, one by one, pieces of the puzzle are added, and we see a clear picture emerge. In the book of Proverbs, God gives us a clear picture, though an unflattering one, of a fool.

A fool can easily be identified by at least ten characteristics described by King Solomon. A fool "refuseth instruction" to the detriment of his own soul (Proverbs 15:32). He just won't listen when given wise counsel. The "words of the pure are pleasant words" (15:26) but, the words of "a fool's lips enter into contention" (18:6-8) and, it is to his own "destruction." He tends to be looking for trouble and is usually harsh in his words. "He that uttereth a slander is a fool" (10:18). Criticizing others has become his favorite sport. "The way of a fool is right in his own eyes" (12:15) and, "it is as sport to a fool to do mischief" (10:23). He seems to always think he is right and that wrong is right. A "fool layeth open his folly" (13:16) and, perhaps he does so because "the fool rageth and is (over) confident" (14:16). As someone once said: "It is better to be thought a fool than to open your mouth and remove all doubt." Proverbs also conveys the concepts that a fool will not heed reproof (17:10), speaks when he should listen (17:28), will be continually "meddling" to stir up strife (20:3) and "uttereth all his mind" (29:11). This sounds like a busybody who delights to gossip continually about others or inserts themself into the affairs of others

As we look carefully at this picture of a fool, we should each ask ourselves if any of these qualities describe us. If so, we should do something about it. Take one or two of these practices you know you need to work on, ask the Lord to enable you to change your pattern, then ask a godly loved one to hold you accountable in this area. In so doing, allow God to transform you.

THE VENOM OF A TALEBEARER
Proverbs 11:13

The website *The Wartburg Watch 2014,* posts a heart-rending article entitled, "When Pastor's Breach Trust: My Testimony of Betrayal." The author gives her testimony about pouring her heart out to a new pastor as she sought refuge in his church. Some time later, she shared her concern when a convicted pedophile was attending un-supervised. The pastor responded with coldness and curt greetings. Then he contacted her former pastor, divulged confidential information, and later shared the same with others in the church. The result was devastating hurt. We live in an age when slander, gossip, and false accusations are frequent in tabloids. People in the media seem to think they can act this way without consequence. Unfortunately, believers too often mirror this kind of conduct today.

The Bible is not silent on this issue. Proverbs 20:19 describes those who don't keep confidentialities: "He that goeth about as a talebearer revealeth secrets...." This truth is emphasized by repetition. Proverbs 11:13 explains, "A talebearer revealeth secrets: but he that is of a faithful spirit concealeth the matter." It has become commonplace, even in Christian circles and by leaders in ministry, to immediately spread whatever dirt they hear. They often dig for information with probing questions. Proverbs 16:27 describes the character of those who practice this sin: "An ungodly man diggeth up evil: and in his lips there is as a burning fire." It is as simple as that. It is ungodly and sinful to betray confidences, spread rumors or lies, or make in-quiries so one can gossip. The consequences of this action are found in the next verse: "A froward man soweth strife: and a whisperer separateth chief friends" (16:28). Proverbs 18:8 says: "The words of a talebearer are as wounds..." Many have lost friends, and many stop attending churches when talebearers weave their evil web. Once such intentional hurts are inflicted, the relationships are irreparable.

God's solution to this problem is in Proverbs 26:20: "Where no wood is, there the fire goeth out: so where there is no talebearer, the strife ceas-eth." *Have you been guilty of being a talebearer?* If so, honor the Lord by confessing this to your victim. This will deter you from repeating this sin. When others come to you with tales about someone else, tell them you want both of you to immediately call this person to inform them about a rumor being spread at their expense. This will be a deterrent to others. Let's stop the cycle of tale bearing.

LISTEN TO WISE COUNSEL
Proverbs 12:15

In his book, *The Untold Secret That Creates Wealth*, author John Beehner recounts an experience with a successful Christian entrepreneur by the name of John Smith. By the age of 28, Mr. Smith had built a chain of 20 athletic stores. At one time each store was averaging 2 million in sales per year. Then the marketplace began to change with the emergence of Walmart and Kmart. Despite the competition and slumping sales, Mr. Smith pressed forward with expansion. Some advised him to sell while he could make a profit. After things worsened still, he had the opportunity to sell the remaining stores for more than 2 million dollars, but John refused. Ultimately, Mr. Smith was forced to close down completely, while still owing nearly 1 million dollars. If he had listened to wise counsel, he would have been able to remain financially secure.

Three times in the book of Proverbs, God instructs us about the wisdom and necessity of listening to wise counsel from others. Proverbs 12:15 says, "The way of a fool is right in his own eyes; but he that hearkeneth unto counsel is wise." It is a sign of wisdom, humility, maturity, and good sense to listen to and heed good counsel. It only proves us to be arrogant, or a fool, when we refuse. Proverbs 11:14 tells us, "Where no counsel is, the people fall; but in the multitude of counselors there is safety." There is a good reason why presidents and prime ministers have a cabinet and advisers to guide them when making important decisions. Likewise, in wisdom, God ordained that churches be run by a multitude of spiritually capable elders. In both instances, this practice minimizes wrong decisions and provides greater safety for the people they serve. In Proverbs 19:20, the Lord's instructions to us are, "Hear counsel, and receive instruction, that thou mayest be wise in thy latter end." In other words, we are implored to listen carefully to, and learn from, those with wise counsel.

Are you facing an important decision? We encourage you to seek out wise counsel. Wise counsel is not a friend who will only tell you what you want to hear. Wise counsel will tell you what God wants you to hear, and that means its advice will be consistent with biblical principles. When that's the counsel you hear, listen. Doing so will avoid problems, make life easier, and demonstrate godly wisdom.

YOU THINK YOU'RE SMART
Proverbs 12:30

When I was ten years old and my oldest sister, Peggy, was nineteen, I trapped her in her bedroom. She had just gussied up her hair when I appeared with an ice-cold glass of water and threatened to throw it on her. While we both laughed at the prank, she begged me not to throw it on her. I made her get down on her hands and knees, give me compliments, and beg for mercy. After several minutes, I turned as if to leave and show her mercy, then I whirled back around and let her have it. She took it good-naturedly. Through laughter, she said: "You think you're smart, don't you, you little rat?"

In an article entitled: *Average Americans Think They're Smarter Than the Average American*, author Marina Koren says, "Fifty-five percent of Americans think that they are smarter than the average American, according to a new survey by YouGov, a research organization that uses online polling."[1] *How about you? Do you think you are smart?* God's standard for a smart Christian is found in Proverbs 11:30: "...he that winneth souls is wise." There is more than one proper motive for intentionally seeking to lead others to eternal salvation. It could be because we realize doing so is "your reasonable service" (Romans 12:1-2). After all, the Savior endured much to redeem us from sin. It is only reasonable to serve Him in this way. We should also realize this is God's *primary mission* in life for every believer. Second Corinthians 5:18-20 informs us all believers are to serve as "ambassadors for Christ" because He gave all of us "the ministry of reconciliation." This means we are all to see ourselves as "fishers of men" (Matthew 4:19). Seeking to lead others to Christ is NOT just for a select few who have some sort of special gift. *Compassion for the fate* of an eternally lost soul should also motivate us. Jude 23 puts it this way: "...others save with fear, pulling them [with Scripture] out of the fire...." It is also proper to be motivated by *eternal reward*. Daniel 12:3 says, "And they that be wise shall shine as the brightness of the firmament; and they that turn many to righteousness as the stars forever and ever."

If we are truly smart, we'll arm ourselves today with gospel tracts and look for an opportunity to share the plan of salvation with a lost soul.

IT'S THE COMPANY YOU KEEP
Proverbs 13:20

God's Word likewise seeks to convince us of the same principle. When writing to his son about sinners, Solomon says, "My son, walk not thou in the way with them; refrain thy foot from their path" (Proverbs 1:15). Then, he tells him why this is so important in Proverbs 22:24-25, "Make no friendship with an angry man...lest thou learn his ways, and get a snare to thy soul." Further reinforcing this truth, Solomon adds, "He that walketh with wise men shall be wise: but a companion of fools shall be destroyed" (Proverbs 13:20). We might try to convince ourselves that we won't be ill affected by time spent with unwise, or ungodly, people. However, God's Word is consistent and clear about this principle. The Apostle Paul tells us in I Corinthians 15:33, "Be not deceived: evil communications [companionship, association together, or company] corrupt good manners." Before long we will begin to think, talk, and act just like the people with whom we spend our time. You can count on it.

Solomon may have learned to make wise choices in companions from his father, David. His testimony was, "I have not sat with vain persons... with dissemblers...and will not sit with the wicked" (Psalm 26:4-5). David had established a standard by which he chose his friends: "I am a companion of all them that fear Thee, and of them that keep Thy precepts" (Psalm 119:63).

Do you have the right kind of friends, truly godly ones? Allow the Lord to influence you through His Word to avoid ungodly old friends and begin making friends, and spending time, with those who are godly. The decision you make on this issue will have far-reaching spiritual affects for the rest of your life.

IT MAKES ALL THE DIFFERENCE
Proverbs 17:27

We once had a friend named Richard who was a handyman who fixed small motors and engines. He had a faithful dog that kept him company everyday in his shop. This dog followed Richard around like a shadow, jumped to greet him, gave him affection, and acted like she thought he was the best man in the world. One day while observing all this, I complimented the dog. Richard smiled and said, "You know, she's the same every day, and after all these years, she's never complained once."

It's a shame more people don't have the same kind of disposition that Richard's dog had: a good attitude. But it is possible. *Remember God's prophet Daniel?* When Nebuchadnezzar conquered Jerusalem, Daniel, along with others, was taken captive to Babylon. In this process, he was forcibly stripped of his freedom, homeland, name, and, ultimately his manhood (Daniel 1). He was placed in the charge of "the prince of the eunuchs" (1:7), which meant he was castrated to make him a safer subject in proximity to the king and his realm. Daniel could have responded to all these brutal events with anger and resentment, but he didn't. The queen described Daniel as one who had "an excellent spirit" (5:12). It was because of this quality that Daniel had been elevated to "master" of the king's magicians and astrologers. As the king observed Daniel, he elevated him further for his good attitude. Daniel 6:3 states, "Then this Daniel was preferred above the presidents and princes, because an excellent spirit was in him; and the king thought to set him over the whole realm."

A famous preacher once commented that he believed attitude was more important than facts, education, money, circumstances, failure, or skill. It will make you or break you.[1] Proverbs 17:27 says it this way: "He that hath knowledge spareth his words: and *a man of understanding is of an excellent spirit.*" Like Daniel, each of us can make a conscious choice to have a good spirit, or attitude, no matter what our circumstances. We can choose not to complain, be bitter, resentful, or negative. We can choose to exalt our Savior with not just a good attitude but with "an excellent spirit." *Is this going to describe you today?*

RESPONDING TO
BEING WRONGED
Proverbs 19:11

In the Internet article, "How Do You Respond When Someone Has Offended You?" author Brian Ford refers to a deep hurt he experienced. Without specifying the offense or the offender, he related how he became angry toward the person he believed had wronged him. Then, while reading the account of Joseph in Genesis (Chapters 37-40), he states, "God dealt with my heart." After being betrayed and sold into slavery, Brian concluded, "If there was anyone that had just cause to be offended it was Joseph." Yet, when reunited with his brethren years later, when he could have had them imprisoned, enslaved, or killed, Joseph chose forgiveness instead. This biblical example drew Brian away from the shores of bitterness and into the harbor of victorious forgiveness.

Yes, there is a season for everything under the sun, and, sometimes, it is necessary to correct the wrong when we are offended. However, most of the time there are better options. We who claim the name of Christ can choose to have three primary positive responses when offended by a wrong doer. Proverbs 19:11 counsels, "The discretion of a man deferreth his anger: and *it is his glory to pass over a transgression."* The flesh wants to exact our pound of flesh from the one who hurts us or give them a piece of our mind. Yet God says it is a glory (an ornament, beauty, or honor) to let the offense pass without any action. Proverbs 17:14 gives us a wise motivation for not responding to an offence: "The beginning of strife is as when one letteth out water: therefore leave off contention...." The point here is, once open strife begins between two parties, it quickly becomes like raging waters released in a flood. It destroys those in its path and carries them to places they don't want to go. Finally, the best course of all is Ephesians 4:32, "...*Be ye kind one to another...forgiving one another, even as God for Christ sake hath forgiven you."* This step is perhaps the most difficult of all. Yet, like Joseph of old and author Brian Ford, it is possible if we allow God to speak to and control our heart.

How will you choose to respond the next time you are wronged by someone? Purpose now to pass over it rather than giving Satan the victory. When strife has begun, let it end with you, and pray for God's grace to simply forgive them. This would be real Christ-honoring transformation.

I WISH I HADN'T SAID THAT
Proverbs 21:23

One Sunday morning an elder entered the bathroom just prior to the start of the service. Once in the room, he fell onto the tile floor and hit so hard it made a loud noise. It obviously hurt, frustrated, and embarrassed him. His immediate response was to utter something I'm sure he wished he hadn't said. The result of this "slip of the tongue" caused even more embarrassment, and we who heard it were embarrassed for him.

In one way or another, we can all relate to the evils of the tongue. James 3:5-8: describes it this way, "Even so the tongue is a little member, and boasteth great things...And the tongue is a fire, a world of iniquity...it defileth the whole body...The tongue...is an unruly evil, full of deadly poison." Even David, the man after God's own heart, struggled to control his tongue. But he didn't rationalize, excuse, or ignore his sins of the tongue. Instead, his mindset was recorded in Psalm 17:3b: "...I am purposed that my mouth shall not transgress."

The Scriptures give us ample reason to guard our speech. Solomon counseled: "Whoso keepeth his mouth and his tongue keepeth his soul from troubles" (Proverbs 21:23). I Peter 3:10 states, "...He that will love life and see good days, let him refrain his tongue from evil, and his lips that they speak no guile." So, we should be motivated by self-preservation to want our tongue controlled. But there are also important spiritual reasons. James tells us it is a matter of testimony: "If any man among you seem to be religious, and bridleth not his tongue, but deceiveth his own heart, this man's religion is vain" (James 1:26). James is saying there is emptiness in one's testimony when the walk doesn't match the spiritual talk. It doesn't matter how rough a background we came out of, or for how many years filthy talk was a habit of life. When we know Christ, He impresses our heart to cooperate with Him to clean up the content of our speech. With this very thing in mind, the Apostle Paul writes, "Let no corrupt communication proceed out of your mouth, but that which is good to the use of edifying..." (Ephesians 4:29).

Today, let's take this matter seriously. As David, let's purpose not to sin with our lips and pray as he did, "Set a watch, O Lord, before my mouth; keep the door of my lips" (Psalm 141:3).

RESPONDING PROPERLY TO BACKBITING

Proverbs 25:23

In October of 2013, twelve-year-old Rebecca of Lakeland, Florida, took her life after being bullied by several other teens. A series of events, including malicious cyber messages to and about Rebecca, drove her to a tragic end. Even after her death, one of the girls callously admitted she had bullied Rebecca, bragged about it, and stated, in crass terms, that she couldn't care less about what happened.

While the above might sound shocking, it has become commonplace in our society. In fact, in differing degrees, it is common even in Christian circles. Believers of all ages allow themselves to participate in verbal bullying, and many of us enable perpetrators by listening to things that should never be spoken. The Bible gives us an answer about how every godly Christian should respond to vicious words spoken against someone else. God tells us in Proverbs 25:23, "The north wind driveth away rain: so doth an angry countenance a backbiting tongue." The word "backbiting" means to attack the character or reputation of a person who is not present or, to speak slanderously of one who is absent. Oftentimes, one who is backbiting is given an ear with the rationalization that the perpetrator is a friend who needs a sounding board because they are hurting. The listener believes counsel can be given. But such concepts are contrary to the instruction of God's Word. Malicious talk about someone who is not present doesn't seek to solve the problem. It is an exercise in sin. Our response should be to let the guilty party know with certainty that it is wrong and that we want no part of such conduct. In II Corinthians 12:20-21, the Apostle Paul warned he would give an even stronger response to those who backbite or slander another. He would publicly "bewail many." *What do you think? Would confronting the backbiter in God's way deter such sinful actions and perhaps aid in the health of the local church?*

If you have been guilty of backbiting another, this is your opportunity to glorify your Savior. We suggest you stop this action immediately and, whether past or present, apologize, without excuse, to the one you victimized. When you hear backbiting, choose to respond as instructed above. You will either be the problem or the solution. *From this point on, which will you be?*

TAKE RESPONSIBILITY
AND CONTROL

Proverbs 25:28

Author Vicki Halsey, Ph.D. addresses an important cultural lie in her daily blog. She writes, "One of my pet peeves is people who use their personality as an excuse for their behavior. *"I can't help it, that's just who I am"* is often uttered to rationalize or justify an action, position, or attitude. In some ways it's almost the perfect defense to any argument, isn't it? *'You mean you want me to change who I am?'* "[1] The point Vicki is making is that our society has been brainwashed into making excuses for bad behavior rather than standing up and taking responsibility for doing wrong. Instead of making excuses for bad behavior, Vicki is advocating we choose to make an intentional change toward correct behavior. The Word of God teaches the same thing.

In Proverbs 25:28, King Solomon writes, "He that hath no rule over his own spirit is like a city that is broken down, and without walls." In biblical days, tall, thick walls encompassed ancient cities. They protected against invading armies who would come in and destroy the inhabitants. Walls that were broken down essentially invited others to conquer the city. In the spiritual realm, a Christian who does not control his own spirit, [one's thinking, actions, and attitudes] is leaving himself open to the attack of Satan and the flesh. Instead of leaving ourselves so vulnerable, we need to take responsibility for bad behavior and take control of our spirit. Our victory must be through God's power, but we have the obligation to yield our spirit to the Lord and control it. This is why, throughout Scripture He gives us commands such as "use not liberty for an occasion to the flesh…"(Galatians 5:13), "…let not sin therefore reign…" (Romans 6:12), and "let no corrupt communication proceed out of your mouth…" (Ephesians 4:29). God expects us to control our spirit, rather than allowing it to control us. When we fail, let's own up to it rather than make excuses.

Have you believed the cultural lies that you can't help sinful actions or that they're not your fault? Let today is the day you take responsibility for wrong behavior, choose to control your spirit, and ask God to help you to do both.

EVENTUALLY YOU'LL GET BIT

Proverbs 26:17

Before coming to a better understanding of grace and liberty, my wife and I both came from a legalistic background. During our first few weeks of marriage, a woman I had only met once came up to us and abruptly said to me, "Oh, you're the one who won't let his wife wear pants." She then told my wife that she didn't need a husband to tell her what to do. We didn't respond sharply, but her statements were offensive and her opinion simply unwanted. I later learned this was common conduct for this woman. She didn't seem to care that she was interfering or creating a negative reputation for herself.

God gives us some wise counsel about needlessly involving ourselves in the affairs of others. Proverbs 26:17 says, "He that passeth by, and meddleth with strife belonging not to him, is like one that taketh a dog by the ears." Picture yourself walking by a Pit Bull and then abruptly lifting the dog into the air by its ears. In nearly every instance, the dog would turn its head and bite you hard. This is what we can expect when we meddle in someone else's affairs. It will usually come back to bite us, and we'll deserve it. When heated emotions between others are involved and we insert ourselves, the reaction toward us will almost surely reap a harvest of undesirable consequences. We will seldom be appreciated, and we may justifiably receive a very angry response. Christians aren't immune from meddling in the lives of others. Paul told the saints at Thessalonica: "For we hear that there are some which walk among you disorderly, working not at all, but are **busybodies**" (II Thessalonians 3:11). A common thread among those who have this habit is too much idle time. In I Timothy 5:11-13, Paul described the danger of "younger widows" who "learn to be idle…and not only idle, but tattlers also and busybodies, speaking things which they ought not." One who constantly gives their opinion when it is not asked for needs to learn several lessons: advice not asked for is advice not wanted; some things are better left unsaid; and when we stick our nose into someone else's business, we are just asking for trouble.

The next time you are tempted to "put your two cents in" to someone else's business remember, God simply doesn't want you to do so. Instead, busy yourself doing something truly productive in the cause of Christ.

POLITICALLY INCORRECT
IS CORRECT WITH GOD

Proverbs 28:4

*H*ave you heard about the experiment with a frog placed *in a pan of water on the stove?* Some say if you gradually turn up the temperature until the water reaches a boiling point, the frog won't realize it is being cooked alive and will simply stay in the water. Whether this is true or not, it seems to illustrate the political and moral condition in America. Over the past four decades, the media and many politicians have been pushing homosexuality as being right and desirable. They insist abortion is a woman's right while ignoring the rights of babies in the womb. And they promote immorality, such as casual sex. Those who object to this standard of sin are viciously attacked. They are labeled, as having a phobia, being narrow minded, intolerant, ignorant, extreme, and politically incorrect. Americans, and some Christians, have been gradually desensitized by this campaign of propaganda. In many cases, believers are intimidated into complete silence, and others have come to embrace and defend these sins the Bible speaks against. *How should Christians respond to the moral issues of our day?*

Proverbs 28:4 says, "They that forsake the law [God's standards] praise the wicked: but such as keep the law contend with them." In order to embrace and defend the moral decline of our day, one has to forsake God's standards recorded in the Holy Scriptures. One must deem them outdated, irrelevant, and without authority. It amounts to abandoning God's Word to become loyal to an alternate ideology. Many who do so still "have a form of godliness" in worship or speech. How the Lord responds to this is soberly explained, "He that turneth away his ear from hearing the law, even his prayer shall be abomination." (Proverbs 28:9). *How then is the believer today supposed to respond to the moral decay?* According to Proverbs 28:4, we are to "contend with them" when unbiblical and ungodly ideas are being promoted. We don't have to protest in the streets, do acts of violence, or become obnoxiously argumentative, but **we should speak up**. We should respectfully explain and support the standards outlined in the Holy Scriptures and stand with others who are doing likewise.

In these "latter times some shall depart from the faith, giving heed to seducing spirits, and doctrines of devils..." (I Timothy 4:1). Instead of being swept away to the wrong side of moral issues, be brave enough to be "politically incorrect" but correct in the sight of God.

TRUTH AND PRACTICE

Proverbs 30:5-6

We all know from civics classes or TV shows, whenever anyone takes the stand in a courtroom, they are required to answer a question. They are asked, by way of an oath: "Do you swear the testimony you are about to give will be the truth, the whole truth and nothing but the truth, so help you God?" Giving a testimony in a courtroom is a solemn matter. Likewise, whenever anyone handles the inspired Word of God, it too is a solemn matter that requires the utmost carefulness and truthfulness.

Repeatedly, the Lord emphasizes that no one is to add to or take away from the divine words He has given. Proverbs 30:5-6 tells us, "Every word of God is pure…Add thou not unto His words, lest He reprove thee, and thou be found a liar." There is a big difference between explaining the content of Scripture as opposed to adding things God never intended. God's servant Nehemiah "…read in the book in the law of God distinctly, and gave the sense, and caused them to understand the reading" (Nehemiah 8:8). Explaining the meaning of Scripture has the godly intent of helping others adhere to God's will through His Word. Adding to Scripture implies a devious motive (II Corinthians 2:17). Then, in both Deuteronomy 4:2 and 12:32, Moses wrote, "Ye shall not add unto the word which I command you, neither shall ye diminish ought from it, that ye may keep the commandments of the Lord…which I command you." Again we see the warning not to add to God's words, and here we see taking words away is strictly forbidden. We too are to give the truth, THE WHOLE TRUTH, and nothing but the truth. Revelation 22:19 reveals how grave this issue was when kingdom saints under the Law of Moses were warned, "And if any man shall take away from the words of the book of this prophecy, God shall take away his part out of the book of life…." We hasten to add here that all today who have trusted in the finished work of Christ as their only hope for eternal life have eternal security. We are "sealed unto the day of redemption" (Ephesians 4:30). Nonetheless, we too should be careful not to add to or take away from God's words.

In every dispensation, God's primary purpose for His Word is that we do not change it, but allow it to change us (Romans 12:2). Every day look for something in Scripture to put into practice.

A VIRTUOUS WOMAN
Proverbs 31:10

Proverbs 31:10 asks the question, "Who can find a virtuous woman?" Webster's dictionary defines the word "virtuous" as "general moral excellence, goodness of character, or chaste." The end of verse ten goes on to say if you can find such a woman: "her price [or worth] is far above rubies." The standard here is not an unrealistic perfection in all areas of life. Instead, it is an inward beauty of character and morals that can make any woman who seeks to cultivate these qualities a highly valued woman to all who know her.

We actually have several biblical examples of virtuous women. Ruth was told all the city knew she was a "virtuous woman" (Ruth 3:11), for her devotion to Jehovah, loving care for her mother-in-law, work ethic, and humility to listen to instruction. The virtue of Sarah is described in I Peter 3:4-6 for her submission to her husband with a "meek and quiet spirit, which is in the sight of God of great price." Proverbs 31 emphasizes several qualities of a virtuous woman. She is worthy of her husband's trust (v. 11), will always do her husband good and not evil (v. 12), and diligently and consistently "worketh willingly" to advance family finances (vs. 13-24). She conducts herself with "strength and honor" (v. 25), "openeth her mouth with wisdom [or discretion], ...and kindness" (v. 26), and "looketh well to the ways of her household" without engaging in "idleness" (v. 27). Verse 30 seems to also imply that while she may possess or desire outward beauty, she realizes this is "vain", or empty, and fleeting. Therefore, she places a higher value on the inner beauty of the virtues studied above, and she does so because she has godliness, or is "a woman that feareth the Lord."

If you are a man who has found a virtuous woman, you are greatly blessed. Proverbs tells us "a prudent wife is from the Lord" (19:14) and she is "a crown to her husband" (12:4). Tell your virtuous woman today that you greatly appreciate her godliness, which makes her a true "trophy wife." If you're not yet married, this is the kind of woman you should be looking for. If you are a woman who is not satisfied these qualities are developed fully enough in you, don't be discouraged. Instead, ask the Lord to help you grow in these virtues, and prayerfully work on several of them today.

A LIVING SAVIOR

Romans 1:4

This author's unsaved brother relates the story of an acquaintance with a Hindu man from India. This man said, "Our faith is the only true religion in the world." My brother's emphatic response was, "Followers of every religion in the world think they are right and that theirs is the only true religion." My response to my brother is that the faith of Christians is not a blind faith, but a faith based on the rock solid foundation of fulfilled prophecy, a risen Savior, and historical accuracy.

To begin with, everyone has faith. Even atheists have faith that there is no God, heaven, or hell. Yet, in a time of tragedy (such as it was on 9/11), nearly everyone, even atheists, instinctively use God's name asking for His help. Romans 1:19 refers to mankind's God-consciousness when it says, "… that which may be known of God is manifest in them, for God hath shewed it unto them." Other religions have mortal prophets who promoted their philosophies, but Christians have a Divine Savior who has many documented miracles to back up His teachings. Other religions have leaders that simply died, but Christians have a Redeemer who paid for their sins through His death. Then the Lord Jesus "…shewed himself alive…by many infallible proofs…" (Acts 1:3), and He is "…declared to be the Son of God with power…by the resurrection from the dead" (Romans 1:4). The resurrection of our Savior was "…seen of above five hundred brethren at once…" (I Corinthians 15:6), and was witnessed by unbelieving Roman soldiers. Other religions often produce cruel, savage, and ruthless behavior on the part of their followers, such as we see in Muslim countries. While professing Christianity has produced many atrocities, such as the Spanish Inquisition, true Christianity seeks to follow "…the doctrine which is according to godliness" (I Timothy 6:3). There are countless examples of Christians living transformed lives that honor Christ and society. Other religions have books they follow, but Christians have an inspired Bible that has been proven true though hundreds of fulfilled prophecies, historically correct accounts, and archeology that constantly confirm its accuracy. Moreover, God's Word has power to transform lives into godliness superior to any book used by other faiths.

Believer, you need not cower in the face of those who ridicule your faith in the Lord Jesus Christ and the Bible. Stand strong in the abundance of evidence proving our Bible is true and that Jesus Christ is the true only Savior.

ACCUMULATED WRATH
Romans 2

Four children were playing together when one began to misbehave by hoarding all the toys. When reasoning and spanking didn't work, time out on the couch followed. This child was told to sit there and watch the clock until the big hand was on the ten. Unfortunately, the child repeatedly slithered off the couch. Each time an additional ten minutes was added to the time out along with the warning that a spanking would result for continued disobedience.

Every unsaved individual lives on a precarious slippery slope. At any moment they could be swept into eternity where all the lost will stand before a just God who will severely judge their sins. Paul calls this "…the day of wrath and revelation of the righteous judgment of God…"(Romans 2:5). They may think they can "…escape the judgment of God" (2:3), but eternal punishment is certain for every individual who "…despiseth…the riches of His [God's] goodness and forbearance and longsuffering..."(2:4). Presently, God offers forgiveness and eternal life to all who will trust in Christ. But those who stubbornly resist the wooing of the Holy Spirit and reject faith in Christ Jesus are accumulating punishment and intensifying God's wrath with every rebellious act. Romans 2:5 describes it this way: "But after thy hardness and impenitent heart treasurest up unto thyself wrath against the day of wrath and revelation of the righteous judgment of God." Like water being restrained behind a huge dam, God's wrath is presently held back by His love, grace, and mercy. But just as an abundance of stormy rain can cause the water to break over a dam in angry swirls of destruction to all downstream, eventually God's wrath will be released to punish every lost soul. It won't be God's fault when His wrath falls on lost souls either. Grace has been patiently offered to all. Until the day when divine punishment falls on lost souls, the sin of every unsaved individual accumulates and increases the torment they will experience in eternity.

A lost soul was recently telling me about talking with a friend who, at the age of twenty-two, died in a fatal car wreck. My friend said, "He had no clue his life would be over in thirty minutes." We who know Christ as Savior must keep in mind the looming wrath of God on lost souls who are within our sphere of influence. Speak to a lost soul about their need of eternal life today. Tomorrow may be too late.

LET GOD BE TRUE

Romans 3:3-4

During the 2013 season, Bill Belichick, coach of the New England Patriots, made a controversial call to run a play on fourth down rather than punt the ball back to the Indianapolis Colts. The Patriots failed to convert that fourth down and they lost the game. Media and fan scrutiny was blistering. As Belichick spoke to the team days later, he told them not to listen to all the negative noise, but to focus on their preparation for the next week. That was good advice.

In the context of many in his day vocally rejecting his new Gospel of Grace, the Apostle Paul writes Romans Chapter 3. Critics used three basic arguments. First, he writes, "For what if some did not believe" (vs. 3). Apparently, when Paul proclaimed forgiveness of sins through faith in the payment that the Savior made for us on the cross, many dismissed his message as only nonsense or man-made fiction. They simply would not consider or accept God's offer of forgiveness by grace alone. Most Jews either clung to a system of works in an empty attempt to merit eternal life, or they placed their confidence in their heritage as God's chosen people. Secondly, some chose not to believe that a loving God would punish people who sin for all eternity in the torment of the Lake of Fire. Paul responds by asking, "Is God unrighteous who taketh vengeance?" (vs. 5). His point was that our "unrighteousness" is in such contrast to the holiness of the Lord that our sinful works magnify the righteousness of God. In other words, our pure, sinless, and holy God cannot dwell in the presence of sin. Therefore He is right to banish sinful souls away from His presence for all eternity, especially since they rejected His offer of eternal life through His Son. Third, others simply thought salvation by grace alone was too easy. So, they mocked this message when they "slanderously reported" that Paul taught it was okay to live it up in sin since grace covers all our sin (vs. 8). Throughout Paul's letters, he constantly proclaims that grace teaches us to live "soberly, righteously, and godly in this present world" (Titus 2:12).

These three arguments sound familiar because Satan is still using the same lies to blind lost souls to their need for salvation in Christ. Don't you believe them or listen to all the noise. "Let God be true, but every man a liar" (Romans 3:4). Stand firm in your faith.

I'M SO BLESSED

Romans 4:6-8

We've had a number of Christian friends who regularly give edifying, memorable responses when greeted with the question: "How are you doing." One friend says, "I'm doing great, and I'm on the right side of the grass." Another responds, "I'm doing better now that you and the rest of the saints are here." Still another says, "I'm doing better than I deserve. Thank God for His grace." But my favorite comes from a radiant Christian man who says, "I'm blessed! Just think about all these wonderful things in life and God's eternal life too."

In Romans Chapter 4, the Apostle Paul is talking about those who have "the righteousness of the faith" (vs. 11), and he describes them as being truly blessed by God. When Scripture describes anyone as having righteousness, it means they are divinely justified or declared without sin. In every dispensation, past or present, righteousness has always been on the basis of faith. Even when God required Abraham to leave his pagan family and homeland, it was his faith in God's promises that gave him the inheritance of eternal life. It was not his works, or acts of obedience, that saved him. Romans 4:3 declares, "Abraham believed God, and it (his faith) was counted unto him for righteousness." Explaining it further, Paul says of Abraham that he "believeth (or believed) on Him that justifieth the ungodly, (and) his faith is counted for righteousness" (vs. 5). Abraham was not an exception in being justified by faith apart from works. Paul uses David in the same context saying, "Even as David also describeth the blessedness of the man, unto whom God imputeth righteousness without works" (vs. 6). Notice here that the Scripture describes those who accept imputed righteousness, or eternal life, by faith alone, as being blessed. *How were they, and how are we today, blessed?* Verse seven says, "Blessed are they whose iniquities are forgiven, and who sins are covered." What a wonderful gift to be completely forgiven of all our sins and accepted by God. Our blessed condition is further described when Paul refers to how secure our position is in Christ: "Blessed is the man to whom the Lord will not impute sin" (vs. 8). Praise His Name, our imputed righteousness is so permanent that we are assured eternal life. What a blessing to be eternally secure in salvation.

Have you recently thought about how truly blessed you are? Why not pause right now to give thanks and praise to your Savior for being so blessed.

PAIN CAN BRING GAIN

Romans 5:3-5

Growing up in Nebraska, I vividly remember cold fall days, when the trees lost all their leaves, and dreading the much colder winter days that lay ahead. I hated fighting frostbite, scraping ice off windshields, shoveling snow, and being chilled to the bone. Maybe I'm too soft, but I never really understood it when friends say, "I love the changes of seasons, even the cold and snow." When I hear things like this I'm thinking, "Are you crazy?"

I've heard some of the saints jokingly make similar comments about Paul's testimony when he said, "…we glory in tribulation…" (Romans 5:3). Paul wasn't insincere when saying this, nor had he been hit in the head with one too many rocks. He really meant it. Because he had come to realize that the pain of trials could bring real gain in his spiritual maturity, he chose to look at these difficult situations through the lens of faith. **There were four reasons why Paul rejoiced in any trial** that came his way. First, he had learned that "tribulation worketh [or produces] patience" (vs. 3b), which means an endurance. Just as hardship in exercise produces stronger muscles, hardship in life produces experiences where God carries you through and reminds you He can do so again. Secondly, "experience [produces] hope" (vs. 4b). Hope means a confident expectation. Trials endured through God's grace bolster us with the confidence that we can face anything in the strength of the Lord. Thirdly, Paul glories in tribulation because he has learned that "hope maketh not ashamed" (vs. 5). The word "ashamed" means to disgrace or shame down. A believer need not be ashamed before the lost when demonstrating life-changing faith. Face trials with an endurance from God. Remember past victories through God's grace. Then face current problems confidently, expecting God's enablement. Finally, Paul glories in tribulation "because (through it all) the love of God is shed abroad on our hearts by the Holy Ghost which is given unto us" (vs. 5). Paul learned that he better sensed the love of God for him during times of trial than any other time. Perhaps this was so because of a greater quietness and dependence on the Lord.

You don't have to be crazy to rejoice and glory in trials. You simply have to realize that the pain of hardships can produce real spiritual gain. Rejoice in God's enablement through past trials and trust that He will enable you in whatever lies ahead.

WALK IN THE NEWNESS OF LIFE
Romans 6:4-18

When I returned to my 30th high school reunion, I had six people ask the same basic question, "What happened in your senior year to make you so different from what you were before?" To be absolutely clear, I fully realize I still struggle with the old man every day. I am not as consistent as I want to be and have miles to go to become the man God wants me to be. But by the glory of God, when I was saved as a senior in high school, Christ radically changed my life and gave me a desire to live for Him.

When the Apostle Paul described how a believer should live after salvation, he said, "…we also should walk in newness of life" (Romans 6:4). We don't have to wonder what he means by this statement, because he tells us in the remainder of the chapter. Newness of life means that "…henceforth we should not serve sin" (vs. 6). Every lost soul inherently is under the bondage of sin. We often serve sin by practicing things we know are wrong and foolish, because we lack the power from within to live otherwise. Newness of life means one purposes to live "unto God" (vs. 10). That doesn't mean living in sinless perfection, but it does mean honestly purposing to live for Christ and seeking to rise above constant sinful practices. Newness of life means one must "…reckon [or count] ye also yourselves to be dead indeed unto sin…" (vs. 11). Consciously, we must consider ourselves dead to living in old sinful ways and dead to the power of sin to control us. Newness of life means considering ourselves "alive unto God through Jesus Christ our Lord" (vs. 11). We are to view ourselves as a new creation in Christ with life, responsiveness, and desire to live unto Christ rather than self. Newness of life means seeking not to "…yield ye your members as instruments of unrighteousness unto sin: but yield yourselves unto God, as those that are alive from the [spiritually] dead" (vs. 13). Believers should realize we are all servants either to sin or to the Lord (vss. 16-18). Believers living transformed lives purpose to yield their bodies to Christ and to the working of the Holy Spirit within as He leads us to live in godliness.

Are you living in newness of life? If others around you can't see a transformed life, make it a daily matter of prayer.

ONGOING WARFARE

Romans 7:15-22

After the end of World War II, there was an often silent, but ongoing, warfare between the United States and the Soviet Union. At times it became more visible, as during the Cuban missile crisis that threatened nuclear holocaust. Most of the time it was a more subtle warfare of espionage, jockeying for position, influencing public opinion, and recruiting others to one's side in this conflict. We couldn't always see it, but it was always there nonetheless.

Every believer is engaged in an ongoing spiritual warfare that takes place within us. Ephesians 4:22-24 identifies the combatants as the "old man" or old nature, and the "new man" or new nature. These two are constantly at odds, seeking to either pull us as believers into some form of sinful activity or pull us toward Christ-honoring conduct. The Apostle Paul acknowledged that he too struggled as this warfare waged within him. He stated, "For what I do I allow not: for what I would, that do I not; but what I hate, that do I" (Romans 7:15). Every believer can experientially identify with this inner conflict. We want to live apart from sin, as did Paul, but the "... sin [nature] that dwelleth in me" (vs. 17, 20b) is constantly luring us away from the proper path. When believers are in a good place spiritually, they can say with Paul, "...I delight in the law of God after the inward man" (vs. 22). *Why, then, if we yearn to live for Christ and do what is pleasing to Him, do we so often fail in sin?* Romans 7:23 describes it this way, "But I see another law (or fixed principle) in my members, warring against the law of my mind, and bringing me into captivity to the law of sin which is in my members." The bad news is that this unseen spiritual conflict will continue within us until the day we go home to be with Christ or until He comes for us in the Rapture. The good news is twofold. One day we will be free of this conflict. The old nature will be eradicated when we are taken to our heavenly home. Then we will live in continual victory. But until then, we have God's written Word and indwelling Holy Spirit to strengthen our new nature. To the extent we avail ourselves of both, we'll find victory.

You are not alone in this battle or in failures. Stay homesick for heaven, stay in the Word, and seek to yield yourself to the Holy Spirit.

A LIFE AND DEATH MATTER

Romans 8:6

In 1983, singer Karen Carpenter died of complications due to anorexia. For many of us, this startling news was our first exposure to this eating disorder. Like others who struggle with this problem, Karen saw herself as overweight and unlovable. Consequently, she starved herself into massive weight loss. In 1975, at 90 lbs., she collapsed on stage. Family members then realized her improper diet was a life-and-death matter, and they tried to intervene. Unfortunately, Karen did not fully cooperate. Eventually, she died.

The Apostle Paul refers to a spiritual life-and-death matter when he wrote, "For to be carnally minded is death; but to be spiritually-minded is life and peace" (Roman 8:6). Thankfully, no one who trusts in Christ alone for eternal life will ever lose his or her salvation. Once saved, we are sealed until the day of redemption, and nothing can separate us from the love of God or from our heavenly inheritance. However, if we choose to persist in a wayward walk from Christ, we can become effectively, spiritually dead while still having eternal life. Paul warns believers about the possibility of becoming so hardened in sin that we develop a seared conscience (I Timothy 4:2), becoming "past feeling", and alienated from the daily "life of God" (Ephesians 4:17-19). This is why, in Romans 8:6, Paul urged believers to be spiritually-minded and not carnally minded. What Paul was specifically referring to, in this context, was the danger of continuing under the bondage of the Mosaic Law. It was a fleshly system of animal sacrifices, circumcision, and human works. In preceding chapters, Paul taught these saints that they were not under the law, but under grace. They were dead to the demands of the law. There was now no condemnation to those who left all the practices of the Law behind. Unfortunately, some were still so preoccupied, or "minded," with the Law, they insisted on following it. Paul's message to them was that submission to legalism not only brought bondage; it also produced spiritual death. Paul urged them to be spiritually-minded instead by embracing grace as their instruction for today and following these principles whole-heartedly.

Placing ourselves under legalism isn't the only thing that can choke out our spiritual life. Persisting in sin, neglecting the Word of God, and not seeking daily spiritual transformation does too. Choose to be spiritually-minded by making your walk with Christ your highest priority today. "Life and peace" will follow.

A BURDEN FOR THE LOST
Romans 9:2-3

I have known two consistent soul-winners who had an exceptional burden for lost souls. One was a man who came to know Christ in his late forties. He sold his business, entered the ministry, and witnessed constantly. I've seen him in tears and in prayer for someone he knew needed Christ. The other was a simple, quiet, but genuine man who spoke often about how heavy his heart was for those headed for eternal punishment. He sacrificed financially to print and distribute well over 7 million gospel tracts, and he did so even in very poor health. Neither of these men ministered to lost souls to boast to others about how many they lead to Christ. They quietly, and humbly, went about the work of sharing the gospel, therein giving Christ the glory.

Quite probably there was no other mere man who had a greater burden for lost souls than the Apostle Paul. His testimony was, "...I have great heaviness and continual sorrow in my heart. For I could wish that myself were accursed from Christ for my brethren, my kinsmen according to the flesh" (Romans 9:2-3). Note that he said he "could" wish himself accursed, not that he did. Paul knew that his soul, like that of everyone in the Dispensation of Grace who trusts in Christ, was eternally secure. Taking someone's place in the Lake of Fire is simply not possible. Paul had such a heavy burden for the lost that he could contemplate such a scenario. It was this burden that motivated Paul to go into hostile synagogues to share the gospel, to suffer the perils of dangerous travel and assassination plots to further spread the offer of salvation through faith in Christ, and to work tirelessly for years. *What produced this kind of burden?* He knew that every soul who dies without Christ would be cast into the Lake of Fire to be tormented day and night forever (Revelation 20:15). He knew those in the fire of eternal punishment will have no rest day or night for all eternity (Revelation 14:11). He knew those in hell will experience an intense burning torment that is hard to fathom, especially since it will never end. The only solution was to reach lost souls before they stepped into eternity.

At least mentally, we should take a tour of a hospital burn unit to witness the suffering. Then we should pray for a greater burden and consistency to share the gospel with lost souls.

HOW FAITH GROWS
Romans 10:17

We had a loved one who, for decades, resisted saving faith in the Lord Jesus Christ. Several family members made a point of sharing the gospel with her throughout the years. On more than one occasion, she responded by saying, "I wish I could have faith like you do, but I just don't." We prayed often for her salvation and looked for opportunities to lead her to Christ. Thankfully, toward the end of her life, she made a profession of faith.

We learn from Hebrews 11:6 that without faith it is impossible to please God. This begs a question: *"How can faith grow in one who does not have faith?"* There are actually two different kinds of faith needed by every individual. The first is saving faith in the Lord Jesus, trusting in His death, burial, and resurrection alone as one's only hope for forgiveness and eternal life. The second is a walk of faith, believing and trusting the Lord every day after salvation. In both instances, there is a way for faith to grow even within someone who resists a faith that will please God. The Apostle Paul tells us, "So then faith cometh by hearing, and hearing by the Word of God" (Romans 10:17). The more exposure one has to the Scriptures, the more likely it is for faith to grow within. God's Word is powerful and pierces through pride, fear, and resistance. God's Word plants the seed of faith in all who are exposed to it, waters that seed so it may grow, and washes resistant thinking away. It is for these reasons that, when we witness to a lost soul, the most important thing for us to share is God's Word. God uses it more than our reasoning or our testimony. So use the Scriptures generously when dealing with one who needs salvation. The same principle is true for the believer who needs to grow in faith in their daily walk. God's Word renews and transforms the mind. Hearing or reading the Scripture reveals God's will and awakens a desire to obey. Through the internal working of the Holy Spirit, His Word empowers the believer to walk by faith in obedience. It may seem like an overly simplistic principle, but it is true nonetheless.

Believer, you already have saving faith. If you are struggling in some area of your daily walk, faithfully expose your mind and soul to more of God's Word, particularly those passages dealing with your area of need. It works!

WHY ARE THERE SO FEW?
Romans 11:3-25

Perhaps every grace believer has asked the question, *"Why are there so few grace churches? After all, we have the truth."* This relevant question has several answers. We need to be doing a far better job of evangelizing the lost and sharing mystery truths. We need to be more faithful to instill a deep conviction for grace truths in our families, so our message is not lost in future generations. We are also likely very near the Rapture. Paul taught that, in the last days of grace, people would become more resistant to God's truths. However, if we focus on the question of why there are so few grace churches, we will miss the more important issues.

As Paul addressed the setting aside of Israel in Romans Chapter Eleven, he recounts the history of the Jews in the days of Isaiah. Like Elijah before him, Isaiah believed, "I am left alone" (Romans 11:3). He felt like he was the only one left following the Lord. But this wasn't what God wanted the prophet to focus on. Nor did the Lord want believers in Paul's day, or ours, to focus on the sea of unbelief. Isaiah was to be encouraged to know he wasn't the only faithful believer; God had seven thousand others (Romans 11:4). Isaiah may not have known them, but they existed nonetheless. As Paul discussed the unfaithfulness of Israel, there are several more things to see. His readers needed to look for God's sovereign purpose being accomplished in these events. He told them the fall and diminishing of Israel resulted in "the riches of the Gentiles" in our present Dispensation of Grace (vs. 12). Moreover, God was using the salvation and transformation of Gentiles to "provoke them [Israel] to jealousy" (vs. 11). Likewise, our focus today should not be on the negative of so few responding to the gospel or remaining true to grace teaching. Instead, we should focus on God's sovereign purpose of using us to accomplish His will. Moreover, Paul continues by sharing his steady focus on fulfilling his mission as the Apostle to the Gentiles and seeking to win souls whenever, and wherever, he could (vss. 13-14). He warned believers not to be proud or "high-minded" (vss. 20, 25) as one of the few who are doing what is right. Instead, remain humble and faithful to the Lord.

Forget about how few there are of like precious faith. Stay focused on being used of God to complete your personal spiritual mission.

A LIVING SACRIFICE
Romans 12:1-2

About four months after trusting in Christ, this writer was challenged, and specifically asked, to dedicate the rest of his life to the Lord. This was not emotionalism. It was a positive biblical encouragement to make a conscious decision to give my life to Christ in a dedicated way.

The Apostle Paul told us to do this very thing when he wrote, "I beseech ye therefore, brethren, by the mercies of God, that ye present your bodies a living sacrifice, holy, acceptable unto God, which is your reasonable service" (Romans 12:1). A beautiful illustration from the Old Testament is being used here. The word "present" has the connotation of an intentional act of bringing a gift to the Lord as an act of worship and devotion, with no thought of ever taking it back. From this point on, that gift belongs to the Lord. Paul is picturing our need to give ourselves irrevocably to the Lord and see ourselves as belonging to Him. The word "sacrifice" refers to a consecrated or dedicated present, voluntarily given to the Lord. God would accept nothing less than a perfect animal brought to be consumed as a burnt sacrifice. Ultimately, this offering pictured the pure, sinless, perfect sacrifice of the body of the Lord Jesus for the sins of all mankind. But Paul also used this example to picture the purity in body expected of all believers who dedicate themselves to the Lord. This is why Paul specifies that our bodies are to be "holy, acceptable unto God" (vs. 1). When an animal was offered to the Lord, nothing was held back. The entire body of the animal was given to God to be consumed in fire, with the exception of a small portion used by the priests in the service of the Lord. Likewise, believers need to give themselves to the Lord with nothing held back. Note that we are to be an offering that now lives for Him. Paul emphasizes that offering ourselves to the Lord in this way is our "reasonable service" and cannot properly be done while being "conformed to this world" (vs. 2). Instead, we need to be seeking to be "transformed" each day into a better image of Christ.

This concept is just as important as any other instruction in Paul's letters. *Have you ever consciously presented your body and life to the Lord as an act of worship, surrender, and dedication? If you haven't, would you do so right now?*

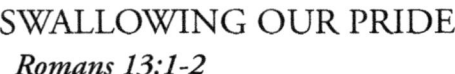

SWALLOWING OUR PRIDE
Romans 13:1-2

To prepare for the ministry, I attended a very legalistic Christian university. They had an extremely conservative dress code, demanded short hair cuts for men, required attendance at all functions and classes, and strictly enforced all of their rules. Violators were sometimes unceremoniously expelled. It was a difficult adjustment for many coming out of high school, especially when human shortcomings were apparent in those in authority. Nonetheless, I chose to swallow my pride and submit to these rules, believing doing so would honor the Lord.

When Paul wrote to the believers at Rome, he told them, "Let every soul be subject unto the higher powers. For there is no power but of God; the powers that be are ordained of God. Whosoever therefore resisteth the power, resisteth the ordinance of God..." (Romans 13:1-2). It is noteworthy these God-inspired instructions were given when the ruthless Roman Empire was at its height. They swept into countries without mercy, slaughtered thousands, made examples of dissidents through public crucifixion, forced slavery and high taxation, and left an occupying army to enforce their tyranny. It is in this context that Paul instructed believers to swallow their pride and submit to these governing higher powers. In fact, they were to view these powers, though often cruel and corrupt, as being placed over them by God. To be defiant and rebellious was to disobey the command of the Lord to submit to them. Beyond this instruction, Paul cites additional reasons to submit themselves. They were to view even these oppressors as "...the minister of God to thee for good..." (vs. 4). Their rule brought orderliness in society, general protection against crimes, and a deterrent to wrongdoers. Because God instructed compliance, they must submit themselves "...for conscience sake" (vs. 5). They could not maintain a clear and sensitive conscience before the Lord and defy these higher powers. They were also to obey for testimony sake. Paul told them it was "...high time to...put on the armour of light..." without making "...provision for the flesh" to walk disorderly (vss. 11-14). Therefore, they were to pay taxes and give honor to those who sat in positions of authority (vss. 6-7).

These principles are still true for us today. We must view all who are in positions of authority as God's instruments placed over us for our ultimate good. Therefore, we must be cooperative, respectful, and obedient to their governing, even if it means swallowing our pride. *Will you choose to do that today?*

ALLOWING DIFFERING CONVICTIONS

Romans 14:4-18

We had someone who gave us a hard time every year about celebrating Christmas. He called our Christmas tree a "Baal pole of false worship," reminded us Christ was not born in December, criticized the exchanging of gifts as pagan, and more. While not really hostile in tone, he was clearly standing in judgment of us without allowing us to follow our own conscience. Interestingly, now, years later, he and his wife go all out in celebrating Christmas.

Even in Paul's day, there was a problem with believers attempting to force their opinions on others and standing in judgment of one another when their conclusions differed. We call these conclusions "opinions" and not "convictions" because there is a difference. One should only claim a conviction if it is clearly specified in Paul's letters, widely seen by other believers, and void of cultural distinctions exclusive to Israel (such as the arranged marriage of Isaac and Rebecca). Otherwise, a conclusion is only an opinion. But even when one has a conviction from Paul's epistles, it is vital to hold that belief in a proper way. It is only acceptable for us to stand in judgment of others who do not adhere to our standard when sin is involved. Paul warns, "Who art thou that judgest another man's servant? To his own master (the Lord) he standeth or falleth" (Romans 14:4). We are to respectfully "let every man be fully persuaded in his own mind" (vs. 5). Just as we have liberty, others do too. "Happy is he that condemneth not himself in that thing which he alloweth" (vs. 22). The matter is really between each individual and the Lord. Paul further demonstrates that the Lord grants latitude to believers. Examples include esteeming one day above another (vs. 5) and deciding what or how one eats (vs. 6). Rather than judging one another for holding a different position, the Lord would have us remember that each of us will stand before "the judgment seat of Christ" (vs. 10). Therefore, we must choose to be far more concerned that we not "put a stumblingblock or an occasion to fall in his brother's way" (vs. 13), than that we stand in judgment or act condescendingly. Instead, we must demonstrate a gracious attitude, even when we disagree with another's conclusion, especially on secondary, nonessential issues.

Have you struggled to graciously allow for a differing conclusion in another believer? Acknowledge this to the Lord, ask for His enablement, and, if needed, apologize to the one you've judged.

FILLED WITH JOY AND PEACE
Romans 15:13

When each of our daughters was born, my wife and I were filled with joy over this new life that had been entrusted to our care. We thought about them constantly, talked about them, and were eager to share them with others. They had irrevocably changed our lives for the better, making us more complete. They are, quite simply, our pride and joy. It's natural for parents to have a huge sense of joy over a child. It should also be natural for all of us, as believers, to have a similar spiritual joy in our salvation. The Apostle Paul actually prayed for such a sense of joyous well being in his converts, saying, "Now the God of hope fill you with all joy and peace in believing, that ye may abound in hope, through the power of the Holy Ghost" (Romans 15:13).

Paul wasn't asking the Lord to give believers a subdued sense of joy that no one could see. He wanted them to be bubbling over with joy. Paul may have had several Old Testament examples in mind. When Israel returned from captivity, David said, "Then was our mouth filled with laughter, and our tongue with singing, then said they among the heathen, The Lord hath done great things for them" (Psalm 126:2). Isaiah's testimony was, "I will greatly rejoice in the Lord, my soul shall be joyful in my God, for He hath clothed me with the garments of salvation, He hath covered me with the robe of righteousness...as a bride adorneth herself with her jewels" (Isaiah 61:10). It is this kind of joy that should regularly permeate every believer "in believing." Our joy should not be dependent upon material things or circumstances. It should be a constant part of who we are. Our faith in Christ should fill our mouths with singing and praise. Our souls should rest in the assurance of eternal security. Our joy should enable us to "abound in hope" [or confident expectation], as we wait to be taken into the presence of Christ. Thankfully, this condition of joyous victory is not achieved by our own effort. It comes through "the power of the Holy Ghost" as we walk in close communion with the Lord and His Word each day.

Since Paul prayed for others that new life in Christ would produce joyous victory, we should too. Right now is a good time to ask the Lord to make your salvation your pride and joy.

WISE AND SIMPLE
Romans 16:19

In the 1960's, Art Linkletter had an entertaining show called "Kids Say The Darnedest Things." He would ask five children different questions about life. The responses were often amazing and hilarious. In childlike innocence, unsoiled by the ways of the world, they would be forthright with their answers. They usually had no idea what their host was talking about, which made them precious and endearing. While listening, it made one wish their innocence would never be lost.

As children of God, the Lord has this same desire for us. The Apostle Paul tells the saints, "...I would have you wise unto that which is good, and simple concerning evil" (Romans 16:19). As sons and daughters of God, we should mature in the content of our prayer, our ability to discern the will of God, effectiveness in sharing our faith, and in all things pertaining to godliness. The Lord desires our growth in discerning bad doctrine and false teachers, so that we might become "...wise as serpents, and harmless as doves" (Matthew 10:16). It pleases a parent when their child is able to grow into a properly functioning adult. Likewise, it pleases the Lord when His children are able to "...grow up into Him in all things..." (Ephesians 4:15), meaning all things that are good and Christ honoring. Yet there is a flip side. The Lord would also have us remain "...simple concerning evil." We must seek to maintain our innocence and distance from the filth and corruption in our society. We should have no idea what others might mean in dirty jokes, sexual perversions, and sinful trends. God's standard for us is to "...have no fellowship with the unfruitful works of darkness, but rather reprove them. For it is a shame even to speak of those things which are done of them in secret" (Ephesians 5:11-12). As we draw closer to the Rapture, it seems like the sinful activities once seldom practiced or only done in secret are now paraded in public and aggressively promoted to all. Nonetheless, it must be our goal to remain wise to what is good and simple to what is evil.

How are we to maintain such innocence today? It begins with a purpose to do so. Then we must seek to insulate our family and ourselves in practical ways from exposure to sinfulness. Also, we must make friends and spend time with godly people and saturate ourselves daily with God's Word. Take positive specific steps to do so today.

GOD CAN USE ANYONE
Matthew 1:1-17

If you've ever wondered if God could use you in a significant way, remember that God uses nobodies. Abraham came from the family of an idolater. Joseph was a slave. Gideon was a simple farmer and hard to convince that God was going to use him. Saul was a fearful man. David was a simple shepherd and the family's last choice. Solomon was the son from a union begun in adultery. Hosea had an adulterous wife. Jeremiah wept frequently. Peter was a rugged fisherman with no particular education. Matthew was a hated tax collector, and Paul was a vicious persecutor of Christians. These examples prove God can use anyone.

Four women in the lineage of the Lord Jesus Christ continue to prove this point. Matthew 1:3 refers to "Thamar," which is spelled "Tamar" in the record of Genesis 38:6. She was the daughter-in-law of Judah, originally marrying his firstborn son. When Judah's second son refused to give her children, and Judah delayed in giving her his third son to provide children, she used cunning to become pregnant by her father-in-law. Even though this was a sinful union, she is in the line of Christ. "Rachab" (Matthew 1:5) refers to "Rahab the harlot" in Joshua 6:17. Hebrews 11:31 tells us it was "by faith" she protected the Jews who came to spy out the Promised Land before it was conquered. Though a Gentile with a morally sinful past, God used her. Ruth (Matthew 1:5) was a Gentile Moabite who married the son of Naomi when their family traveled outside Israel during famine. She chose faith in Jehovah, and followed Ruth back to Israel to care for her. With a willingness to work and be counseled, she was married to Boaz. She is likewise in the line of Christ though a Gentile woman with a background in idolatry. "Bathsheba" is not specified in Matthew 1:6, but she is referred to as "her that had been the wife of Urias" with whom David begat Solomon. II Samuel 11 and 12 records the events surrounding this union with David, which included a provocative public display, and consensual coupling with David in an adulterous affair. Nonetheless, she too is in the line of Christ.

The encouraging lesson from all these examples is that God can graciously use anyone, even those with a past of sinful mistakes. One only need turn to the Lord in faith, be willing, and be available in His cause. Prayerfully report for duty right now.

GIVING GIFTS
Matthew 2:1-11

When foreign diplomats or heads of state come to America to see top U.S. officials, they customarily come bearing gifts. These gifts range from simple chocolates, to jewelry or artwork worth hundreds of thousands of dollars. By law, these gifts must be turned over to the national archives. However, "in all cases, officials accepted the lavish items because 'non-acceptance would cause embarrassment to donor and U.S.', according to the document provided by the State Department."[1] There is usually no attempt to bribe the recipient. Instead, it is a proper custom, rooted in thousands of years, intended to demonstrate respect, appreciation, gratitude, or honor. For instance, when the Queen of Sheba came to see for herself the greatness of Solomon, she came with "spices and very much gold, and precious stones" (I Kings 10:2).

Throughout the Scriptures, God consistently teaches that true worship of the Lord always includes giving gifts back to Him. David would not accept someone else giving him animals to sacrifice to the Lord. He said, "I will surely buy it of thee at a price: neither will I offer burnt offerings unto the Lord my God of that which cost me nothing" (II Samuel 24:24). Likewise, when the wise men came "to worship" the newborn Savior, they "opened their treasures, (and) they presented unto Him gifts: gold, and frankincense, and myrrh" (Matthew 2:2,11). The principle is the same in todays Dispensation of Grace. The Apostle Paul urged the Corinthians to be certain, to regularly and consistently, give back to the Lord "upon the first day of the week" (I Corinthians 16:1-3; II Corinthians 8:7, 9:6-8).

There is an important practical lesson for us here that we should not miss. When we worship the Lord, we should worship Him first by giving ourselves to Him as His servants (II Corinthians 8:5). We should also come with praise and acknowledgment of His greatness. But proper worship of the Lord should always proceed from a thankful heart for all His abundant blessings and include willingly giving back to Him financially, as God has prospered us. When you worship the Lord this week, don't forget to give Him gifts worthy of His name and all He has done for you. Our worship is simply not complete without giving.

UNDETERRED IN MINISTRY
Matthew 3:5

Jonathan Edwards (1703-1758) was considered by many to be the most powerful and effective preacher ever heard on the American continent. His sermon, "Sinners in the Hands of an Angry God," led many to trust in Christ alone for eternal life. Yet he was not without critics. "Oliver Wendell Holmes described his sermons as 'barbaric.' Mark Twain called him 'a drunken lunatic.'"[1] But whether praised or criticized, Edwards continued preaching God's Word undeterred.

The ministry of John the Baptist was both accepted and rejected. The common people of his day widely accepted him as a man of God. Many from Jerusalem, Judea, and Jordan went out to him to be baptized (Matthew 3:5). Herod was deterred from putting John to death because "he feared the multitude, because they counted him as a prophet" (Matthew 14:5). Yet the religious leaders of Israel, jealous of his popularity, did not accept his ministry. The Savior exposed their attitudes, saying, "John came neither eating nor drinking, and they say, he hath a devil" (Matthew 11:18). With no true accusation to level against John the Baptist, they manufactured a smear campaign to oppose him. Herod had John the Baptist beheaded after John rebuked him for having his brother's wife. Yet, he was so fearful of John, he believed God's servant had "risen from the dead" and he associated "mighty works" with John (Matthew 14:1-2).

As John the Baptist was not primarily concerned about whether or not mere men accepted his ministry, neither should we be concerned whether or not mere mortals accept our ministry. Like the Apostle Paul, we should strive to say, "...With me it is a very small thing that I should be judged of you, or of man's judgment: yea, I judge not mine own self...but He that judgeth me is the Lord" (I Corinthians 4:3-4). If we allow ourselves to be concerned about the opinions of others regarding our ministry for the Lord, their negativity may well intimidate us into silence. For the sake of lost souls who need to hear us share the gospel, for the cause of Christ, and because the need is great, we must boldly continue undeterred in ministry regardless of whether others accept or approve of our sharing truth from God's Word. Today, seek only to "be found faithful" to the Lord (I Corinthians 4:2) by sharing the gospel with a lost soul and a truth from God's Word with another believer.

THE LOST MUST REALIZE
Matthew 3:9-12

Carol had come to a Bible study for about two months. While clearly interested in spiritual things, the church she attended had instilled in her a false hope in faith plus works for eternal life. When she turned to me to ask a question about heaven, because a strong relationship of trust had been established, I responded in a way I never had to any lost soul. I asked exactly why God should allow her into heaven. When she answered with a mixture of faith and works, I told her, "I'm sorry to say, you are not going to make it to heaven." This so shocked her, and shook her previously held confidence that she sincerely wanted to know more. The result was, moments later, Carol gloriously trusted in Christ alone by grace alone for eternal life.

When the religious leaders of Israel, the Pharisees and Sadducees, came to observe the multitudes being baptized by John the Baptist, he was very direct with them. He called them a generation of vipers for their spiritual hypocrisy. He also warned of God's "wrath to come" (Matthew 3:7). He explained they did not automatically have eternal life simply because they were the descendants of Abraham, who believed God's promises to him and had his faith counted for righteousness. The response of John the Baptist seems very harsh and would not be the usual approach to an unsaved soul. However, it was exactly what these hard-hearted individuals needed to hear. Steeped in their spiritually dead religious pride, if there was any hope for them to come to eternal life, their false confidences needed to be shaken. They needed to realize their unrighteous condition and the gravity of eternal punishment awaiting them. They needed to know that they were spiritually lost, and that now was the time to respond in faith, that they might escape the eternal punishment of their sin in unquenchable, everlasting fire.

When we witness to lost souls, we should normally use a much less abrasive approach. Nonetheless, no lost soul is likely to trust in the finished work of the Lord Jesus Christ, apart from all works or personal righteousness, unless we help them see that these things cannot save them from eternal punishment. Every lost soul must first understand their lost condition, that they are helpless to do anything of themselves to merit eternal life, and that they must trust in Christ alone for eternal life. Make sure your witnessing is always this clear.

AVENUES OF ATTACK
Matthew 4:1-11

In April 1775, Paul Revere instructed three Boston patriots to put lanterns in the steeple of the Old North Church to report movement of British troops. Though the lights were only there for under a minute, across the Charles River in Charlestown, fellow Americans understood the signals. Subsequently, Paul Revere and William Dawes rode by horseback alerting nearby towns that the British were coming.

In the spiritual realm, it is important for Christians to understand that the attacks of Satan are coming to defeat us. I John 2:16 shines the light of understanding on the three primary avenues of his attack: "the lust of the flesh, and the lust of the eyes, and the pride of life." We see all three of these present when the Spirit of God led the Savior into the wilderness where He was "tempted of the devil." Satan began by questioning, "if thou be the Son of God, command that these stones be made into bread" (Matthew 4:3). The Savior surely had the power to do so, but this was an appeal to the flesh. Christ was to endure victoriously these temptations as the Son of Man, and not as the Son of God with miraculous enablement to satisfy His hunger. Next, Satan tempted the Lord to throw Himself from the pinnacle of the temple that angels might protect Him (vss. 5-6). This temptation was an appeal to "the lusts of the eye" because it would have been a spectacle to see angels intervene. However, just as it would be improper for believers today to pursue reckless behavior to prove God's care, it was also outside the will of God for the Son of Man to engage in such rash conduct. Finally, Satan offered the Savior all the kingdoms of the world if He would only worship him (vss. 8-9). This temptation appealed to the "pride of life," as it would be gratifying for the Savior to have the worship of the world. But this was not the proper time, place, nor means for the Savior to achieve this end.

We, too, should be keenly alert to the ongoing temptations of Satan. Moreover, if we, like the Savior, arm ourselves with relevant verses to answer these temptations, we will have a far better chance to emerge victorious. Right now would be a good time to memorize a verse, or place verses in a prominent place, that apply to each of the three avenues where Satan will try to defeat you.

DROPOUTS
Matthew 5:1

It is estimated that annually 1.2 million students drop out of high school in the United States. In 2009 it was fully 8.1% of high school students.[1] One source refers to this as "The Silent Epidemic" because this problem receives so little press.[2] However it is a big problem with long-range effects. Students who drop out of high school in the United States are more likely to be locked into low-paying jobs, be unemployed, be homeless, be incarcerated, be on welfare, and have children at an early age.

It is a sad reality that there have always been a high percentage of people who once followed the Lord Jesus Christ who become spiritual dropouts. Matthew 5:1 records that "multitudes" followed the Savior early in His ministry. But their true motives and spiritual depth was revealed when He told them, "Ye seek Me, not because ye saw the miracles, but because ye did eat of the loaves, and were filled" (John 6:22-26). It was shortly after these events when the Savior began to teach deeper truths. Many concluded, "This is an hard saying…From that time many of His disciples went back, and walked no more with Him" (John 6:53-66). For a time, there was enough spiritual interest and receptivity to make people listen. But eventually the majority fell away. In essence, many who once followed Christ wanted to make little mental effort or personal commitment. When it came to paying the price of personal persecution that came with following the Savior, very few remained faithful. As a nation, eventually the multitudes joined with the spiritually hardened religious leaders of Israel, to first oppose the Lord Jesus Christ, then to call for His crucifixion. You might say the multitudes were fickle and shallow in their spiritual interest.

Dear one, how deep is your interest in the things of God? Are you interested in following Him primarily when you want Him to intervene in your circumstances? Do you seek to know more of Him and His Word only for a time, or when it is convenient? Surely the Lord Jesus, who suffered and died for us, is worthy of our complete and consistent, sold out, loyal participation. Through good times and bad, purpose now to be a dedicated believer who makes prayer, the study of His Word, sharing the gospel with the lost, and regular worship your constant practice.

ARE YOU A HOARDER?
Matthew 6:19-24

Hoarding is an obsessive-compulsive behavior of acquiring different things in large volumes, while failing to throw away things of little or no value. Television shows document examples of people with voluminous stacks of magazines, newspapers, artwork, clothing, and just plain junk that residents literally cannot walk freely in their homes. Many people are "pack rats" displaying similar characteristics, but hoarding rises to a level of excessive extreme. In many cases, a hoarder's passion for possessions consumes their lives, personal space, and relationships.

While speaking to His disciples, the Lord Jesus Christ told them, "Lay not up for yourselves treasures upon earth, where moth and rust doth corrupt...But lay up for yourselves treasures in heaven..." (Matthew 6:19-20). There were several reasons for this instruction to His apostles. In the past, God miraculously provided manna for Israel's daily need for food in their wilderness wanderings. Christ required His apostles to trust that He once again would provide supernaturally for them in the days ahead, through the years of tribulation, and into the Millennium. He explained that earthly riches are often corrupted by moth or rust, and stolen by thieves. Instead of these fleeting riches, the Savior wanted His followers to be living and serving Him so that they would have secure riches in the figurative vaults of heaven. He further explained, "For where your treasure is, there will your heart be also" (vs. 21). If their true riches were in heaven, their hearts would be fixed on living for Christ. But if their primary treasures were on earth, these would capture their affection and devotion. Moreover, whether choosing Him or the riches of earth as their "master," they would love the one and hate the other (6:24). Therefore, the Lord Jesus was urging them to make serving Him the primary focus of their lives.

While these instructions and promises had exclusive fulfillment to Jews under the Law in the tribulation and Millennium, there is a basic principle that applies to us in a secondary sense. We, too, must be careful not to be consumed by hoarding earthly treasures. Paul warns believers today, "No man that warreth (for the Lord) entangleth himself with the affairs of this life; that he may please Him who hath chosen him to be a soldier" (II Timothy 2:4). Make the Lord Jesus your true master, love Him above earthly gain, and "lay up in store"(I Timothy 6:19) a wealth of eternal riches through a life of genuine faithfulness to Christ.

A CRITICAL SPIRIT
Matthew 7:1

We all know people who have a critical spirit. They almost always seem to be criticizing, finding fault, and tearing others down. Constructive criticism, on the other hand, is always expressed face to face, from a good spirit, and with the intent to build another up. But one with a critical spirit gravitates to a pattern of dwelling on the negative, looking for flaws, complaining continually, and being often upset about something.

In Matthew 7:1, the Savior told the Jewish multitudes being promised the Millennial Kingdom, "Judge not, that ye be not judged." Unfortunately, this verse has been widely misunderstood. The Lord Jesus was clearly NOT forbidding making any judgments about people or conduct. In verse 6, He gave instruction not to give "that which is holy to dogs." In verse 15, He warns to "beware of false prophets." In both instances making some judgments were necessary. Later in Hebrews 5:14, it is promised that saints with a kingdom hope (who will first go through the seven years of tribulation) will "have their senses exercised to discern both good and evil." During this time, false teachers and evil influences will abound, and a keen sense of discernment, anchored in Scripture, will be essential. *What then did our Lord mean when He told His followers to judge not?* In essence, He meant they must not allow a negative judgmental spirit to dominate their daily walk. Once the persecution of the tribulation unfolds, believers who choose to be harsh in judgment and constantly find fault with others (Matthew 7:2-4) will be dealt with in a similar fashion by the forces of the Anti-Christ. Moreover, the Lord was seeking to impress on His followers that there must be a difference between them and the hypocritical leaders of Israel. They were like the self-righteous publican thinking himself better than the humble sinner who prayed in the temple (Luke 18:9-14). The Savior was urging believers to cultivate a humble and sincere godliness all could readily see.

While this passage has primarily application to Jewish believers awaiting or going through the Tribulation, there are two principles for us to glean. We, too, must guard against having a persistent, fault-finding, critical spirit. This leads to a soured negative existence and a testimony rooted in pride. Yet we must not fail to judge bad doctrine or sinful behavior and distance ourselves from both, for "he that is spiritual judgeth all things" (I Corinthians 2:15). *Are you striving for balance in both areas?*

TOTAL COMMITMENT
Matthew 8:18-22

A sincere Christian businessman once told this author, "When I retire, I intend to dedicate the rest of my life to serving the Lord." His involvement in the local church was fairly limited, and, once he retired, he moved far away from any grace church. His final years were spent largely without any meaningful spiritual ministry.

In Matthew 8:18-23, two disciples offered to follow the Savior. The first said, "I will follow Thee whithersoever Thou goest" (vs. 19). Our Lord's response was, "the foxes have holes...but the Son of man hath not where to lay His head" (vs. 20). In divine wisdom, the Lord Jesus knew this man needed to understand there would be hardship and sacrifices for those who followed Him. The second man, likewise, expressed a willingness to be our Lord's disciple, but he asked, "...first to go and bury my father" (vs. 21). This was not a request for a temporary leave of absence. If his father had just recently died, he would surely have been attending to the needs for burial at the time. Instead, he was asking for a delay in fully following the Lord for what likely may have been many years. The Savior's response was, "Follow Me; and the let the (spiritually) dead bury the dead" (vs. 22). In both instances, the Lord Jesus Christ was explaining He expected complete and immediate commitment in following Him, not delays or half-heartedness. These were requirements for Jews in this day to receive eternal life and enter the Millennial Kingdom. He more fully explained in Luke 14:26 saying, "If any many come to Me, and hate not (comparatively) father, and mother, and wife, and children...he cannot be My disciple." Being a true believer in this era meant complete commitment because, "No man having put his hand to the plough, and looking back, is fit for the kingdom of God" (Luke 9:62).

Today, under Grace, such exacting standards are not demanded to be a follower of Christ. Still, we see tremendous dedication in the lives of grace believers like the Apostle Paul, Titus, Timothy, and more. Surely the Savior expects us to similarly be "sold out" in our daily walk because we are told, "...that He [Christ] died for all, that they which live should not henceforth live unto themselves, but unto Him which died for them, and rose again" (II Corinthians 5:15). *Is your life one of total commitment to the Lord, or one of delay and half-heartedness?* Today, make your first priority your Savior.

LABORERS FOR THE HARVEST
Matthew 9:35-38

When this author's father was a young man, he worked the family farm with horses. When it came time to harvest crops, it was very labor-intensive. Workers commonly traveled from one region to another to work for several weeks until the fields were empty of grain. It was a time of hard work, but working side by side forged life-long friendships, and all the workers were rewarded with generous pay.

As the Lord Jesus Christ "went about all the cities and villages…preaching the gospel of the kingdom…but when He saw the multitudes, He was moved with compassion on them…" (Mathew 9:35-36). When many of us see masses of people, we often focus with irritation on their sinful conduct. It is noteworthy that when our Savior saw people, He saw their spiritual need and was moved to work to rescue them from eternal punishment. As the Son of God, He knew many were indifferent to His message of salvation and that most would turn away from Him, particularly around His crucifixion. Nonetheless, He knew some would respond and be saved. Therefore, He told His disciples, "The harvest truly is plenteous, but the labourers are few…(vs. 37).

We must not allow Satan to convince us that no one wants to listen or respond in saving faith to our gospel of grace. The field of souls is still ripe for harvest, many will still trust in Christ when they hear the gospel, and there is still an urgent need for workers. Like our Lord, we need to cultivate a compassion for lost souls in danger of eternal torment and allow a burden for their souls to motivate us to share with them the good news of eternal life. We also need another new perspective. Of the tens of thousands to whom the Lord ministered, only about one hundred and twenty actually believed on the Lord Jesus and remained faithful to Him until His ascension. Still, the Savior considered this a plenteous spiritual harvest of souls. In our era, when some ministries fill arenas and boast great numbers, we sometimes forget what our Savior considers successful ministry. We, too, need to begin to look at one, two, or three souls that we lead to a saving knowledge of Christ as a plenteous harvest, and begin to get busy giving out the gospel. Share a gospel track or a simple explanation of salvation with a lost soul today. You can forge life-long relationships and be richly rewarded in eternity.

TWO BY TWO
Matthew 10:1-5

Often when missionaries return home from the foreign field on furlough, they decide not to return. Author, Gordon Franz attributes the high attrition rate for missionaries to loneliness and discouragement.[1] He also suggests this problem could be solved by following a more biblical example.

Have you ever noticed that in Scripture, when the Savior sends people out in ministry, it is nearly always in pairs, and not alone? In our text, the apostles are listed in pairs, either brother with brother, or friend with friend. Likewise, when seventy disciples were sent out to harvest eternal souls with their Gospel of the Kingdom, Christ "sent them two by two" (Luke 10:1-2). There were likely multiple reasons for following this pattern. The Savior told them, "Behold, I send you forth as sheep in the midst of wolves...But beware of men: for they will deliver you up to their counsels, and they will scourge you in the synagogues..."(Matthew 10:16-17). These brave souls were going to minister in spiritually hostile territory. Going in pairs may have brought greater safety by making a violent attack less likely. Working in pairs likely helped lessen discouragement, and was more effective in answering questions or objections. Two heads have always been better than one. The reason for going in pairs may have been to follow the divine principle of Deuteronomy 19:15, which says, "...at the mouth of two witnesses, or...three witnesses, shall the matter be established." In other words, it gave them greater credibility. Moreover, working together enabled them to forge a strong bond with another believer as they ministered together. It is noteworthy that as these apostles continued their ministry in the Book of Acts, Peter and John continue ministering as a team (Acts 3:1-3).

God the Holy Spirit confirms this principle when separating and ordaining the Apostle Paul for ministry. "The Holy Ghost said [to prophets and apostles in the church at Antioch] Separate Me Barnabas and Saul for the work whereunto I have called them" (Acts 13:2). Paul also continues this pattern of ministering with others throughout his lifetime. The lesson to learn from all this is, whenever possible, when you go to minister, especially to share the gospel, it is wise to enlist someone to go with you. They can pray for you and for the lost as the gospel is presented. They can help give biblical answers to honest questions. You can also encourage one another to be faithful and enjoy sweet fellowship together.

FORGETTING TRUTH
Matthew 11:4-6

If you've ever been frustrated because you easily forget biblical truth you once learned, you are not alone. Many sincere believers struggle with this problem, and this author is one of them. By Wednesday, I usually have a hard time even remembering what I preached on the previous Sunday. My mind works forward to future responsibilities and not so well looking back to the past. For many of us, our minds are like a colander that allows truth to be washed away. Therefore we need constant review of biblical truths.

Even John the Baptizer had this problem. While imprisoned for some time and abandoned by Israel, this great man of God became discouraged and confused. John knew our Lord to be the Messiah, for when John baptized Christ, John witnessed the Spirit of God descend upon the Savior and heard the Father's voice from heaven declaring Christ to be His Son (Matthew 3:13-17). But John was anticipating the Savior to quickly establish His kingdom on earth. With this delay and John's persecution, he sends his disciples to Christ asking, "Art thou He that should come, or do we look for another?" (Matthew 11:3). The response of the Lord Jesus is encouraging because it was not harsh. Instead it was patient and loving. Beyond the miraculous events John personally witnessed confirming our Lord was the promised King of Israel, he should have also remembered key Old Testament prophecies of the Messiah. Isaiah 35:1-5 predicted the Messiah would open the eyes of the blind and ears of the deaf. Isaiah 61:1-3 declared Israel's promised one would have the Spirit of God upon Him as He preached to the meek and brokenhearted, and that He would proclaim "the acceptable year of the Lord" [establishing a kingdom on earth for Israel]. The Lord Jesus told the disciples of John to return to him and confirm "again" that the blind were being healed, the dead raised, and the Gospel of the Kingdom was being "preached to them" (Matthew 11:5). All these things demonstrated that the Lord Jesus was Israel's Messiah.

When you forget great spiritual truths previously learned, be encouraged that the Lord understands, "For He knoweth our frame; and remembereth that we are dust" (Psalm 103:14). He knows we will need constant review or we will forget. This is exactly why He provided us with His written Word. Make it your priority to read it every day.

*For a more detailed study in the book of Matthew, see the author's book, *God's Meaning in Matthew*.

OPPOSING A SPIRITUAL RESPONSE
Matthew 12:22-24

Two professing Christian couples have stood in the way of allowing spiritual ministry to their children, and do not allow their children to have a positive spiritual response. One refuses to give, or allow anyone else to give, any biblical input to their children, saying, "We want them to make up their own mind." An appeal was made to the other couple that, even if they wouldn't attend any church, they could at least have Bible study at home. Their response was, "They already know everything they need to know about the Bible."

When our Lord healed one who was blind, deaf, and possessed with a demon, the Pharisees publicly described the Savior saying, "This fellow doth not cast out devils, but by Beelzebub the prince of devils" (Matthew 12:24). Second Kings 1:3 reveals Beelzebub to be the false god of the Canaanites, and worshipping him was considered to be most vile of all demonic worship. The Jews in Jesus' day associated this name directly with Satan (Mark 3:26). This was not the first time the religious leaders of Israel had opposed God's messenger. They previously accused John the Baptist of having a demon (Matthew 11:18). Likewise, they had previously said the same of our Lord when He healed "a dumb man possessed with a devil" (Matthew 9:32-34). These Pharisees were becoming progressively more spiritually hardened and bold in their opposition of the Lord Jesus Christ. Stephen hit the nail on the head when describing them: "...Ye do always resist the Holy Ghost, as your fathers did, so do ye" (Acts 7:51).

It is a very dangerous thing to seek to turn others away from faith in, or faithfulness to, the Lord Jesus Christ. The Lord explained about those who do so, "...it were better for him that a millstone were hanged about his neck, and that he were drowned in the depth of the sea" (Matthew 18:6). The same warning is issued again in Mark 9:42 and Luke 17:2. These are stern warnings about eternal consequences for those guilty of negatively influencing, or preventing, spiritual ministry to others. For the lost, doing so will add to their sins and intensify their eternal punishment. For those who are saved but likewise hinder a spiritual response, surely there will be great accountability at the Bema Seat of Christ. We do well to warn those who oppose the cause of Christ that our Lord views this very seriously. *Do you know someone with whom you should share this article?*

YOU WOULDN'T BELIEVE
Matthew 13:3

Most of us are familiar with the phrase, "You wouldn't believe me if I told you." There are actually several instances in the Scripture when something very similar takes place. The prophet Habakkuk declares to Israel that God was going to raise up the dreadfully violent Chaldeans to plunder the land. But his explanation included, "…for I will work a work in your days, which ye will not believe, though it be told you" (Habakkuk 1:5).

We learn from Matthew 13:3 that the Lord Jesus "…spake many things unto them in parables." A parable is a similitude or comparison, but the root word means something thrown alongside. At this point in our Lord's ministry, it was apparent the nation of Israel was largely rejecting Him as their Messiah and King. Therefore, going forward, except when speaking to His apostles, He nearly always addresses the masses in parables. In effect, He was walking away from aggressive ministry to the nation to focus His time and attention on preparing the "little flock" of believers for future ministry after His departure. But, as He walks away from Israel as a whole, He throws alongside those who would not respond to Him in faith, a number of parables. We do well to fully understand these parables were *NOT to reveal spiritual truths* or make them easier to understand. *It was to conceal spiritual truths* and make it more difficult for His enemies to mount further attacks against Him. Matthew 13:13-15 makes this abundantly clear when Christ explains to His disciples why He now spoke in parables, "because they seeing see not, and hearing they hear not, neither do they understand… For this people's heart is waxed gross, and their ears are dull of hearing, and their eyes they have closed…."

It is always a serious and dangerous thing to have the privilege of being exposed to spiritual truth, and then refuse to respond as the Lord would have us respond. God's divine purpose in giving divine truth is that it might change us, or transform us for the better. This is true for the lost that need to respond to the gospel and be saved from eternal punishment through faith. But it is equally true for believers who are to allow God's Word to change their daily walk. *Are there any areas in your life where the Lord has shown you His will and you have remained unchanged?* Right now is the time to surrender to His Will.

PLUCKING UP THE SEED
Matthew 13:18-44

Growing up on a farm, every spring we would pre-pare the ground, then sow seeds for a harvest of oats. Nearly every year seagulls followed behind the wagon, and would eat a good deal of the seed. As soon as we finished sowing the field, we would harrow the ground to cover the seed, but it always bothered me that we were losing too many seeds to the birds.

We have a parallel of this experience in our Lord's parable of the sower in Matthew Chapter 13. The key elements are "a sower went forth to sow," what was being sowed was "the word of the kingdom," and "the wicked one...catcheth away that which was sown in his heart" (vs. 19). It will greatly help our understanding if we remember the context preceding this parable. The Lord Jesus had come offering eternal life in the Millennial Kingdom to Israel if she would follow Him by faith as her promised King and Messiah. Even though fulfilled prophecy, many miracles, and His pow-erful preaching authenticated our Lord's ministry, most in Israel remained in unbelief. Verse 37 identifies the sower in this parable as "the Son of man," the Lord Jesus Christ. What was being sown to Israel was "the word [offer or promise] of the kingdom" (vs. 19). "The wicked one" who caught away the seed (vs. 19), is identified as "the devil" (vss. 37-39). It is also noteworthy that there were human "children of the wicked one" seeking to turn others away from saving faith in the Savior.

While the circumstances surrounding this parable and its primary ap-plication deal directly with Israel, there are secondary applications for us today that we should not miss. Satan still seeks to steal away the seed of gospel truth when it is sown in the life of an unsaved soul. As he did with Israel, Satan attacks, either through evil men or his fallen angels, those who hear and may respond to our gospel of grace. Paul tells us "the god of this world hath blinded the minds of them which believe not, lest the light of the glorious gospel of Christ...should shine unto them" (II Corinthians 4:4). Knowing that Satan and his forces seek to thwart a lost soul coming to Christ when we share the gospel, we should be much in prayer, gener-ously use God's powerful, written Word, and follow up soon on those who have heard how to be saved, before Satan gobbles up the seeds of truth and conviction.

THE INFLUENCE OF THE WOMAN
Matthew 14:11

A woman in the town where we live was such a nasty, nosy, in your face type of person that, instead of referring to her as Eva, many called her "Evil." Not surprisingly, she raised a daughter who followed in her mother's pattern of ungodliness. Those who really know these women want little to do with them.

Herodias was the same kind of evil woman, yet even worse. She was an immoral woman who had a consensual union with Herod after leaving her husband, Herod's brother. When John the Baptist rebuked them for this union, he was imprisoned. Angry and vindictive, Herodias wanted John put to death. When Herodias' daughter went to dance seductively before Herod during his birthday banquet, she was "before instructed of her mother" to ask for "John (the) Baptist's head in a charger" (Matthew 14:8). Herod complied, but he did so by going against his better judgment because he feared the multitudes that considered John a prophet. What Herodias could not achieve outright, she did by coercion, manipulation, and trickery.

The mother of Solomon stands in stark contrast. "The prophecy that his mother had taught him" included a strong warning to beware of "wine...lest they [kings] drink, and forget the law and pervert...judgment" (Proverbs 31:1-5). The law, or strong commands, of his mother was given "to keep thee from the evil woman" (Proverbs 6:6, 24). She told Solomon to look for "a woman that feareth the Lord" (Proverbs 31:30) and gave a lengthy description of how such a woman conducts herself (Proverbs 31:10-31). These qualities in a woman were of great price in the days of Solomon, and they are just as important today. We learn from Titus 2:3-5 that older women are to teach younger women about "behavior as becometh holiness... [and is] discreet." Mothers are also to teach their children to "know how to possess his [or her] vessel in sanctification and honor" and not to "defraud" others in areas of temptation, such as wearing revealing clothing, or being sexually aggressive outside of marriage (I Thessalonians 4:3-6).

We urge women who read these descriptions to purpose to eradicate the qualities of ungodliness, and avoid those who revel in them. But do more. Seek to build true godliness into your life. To the men, we urge you to look for a truly godly woman as your soul mate in marriage. And if you have found such a woman, tell her today how thankful you are for her godly example.

HELPING THE BEREAVED
Matthew 14:12-14

What should you do when a friend loses a loved one in death? Many are so uncomfortable and so unsure what to say, they simply avoid these friends. Others offer platitudes in an attempt to give comfort, while some urge their grieving friend to move on with life. There are actually three passages that give us keen insight for what do to help the bereaved.

The book of Job gives a lengthy account of four friends who came to give comfort as soon as they learned of Job's sorrows. Their initial responses were very good. They immediately came to spend time with Job to demonstrate compassion and comfort. Then they wisely sat in silence with Job for seven days, letting their presence voice their love. Only when they began to speak, and render conclusions, and judgmental ultimatums did they undo the previous good. We learn from these examples that when others grieve, we simply need to be there, be quiet, be a good listener, and be nonjudgmental. When Mary came to our Savior grieving and weeping over the loss of her brother Lazarus, "Jesus wept" (John 11:35). There is nothing wrong with men or women allowing the sorrow of a friend to touch their own soul so that they literally weep with those who grieve. When these emotions are genuine, they express a love, connection, compassion, and understanding that no mere human words can convey adequately to those in mourning. The lesson here is to allow yourself to cry with those who sorrow, if your tears are genuine. Paul put it this way, "Rejoice with them that do rejoice, and weep with them that weep" (Romans 12:15). When John the Baptist was murdered, his (John's) disciples came and "told Jesus" (Matthew 14:3-13). Our text says that Jesus "departed...into a desert place." However, Mark 6:31 specifies, "He said unto them [the disciples of John], Come ye yourselves apart into a desert place, and rest awhile." Luke 9:10 tells us Christ "took them, and went aside privately into a desert place." We learn from our Lord's response that those who are grieving need time to rest, not in solitude, but with a compassionate friend who will attend to their physical and emotional needs while their spirits grieve and begin to heal.

Arm yourself with these principles for action when someone is grieving. In fact, it would be good to record these principles in your Bible so you have a quick reminder the next time they are needed.

GIVING THANKS
Matthew 14:15-21

While attending a Christian college to prepare for the ministry, one of my precious memories was that of several thousand students gathering for the evening meal, and collectively giving thanks to God. Giving thanks before eating is something we have practiced regularly since trusting in Christ for salvation. It has even been a testimony at restaurants where we occasionally have people thank us for this example.

When the Savior prepares to miraculously feed "five thousand men, beside [or in addition to] women and children" (Matthew 14:21), He first pauses to give thanks to the Father. Matthew 14:19 simply says, "and looking up to heaven, He blessed [meaning to thank or invoke a benediction], and break, and gave the loaves to his disciples." John writes, "and when He had given thanks, He distributed to His disciples" (John 6:11). Surely the Lord's purpose in providing this clear record is to enable us to realize that if even the Son of God stopped to give thanks before eating, we should also do so every time we are blessed of the Father to have something to eat.

Not only do we have this example from the Lord Jesus Christ, we have other Scripture that likewise teach the practice of giving thanks before eating. Romans 14:6 tells us, "He that eateth, eateth to the Lord, for he giveth God thanks; and he that eateth not, to the Lord he eateth not, and giveth God thanks." The point here is essentially that unbelievers do not give God thanks before eating because they are not acknowledging the Lord. But, believers are to give thanks before eating because they are to acknowledge the Lord as the true provider of their daily food. Similarly, we learn from I Timothy 4:3-4 that "God hath created [meats] to be received with thanksgiving of them which believe and know the truth. For every creature of God is good, and nothing to be refused, if it be received with thanksgiving."

On the basis of these Scriptures, we encourage every believer to cultivate the practice of stopping to pray consistently before each meal. However, we urge you not to do so with mechanical memorized prayers, or as a mere ritual. Instead, speak to the Lord from a thankful heart, acknowledge Him as the real provider of the food, and give Him thanks for His generous provision.

MEN REPORTING FOR DUTY
Matthew 14:34-36

After the Japanese bombed Pearl Harbor on December 7, 1941, American men really stepped up to the plate. In great numbers, and with a strong loyalty to their country, they voluntarily reported for military duty. Our victory in WWII came largely through the responsiveness of these brave men.

Matthew 14:35-36 touches on an extremely important timeless principle that we don't want to miss. When the Savior came into the land of Gennesaret, "And when the **men** of that place had knowledge of Him, they sent out into all that country round about, and brought unto Him all that were diseased...[and each one was] made perfectly whole." Please notice that it was the **men** who led the way here, and not the women. Men have been sold a false bill of goods from Satan to believe that being spiritually-minded is something unmanly. On the contrary, it is manly, as well as Biblical, for **men** to take the spiritual leadership in their home and church. Men should be ashamed when they shy away from prayer, Bible study, church attendance, and general spiritual leadership. In fact, God makes the point over and over in Scripture that **men** should be the driving spiritual force leading their families toward a closer walk with the Lord. Joshua stood before the spiritually anemic men of Israel and told them, "Choose you this day whom ye will serve...but as for me and my house, we will serve the Lord" (Joshua 24:15). Gideon asked, "Where be all his miracles which our **fathers** told us of, saying, Did not the Lord bring us up from Egypt?" (Judges 6:13). The Psalmist wrote, "Give ear, O my people...I will utter dark sayings of old: Which we have heard and known, and our **fathers** have told us...which he commanded our **fathers** that they should make them known to their children: that the generation to come might know them...That they might set their hope in God" (Psalm 78:1-9). Paul wrote, "And ye **fathers**, provoke not your children to wrath: but bring them up in the nurture and admonition of the Lord" (Ephesians 6:4).

It is not an accident Matthew 14:35 records the **men** taking the spiritual leadership in bringing many to the Lord Jesus Christ. God places this in His Word to encourage men to be spiritually-minded, involved, proactive, and to provide consistent spiritual leadership in their home and church. We are in a serious warfare with Satan. Godly men are desperately needed. Don't be AWOL. Step up to the plate.

GENUINE OR HYPOCRITE?
Matthew 15:1-9

When your author first became concerned about where he'd spend eternity, he first went to his denominational pastor asking if he could tell him how to have eternal life. This pastor did not have the foggiest idea, but he vehemently opposed my going to another church, and made a huge public ruckus.

When the scribes and Pharisees came from Jerusalem to question and oppose the Lord Jesus Christ, His answer was surprising. He confronted them about their inconsistencies in placing their traditions over the written commandments of God. Then, He plainly told them, "Ye hypocrites, well did Esaias [Isaiah] prophesy of you, saying, This people draweth nigh unto me with their mouth, and honoureth Me with their lips; but their heart is far from Me" (Matthew 15:7-8). This strong rebuke was intended to jar these spiritually dead men out of their cold lethargy, and into a living relationship with Him.

Only going through the motions of religious activity without a genuine, heartfelt desire to have a close, pleasing relationship with the Lord is hypocritical behavior in any dispensation. We can attend church services, dress up nicely, act spiritually, even read our Bible, then go out and live just as sinfully as the world. When this happens, we resemble the scribes and Pharisees, who the Savior so sharply rebuked. The Apostle Paul warned the saints at Ephesus about persisting in a cold, unemotional, spiritually dead internal condition. He explained that even believers could eventually become so spiritually hardened that their "understanding [becomes] darkened" and so blinded to God's truth that they could become "past feeling" (Ephesians 4:17-19). These examples are intended to encourage us to be genuine in our walk with the Lord, fervent in spirit, and intentionally cultivating a close walk with the Lord. We can accomplish this through regular study of His Word, with a consistent pattern of putting biblical truth into practice in our lives each day.

It is more than appropriate, when we read about biblical examples that had hearts far from the Lord, for us to ask ourselves about the condition of our own heart. *Is our heart only lukewarm for Christ? Is our heart likewise far from the Savior who died for us? Are we only going through the motions of religious activity?* If our hearts are not in the right spiritual condition, we can choose right now to begin to respond with genuine zeal and obedience toward our Savior.

EMOTIONS IN CHECK
Matthew 16:21-23

In many Christian circles emotions seem to be controlling the lives and even actions of many professing Christians. A church in Lakeland, Florida, televises services where people practice what they call "holy laughter." They literally roll on the floor while laughing uncontrollably, which defies the instruction from I Corinthians 14:27-34 about being in control of one's spirit, and doing things in an orderly fashion. Similarly, the trend today is to constantly ask others, "How do you feel about that?" Christians are not to be dictated by their feelings. What we believe, how we act, and even the way we feel is supposed to be subject to God's Word. It should never be a matter of how we feel, but as Galatians 4:30 says, "Nevertheless, what saith the Scripture?"

Prior to Matthew Chapter 16, the Savior had not disclosed to His apostles that He was going to suffer, die, and rise again from the grave. Luke 18:34 confirms "...this saying was hid from them, neither knew they the things which were spoken." Once he understood, Peter did not take this announcement well. "Peter took Him, and began to rebuke Him, saying, Be it far from thee Lord: this shall not be unto Thee" (Matthew 16:22). Peter had always reverenced the Savior, standing in awe of His power, doctrine, and commanding presence. But, this news completely upset his plans and his emotions began to control him. The Savior's response to Peter was very strong. He "said unto Peter, Get thee behind Me, Satan: thou art an offense unto Me..." (Matthew 16:23). This verse implies Satan was behind Peter's heightened, fleshly, emotional response. Satan was distracting Peter from seeing the greater truth and need for the Savior to fulfill prophecy, and the needed task of going to Jerusalem to die for the sins of all mankind. Isaiah 53:7-12 explained the Messiah must be brought as a lamb to slaughter, to pour out His soul unto death and become an offering for sin. Peter was allowing his emotions, or his flesh, to rule him rather than His head and God's will. This is a common mistake occurring regularly in these closing days of the Dispensation of Grace.

Christians should rejoice over their salvation, eternal security, heavenly hope, and regular service for Christ. However, we need to be on our guard to monitor, control, and bring our emotions into conformity to the Word and will of God in all areas. *Are you being careful in this area?*

102

AN IMPORTANT PRIORITY
Matthew 17:1-3

What do you set as your priority as you start your day? For some it is to begin by bathing and brushing their teeth. The ladies often fix their hair and makeup. Men generally shave in the morning. Most begin with a fresh set of clothes. Many always drink coffee and read the newspaper. But the most important priority to begin your day is to spend time in prayer.

Matthew 17:1-2 records the Lord Jesus Christ being transfigured on a high mountain before Peter, James, and John. However, Luke 9:28-29 tells us the Savior "went up into a mountain to pray. And as he prayed, the fashion of his countenance was altered, and His raiment was white and glistering." We are reminded by this example of the Son of God, and many others, how important it is to pray. The Lord Jesus spent time in prayer before walking on water. Later He prayed before being arrested prior to His crucifixion. Here we see the Lord praying before He was transfigured. Each of these important events was bathed in prayer before proceeding. While the Savior ministered to His apostles, He constantly instructed them to be men of prayer. He told them to pray for those who would persecute them (Matthew 5:44), pray to the Father in secret, or in a private way (Matthew 6:5-7), pray the Father would send forth laborers to harvest eternal souls through ministry (Matthew 9:38), and to pray that they enter not into temptation (Matthew 26:41).

God places all these instructions about prayer in His Word and provides the example of the Savior being devoted to prayer so that believers in every dispensation can see how important it is to cultivate the holy habit of prayer. We are to be "praying always" (Ephesians 6:18). May we allow this simple reminder, and this profound principle, to transform our lives immediately. We urge you to pause after reading this devotional to spend time in prayer. We encourage you to make a time of prayer your highest priority as you begin each day. We suggest that, as the Savior did, you particularly spend earnest time in prayer prior to any important decision or event. God desires your fellowship in prayer, your dependence upon Him demonstrated through prayer, and your access to richer blessings through prayer. Make it a priority beginning right now.

WHAT WILL ETERNITY BE LIKE?
Matthew 18:1-6

As a young man fresh out of Bible College, I worked as an assistant pastor in a denominational church for several years. There were several fundamental churches in this city. The pastors and assistant pastors met once a month for a time of fellowship and encouragement. While many of the experiences were edifying, one thing always bothered me. Each month these pastors would "count scalps," so to speak, by bragging about how many baptisms, new memberships, or attendance records they had recently.

If you've ever wondered what eternity will be like, you are not alone. One day the disciples "...came...unto Jesus, saying, Who is the greatest in the kingdom of heaven" (Matthew 18:1). The apostles were anticipating a Millennial Kingdom virtually identical to that of every earthly kingdom before it. They saw the Lord Jesus as King, with them as His loyal subjects possessing positions of honor, wealth, glory, and power. The problem with this concept is that the Kingdom of our Lord will be unique in nearly every way from the kingdoms of mere men. When the Lord Jesus Christ reigns as King over all the earth, the primary focus and activity will be ongoing worship of the King, and the sincere learning His precepts out of a humble heart (Daniel 7:14; Zechariah 14:16; Isaiah 2:2-3). It will not be to exalt men, including the apostles. Instead, it will be as recorded in Isaiah 42:8, "I am the Lord...My glory will I not give to another." This means the answer to the question of the apostles is that the Lord Jesus Christ will be the greatest in the Kingdom, and there will be room for only Him to have the spotlight of greatness and exaltation at this time.

We today share the same fleshly ambitions of the apostles. Therefore, the Lord reminds us, "For this I say...to every man that is among you, not think of himself more highly than he ought to think; but to think soberly... (Romans 12:3). Revelation 4:1-11 paints a vivid picture of the nature of an eternal existence for the saints: "...I looked, and, behold, a door was opened in heaven...The four and twenty elders fall down before Him that sat on the throne, and worship...and cast their crowns before the throne, saying, Thou art worthy, O Lord, to receive glory and honour and power: for Thou hast created all things." May we begin now to rearrange our eternal expectations toward praise, adoration, learning, and service, rather than self-exaltation!

GUARDIAN ANGELS?
Matthew 18:10-14

Through the years your author has listened to people who, with great emotional conviction, claim to have seen their guardian angel. However, it is extremely important for us always to confirm what we believe, including those things we want to believe, with the clear testimony of God's written Word. The Holy Scriptures must be our absolute standard for what we believe on any subject. *But what do the Scriptures teach about having guardian angels?*

There are actually no passages in God's Word that tell us that we, or anyone else, have a guardian angel. Nonetheless, our text in Matthew 18:10 is sometimes used to bolster this concept. It records the Lord Jesus saying, "Take heed that ye despise not one of these little ones; for I say unto you, That in heaven their angels do always behold the face of my Father which is in heaven." Note that our Lord did NOT say any Jewish believer had a guardian angel. We must be slow to draw this conclusion, unless it is clearly stated and then corroborated by other Scriptures that plainly teach such a concept. From Hebrews 1:14 we learn that, at least when it came to Israel in the past, angels were God's "ministering spirits, sent forth to minister to them who shall be heirs of salvation." The Scriptures record multiple instances of God sending angels to minister to individuals, but they are never referred to as a guardian angel nor that they remained permanently with any individual. Matthew 18:10 is only saying that angels, in general, ministered to Jewish saints in different ways, at the specific bidding of the Lord, and that these angels collectively have a direct audience with God the Father. Nothing more is intended.

Is our condition somehow diminished not to have a guardian angel? The answer is "no," not at all. We are already blessed with "all spiritual blessings in heavenly places" (Ephesians 1:3). We have the completed Word of God to guide and empower us each day. The Spirit of God now indwells every believer to comfort, strengthen, teach, and guide us. We also know that even when trials arise, God is able to make "all things work for good to them that love God, to them who are the called according to His purpose" (Romans 8:28). We simply need nothing else. Therefore, rest and rejoice in your blessed condition, which is far better than having a guardian angel.

*For a more detailed study, see the authors book, *God's Meaning in Matthew.*

ETERNAL EXISTENCE
Matthew 19:28-30

Nearly all adults have driven in foggy conditions. Even with our headlights on, oftentimes we can only see ahead a very short distance. When it comes to understanding exactly what eternity will be like for us in the heavens, we can't see into the future with a clear understanding of what lies ahead. God has kept some of the wonders of heaven a mystery. However, the Bible does give us some glimpse into eternity, if we are willing to look carefully.

Believers in the Dispensation of Grace can gain some insight into what things will be like in eternity by studying the promises revealed to Israel about their eternal existence. Jeremiah 31:33 promises, "I will put my law in their inward parts, and write it on their hearts, and will be their God, and they shall be my people." Those in eternity will serve the Lord in pure devotion. Luke 20:33-36 promises, "in the resurrection...neither can they die anymore." Revelation 21:4 adds, "And God shall wipe away all tears from their eyes; and there shall be no more death, neither sorrow, nor crying, neither shall there be any more pain: for the former things are passed away." Sorrow and pain will be replaced by rejoicing and only happy memories in eternity. Zephaniah 3:9 promises, "For then will I turn to the people a pure language, that they may all call upon the name of the Lord, to serve Him with one consent." Everyone may be united in one language and happy service to the Lord. Matthew 19:29 reveals that God will richly reward those who were sacrificially faithful to Him. While many of these promises apply to life for redeemed Jews in the Millennial Kingdom, these descriptions also apply to resurrected Jewish saints who will experience eternal life in the Kingdom while Christ reigns as Lord of Lords.

While we should always be careful NOT to claim promises given to Israel indiscriminately, we cautiously suggest the eternal existence of members of the Body of Christ in the heavens is likely to have some of these parallel blessings. We too will be given new, eternal, pain-free bodies (I Corinthians 15:42-54), have a joyous existence in the presence of Christ, (I Thessalonians 4:17), and will have active service for the Lord (II Timothy 2:12; I Corinthians 6:1-3). Knowing that these things await us, we should set our affections on things above, and living now in light of eternity.

*For more detail see the author's book, Growing in God's Grace.

106

DULL OF HEARING
Matthew 20:17-21

In our family, we have some with a hearing problem. Some of the children actually hear instructions from an adult, and, in disobedience, chose to act as though they hear nothing. Some of the husbands have "selective hearing," meaning they only hear what they want to hear. Ladies, it's in the men's manual. Then we have several who have a genuine loss of hearing, and need a hearing aid to assist them.

The apostles of the Lord Jesus Christ had a hearing problem too. Three times previous to Matthew 20:17-19, the apostles had been told of our Lord's impending death. In Matthew 12:40, the Savior explained He was soon to be three days and three nights in the heart of the earth. Matthew 16:21 records, "From that time forth began Jesus to shew unto His disciples, how that He must…suffer…and be killed, and be raised again the third day." So, the effort to help them anticipate this was continual. Matthew 17:22-23, documents the Savior explaining the same upcoming sequence of events. Now in Matthew 20:17-19, we have a fourth instance of our Lord clearly explaining His upcoming betrayal, mocking, crucifixion, and subsequent resurrection. Yet with all these opportunities to grasp these events, Luke 18:31-34, clearly explains, "And they understood none of these things." The primary way in which these facts were hidden from the apostles was through a self-imposed, selfish, human blindness to God's revealed truth. These men did not want a dying Redeemer. They wanted a conquering King. They had been told, and were telling others, that the Millennial Kingdom was "at hand." With an imminent expectation of this kingdom of rich blessing, they had "forsaken all" (Matthew 19:27) to follow Christ, and they were focused on what they were going to receive for their faith and self-denial. Beyond the personal rewards, they also eagerly awaited Israel's suffering under Roman occupation being replaced with peace, prosperity, and prominence. These things made them dull of hearing when our Lord explained His coming death and resurrection.

While keeping Israel's distinctive context in mind, we must also not miss an application for us today. Sometimes our spiritual receptiveness is no better. If we become to entangled "with the affairs of this life" (II Timothy 2:4), it will drown out our responsiveness to God's Word, God's will, and God's Spirit. Instead, our disciplined focus must be to keep our eyes on "the things which are not seen…but (on) the things which are eternal" (II Corinthians 4:18).

TRIUMPHANT ENTRY
Matthew 21:6-11

Victorious Presidential candidates have a triumphant entry when they enter the convention hall to receive their party's nomination for president. Sports teams have a triumphant entry when they come back to their home city after winning a championship. Generals and armies have received triumphant entries into cities after defeating an opposing military force. However, the greatest triumphant entry of all time belongs to the Lord Jesus Christ.

Matthew 21:6-11 records what is commonly called our Lord's triumphant entry into Jerusalem. It tells us "a very great multitude spread their garments in the way; others cut down branches from the trees, and strawed them in the way" (vs. 8). This was the ancient equivalent of a jubilant ticker tape parade, demonstrating respect, appreciation, and even adulation. The "multitude" in this procession is described as "disciples" in Luke 19:37. They rejoiced "with a loud voice for all the mighty works that they had seen." They may have seen their Messiah heal many diseases, or perhaps they witnessed Lazarus being raised from the dead. But not everyone was happy to see the Lord on this day. John 12:9-11 records the chief priests sought to put Lazarus to death, "Because...by...him many of the Jews went away, and believed on Jesus." The real triumphant entry of the Lord Jesus Christ will be at His Second Coming to earth as the King of kings. At this time He will vanquish the armies of the nations that seek to destroy Israel, the beast, the false prophet, and Satan (Revelation 19:11-16, 20). In that day, as they experience eternal life, "the remnant of Israel shall not do iniquity." Therefore, their Messiah tells them "Sing, O daughter of Zion; shout, O Israel; be glad and rejoice with all the heart" (Zephaniah 3:13-14).

Believers in the Dispensation of Grace await a different triumphant entry of our Savior, when He returns in the clouds to rapture us home into the heavens. No one will be able to prevent Him from accomplishing this for us. With all adoration and glory belonging to the Lord Jesus Christ at this time, all who know Christ will be granted a triumphant entry into a heavenly existence. Our trials, physical or emotional pain, and failures in sinful conduct will all be swallowed up in a victory resounding the eternal praise to Him. We know we lose some battles on this side of eternity, and our enemy is daunting, but praise His name, we are on the winning side. Rejoice in these things my Christian friend.

THE GREATEST COMMANDMENT
Matthew 22:34-40

What is your number one rule? There seems to be one for almost everything. In business, many think it is to believe in yourself, or have the right location. In sports, it may be solid fundamentals, or a strong competitive nature. In looking for a mate, some think it is being attractive, or having a good sense of humor. In Bible study, it is being consistent with the context of each passage, or studying it dispensationally. Nearly everyone has a number one rule for different categories.

When the Sadducees were unsuccessful in snaring the Lord Jesus in words they could use against Him, "a lawyer" (meaning a scribe who was considered an expert in the Mosaic Law) posed a question. He asked, "Master, which is the great commandment in the law" (Matthew 22:36)? During this time period it was debated whether animal sacrifices for sins, requirements for purification, keeping the Sabbath, or circumcision was the most important aspect of the Law. This question was designed to get different groups upset with the Savior for not agreeing with their position. Our Lord's answer was a quote from Deuteronomy 6:5, where Moses implored Israel to keep all the commandments of God. But the Savior specified two commandments as the greatest: "Thou shalt love the Lord thy God with all thy heart, and with all thy soul, and with all thy mind. The second is like unto it. Thou shalt love thy neighbor as thyself" (Matthew 22:37-39). The history of Israel had been that she only half-heartedly loved Jehovah, and surely this was the case with all who questioned the Savior. Religious activities and positions of power did not equate to a complete love for the Lord, or she would have been more responsive to the ministry of the Savior. Israel's history had also been anything but one of love for one another. The Lord Jesus likely included this second rule of importance to strike conviction in this lawyer's heart and in all who were seeking to harm Him. Clearly, their motives and actions were not ones of love, but of sinful deceit and envy.

While these two commandments apply directly to the Jews under the Law of Moses, there is surely a needed application for us under grace. The Lord still desires more from us than a half-hearted love. He wants our genuine love with all of our being. We are also to love one another. Today, let's specifically ask the Lord to help us grow in both areas of love.

IS IT WRONG?
Matthew 23:13-39

Someone my father greatly admired once told him, "If you can't say anything good about another person, don't say anything at all." The godly intent behind this advice so gripped my father that he genuinely tried to live by this principle. He also often repeated this advice to his children, attempting to make a similar impression upon them. While this may be a good general principle by which to live, there are certainly needed exceptions. It is only prudent to warn others about a child molester, a dishonest businessman, those who sell drugs, an ungodly liar, or those with dangerously bad doctrine.

Many Christians in our present day have become convinced it is wrong to say anything negative about those who promote religious error. Their politically- correct concept is that we should only focus on the positive and what we have in common with others in doctrine. But we would do well to re-examine such a perspective. In Mathew Chapter 23, the Lord Jesus took such a strong, vocal, stand against religious error that it must have made the hair of some stand on end. The Savior repeatedly said, "Woe unto you, scribes and Pharisees, hypocrites" (Matthew 23:14, 15, 23, 25, 27). He called them "blind guides" (vs. 16), "fools" (vs. 19), and "serpents" (vs. 33). The Lord Jesus Christ took such a strong stand against these religious leaders because their spiritual influence was making others "twofold more the child of hell" (vs. 15). They clung to man-made traditions while they "omitted...faith" (vs. 23). They consistently opposed true men of God (vs. 34) and were "full of...iniquity" (vss. 27-28). In godliness, the Apostle Paul likewise aggressively opposed false teachers who were leading other souls to eternal damnation. He warned others to separate themselves from those who would "pervert the gospel of Christ" (Galatians 1:7-8). In II Timothy 2:16-18, he even named names because they were "overthrow[ing] the faith of some."

We are not advocating we should be looking for a fight, to dwell frequently on the negative, or constantly expose the false doctrine of others. However, the above examples should remind us there are times when taking a vocal stand is needed and appropriate. As Ecclesiastes 3:1 says, "To everything there is a season, and a time to every purpose under the heaven." Therefore, when sound and trusted Bible teachers warn you against spiritual dangers, thank them for their vigilance. Then, be a Berean searching "the Scriptures daily, [to see] whether these things be so" (Acts 17:11).

THE END OF THE WORLD
Matthew 24:3

The liberal media makes fun of believers by showing a raggedy-dressed man holding up a sign saying, "It's the end of the world." But those with some reverence for the Bible are concerned that our world is soon coming to an end. They view rising crime, atrocities by ISIS, and the risk of nuclear holocaust as real threats to the very existence of planet earth. *Is the end near?*

After viewing the temple, the disciples came to the Lord Jesus Christ asking, "what shall be the sign of Thy coming, and of the end of the world" (Matthew 24:3)? The phrase "the end of the world" has been widely misunderstood. It does NOT mean mankind will be extinguished from the face of the earth, or that the world itself will be obliterated. The consistent testimony of Scripture reveals this will never happen. Jehovah promised Israel the land of Canaan as "an everlasting possession" (Genesis 17:5-8). Jews with the righteousness of faith were told they would be resurrected into a divine Kingdom, and God "shall place you in your own land" (Ezekiel 37:14). Even though the earth eventually will be purged by fire to prepare for an eternal state for Israel (II Peter 3:10-14), redeemed Jews will occupy the earth as "an everlasting possession." The phrase "the end of the world" is a rewording of the phrase "the time of the end" as found in Daniel 8:17; 11:35; 12:9. A careful study of these passages, as in Matthew 24, refers to end times when Israel will go through seven years of prophesied tribulation. The Lord Jesus defined this phrase in Matthew 13:36-43, 48-50 in the parable of the tares and good seed. He described a coming time when lost souls would be gathered and cast "into a furnace of fire...then shall the righteous shall shine forth..." These events refer to the seven years of tribulation culminating with the Savior establishing His world-wide reign which will mark the end of Satan's reign as "the god of this world" (II Corinthians 4:4), and the end of Gentile domination over Israel and her promised land (Luke 21:20-24).

There is an end coming for the world as we know it. The Savior will come to rapture members of the Body of Christ to heaven and subsequently fulfill every promise to Israel. Believers must stand secure in God's promises, and live in constant expectation that He may begin this process at any moment.

WHY WILL THIS HAPPEN?
Matthew 24:21

Many times when great heartaches occur, hurting and confused individuals ask, "Why did God do this to me?" In general, it is important for Christians to understand God does not cause our sorrows! Our pain and hurts come from a variety of sources: the attacks of Satan as with Job; the consequences of unwise choices; "time and chance;" (Ecclesiastes 9:11) propensity to illnesses; and opposition from sinful people. God is simply not always behind what we find hurtful. However, when it comes to Israel's future seven years of agonizing tribulation, God will bring these trials to pass for several specified reasons.

Jeremiah 30:7 refers to these seven years as "the time of Jacob's trouble." Early in Israel's history, God promised to bless her if she followed Him faithfully, and curse her if she would not. These coming years of tribulation will be the consequences of Israel's continual, spiritual rebellion, when God will "punish" her (Zephaniah 1:12). God will use these days, particularly the Second Coming of Christ, "So the house of Israel shall know that I am the Lord their God" (Ezekiel 39:22, 27-29). The Lord will use these intense trials to purify the nation of Israel, or "refine them as silver is refined" (Zechariah 13:9), therein removing the "dross" of rebellion (Ezekiel 22:17-22). When purged from her iniquity, Israel will be prepared to properly worship Jehovah and "offer unto the Lord an offering in righteousness" (Malachi 3:3). The Tribulation will also fulfill prophecy, as God accomplishes the seventy weeks "determined upon thy people" (Daniel 9:24). These terrible days will also punish the entire world justly for its rebellious, sinful conduct. Just as Isaiah 13:9-11 promises, "I will punish the world for their evil, and the wicked for their iniquity" (Isaiah 13:9-11); God will bring the "haughtiness" of even "mighty men" low (Isaiah 2:11,17; 13:6-11). These events will be used to open the hearts of many to saving faith. Revelation 14:1-7 describes thousands who will proclaim "the everlasting gospel" to lost souls in peril of eternal punishment, and many will be saved.

We who have trusted in the Lord Jesus Christ alone for eternal life need not fear these days of tribulation. First Thessalonians 1:10 promises we have been "delivered from the wrath to come." Praise His name for this merciful blessing. Our responsibility is to rejoice in this truth, share the gospel that others may likewise be saved, and rest that even when trials come our way, God's grace will carry us through.

THE DUTY OF BELIEVERS
Matthew 25:1-13

Have you ever been unfamiliar with some kind of food and asked, "What does it taste like?" The inevitable response is, "It tastes like chicken." Everything doesn't taste like chicken, but making this comparison is an attempt to illustrate a description in a way that will make sense to the inquirer. Just as we do today, the Lord Jesus Christ often used the comparative words "like" or "as" to illustrate something with significant spiritual importance.

The parable of the ten virgins is rich with meaning and symbolism. The Old Testament pictured the nation of Israel as the wife of Jehovah (Isaiah 54:5-6). Yet because of constant spiritual adultery, God "put her away" with a "bill of divorce" (Jeremiah 3:8). Though Israel had forgotten the Lord, He promised He would not forget her but would once again woo her, and "betroth thee unto Me forever" (Hosea 2:19-20). In this parable, the Lord Jesus Christ represents the bridegroom, and Israel the bride. It was God's purpose to use redeemed Jews to "restore the preserved of Israel; [and] I will also give thee for a light to the Gentiles" (Isaiah 49:6). The ministry of these messengers is described as "open[ing] the eyes of the [spiritually] blind" (Isaiah 42:5-7). What a marvelous description of lost souls coming to see their need for saving faith. The virgins in this parable were equipped with lamps to provide illumination in the night (Matthew 25:3-4). This pictures the literal and spiritual darkness that will pervade the seven years of tribulation. As "the salt of the earth" and "the light of the world" Israel was told to "let your light so shine before men, that they may see your good works, and glorify your Father which is in heaven" (Matthew 5:16). Empowered with an unction of the Holy Spirit, these Jewish believers, pictured by the ten virgins, are being instructed to fulfill God's will for them. They were to "go forth as brightness, and the salvation thereof as a lamp that burneth" (Isaiah 62:1), leading many to eternal life.

While our program, promises, and people are different in this present Dispensation of Grace, we have many obvious parallels. We too are to be a light in our spiritually dark days, leading many to eternal life by giving out our Gospel of the Grace of God. We too are to be God's evangelists. We too are to live so godly that our life enhances our efforts to lead others to Christ. Make this your goal today.

SPIRITUAL PERSPECTIVE
Matthew 26:6-13

This author's eldest brother once managed a company selling Yellow Page ads in different parts of the country. Our youngest brother traveled some distance to go to work for him. The usual process for new salespeople was to go through a two-day training class, and the newcomers always had questions from the materials already covered. However, our youngest brother was so bright, he was given the training manual to read. Twenty minutes later he came back and announced he was ready to get started. Sure enough, when quizzed, he had thoroughly digested all the material and understood it well.

When Mary anointed the hands and feet of the Lord Jesus Christ with oil, it demonstrated how spiritually perceptive she was. Even though the Savior had been explaining repeatedly to His apostles He was soon to die and rise again, they still did not comprehend it. In fact, at least some of the disciples "had indignation, saying, To what purpose was this waste" (Matthew 26:8)? John 12:4 specifies Judas was responsible for stirring up this discontent and criticism among others. While he may have been an unsaved man, it is not uncommon even for the saints to rile up others with a critical spirit. This is always a serious sin. Proverbs 6:16-19 tells us sowing discord among the brethren is "an abomination." We must be careful not to do so. Even though the disciples did not comprehend our Lord's upcoming death, it appears Mary had remembered this from previous discussions. The Lord explained when Mary anointed Him that "she did it for my burial" (Matthew 26:12). We should also note that using this expensive oil was not a "waste," as expressed by Judas (vs. 8). Anything given as unto the Lord is never a waste, even though the unspiritually-minded may not perceive it this way. Moreover, it was Mary's prerogative to spend her money as she pleased. Peter made this point to Ananias about his finances saying, "Whiles it remained, was it not thine own?" (Acts 5:4) The sum of this record is that Mary's anointing of Christ with oil was "a good work" (Matthew 26:10), and the Savior announced wherever the gospel was preached, it would "be told for a memorial of her" (Matthew 26:13).

Are we spiritually receptive and perceptive enough readily to grasp spiritual things presented to us? May we seek to be so, never stir others to discontent, and remember doing things for the Savior is a good work that will bear lasting reward.

GUILTY HANDS
Matthew 27:15-26

While living in the dorms during my college years, one night a good-natured pillow fight broke out. It began when the one below me swatted me several times with a towel. My response was to reach for a bottle of Chloraseptic and thoroughly spray him down. He proceeded to drag my mattress, and me, to the floor. Then mayhem broke out. We'd been in trouble before, so I quickly put my mattress back on the frame, crawled in bed, and faced the wall, as if asleep. Momentarily, the door burst open with the dorm supervisor sending the rest of my roommates to the dean's office. I continued facing the wall, as if asleep and innocent, but I was neither.

It is true that Pilate sought to set the Lord Jesus Christ free, rather than have Him crucified, but he was not guiltless. After questioning the Savior, he announced to the Jews, "I find no fault in this man" (Luke 23:4); he even calls Christ "this just person" (Matthew 27:24). Luke 23:20 documents he was "willing to release Jesus." Peter says that Pilate was "determined to let Him go" (Acts 3:13). But he did not do so. Instead, he succumbed to the will of the mob. When he "saw that he could prevail nothing, but that rather a tumult [an uproar or disturbance] was made" (Matthew 27:24), he delivered up our Lord to be scourged savagely, beaten, and crucified by the soldiers. As the supreme governmental authority in this region, Pilate's primary duty was to see justice was always done when a subject was brought before him. He had the moral obligation to release anyone who was innocent, regardless of public opinion, and he had ample military forces to put down any unrest. It was a profound miscarriage of justice. Pilate tried to absolve himself of responsibility when he "took water, and washed his hands before the multitude, saying, I am innocent of the blood of this just person" (Matthew 27:4). But God did not hold him guiltless. Shortly before our Lord's death, He explained to Pilate, "He that delivered Me unto thee hath the greater sin" (John 19:11). Israel was the primary guilty party, but Pilate was also guilty by association and by his refusal to stop this wrongdoing.

Each of us does well to realize we are guilty before the Lord when passively going along with sinful actions, even when we are not the primary instigator. Instead, we must oppose and stop wrongdoing when possible.

COME AND DINE

Matthew 28

One of the greatest men in the Old Testament made a serious mistake. While military conquest was still needed, we read in II Samuel 11:1, "...at the time when kings go forth to battle... David sent Joab...But David tarried still at Jerusalem." We are not told explicitly why David was not in battle. Perhaps he was just tired from all the conflict, overwhelmed by the weight of responsibility, or concerned about the dangers that would be involved. Whatever the reason, David squandered an opportunity to be greatly used of the Lord, and he involved himself in actions that were beneath his calling. He involved himself with Bathsheba.

As we read Matthew Chapter 28, we should realize we are looking at only a brief overview of events after our Lord's resurrection. To see a more complete picture we should consult the other Gospels. After our Lord's death, the apostles were a defeated band of followers. From our Savior's repeated instructions, they should have known He would rise from the dead in three days. Yet when the women at the tomb announced that Christ had risen, "their words seemed to them as idle tales" (Luke 24:11). Even after the Lord Jesus appeared to them, the apostles "were terrified and affrighted, and supposed that they had seen a spirit" (Luke 24:36-48). Knowing how defeated His disciples would be, Christ gave instructions through an angel (Matthew 28:7) for them to meet Him in Galilee (some 70 miles north of Jerusalem) at the Last Supper (Matthew 26:32), and by angels at the tomb. There was also a specific place where "Jesus had appointed them" (Matthew 28:16) to meet Him, which was likely upon a nearby mountain where He had been transfigured. John 21 provides details that while this defeated band of believers awaited His appearing for eight days, they went fishing. Though they did not recognize Him at first, the Savior provided them with many fish. Then He invited them to draw near to Him by saying, "Come and dine" (John 21:12). It was during this time with the Savior that He comforted them and urged them to continue following Him by getting back to ministering to those who needed to hear the gospel.

It is understandable when circumstances and opposition from our spiritual enemy occasionally overwhelm God's servants. But we must not remain sidelined for long. Come and dine in fellowship with Christ and His written Word. Then get quickly back in the battle.

*See *God's Meaning In Matthew* for more detail.

NOT A PERFORMANCE SYSTEM
I Corinthians 1:2

Ionce had the joy of sharing a clear gospel and leading a young couple to a profession of faith in the Lord Jesus Christ. Immediately, they began attending our church, but after a few months they stopped coming and demonstrated no evidence of further interest in spiritual things. One well-intentioned lady referred to this absent couple and said: "Pastor John, they must have been your converts because they certainly weren't the Lord's converts."

It is important for us to remember a lesson from the believers at Corinth. Acts 18 records the Apostle Paul preaching in this city with many trusting in Christ as their Savior. Then, for 18 months, he stayed and ministered the Word of God to them. After professing Christ, there was a time of spiritual growth, but they soon drifted into terrible carnality. They became very judgmental toward Paul (I Corinthians 4:3). Gross immorality became common with them (5:1). They reveled in the sin of others (5:2) and were puffed up in pride over their biblical knowledge (8:1). Paul called them "carnal" and "babes" "in Christ," who had not grown into spiritual maturity (I Corinthians 3:1-3). But he never questioned their salvation! Notice he referred to them collectively as "the church of God" who were "...sanctified in Christ Jesus, [and] called to be saints..." (I Corinthians 1:2). He is even clearer when he lists a host of people identified by various sins, adding, "And such were some of you, but ye are washed, but ye are sanctified, but ye are justified in the name of the Lord Jesus..." (I Corinthians 6:11). Even though these Christians were living a sinful lifestyle with little apparent spiritual interest, Paul still never questioned their salvation. This is because Christians today are "...not under the law, but under grace" (Romans 6:14), and grace is not a performance system. Grace is the rich mercy of God. Some would object that the Savior said: "...by their fruits ye shall know them" (Matthew 7:16, 20). However, our Lord was talking about how to discern false teachers in the tribulation, not believers today. He was teaching the Jews still under the Law in a different program, with different requirements. It is a wonderful testimony when true godliness is exhibited in believers but today one can still be truly saved, yet not be living for the Lord.

Believer, don't question your salvation or that of others, when a lack of spiritual interest, or sin, is present. Remember, grace covers this too.

BEING PERFECT

I Corinthians 1:2

When I met the woman who was to become my wife, I was convinced she was "the one." I called my parents telling them I had found the woman to share the rest of my life with, and she was "perfect." I went on to extol her beauty, charm, love for the Lord, and more. She would have never described herself as perfect, but in my eyes, she certainly was.

As the Apostle Paul opens I Corinthians Chapter 1, he reminds believers they will be "blameless in the day of our Lord Jesus Christ" (1:8). It is important for us to realize there are two aspects of a Christian's perfection. The first is our position before God the Father. Because, through faith, we have been "made the righteousness of God in Him [the Lord Jesus Christ]" (II Corinthians 5:21). Our position before the Father is now one of perfection in the identity of the Savior. The Father now sees us as holy and perfect. This position will never change. Our daily practice after salvation is also to be "perfect." We have been "called to be saints" (I Corinthians 1:2), and the Lord expects us to seek to live up to a standard of holiness. *What does that mean?* In Philippians 2:14-15 we are told this includes doing "... all things without murmurings and disputings: that ye may be blameless and harmless, the sons of God, without rebuke...." A standard of perfection then includes a proper attitude free of argument. The Apostle Paul told the saints at Thessalonica: "...I pray God your whole spirit and soul and body be preserved blameless unto the coming of our Lord Jesus Christ" (I Thessalonians 5:23). The emphasis here is purity in mind, emotion, and body. All three are important. If we are to stand before the Savior and "not...be ashamed" (II Timothy 2:15), we must consistently be "rightly dividing the Word of truth." However, be certain to digest all the above verses that show how we live is as important as how we understand God's Word. We should also be motivated by the truth of II Corinthians 5:8-11. In eternity, all our life after salvation will be judged, "whether it be good or bad," and we will all "give an account of himself to God" (Romans 14:12).

While perfection in lifestyle doesn't mean sinlessness, we should daily be striving to practice genuine holiness in all areas. Raise your personal standard high. You bear the name of Christ!

GOD IS FAITHFUL
I Corinthians 1:9

We have a Yellow Labrador named Molly. Recently, when my wife, Terri, was sick, Molly would not leave her side. When Terri couldn't sleep in the night, Molly stayed by her side while she read and watched TV. When Terri slept in another room so I could get a better night of sleep, Molly stayed by her side. Whenever Terri moved about the house, Molly remained close. Our Molly is a gentle, loving, and faithful companion.

Intended with reverence, the faithfulness of our Molly reminded me of someone who is far more faithful. Several times in Scripture, we are told: "**God is faithful**..." (I Corinthians 1:9; 10:13; Deuteronomy 7:9). The definition of the word "faithful" means to be trustworthy, sure, or true.[1] Unlike mankind, who is only sometimes faithful, the Lord repeated these assurances to give us an unwavering confidence in Him. This is an unchanging principle, regardless of which dispensation in which the believer lives. As God explained Israel's special privileged position before Him, Moses described the Lord as "...the faithful God, which keepeth covenant and mercy with them that love him ...to a thousand generations" (Deuteronomy 7:9). The Lord wanted Israel to be thoroughly certain that He would keep every promise made to her including dealing with her with longsuffering. When Paul told the Body of Christ "God is faithful," it is in the context that the Lord will "...confirm you unto the end, that ye may be blameless in the day of our Lord Jesus Christ" (I Corinthians 1:8-9). This is a concrete guarantee that, in this Dispensation of Grace, our positional standing of complete righteousness before the Lord will never change. This is because our standing is based on God's faithfulness, not our faithfulness. When Paul explains, "there hath no temptation taken you but such as is common to man: but God is faithful, who will not suffer you to be tempted above that ye are able; but will...make a way to escape" (I Corinthians 10:13), it was a divine pledge that victory over sin is possible. One need only believe this is true, be strengthened through a daily walk with the Lord, and look for ways to flee from any present temptation.

These three examples represent how faithful the Lord is. It is important for us to remember that God is faithful in every respect. We can trust Him explicitly. May we now purpose to be found faithful to Christ in every aspect of our walk before Him.

GOD CAN'T USE ME
I Corinthians 2:1-5

I was approaching my senior year in high school when I first heard the Gospel of Grace and trusted in Christ alone for eternal life. Only a few months later, my heart began to be burdened to use the rest of my life in the ministry of my Savior; but a great internal struggle ensued. I reasoned that I was not smart enough, talented, nor capable of great things. I lacked biblical knowledge, was fearful about such a commitment, and much more. Moreover, I saw others who were dynamic, and I thought I could never reach their levels of ministry, so perhaps God could not use me in His service. Then, giving me perspective, the Lord brought other imperfect biblical figures to my attention.

Throughout the history of mankind, God has always used flawed human instruments. He could have chosen to use only holy angels or individuals empowered to some sinless condition. Instead, God chose to use ordinary men and women, all of who had glaring inadequacies. Noah was guilty of drunkenness. Abraham was too old to begin a new nation. Isaac was a daydreamer. Jacob was a liar and schemer. Leah was unattractive. Joseph was abused in youth. Moses could not speak well, and had fits of temper. Deborah was a woman in a man's world. Gideon was afraid to make himself available to the Lord. Rahab was a prostitute. David committed adultery and murder. Elijah wallowed in self-pity with suicidal desires. Isaiah preached naked (at God's instruction). Jonah ran away from God's appointed ministry. Job had a discouraging wife, and was overwhelmed when tried. Peter was impulsive and hot-tempered. The twelve disciples of Christ were slow to comprehend many simple truths, and deserted Him when under pressure. Martha worried about incidental things.

God also used the Apostle Paul despite numerous deficiencies. He had been a persecutor, did not have "…excellency of speech or of wisdom…" and he ministered "…in weakness…and in much trembling…" (I Corinthians 2:1-4). *Why then did God use an imperfect vessel such as Paul?* It was so the "…faith [of others] should not stand in the wisdom of men, but in the power of God" (vs. 5). Moreover, God receives glory when weak human vessels are used.

If you feel unworthy or incapable of being used by God, you've just met the first qualification. Now, report for duty to your heavenly Commander in Chief today.

YOU HAVE NO IDEA
I Corinthians 3:3-6

When my wife and I were expecting our first child, it was an exciting time of anticipation. We were so looking forward to having a child of our own. We made preparations in the house, chose names, bought clothes and diapers. We just had to wait until the proper time for our baby to come. Especially in the final months, we had people tell us how much our lives would change, that we were going to have an indescribable love for our child, and that this new life would become our world. One time in particular, we said, "We know." Then this Christian couple looked at us and said, "You have no idea. You have to experience it to fully understand."

In I Corinthians 2:9, the Lord tells us: "…Eye hath not seen, nor ear heard, neither have entered into the heart of man, the things which God hath prepared for them that love Him." Interestingly, Isaiah 64:4 says almost the exact same thing. It differs only that Isaiah closes his verse referring to those that "waiteth for him." Whether for Israel in her earthly Kingdom hope, or for the Body of Christ in our future heavenly existence, what God has prepared for us is so spectacular that we really have no idea how magnificent it is going to be. But, both Israel and the Body of Christ have a glimpse of their eternal future. Israel is promised she will become the light of the world (Isaiah 60:1-3), Christ will be her light source (Isaiah 60:19-20), she will be righteous (Isaiah 60:21), have no sorrow (Revelation 7:17), and forget all past sorrows (Isaiah 65:17). We, the Body of Christ, are promised new heavenly resurrected bodies free from all pain (I Corinthians 15:35-36; Philippians 3:21), to forever be in the presence of our wonderful Savior (I Thessalonians 4:17-18; Colossians 3:4); and we will be richly rewarded for any service done for Christ after salvation (I Corinthians 3:13-14; Ephesians 6:8).

Even with all this information about eternity, we really have no idea how fantastic it will be. We will have to experience it to fully comprehend it all. *How should this affect us now?* We should be rejoicing in these riches, longing to be with Christ, living in preparation for eternity, and remembering that problems here pale in comparison to what awaits us in heaven. Today, lift the spirit of another believer with the promise of what God is preparing for us.

WILL YOU PLEASE JUST GROW UP?
I Corinthians 3:1-6

We have friends who have a niece who is extremely immature. She has been so babied by her parents that, into her twenties, she never had to fix her own plate at meals, do her laundry, lift a finger to help around the house, get a job, or do anything other than play video games. On the rare occasions she wouldn't completely get her way, she would throw tantrums to manipulate adults around her. On one instance, she screamed at her aunt, slammed doors, scratched her own face and hacked on her hair. Her aunt and uncle told her: "Will you please just grow up!"

It seems to be ingrained in our human nature readily to see immaturities in others, but not so easily in ourselves. The Apostle Paul addresses this problem when he tells the saints at Corinth: "And I, brethren, could not speak unto you as unto spiritual, but as unto carnal, even as unto babes in Christ" (I Corinthians 3:1). There were four characteristics that made this conclusion obvious. Paul said, "I have fed you with milk, and not with meat; for hitherto ye were not able to bear it, neither yet now are ye able" (I Corinthians 3:2). Just as an infant cannot digest solid food, immature believers cannot digest anything but the simple basics of biblical teaching. Hebrews 5:11-14 explains why this is so in any dispensation. A disinterest in biblical teaching and a lack in using God's Word to hone one's "senses... to discern both good and evil" will always result in spiritual immaturity. Until changed by a genuine interest in God's Word, and time properly studying Scripture, no believer will truly grow to be a mature child of God. I Corinthians 3:3-6 reveals there are three other characteristics that prove one has not grown to spiritual adulthood. Paul rebukes them for "envying" one another, having avoidable "strife" with other believers, and creating "divisions" because they inappropriately exalted one teacher over another.

As we looked into the mirror of God's Word today, did you see your own reflection? If so, good! Being able to acknowledge one's problem is the first step toward victory and maturity. Today, take at least one of these four characteristics and take positive, concrete steps to correct the problem. Only if we are willing to allow God to change us, are we truly spiritually mature or growing to that end.

PAYDAY SOME DAY
I Corinthians 3:8

While our children were growing up, our family had a small janitorial business to finance having them in a Christian school. We took the children with us, even if all they were able to do was gather the wastebaskets. One day the girls were less than enthusiastic about their participation. So, without really thinking it through, I told them: "If you work hard with a good attitude, when you graduate high school, mom and I will buy you a car." I only promised that once, but they never let me forget it nor allowed me not to follow through on my promise.

Our Heavenly Father has a fantastic promise for every blood-bought believer. Referring to the time when we graduate from this life into eternity, I Corinthians 3:8 says "...every man shall receive his own reward according to his own labor." With absolute certainty, we are assured the Lord will handsomely reward us for service done for the Lord Jesus Christ after salvation. Reconfirming this confidence, the Apostle Paul tells us in I Corinthians 15:58: "Therefore, my beloved brethren, be ye stedfast, unmovable, always abounding in the work of the Lord, forasmuch as ye know that your labor is not in vain in the Lord."

We should also comprehend our reward will be proportionate to our effort in service. As stated above, everyone will be given "reward ...according to his own labor" (I Corinthians 3:8). If we choose to do little or nothing for the Lord after salvation, this will be reflected in little reward received. II Corinthians 9:6 states it this way: "...He which soweth sparingly shall reap also sparingly; and he which soweth bountifully shall reap also bountifully." As a high school yearbook reflects one's participation, or lack thereof, in school activities, our records in eternity will correspond with our service and reward. That makes it important for us to busy ourselves now with activities that will matter once we reach eternity. We can serve Christ by inviting or transporting folks to church, presenting the gospel, handing out gospel tracts, serving in the church nursery, teaching the Scriptures, assisting in youth ministries, giving faithfully, doing follow-up on visitors, befriending new comers to church, and much more. The limit on serving Christ is only our imagination and our willingness. If you properly desire reward in eternity, it is imperative that you choose to consistently serve the Lord now. Let today be the start of consistent service for the cause of Christ.

DON'T DRINK THE KOOL-AID
I Corinthians 3:3-8

On November 18, 1978, cult leader Jim Jones and more than 900 of his followers committed mass suicide in the jungles of Guyana. Jones was a charismatic leader who drew people in with promises of building a utopia- type community, where everyone would be equal. Once within the group, complete loyalty was demanded. Under investigation by the U.S. government, Jones convinced his followers to drink cyanide-laced Kool-Aid. Many were so enthralled with Jones that they believed whatever he told them and did whatever he said. The results were devastating.

While the example of Jim Jones is extreme, the truth is "man-followers" have always existed, even among God's people. The Apostle Paul rebuked the saints at Corinth saying, "...there is among you envying, and strife, and divisions, are ye not carnal, and walk as men? For while one saith, I am of Paul; and another, I am of Apollos; are ye not carnal (I Corinthians 3:3-4). Apparently these believers, like some today, had become enamored with those who had ministered to them. They would champion one over the other, give them their undying loyalty, and continually extol their virtues. Apollos was "...an eloquent man, and mighty in the Scriptures..." (Acts 18:24). This capability drew an avid following, which championed him as its leader (I Corinthians 1:12). The Apostle Paul was less polished yet God enabled him to perform "...the (miraculous) signs of an apostle...and wonders, and mighty deeds" (II Corinthians 12:12). In either event, believers were placing their focus on these men rather than upon the Lord Jesus Christ. Today such loyalties would manifest itself in treating their teachers like a celebrity, following them around the country, seeking photo ops with them, and continually quoting them. But none of this is God's way. Paul told these saints that those who planted the seed of God's Word in their lives were not "any thing" (I Corinthians 3:7). Paul continued: "...these things, brethren, I have in a figure transferred...that ye might learn in us not to think of men above that which is written, that no one be puffed up for one against another" (I Corinthians 4:6). Since Paul and Apollos were truly godly men, their desire was to see people give their love, loyalty, and enthusiasm to the Lord instead of to them.

Dear believer, don't drink the Kool-Aid of becoming overly enamored with those who minister for the Lord. Be thankful for their ministry, but keep your focus on the Lord Jesus Christ.

A JUDGMENTAL SPIRIT
I Corinthians 4:3-5

One day a brother whom seldom had much contact with his sister called her to set her straight. He'd heard that his sister's adult daughter had medical bills she was struggling to pay. "Why aren't you helping her with those bills?" She answered that she and her husband had helped her and listed a number of examples. Then he proceeded to tell his sister what money-hungry people she and her husband were for having cleaning jobs at night in addition to their regular jobs. The sister explained the income from these jobs was a designated college fund for their children. Then the brother retorted, "You're doing too much for your kids...."

Even for Christians, the habit of a judgmental spirit is a frequent problem that sours one's spirit and ruins relationships. Therefore, the Scriptures deal with this extensively. In Romans 14:4, Paul tells believers at Rome: "Who art thou that judgest another man's servant? To his own master he standeth or falleth...." The point was we have no right to judge another believer. The Lord Jesus alone is our judge. John 5:22 confirms: "For the Father...hath committed all judgment unto the Son." Therefore, when we venture into this area of judging others, we are overstepping proper boundaries intended by the Lord. We have neither the qualification nor enough complete information to stand adequately in judgment of another believer. When believers at Corinth became critical of the Apostle Paul, he told them: "But with me it is a very small thing that I should be judged of you, or of man's judgment: yea, I judge not mine own self. For I know...He that judgeth me is the Lord. Therefore judge nothing before the time, until the Lord come, Who both will bring to light the hidden things of darkness, and will make manifest the counsels of the heart..." (I Corinthians 4:3-5). Paul writes in another letter: "Let us not therefore judge one another any more: but judge this rather, that no man put a stumblingblock or an occasion to fall in his brother's way" (Romans 14:13). As the saying goes, "That's so simple, even a fifth grader can understand it."

Believer, have you allowed a judgmental attitude to sour your spirit? Are you often critical of others? This horrible habit so dishonors the Lord that He will one day judge these actions at the Bema Seat. Let today be a turning point when you intentionally turn from judging others.

NOBODY WILL EVER KNOW

I Corinthians 4:5

On February 24th, 2002, eight-month pregnant Laci Peterson, of Modesto, California, went missing. Investigators learned her husband, Scott, had been carrying on affairs and that he had made several incriminating statements to his mistress fourteen days prior to Laci's disappearance. Prosecutors believe Scott killed Laci and dumped her body in the ocean weighed down by chains. In mid-April, 2003, the partial bodies of Laci and her unborn son washed ashore. Apparently, Scott thought nobody would ever know about his affairs, discover the bodies of his family, or learn of his attempt to flee the country. But, Scott was arrested, his actions made public, and he was convicted of murdering his family.

Scott Peterson is admittedly an extreme example of a sinful person thinking no one will ever find out. However, most people who sin probably think their sin and motives will not be discovered. But such a notion is just not realistic. God always knows exactly what we do. When King Asa "... relied not on the Lord..." he learned, "the eyes of the Lord run to and fro throughout the whole earth..." (II Chronicles 16:7-9). The message was that God saw what he did. King David acknowledged the Lord "...knowest my downsitting and mine uprising, thou understandest my thought afar off...for there is not a word in my tongue, but, lo, O Lord, thou knowest it altogether..." (Psalm 139:1-10). Solomon learned "...God shall bring every work into judgment, with every secret thing, whether it be good or evil" (Ecclesiastes 12:14). Not only does God know our sin, it appears the sin of believers will be revealed when judged in eternity. Paul wrote that when Christ comes for us He "...will bring to light the hidden things of darkness, and will make manifest the counsels of the heart..." (I Corinthians 4:5). Paul is implying the sins of believers will be public at the Bema Seat when he wrote, "Some men's sins are open beforehand going into judgment; and some they follow after" (I Timothy 5:24; compare II Corinthians 5:8-11; Luke 12:2-3).

It is extremely sobering to think that when we stand before the Savior for Him to judge our life after salvation, that our sins will be exposed. That is exactly the point. The Lord informs us of this concept to motivate us toward a more pure walk with Him. Don't be paralyzed by this future scene. Be motivated to live in such a way that you will be richly rewarded and highly praised at this time.

ALL CLEANED UP
I Corinthians 4:9-11

One of our grandchildren had just been bathed, dressed in clean clothes, and readied to walk out the door. While her mother attended to another child, she promptly got all messed up again. When mom discovered what had happened she, with a frustration in her voice, called her by the first, middle and last name, saying, "...I just got you all cleaned up. Now look at yourself."

When the Apostle Paul addresses the saints at Corinth, some of them were returning to the filth pit of sinful practices they knew prior to their salvation. He tells them: "Be not deceived: neither fornicators, nor idolaters, nor adulterers, nor effeminate, nor abusers of themselves with mankind, nor thieves, nor covetous, nor drunkards, nor revilers, nor extortioners, shall inherit the kingdom of God. And such were some of you: but ye are washed, but ye are sanctified, but ye are justified in the name of the Lord Jesus..." (I Corinthians 6:9-11). Sinners, such as those described above, cannot enter eternal life in the identity of sin. But when the Corinthians trusted Christ, all that guilt was taken away. They now stood in the pure identity and righteousness of Christ (II Corinthians 5:21).

For Israel, in the Old Testament, their future promises picture what we, and believers at Corinth, already possess. Jehovah promised Israel: "In the day...I shall have cleansed you from all your iniquities..." (Ezekiel 36:33). God will command them: "...Take away the filthy garments from him. And...I have caused thine iniquity to pass from thee...I will clothe thee with a change of raiment" (Zechariah 3:4). One day, Israel will say in rejoicing: "...for He hath clothed me with the garments of salvation; He hath covered me with the robe of righteousness..." (Isaiah 61:10). When Paul tells the Corinthians they were now washed from their sin, justified in Christ, and sanctified unto God, he wanted them to realize they should live up to their new standing in Christ, not down to the depths of sinful conduct prior to salvation. This is why he explains some things are "not expedient" (meaning advantageous or profitable), that they must not be "brought under the power" of any sin, or use their body for anything "...but for the Lord" (I Corinthians 4:12-13). Instead, they were to live their lives as a "new creature" (II Corinthians 5:17), living up to their clean condition in Christ.

If old sinful practices have crept back into your life, forsake them today. Honor Christ anew.

A POSITIVE SPIRITUAL INFLUENCE
I Corinthians 4:15

While a youth pastor ministered in a church, there was one young man in particular that was given a great deal of extra love and care. This teen struggled to fit in and get along with the others. To help this young man, every week the youth pastor took this young man along on his visits to those on his bus route. They prayed together, talked about the Lord and the Scriptures. They also joked and laughed. More than thirty years later, these two were reunited for an afternoon. The man now grown told his former youth pastor: "You were the best spiritual influence I had in my whole life. You showed me love, a Christ-like example, and patience. You saved my life...and enabled me to be where I am in my Christian walk today."

When the Apostle Paul addresses the saints at Corinth, he tells them: "... though ye have ten thousand instructors in Christ, yet have ye not many fathers..." (I Corinthians 4:15). Paul was saying that he was a spiritual father, and a positive spiritual influence, to them. *How was this so?* In the same verse, he told them: "I have begotten you through the gospel." The person who leads us to a saving knowledge of the Lord Jesus Christ is certainly a positive spiritual influence. But there were other ways Paul was a spiritual father figure. In I Thessalonians 2:7-12, he gives a vivid list of ways he influenced them spiritually. Most of the time, he was "gentle" with them as he encouraged their spiritual growth (vs. 7). He was "affectionately desirous" toward them (vs. 8), meaning he gave them a pure godly love. He was "willing to have imparted unto you, not the gospel of God only, but also our own souls, because ye were dear unto us" (vs. 8). As he had been willing to sacrificially spend and be spent for the saints in Corinth, so it was here. Paul also left them a godly example in a good work ethic (vs. 9), while living before them "holily and justly and unblameably..." (vs. 10). Finally, depending on what they needed, he "exhorted and comforted and charged every one of you" (vs. 11).

Paul left a positive spiritual impact on others because he intended to do so. It is time for you to do the same, without delay. Before going to sleep tonight, *who will you reach out to so that you might befriend them, and begin a mentoring process in the things of the Lord?*

YOUR PASSOVER SACRIFICE
I Corinthians 5:7-8

On January 13, 1982, Air Florida Flight 90, smashed into the ice covered Potomac River just outside Washington, D.C. With fractured arms and shattered legs, six souls swam past fellow passengers to the surface. When a helicopter arrived lowering a lifeline to pull out 46-year-old, Arland Williams Jr., twice he handed the ring on the lifeline to another passenger. When the helicopter returned for the third time to get Arland, hypothermia had claimed him. He had given his life in an unselfish way to save others.[1]

In I Corinthians 5:7-8, the Apostle Paul reminded believers in the Dispensation of Grace about another unselfish sacrifice of life for others. He said, "Purge out therefore the old leaven, that ye may be a new lump, as ye are unleavened. For even Christ our Passover is sacrificed for us." The Passover Feast was an annual observance initiated by the Lord to commemorate Israel's deliverance from the cruel bondage of Egypt. In the first observance, a perfect lamb was slain for each family. The blood was to be placed upon the doorposts so the Lord's angel of death would passover their household without slaying their firstborn. The occupants inside were to consume all of the Lamb and do so with unleavened bread. Leaven was essentially yeast that spread throughout the dough. Even a small amount was effective. The leaven pictured sin. Therefore, at the annual observance, all leaven had to be removed from every Jewish home. *Why would Paul tell saints today about the Jewish Passover?* He does so reminding them that the Lord Jesus was the ultimate Passover Lamb that every previous sacrifice had pointed to. Our Savior was the perfect, sinless Lamb who sacrificed His life to atone for our sins so that God's eternal wrath would not fall on us. Then, remembering the sacrifice of Christ for us, Paul urged the sinning saints at Corinth to purge out the leaven-like sinful practices in their lives. Symbolically, they were to "keep the feast" by living apart from "the leaven of malice and wickedness, but with the unleavened bread of sincerity and truth" (I Corinthians 5:8).

Are you grateful enough to your Savior, who willingly laid down His life for you, that you are seeking to purge out sinful practices in your life? Purging sin out of your life demonstrates the "sincerity and truth" Christ longs to see in you.

STAY AWAY
I Corinthians 5:11

A professing Christian couple was living in open sin, causing another Christian couple to withdraw their fellowship. When invited to the home of a third Christian couple where all the above parties would be present, the couple who had distanced themselves explained that they could not attend and why. The hosting couple emotionally exclaimed, "What difference does it make, and who really cares what they do." When our text, in I Corinthians 5 was explained, it was brushed aside as being irrelevant for our day and time. In these apparent last days before our Savior returns to rapture us into the heavens, Christians have often become desensitized to the rampant practice of sin all around us. Even in Christian circles, the sins of the world are becoming commonplace and accepted. But, sin is still wrong, and God's instructions to distance ourselves from these practices are as relevant as if God had sent them to us for the first time this week.

We can't, nor should we, separate from everyone who practices sin. In fact, I Corinthians 5:10 tells us not to refuse to keep company with lost souls "for then must ye needs go out of the world." Moreover, these lost souls need our ministry to bring them to a saving knowledge of Christ. However, God's standard for us is different with professing Christians who practice six very specific sins. In verse eleven, the Lord tells us "**not to keep company**, if any man that is called a brother be a fornicator [any sexual sin], or covetous, or an idolater, or a railer, or a drunkard, or an extortioner; with such an one **no not to eat**." By the way, there is no exception even for family members in this standard of separation. *Why?* I Corinthians 5:6 explains the "leaven" of sin can spread to us and pull us into these sinful practices. II Thessalonians 3:14 gives a second reason: God uses your withdrawal of companionship to bring them to a condition of being "ashamed" of their sin and willing to change. So, we should not be naïve enough to think we couldn't be drawn into sin, nor should we refuse to be God's instrument to evoke divine conviction and needed change in others.

Does the lifestyle and conduct of professing Christians make any difference in deciding whether or not to share time and meals with them? According to I Corinthians 5:11, it should! *Now that we know, will we have the courage to obey?*

ARE LAWSUITS FORBIDDEN?
I Corinthians 6:1-7

According to "Top Ten Frivolous Lawsuits" posted on the Internet site Legalzoom, in 1991, Richard Harris sued Anheiser-Bush for $10,000. He claimed to suffer from emotional distress, with mental and physical injury due to what he viewed was false advertising. He stated that when he drank beer, he did not have any luck with the ladies, as he perceived the ads promised on TV. Harris also did not like that he sometimes got sick after he drank. The case was thrown out of court. We are living in a sue-happy world of frivolous lawsuits. But bringing foolish matters before courts of law is nothing new.

The Apostle Paul wrote to the Corinthians saying, "Dare any of you, having a matter against another [believer], go to law before the unjust, and not before the saints? (I Corinthians 6:1). We are not told exactly what kind of matters these believers were bringing before the courts. Paul puts these into one simple category when he says, "…are ye unworthy to judge the small-est matters?" (vs. 2) In other words, these believers were suing one another over frivolous issues. It is important for us to understand that Paul was not forbidding these saints any lawsuit over weighty issues, nor is the Lord forbidding believers today the protection of authorities or the legal system when truly important issues are at hand. Romans 13 explains, "the powers that be are ordained of God" (vs. 1) as a deterrent to evildoers (vs. 3) and a protection to the innocent. First Peter 2:13-17 essentially says the same thing. Therefore, if another believer steals your car, threatens your family, or murders a loved one, the Scriptures do not prohibit you from taking every reasonable legal action against them. These are important weighty issues that our governmental authorities are divinely designed to handle. On the other hand, "the smallest of matters" (I Corinthians1:2) are things we ought not to sue another believer over. Instead, we should "rather take the wrong" (vs. 7) so the testimony of Christ is not soiled before the unsaved public and authorities. When the Corinthians were being sue-happy, Paul told them: "…there is utterly a fault among you…I speak to your shame…" (vss. 7, 5). What they should have been doing instead was peacefully setting aside these small matters by simply suffering the wrong without legal action.

If you ever consider a lawsuit against another believer, be certain it is over a truly weighty issue. Otherwise, let the issue be judged at the Bema Seat.

HOW DOES GOD SEE YOU?
I Corinthians 6:9-10

If you've ever been an adult working with children, you've probably had an incident somewhat similar to my Aunt Ann. Her son was a big boy with a constant stuttering problem. As a result, kids would frequently tease him, causing him to be a brute and bully. When he mistreated several of his cousins at a family reunion, the children ran to the adults for protection and explained what had happened. Ann's response was, "Oh no, my boy would not do anything like that." Ann had repeated this kind of denial several times to administrators in the school where her son attended. She simply would not see or acknowledge anything but the good in her son.

When the Apostle Paul writes to the saints at Corinth, he describes how the Lord views all the children of God who have placed their faith in Christ alone for eternal salvation. Paul states, "Know ye not that the unrighteous shall not inherit the kingdom of God? Be not deceived: neither fornicators, nor idolaters, nor effeminate, nor abusers of themselves with mankind, nor thieves, nor covetous, nor drunkards, nor revilers, nor extortioner, shall inherit the kingdom of God" (I Corinthians 6:9-10). It is noteworthy that the believers to whom these words were written, though saved by the blood of Christ, were still practicing these very sins. First Corinthians 5:11 implies many were guilty of being "...covetous, or an idolater, or a railer, or a drunkard, or an extortioner...." While any saint can commit any sin given the right opportunity and the wrong spiritual condition, it seems these saints were particularly sinful. But God did not view them this way. By virtue of their faith in Christ, they had been made "...the righteousness of God in Him [Christ]," (II Corinthians 5:21) and forgiven "all trespasses" (Colossians 2:13). On this basis of imputed righteousness, God only saw these saints as holy and not in their present practice of sin. It was for this reason, after Paul's list of heinous sins many of them were practicing, he says, "And such were some of you: but ye are washed, but ye are sanctified, but ye are justified in the name of the Lord Jesus..." (I Corinthians 6:11).

As God's children, we should rejoice that He sees us, not in the filth of sins we sometimes practice but only in the holiness of Christ. Nonetheless, we must put off these sins and seek to walk in newness of life.

INSEPARABLY LINKED
I Corinthians 6:15-19

Matt Damon and Greg Kinnear play the role of adult conjoined twins in the movie *Stuck On You*. They share a common liver but otherwise have separate bodies, personalities, and dreams for life. However, whenever one plays baseball, acts in plays, or does anything else, the other twin must also be involved because they are inseparably linked. While this movie is a comedy about the problems with conjoined twins, there are sobering examples in real life. However joined, whenever one moves or decides to do anything, it affects the other.

In a very real sense every believer who has trusted the Lord Jesus Christ alone for eternal life has a similar relationship with the Savior. Through grace and faith, we are inseparably linked with the person of Christ. II Corinthians 5:21 states: "For He [the Father] hath made Him [the Son] to be sin for us, who knew no sin; that we might be made the righteousness of God in Him." After salvation, the Lord no longer sees us in our old identity of sin. Instead, He sees us in the righteousness and holiness of His Son. This change in identity is so complete that there is more than the forgiveness of sins and a new standing to consider. Ephesians 5:30 describes it this way: "For we are members of His body, of His flesh, and of His bones." This is the most complete and intimate link to the Lord Jesus possible. In I Corinthians, Chapter 6, the Apostle Paul told the Corinthians: "Know ye not that your bodies are the members of Christ? ...your body is the temple of the Holy Ghost which is in you..." (I Corinthians 6:15,19). With the Holy Spirit inseparably living within, everything they did and everywhere they went, involved God's Spirit. Some of the believers at Corinth were engaging in horrible acts of immorality. Paul is explaining to them that their identity is so close and intimate with the Lord Jesus Christ that, when they committed fornication, they were involving the Savior. He tells them: "...shall I then take the members of Christ, and make them the members of an harlot? God forbid" (v. 15). They simply must not. They must choose to "glorify God in your body, and in your spirit, which are God's" (I Corinthians 6:20).

Remember, every thing you do today with your body affects God the Son and God the Holy Spirit. Be sure to be pure.

A WEAPON OR A BOND
I Corinthians 7:1-7

I received a phone call requesting prayer from the mother of a daughter who had been married for nearly fifteen years to a good man. This daughter had foolishly and emotionally recoiled from sexual relations with her husband. He had been extremely patient, but after several years of this, he was nearly through with the marriage. He wanted and needed the normal physical union between a man and wife. If she remained unwilling, he would simply go elsewhere to meet his needs.

While it is a mature subject, the Bible has a great deal to say, in a tasteful way, about the sexual union between a man and wife. God tells us: "Marriage is honourable in all, and the bed undefiled..." (Hebrews 13:4). As a pleasurable gift intended of the Lord to continually strengthen the bond between a man and wife, Proverbs 30:18-19 describes this physical relationship as "wonderful." This "one flesh" interaction is so important Paul tells both the man and woman to carefully maintain this practice. Both are to willingly render "due benevolence" to one another to meet their mate's need "...that Satan tempt you not for your incontinency" (I Corinthians 7:3-5). It is a foolish thing to use sex as a weapon to manipulate, or punish one's mate. Doing so weakens the bond and tempts both parties to fulfill this need, in a sinful way, with someone else. Instead, both the husband and wife are responsible to initiate this sexual experience. There is a wonderful example in the book of Song of Solomon where the wife seeks out her husband for such an encounter (3:1). She confirms her love for him (3:2), holds him close (3:4), expresses "great delight" in her husband's caresses (2:1-6), compliments his comeliness (5:10-16), and willingly gives herself to him (7:10-13). This is actually the way both genders are to respond within the bonds of holy matrimony. It is not the husband's duty to be the initiator all the time, nor is it only the wife's responsibility. Both are to equally participate in this way. To refuse to take action because "that's just not me" or "I'm not in the mood" are flimsy and foolish excuses to rationalize disobedience in a very important area of marriage.

If you are married, we urge you to not neglect your responsibility in your physical union with your mate. God intends it for pleasure, but also to bring strength and longevity to your marital bond.

WHOM TO PLEASE
I Corinthians 7:32-34

Singer Ricky Nelson once had a hit song entitled, "I Went To A Garden Party." In the chorus, he repeats the words: "You can't please everyone, so you've got to please yourself." This kind of philosophy seems to be drummed into our heads from every source: the media that seeks to brainwash us with ungodly standards, coworkers, and even family who embrace wrong concepts. We hear things like: "You've got to look out for number one," and, "If you don't look out for yourself, who will?" But especially for Christians, there is a far higher standard by which to live.

We, who know the Lord Jesus Christ as Savior, should never forget we owe a debt of love and gratitude to Him who purchased our salvation with His life's blood. Our constant goal ought to be to please Him rather than ourselves. Paul urges us to "...live unto the Lord [because]...we are the Lord's..." (Romans 14:8). Then he reminds us that believers "...should not henceforth live unto themselves, but unto him which died for them and rose again" (II Corinthians 5:15). Paul also tells Christians who are married, to consciously and constantly seek to please one's mate. The proper role of the husband is described being concerned "...for the things of the world, how he may please his wife" (I Corinthians 7:33). The instruction here is for a husband to provide well, bring security to his wife, and do the many things he learns will please her. Likewise, Paul tells Christian women: "...she that is married careth for the things of the world, how she may please her husband" (I Corinthians 7:34). In neither instance is Paul talking about or sanctioning any form of worldliness. Instead, he is teaching a genuinely godly individual will seek to do all the things they know will please their mate. It should be uppermost in their thinking and activities. If one's marriage partner expresses that something is important to them, immediate action should be taken to comply or supply what will please them. Following this course is not only God's revealed will; it also brings greater harmony, stability, and happiness to any marriage. But when an individual only lives to please oneself, instead of one's mate, the marriage often crumbles around them.

Who are you going to try to please today? If you're married, we urge you to please the Lord by seeking to please your mate. Doing so will pay high dividends here and in eternity.

135

YOUR MISSION IN MARRIAGE
I Corinthians 7:33-34

We once knew a godly Christian lady who was married to an unsaved man. He never attended church, and when we went to visit at the house, he always went out of his way to be rude. For twenty years this godly woman lived a Christ-like life before her husband. Then one day, God broke the heart of her husband. He trusted Christ as Savior, and thereafter lived a consistent life for Christ. All this happened because this godly wife accomplished her God-given mission in marriage.

First Corinthians Chapter 7 discusses multiple aspects of marriage. Notice verse 14 says, "...the unbelieving husband is sanctified by the wife...." The word "sanctified" means to set apart. When a believer is married to an unbeliever, the one who is unsaved is in a special place. As they witness the godly attitude, actions, and practices of the saved mate, God can use this in a powerful way to draw them to salvation. This is true for both men and women. Ladies, don't underestimate your influence on an unsaved husband. In a dialogue in the movie, *My Big Fat Greek Wedding*, the mother says, "The man may be the head of the family. But the woman is the neck, and she can turn his head whichever way she wants." In seriousness, the goal should not be one of manipulation, but one of godly influence. Most only look at marriage for what they can selfishly get out of the relationship, but believers have a higher standard. Verses 33-34 explain that a godly mate "...careth for the things...**how he may please** his wife...(or) **how she may please** her husband." When our goal is to please our mate, it affects how much, how often, and with what spirit we do things for them. Done out of love and unto the Lord, this is a powerful testimony that God can use. I Peter 3:1-2 addresses this very thing saying, "...if any obey not the word, they also may without the word be won by the conversation [or manner of life] of the wives, while they behold your chaste conversation...." We would suggest that even Christians with a believing mate have the divine mission to be a godly influence and spiritual encouragement.

If you're married, how are you doing on your mission field in your marriage? What can you do today to please your mate and be a godly example that would draw your mate closer to the Lord?

PUFFED UP BELIEVERS?

I Corinthians 8:1

During a Sunday morning service, we had a dear saint stand and do something that made us cringe. Unfortunately, while expressing thanks for the preciousness of rightly dividing the Word of God, he compared us to a denomination, saying how foolish and incorrect they were in interpreting God's Word. We've seen wild Tom Turkeys all puffed up, spreading their feathers and strutting their stuff to impress the ladies around them. Sadly, this was the impression our Christian friend was leaving with those who were visiting from the denomination he was ridiculing.

The knowledge that God has placed divisions in His Word is, indeed, precious. It helps us better understand truth in Scripture and dissolves what otherwise would seem to be contradictions. But there are *two dangers* we should be keenly aware of and avoid. The first is *to search only for "knowledge" when we read God's Word*. Please don't misunderstand what we are trying to say. The knowledge of sound doctrine, or information, from God's Word is essential. Paul told the saints at Corinth that when he ministered to them: "...what shall I profit you, except I speak to you...by knowledge... or by doctrine" (I Corinthians 14:6). He encouraged believers to "...give attendance...to doctrine (I Timothy 4:13), to be "...nourished up in...good doctrine" (I Timothy 4:6) and to become skilled in sound doctrine (Titus 1:9; 2:1). But *the trap that many fall into is thinking that information is all they should be looking for when studying God's Word.* When this happens, it only leaves us "puffed up" with pride. Our study will then, in effect, leave us worse off in pride and less pleasing to the Lord. The second trap is *failing to look for application to change our lives*. Paul told the saints in Romans 6:17: "But God be thanked...ye have obeyed from the heart that form of doctrine which was delivered unto you." God is not impressed with how much we know, unless it shows itself in a transformed life of greater godliness. Therefore, after every time in the Scripture, we should always be able to answer the question: *"So what difference does God want this information to make in my life today?"* This is the most essential aspect of every Bible study. Demand of yourself, and anyone who teaches God's Word, that this kind of application is being made.

Let's not be puffed up over how much doctrine we know. Let's be transformed into lives of greater godliness!

LOVING GOD
I Corinthians 8:3

Many people have silly standards by which they decide whether someone loves them. As children, many of us plucked petals from a flower saying, "He loves me, he loves me not" and hoped for the right answer. Cher once sang a song saying, "How will I know if he really loves me..." concluding "...it's in his kiss." *But how do we Christians determine love?* We know that God loves us because "...while we were yet sinners, Christ died for us" (Romans 5:8). *But what about whether or not we truly love the Lord?* I Corinthians 8:3 says, "But if any man [or woman] love God; the same is know of Him." *But how would we, or others, know if we really love the Lord?*

Let's begin by realizing that God greatly desires that we freely give Him our love. He instructed Israel: "...what doth the Lord thy God require of thee, but to...love Him..." even to "...love the Lord your God with all your heart and with all your soul" (Deuteronomy 10:12; 13:3). Dozens of passages in the Old Testament repeat this command. Then the Savior quotes these verses, calling this "the great [or greatest] commandment" (Matthew 22:37-38). God's desire is the same for us in the Dispensation of Grace. The Apostle Paul encouraged the saints to grow in their love for the Lord saying, "Grace be with all them that love our Lord Jesus Christ in sincerity..." (Ephesians 6:24). We don't have to rely on the standards of the world, or fickle emotions, to know if we really love our Lord. The Savior told His apostles: "If ye love Me, keep My commandments" (John 14:15). Love always demonstrates itself! One's love for the Lord is demonstrated through willing obedience to the will of God. David said, "Ye that love the Lord, hate evil..." (Psalm 97:10). Loving Him means hating what He hates. Paul implies two standards for those who truly love the Lord. We will seek to edify other believers rather than acting puffed up against them. And we will be careful not to become a "stumbling block to them that are weak" (I Corinthians 8:1-13). In other words, if we really love the Lord, it will manifest itself in our demonstration of love for other Christians.

Pause for a moment to ask yourself: *"Is it known of me that I truly love the Lord?"* Let that question motivate you today to zealously love your Savior and demonstrate love to others who also know His salvation.

A WEAKER CONSCIENCE
I Corinthians 8:4-13

My father had a good friend and neighbor, named Clarence, with whom he grew up. The friendship was so strong that this man served as his best man during the wedding of my mother and father. Clarence also had a clear testimony of knowing Christ as his Savior, godly deportment, and consistent involvement at church. For decades after my parents were married, Clarence and his family visited our home, but then it abruptly stopped. The deal breaker was that our parents frequently played innocent card games when hosting guests. Without a clear verse to substantiate his position, Clarence believed playing any kind of cards was sinful, so he separated company with my parents.

Christians should always have concrete Pauline Bible references to prove any standard they seek to uphold. Without this as our basis, anyone can consider, in their own mind, that virtually anything is a sinful practice, i.e.: wearing blue jeans, eating products with sugar, dying gray hair, or even owning a car. To avoid foolish conclusions and legalistic practices, we must base what we seek to live out primarily from the epistles of the Apostle Paul. But beyond this, it is important that we who understand the liberties of living under grace not be calloused in what we allow for ourselves. The Apostle Paul addresses this in I Corinthians 8:4-13. The specific issue was that some believers who realized idols were only dead inanimate objects were purchasing and eating cheaper meat that had been offered to idols. Paul admonished: "But take heed lest by any means this liberty of yours become a stumbling block to them that are weak…and through thy knowledge shall the weaker brother perish, for whom Christ died" (vss. 9,11). The word "perish" here means to mar or destroy. Paul is certainly not referring to a Christian "brother" losing his salvation or suffering eternal punishment. Paul is saying it is wrong to stubbornly insist on using one's liberty to practice things that offend other believers. It is far better to abstain in their presence or to forgo one's liberty altogether. Our impact on other believers is so important Paul strongly states, "But when ye sin so against the brethren, and wound their weak conscience, ye sin against Christ" (vs. 12).

Sincere Christians need to reevaluate choices, like consuming alcohol, styles in hair or clothing, and places that one goes. If the practice is questionable, particularly being addressed in Paul's epistles, choose to avoid it (vs. 13).

WHY IS IT INCLUDED?
I Corinthians 9:7-10

Years ago I dabbled in carving Scripture verses into parcels of wood. I took a number of these plaques to family camp to sell at a modest price. Along with many references from Paul's epistles, I had several key Old Testament verses that stated timeless principles. I was somewhat surprised that not one of the plaques with an Old Testament verse sold. Believers did not seem interested in verses that were not written specifically to believers in our present Dispensation of Grace. But, we would do well not to avoid or neglect non-Pauline passages of Scripture.

The Apostle Paul tells us something very noteworthy in I Corinthians 9:7-10. When he refers to the timeless principle of financially supporting one who ministers to you, he uses the logic of a soldier not going to war bearing his own expenses, and a farmer not being excluded from eating the fruit of his labors (vs. 7). He added, "For it is written in the law of Moses, Thou shalt not muzzle the mouth of the ox that treadeth out the corn. Doth God not take care of the oxen? Or saith He [the Lord] it altogether for our sakes? For our sakes, no doubt, this is written: that he that ploweth should plow in hope and...should be a partaker of his hope" (vss. 9-10). In these verses, Paul emphasizes the Old Testament was not written only for the benefit of the Jews governed by the Law of Moses. It was also written and included in our Bible for the benefit of believers in the Dispensation of Grace. Other passages confirm this truth, II Timothy 3:16-17 explains, "All Scripture [including the Gospels, the Old Testament and Jewish epistles] is given by inspiration of God and is profitable...that the man of God [in any dispensation] may be perfect, thoroughly furnished unto all good works." To neglect these sections in God's Word is to neglect what is divinely intended for our benefit. First Corinthians 10:1-11 states twice that the Old Testament was recorded to provide us today with helpful examples of doing right and wrong. Romans 15:4 explains all these things "...written aforetime were written for our learning..." We certainly need to learn the key doctrines of grace from the Apostle Paul, but we also need to learn from the Scriptures written originally to Israel.

Did you know the Jewish books were written "for our sakes [or benefit]"? Purpose today to invest time reading and benefiting from Jewish sections in your Bible.

AGAINST MY WILL
I Corinthians 9:16-17

Most of the time our grandchildren greet us willingly with hugs and kisses. However, every so often, they stubbornly withhold these expressions of affection. Especially when leaving for the day, the parents of our grandkids usually make them say goodbye with a hug and a kiss, even if they don't seem to want to do so. However, when it is done against their will, it is not nearly as gratifying as when they willingly come to us with those desired hugs and kisses.

It is really no different with the children of God from any dispensation. There is a consistent record in Scripture of God placing a high premium on believers giving Him worship, obedience, or service from a completely willing heart. Moses was instructed to, "Speak unto the children of Israel, that they bring me an offering; of every man that doeth it willingly with his heart..." (Exodus 25:2). Similarly, Paul instructed believers in the Dispensation of Grace about giving to the Lord, saying, "For if there be first a willing mind, it is accepted according to that a man hath..."(II Corinthians 8:12). In either instance, if not done willingly, it is neither pleasing to nor accepted by the Lord. In II Chronicles 17:16, Amasiah is praised because he "...willingly offered himself unto the Lord." Jehovah could have somehow forced the circumstances, but how much sweeter when Amasiah was the Lord's willing vessel. The Apostle Paul grasped this concept writing: "For though I preach the gospel, I have nothing to glory of; for necessity is laid upon me...For if I do this thing willingly, I have a reward; but if against my will, a dispensation of the gospel is committed unto me" (I Corinthians 9:16-17). The "necessity" Paul refers to, we believe, was a burden of heart for his ministry of sharing the message that eternal punishment can be escaped and a fuller abundant life experienced through faith in the Lord Jesus Christ. God was providing open doors of opportunity to share the Gospel of Grace, and He was preparing hearts to hear this message. Paul understood if he ministered willingly, he would have a reward. If he did so unwillingly, he would receive no eternal reward.

These principles are as up to date as if written this morning. If you are struggling in the area of being willingly obedient to the Lord, such as in giving or sharing the gospel, make it a consistent matter of prayer that Christ would change your heart.

WHY PAUL WAS SO EFFECTIVE?
I Corinthians 9:22

We have Christian friends who have a close relationship with an outstanding Bible teacher. They tell the story of going on a cruise with this teacher. At the time, the husband knew Christ as Savior. But the wife was still unsaved and somewhat leery of letting go of the doctrines learned in her church as a child. But the teacher disarmed this lady by seeking her out, sharing a meal with her and her husband, being very personable, and lovingly sharing the Scriptures she needed. The end result was that this lady trusted Christ as her Savior and became a vibrant believer. The couple became lifelong friends with this teacher, who had been so used of the Lord in their lives.

Have you ever wondered how the Apostle Paul had such an effective ministry with so many during his lifetime? He gives his testimony about this in the Scriptures. It began with a genuine burden for lost souls. Paul tells us "That I have great heaviness and continual sorrow in my heart, for I could wish that myself were accursed from Christ for my brethren..." (Romans 9:2-3). Lost souls seem to be able to sense when one deeply cares for their spiritual welfare. Paul was ready to share the eternal life-giving gospel "in season, [or] out of season" (II Timothy 4:2). No matter where he was, from prison or palace, he was constantly giving out the message of salvation by grace alone. He sowed the seed of the gospel frequently enough that many were saved. Paul said, "I made myself servant unto all, that I might gain the more" (I Corinthians 9:19). His attitude was one of surrendering as a willing bondslave to the Savior. Then, he willingly and humbly attended to their spiritual needs. Paul approached the lost in a personable way, finding common ground so he'd have greater credibility when presenting the gospel. He says, "...unto the Jews I became as a Jew, that I might gain the Jews...To them that are without [the] Law, as without Law...I am made all things to all men, that I might by all means save some" (I Corinthians 9:20-22). Paul was also tireless, working night and day (Acts 20:31; I Thessalonians 2:9; 3:10), as he cared and prayed for those he led to Christ.

If you'd like to be more greatly used of the Lord, follow this pattern used by the Apostle Paul and the teacher who reached our friend.

SELF-CONTROL
I Corinthians 9:24-27

We've all seen it. When a young man is seriously interested in developing a life-long relationship with a young woman, he conducts himself more carefully than he otherwise might. He puts his best foot forward with good hygiene, proper language, courteous conduct, and great attention to the wishes of this young lady. When she takes him to meet her parents, he is usually on his absolute best behavior. *Why?* It is because he is pursuing something valuable: the prize of winning the heart of this young lady and the approval of her parents.

When referring to how believers should live each day after salvation, the Apostle Paul used the illustration of an athlete running a race. He asked, "Know ye not that they which run in a race run all, but one receiveth the prize? So run that ye may obtain" (I Corinthians 9:24). Every believer, without exception, should aspire to earning eternal reward. It is not selfish or carnal to desire such things, and it would be utterly foolish to live without this goal in mind. Love for the Lord is one motivation to live a godly dedicated life, and the desire for reward is another. The Lord tells us about the possibility of reward to encourage us to strive to live for Christ in such a way that it will result in rich eternal reward. *How will this be possible?* Paul told us: "And every man that striveth for the mastery is temperate in all things. Now they do it to obtain a corruptible crown, but we an incorruptible...But I keep my under my body, and bring it into subjection..." (I Corinthians 9:25, 27). Before entering a competition, a serious athlete will discipline himself and mold his body into the best it can be. He will abstain from smoking or using drugs, choose to eat properly, exercise, and train hard to maximize his needed skills. In the arena of Christian living for Christ, we too must become "temperate," or demonstrate self-control. We must choose to refrain from sinful things that would hamper our performance, daily feed our souls with the spiritual nourishment of God's Word, and grow in the needed skills as a soldier of Christ. All this requires an intentional mindset, while keeping our eye on the goal of receiving the prize of eternal reward.

Believer, arm yourself today with the mindset that you are preparing for eternity. Therefore, discipline yourself to grow in the grace of our Lord Jesus Christ.

EVERYONE IS GOOD FOR SOMETHING

I Corinthians 10:13

I have a brother who is six years younger than I am. As a youngster, when I was caught doing something wrong, my parents would scold me saying: "You're the big brother, you're supposed to be setting a good example for your younger brother. Shame on you." When I think of my failure as an example or others who likewise failed in the Scriptures, I've often said, "Everyone is good for something, even if it's only to be used as a bad example."

In I Corinthians Chapter 10, the Apostle Paul is dealing with the issue of bad examples. He tells the believers of his day that in Israel's history, many lusted after evil things. Many were idolaters, fornicators, disobedient to the Lord, and constant murmurers (I Corinthians 10:1-10). Given the pattern of sinful carnality that existed in the Corinthian Christian community, the Apostle Paul wanted to give them the solution to these problems. Paul begins by telling them: "Let him that thinketh he standeth take heed lest he fall" (10:12). When believers fool themself into thinking they are just too spiritual to sin like others, they become easy targets for Satan. The truth is, any believer can commit any sin given the right opportunity and the wrong spiritual condition. Beware. Next, Paul informs them: "there hath no temptation taken you but such as is common to man; but God...will...make a way to escape, that ye may be able to bear it" (10:13). We don't really have to sin. We can choose to draw on the power of Christ and find a way, provided by the Lord, to get far away from the sin that tempts us. In verse 14, Paul urges, "...my dearly beloved, flee from idolatry." As pure Joseph fled from the presence of Potiphar's wife, even when she literally tried to pull him to her bed of sin, we are to vigorously and immediately flee from the presence of sin. Paul also didn't want the Corinthians to confuse their liberty with a license to sin. He told them: "...all things are lawful...but all things edify not" (10:23). Our standard must become doing only what will build up other believers and avoiding anything that would lessen the spiritual walk of others. Finally, live by the rule of only allowing self what will give "glory to God" (10:31).

May we all ask ourselves today: *"What kind of spiritual example am I leaving for others?"* Let's choose to be a good example, not a bad example.

PRAYING AT MEALTIME
I Corinthians 10:30

My wife and I were blessed to attend a large Christian university in preparation for our life's work. There was required attendance at evening meals in a huge dining common that seated 3000 people who ate at tables family style. Ministerial students took turns leading the entire group in giving thanks prior to eating. It was a neat experience to have so many pausing in prayer before meals. I often thought, *wouldn't the world be a better place if everyone likewise paused in thanksgiving?* This should be a regular practice for all who know Christ as Savior, and doing so can even be a good testimony.

In the days when the final books were being written to complete our Bible, there was a big controversy about Christians buying and eating cheaper meats that had been offered, in part, to idols. In I Corinthians Chapter 10, the Apostle Paul made a statement we could easily miss: "...why am I evil spoken of for that for which I give thanks" (vs. 30)? In other words, Paul is saying it was his practice to stop and give God thanks for everything he ate. Regardless of how hard we may work to put food on our tables and a roof over our head; ultimately all we have is a provision from the Lord. "Every good gift and every perfect gift is from above, and cometh down from the Father of lights, with whom is no variableness, neither shadow of turning" (James 1:17). This means that our jobs are a blessed provision from the Lord, as is being healthy enough to work, and that makes anything we eat a provision from the Lord, for which we should always pause to give thanks. We would, or at least should, express our thanks to someone who graciously invites us into their home for a meal or helps provide food in our home during a time of need. Likewise, but even more so, we should willingly and sincerely give God thanks for the food He provides for us each day. The Apostle Paul confirms this principle again when he writes, "For every creature of God is good [for food], and nothing to be refused, if it be received with thanksgiving: For it is sanctified [meaning set apart for a holy purpose] by the word of God and prayer" (I Timothy 4:4-5).

Whether in private or in public, we encourage you to pause before every meal to give God thanks for His loving provision.

MEN AND WOMEN'S HAIR
I Corinthians 11:2-15

S everal months ago, our oldest grandson got a pair of scissors and really butchered his hair. His mother was particularly unhappy with him because they were leaving in a few days to see family who live a great distance away. The only way to make his hair look remotely presentable was to basically buzz it all off. *Sound familiar?*

It might be surprising, but God's Word has a great deal to say about the hair of men and women. In the context of proper worship within the assembly at Corinth, Paul told the women that there were at least five reasons why they should wear long hair. First, doing so is a demonstration of godly submission to the headship of God and the man who is the head in her home (I Corinthians 11:5). To do otherwise is an expression of rebellion that "dishonoureth her head." Second, it was "a shame" for a woman to be "shorn [hair cut short] or shaven" (vs. 6). It is believed that prostitutes in the temples of idols wore extremely short hair; so wearing short hair had this evil association. It was also seen as a form of public shame or mourning, as when non-Jewish women were taken captive. Before marrying a Jewish man, she had to "shave her head" and bewail her parents for one month (Deuteronomy 21:10-12). Therefore, Paul said, "…let her be covered" (vs. 6). Third, "…the woman is the glory of the man" (vs. 7). This simply acknowledges the inherent beauty of a woman, making her the ornament, jewel, or honor of her man. Longer hair magnifies that feminine beauty. Fourth, "For this cause ought the woman to have power on her head because of the angels" (vs. 10). Whether these "angels" were human messengers to the church or holy angels observing the conduct of women seeking to honor the Lord, longer hair was considered a proper example. Fifth, Paul teaches that "even nature itself teach [es] you…if a woman have long hair, it is a glory to her…[as a] covering" (vss. 14-15). Conversely, men are not to have long hair because nature teaches it is a "shame" for men to wear long hair (vs. 14), and doing so dishonors their ultimate head: God.

Before the Lord, there is certainly great liberty in acceptable hairstyles and length. However, a woman's hair should always be long enough to be distinctive from a man and a man's hair short enough to be clearly distinctive from a woman. *Is this your standard?*

THERE MUST BE HERESIES
I Corinthians 11:19

It has been my privilege to serve on different boards in ministries that recognize the distinctiveness of the Dispensation of Grace and the ministry of the Apostle Paul. Another board member once casually remarked what a blessing it had been for several years to enjoy sweet unity free of controversy and divisive doctrines. Then he said, "But we must be vigilant, because it seems like every few years, Satan sends some kind of doctrinal problem that threatens the integrity of our message, and the harmony of our fellowship."

In most Christian circles, dangerous doctrines seem to regularly arise. Though it may be surprising to many, these instances are actually necessary. The Apostle Paul wrote, "For there must be heresies among you, that they which are approved may be made manifest among you" (I Corinthians 11:19). The word "heresies" means a disunion, sect, or party. This implies a division that separates those in error from those who are maintaining proper doctrine. These divisive heresies often come from unexpected sources. Paul warned the elders at the church at Ephesus: "...also of your own selves shall men arise, speaking perverse things, to draw away disciples after them..." (Acts 20: 30). Therefore, all the leaders were to be vigilant to protect sound doctrine in their assembly. Leaders of local churches must be ones who are "holding fast the faithful word as he hath been taught, that he may be able by sound doctrine both to exhort and to convince the gainsayers" (Titus 1:9). However, every believer has the responsibility to not be "...tossed to and fro with every wind of doctrine, by the sleight of men, and cunning craftiness whereby they lie in wait to deceive..." (Ephesians 4:14). Instead, we must be wise enough to compare what all teachers promote with the Scriptures to see "...whether those things were [or are] so" (Acts 17:11). Historically, many stubbornly persist in doctrinal error out of foolish loyalty to men, and seem to willingly embrace whatever error their leader teaches. However, some can be rescued by sound doctrine when their primary loyalty is to God's truth. Moreover, those who do stand consistently true and capable in the Word of God are manifest, or "approved," by sound doctrine and behavior that "adorn the doctrine of God our Savior in all things" (Titus 2:10).

Believer, don't despair when division over doctrinal issues comes. These heresies must come to expose those in error and distinguish those who are standing for God's truth.

DO YOU REMEMBER ME?
I Corinthians 11:24-25

We've probably all asked a small child, or an elderly friend: "Do you remember me?" When our youngest daughter and family moved away to Wisconsin, they, of course, took our oldest grandchild. For the first year and eight months of his life, we saw this grandchild every day. We became so attached to him, and his parents too, that our hearts just ached with missing them so much. One of the things that bothered us was the concern that our young grandchild would completely forget us. After a couple months, my wife and I were able to go visit them. When we saw him, we asked, *"Do you remember Grandpa?" "Do you remember Mimi?"*

It is noteworthy that when the Apostle Paul gives his instructions to the Body of Christ about observing the Lord's Supper, he adds an instruction twice. In I Corinthians 11:24-25 he tells the saints to partake of the symbolic bread and drink "in remembrance of me." Surely there is something deeper here than an occasional reminder of the Savior during what could become a religious ritual. Yes, we are to remember the agony He endured for us as His body was broken and His life-blood was spilt to purchase our eternal redemption. Indeed, we must remember this is the foundation for our forgiveness of sin and eternal life. But this writer believes there is something more intended in these words: "…in remembrance of me." The Lord warned Israel, when they obtained their Promised Land and began to enjoy abundant prosperity there, they would "…forget the Lord" (Deuteronomy 6:10-12). Jeremiah tells them "…my people have forgotten me days without number" (Jeremiah 2:32). Surely the instruction in the Lord's Supper to observe it "…in remembrance of me," is also given to help us not forget the Lord in our daily life. Just as we long for our children and grandchildren to remember us with affection, the Lord longs for us to remember Him. He wants us to remember Him when we wake each morning, eat a meal, face a problem, experience prosperity, face a decision, prioritize, deal with temptation, read our Bible, work through difficulties, or go to sleep. He wants to be foremost in our thinking and in our lives. He longs for us to remember Him with loving affection and come often to Him for regular fellowship.

Perhaps today the Lord would ask each of us: "Do you remember me?" Let's choose to remember our Lord frequently throughout this day.

A MELTING POT
I Corinthians 12:13

People seeking a better life have come to America from all over the world. Our country has become a "melting pot" of different cultures that have been blended together into one people. The idea of a melting pot comes from a large kettle of stew where various ingredients are added until a wonderful blend emerges. We, who know the Lord Jesus Christ as Savior, have become a part of a far greater melting pot of people. I Corinthians 12:13 says, "For by one Spirit are we all baptized into one body, whether we be Jews or Gentiles, whether we be bond or free; and have been all made to drink into one Spirit." For several thousand years, the Lord has been taking sinners saved by grace from all over the world and placing them into the Body of Christ. By identification with the Savior, we have become one.

This concept of all believers, regardless of age, color, or previous culture, being blended into one body of believers is more than a doctrinal fact. Our Savior intends for it to have several practical results. We are never to assume the attitude "...I have no need" of another believer (vs. 15-21). Just as a body needs every part: an eye, foot, and ear, we all need every believer. Just as each physical body part is "necessary" (vs. 22), we are to see every member of the Body of Christ as necessary for us to function properly and to be whole. An ear may seem less beautiful than the eyes, but both are truly beautiful when we understand how important each one is to our ability to function in a whole capacity. Similarly, we are to see every believer in "comeliness," or beauty, because they too contribute something critical to the function of the Body of Christ. God has "tempered" us all together with mutual need. Therefore, the desire of the Savior is that there "should be no schism in the body" (vs. 25a). The word "schism" means a split, division, or gap. We must endeavor to keep the unity of the Spirit so that no "schism" exists between believers. Finally, believers are to "have the same care one for another" (vs. 25b). This means we are to nourish, protect, comfort and build up one another.

We should each ask ourselves: *"Am I functioning with other believers the way the Savior intends?" What action can you take today to demonstrate the proper attitude toward other believers?*

PLACED WITH DIVINE WISDOM
I Corinthians 12:18

As a youngster, I attended a one-room country schoolhouse from kindergarten through eighth grade. Amazingly, one teacher taught students in all grades in the subjects required by the state. Every year the teacher organized an elaborate Christmas program. At her discretion, she would dole out parts for skits, and place each student exactly where needed on the stage for the final song. As I think back on it, she always did a masterful job.

As the Apostle Paul explained the role spiritual gifts played in establishing the newly formed Body of Christ, he explained that God was sovereignly placing believers where He needed them to be. Paul put it this way: "But now God hath set the members every one of them in the body, as it hath pleased him" (I Corinthians 12:18). The uses of miraculous instantaneous gifts, or abilities given by God, were particularly needed prior to the completion of the Scriptures. If we can imagine how difficult it would be for us to know what God expected of us, what to believe, or how to function with only a written record of the Old Testament, then we can better understand why these miraculous spiritual gifts were so needed. Once the Bible was complete and began to be more widely circulated, the Lord desired all believers to place their focus on God's Word (II Timothy 3:16-17). Until that was possible, these gifts played a major role in establishing the saints on a solid spiritual path. Paul specified these miraculous spiritual gifts as being ones of wisdom, knowledge, faith, healing, discerning spirits and tongues (I Corinthians 12:7-10). The Holy Spirit distributed these gifts "to every man severally as he will," or "as it hath pleased him" (I Corinthians 12:11, 18), to equip every local assembly with what they needed to function properly until receiving a completed Bible. With these gifts in place, they were able to reach lost souls in any language with the gospel, know sound doctrine, discern false doctrine, and have supernaturally enabled men capable of teaching truth for today. It was a marvelous divine provision.

While the application is somewhat different today, God still sovereignly works to place individuals in every assembly with the needed abilities to minister, so that every saint is contributing a needed aspect of ministry. This is what Paul meant when he referred to us as being "fitly joined together... according the effectual working...of every part" (Ephesians 4:16). *What are you contributing in ministry in your local church?*

MEANINGLESS NOISE AND ACTIVITY

I Corinthians 13:1-7

A pastor was once privileged to lead a church large enough to have a bus route, evening Bible institute, and assistant pastor to work with the teens. It wasn't long after the assistant pastor arrived that he began to see glaring chinks in the senior pastor's armor of daily righteousness. This senior pastor frequently lost his temper with adults who sought to minister with him. He often yelled at, or refused to speak to, co-workers, frequently had his wife in tears, sometimes slammed bus children into the wall when they misbehaved, and alienated virtually everyone around him. Nonetheless, he was a tireless and fairly capable worker. But, sadly, after awhile it didn't matter how hard he worked. He became ineffectual and lost his ministry.

While the above is somewhat of an extreme example, there is a vital lesson for all of us to remember from this true account. In I Corinthians 13:1-3, the Apostle Paul warns believers that spiritual ministry without love is utterly meaningless and unprofitable. He explains that having the miraculous gift of speaking in an unknown language, but doing so without love is <u>nothing more than meaningless noise</u>. If without love, Paul said, "I am become as sounding brass, or a tinkling cymbal" (vs. 1). Paul explains that if he had the capability of "prophecy [meaning eloquence in proclaiming the truth], and understand all mysteries, and all knowledge and...have all faith...and have not love, <u>I am nothing</u>" (vs. 2). Some in Paul's day who possessed these miraculous gifts needed to know their show of ministry had a hollow ring. Then, and now, one might think great abilities make them important, but God measures His servants not by talent, but love. Unless we have love, we are in reality a big zero. In verse 3, Paul adds, "though I bestow all my goods...and give my body to be burned... <u>it profiteth me nothing</u>." That must have been a shocking statement to some who were being impoverished and martyred. Unless they did so with real love, they would receive no eternal reward. This should also speak to us today. No matter how much we work or sacrifice, God will not reward us unless we are permeated with love. These sobering truths should cause us to rethink the condition of our heart. *Above every other quality or capability, love reigns supreme.* Verse 13 tells us the greatest capability is genuine love.

Why not pause right now asking the Lord to help you grow, and consistently demonstrate real love to everyone.

WHAT IS LOVE?
I Corinthians 13:4-6

May 27

The storyline of the 1970 movie, *Love Story*, with Ali MacGraw and Ryan O'Neal, revolves around an upper-class young man falling in love with a middle-class girl. Against his father's wishes, they date, marry, and build a life together. After a fight and separation of several hours, the two reunite. He tries to apologize and she stops him, saying, "Love means never having to say you're sorry." At the end of the film, he repeats this phrase to his estranged father. I remember thinking at the time: "That makes no sense at all."

There seems to be a great deal of confusion over what love is. Some believe it is sex without commitment in marriage, while others think it is only a passionate emotion. But the most accurate explanation of love is found in I Corinthians, Chapter 13. God's description starts with, "Charity [or love] suffereth long, and is kind" (vs. 4a). When someone is difficult, love with great kindness, endures the irritation for a long time. "Charity vaunteth not itself, is not puffed up" (vs. 4b). It is natural to demand our rights with others and exalt ourselves, but real love demonstrates humility toward the one we love. Love "doth not behave itself unseemly" (vs. 5a). The idea here is that love does not go beyond what is appropriate or lose control. Love simply behaves very well. Love "seeketh not her own" (vs. 5). When love reigns, we put the needs and wishes of the one we love ahead of our own. "[Love] is not easily provoked, [and] thinketh no evil" (vs. 5b). Love is not being easily irritated, nor is it suspecting another of wrong doing without proof. Instead, love will think the best of others and demonstrate great patience. Verse 6 says: love "Rejoiceth not in iniquity, but rejoiceth in the truth." Here, the Lord is making a contrast between sinful actions and qualities of virtue. Love takes no pleasure in vices, but is overjoyed when the one loved exhibits good and godly characteristics. The description ends by saying love bears, believes, hopes and endures "all things" (vs. 7). No matter what comes, for better or worse, love endures it all. Even in poor treatment, injustice, selfishness and more, love can prevail if we allow God's love for others to live in us.

Sound impossible? Real love doesn't come naturally. It's supernatural. We need God's strength to exhibit genuine love. Let's pause right now to ask for His power to live in love the way we should.

CHILDISH THINGS
I Corinthians 13:8-10

If you have children, or grandchildren, your house has become a warehouse for childish things. Diapers, bottles, swings, walkers, and lots of toys clutter your home. As they grow and mature, they graduate to different levels of paraphernalia and toys. Recently, our oldest grandchild learned how to ride his bike without training wheels. He was so proud when we could put them away, because he didn't need them any more. Now he rides "a big-boy bicycle."

The Lord temporarily provided miraculous gifts to the Body of Christ, prior to the completion of the Holy Canon. The Apostle Paul wrote to the believers at Corinth explaining God was going to take these away in their foreseeable future. In I Corinthians 13:8, he stated, "whether there be prophecies [meaning men preaching without Paul's letters to guide them in new grace doctrine but having God's divine temporary enablement] they shall fail [meaning to cease]." He continues, "whether there be tongues [meaning the supernatural ability to speak in a previously unknown language], they shall cease; whether there be knowledge [a supernatural enablement to know truth, error, and dynamic discernment], it shall vanish away." He further explained the time and reason these miraculous provisions would end. They would cease when "that which is perfect [meaning complete or full] is come" (I Corinthians 13:10). This was a specific reference to the Scriptures being filled up with the final God-given revelations to Paul. When this was complete, these miraculous sign gifts would "be done away." The reason they would be done away is explained in verse 11: "When I was a child, I spake as a child, I understood as a child, I thought as a child: but when I became a man, I put away childish things." The concept was that these miraculous abilities were for the Body of Christ when yet in an immature state. Now we are to stop depending on, or hanging on, to these things of the past. Instead, as mature believers, we are to place our confidence, attention, and dependence in the completed Scriptures. Like training wheels on a bike, these miraculous abilities were never intended to be permanent. They were only given to serve the purpose of protecting and guiding believers until they could stand and walk in the strength of God's completed Word.

If you have been clinging to these miraculous things of the past, let them go. Move on to a more mature spiritual relationship with the Lord by following these principles in His Word.

FOLLOW AFTER LOVE
I Corinthians 14:1

In 1969, Paul Newman and Robert Redford starred in the movie, *Butch Cassidy and the Sundance Kid.* The film is based on a band of train robbers led by Butch and Sundance. The Union Pacific hired a renowned group, the Pinkerton National Detective Agency, to hunt these robbers down. In the film, this posse was skillful and relentless in their pursuit. Butch and Sundance tried everything they knew to elude them, but they just kept coming, undeterred. Butch turned to Sundance and said, "Who are these guys?"

Having just spent the entire previous chapter extolling the necessity and importance of genuine love in the lives Christians, Paul continued in the next chapter with, "Follow after charity..." (I Corinthians 14:1). The word "follow" means to pursue, follow after, or press forward. If you can picture in your mind the posse, mentioned above, relentlessly pursuing bank robbers [or a dog completely focused on running down a rabbit that is trying to evade him], then you've begun to grasp the concept Paul was communicating. It isn't enough for us to inactively wait for the Lord to fill us with a warm fuzzy feeling of love for others. We are to pursue love by seeking to capture it and make it our own. *But how does one follow after love?* It begins by realizing that brotherly love is the fruit of the Spirit. Galatians 5:23-24 lists it as the first, and by implication, the most important of all the godly qualities that the Holy Spirit seeks to produce in us. Since the Holy Spirit produces love, we can't toil to produce it. God must grow it in us as we grow in Him. However, He does not do so against our will. We must have a surrendered heart to allow love for others to grow. It is in this context that Galatians 5:24 instructs us to "...crucify the flesh with the affections and lusts" (meaning to resist unloving tendencies) and "walk in the Spirit," which would mean to yield to the Spirit when He seeks to grow brotherly love for others. Beyond this, we can pursue love by praying for the welfare and blessing of others. This is not praying for God's judgment upon others who offend us, but praying for their well-being.

Among all the things we pursue in life, brotherly love needs to be near the very top of our list. *Are you pursuing love for others?* Today, do something concrete to demonstrate brotherly love to another Christian.

IS THIS ONE OF YOUR SKILLS?
I Corinthians 14:12

We have friends who have two beautiful daughters. While their girls were still at home and playing sports, we attended one of their games. Like the other parents who had kids on the team, our friends were yelling out constant encouragements from the sidelines: "You can do it," "Good job girl," "Stay alert," and "Be ready." Go to any ball game anywhere in America, and you'll hear these constant encouragements yelled to children from their families.

A local church should be like a close-knit family of believers. We should have a deep love for one another and interest in what each member is doing. We should be cheering one another on with constant encouragement. This is the concept the Apostle Paul repeats in I Corinthians Chapter 14. In verse 12, he tells the saints: "...seek that ye may excel to the edifying of the church." Every individual was being urged to consciously strive for excellence in the skill of encouraging saints in their assembly. It was to be their intentional purpose to "excel" in this needed ministry. We may not think very often about how important this is until we are the one going through a very difficult time and another saint strengthens our weary soul. But this is as important a ministry as any other. When Paul wrote about those "that prophesieth" (vss. 2-3), he was explaining that preaching was to accomplish the purpose of "edification." Prophesying simply meant to proclaim God's truth, in this instance with divine help from the Lord. But God wanted the human instrument to see that the Lord's goal was more than grounding hearers in sound doctrine. It was also to build them up in Christ, "that the whole church may receive edifying" (vs. 5b). But this ministry of encouraging the saints isn't just the preacher's job. It's everyone's job. Paul explained to all the saints that whenever they opened their mouths, it was to be governed by words that were "...good to the use of edifying" (Ephesians 4:29b). The new standard now is: "Let all things be done unto edifying" (I Corinthians 14:26b).

Now that you know it is your job to intentionally strengthen, encourage, and build up other saints around you, *how are you going to let this affect your life? Who in your assembly could use a call or visit from you to encourage them?* The next time you attend a church service, go armed with the intention of purposely trying to encourage others around you.

NOTHING BUT THE TRUTH
I Corinthians 14:15

This oath is repeated in courtrooms: "Do you solemnly swear to tell the truth, the whole truth, and nothing but the truth, so help you God?" Oaths like this may go back as far as the Roman Empire. Truthful testimony, particularly in legal proceedings, is so vital that one form or another of this oath has been commonplace in many countries for centuries.

Christians should be just as concerned about telling the truth in all areas of life. The Apostle Paul tells us one aspect of the whole armor of God that enables us to stand against the wiles of the devil is to "Stand, therefore, having your loins girt about with truth…" (Ephesians 6:14). While this imperative includes divine truth, believers should be truthful in all things. There are two areas in which we should particularly settle for "nothing but the truth." The teaching of God's Word is the first area. We learn from I Timothy 3:15 that the local "…church of the living God, [is to be] the pillar and ground of the truth." Not some truth and some error, but "the whole truth and nothing but the truth," so help us God. This principle is why Paul withstood false teaching that came into the Galatian churches, "that the truth of the gospel might continue with you" (Galatians 2:5). The second area where truth is so important is in music. It must consistently teach sound doctrine and not error. A believer once told our assembly: "Many people mindlessly sing error in church services. It's as if they turn their minds off to the content of the words. But if we wouldn't stand for someone teaching error from the pulpit, we shouldn't stand for anyone teaching error when we sing." He was right! Therefore, as a church, we proceeded to look discerningly at every word in every hymn. If a word needed to be changed, we changed it. If a verse needed to be left out, we left it out. Even if we liked a particular song, if it taught bad doctrine, we no longer sang it. The biblical basis for such a practice, in part, is found in I Corinthians 14:15 when Paul says, "…I will sing with the spirit, and I will sing with the understanding also."

From now on, when you listen to the teaching of God's Word or sing in worship, make your standard "the truth, the whole truth, and nothing but the truth, so help me God."

ARE YOU CONFUSED?
I Corinthians 14:22

My oldest daughter loves to remind me of an incident during her senior year of high school. On a cross-country trip, she was driving and I was navigating. As we went through Memphis, Tennessee, I was reading the map; and she, the signs. When we came to a fork in the road, I insisted we go left, even though she was certain the signs told us to go right. Within about five miles, the interstate abruptly ended and funneled us off into a very rough part of town. She said, "See Dad, I told you we should go right." I was sincere and certain, but I was confused.

Many today seem to be sincerely confused about miraculous sign gifts. God intends for us to see that all of them were only given for a temporary time period, for a specific purpose, and to be used in a specific way. During the Acts era, before Scripture was complete, there was a need for supernatural abilities to guide the early church. I Corinthians 13:10 promised, "when that which is perfect [or complete] is come, then that which is in part shall be done away." Verse eight explains that "prophecies," "tongues," and supernatural "knowledge" would "fail" to continue, or "cease" and "vanish away." Once the revelation of Scripture was complete, all sign gifts ended. The primary purpose of these sign gifts was "not to them that believe, but to them that believe not" (I Corinthians 14:22). When unsaved people in the early Acts era witnessed believers with genuine miraculous abilities, it was a powerful tool in leading them to Christ. While some of these gifts, such as prophecy [meaning to proclaim God's truth], were used for a time to "edify," or build up, saints in new biblical truth, the primary purpose of God was to influence the lost. Whenever gifts, such as tongues (meaning an unknown human language), were given, they had to be practiced as God required. Tongues always had to be interpreted to all (vs. 26). They were only done one at a time (vss. 30-31), never by more than three (vss. 27, 29), never leave the one speaking out of control (vs. 28, 32), and women were never permitted to speak in tongues in public services (vs. 34).

Claims today of miraculous tongues do not follow this divine pattern, nor can they achieve God's original purpose. God is not the author of confusion. If we will only abide by these instructions, confusion on this subject will disappear.

MAKE IT COUNT
I Corinthians 15:9-10

In the 1998 movie, *Saving Private Ryan*, Captain John Miller took his men behind enemy lines to find James Ryan, whose three brothers were recently killed in action. Their mission was to get Ryan out of harm's way so his family would not lose their only remaining son. The film ended with Captain Miller being mortally wounded. With his last breath, he pulls Private Ryan close to him and whispered the words: "Earn this." He wanted Ryan to realize the great sacrifice of human lives spent to secure his safety. Therefore, he needed to live a life worthy of such sacrifice.

Before salvation, Paul had been a merciless persecutor of the Jewish Kingdom Church. He had imprisoned both men and women, causing them to be brutally tortured to death unless they would renounce faith in the Lord Jesus Christ. Then, the Savior confronted Saul, later known as Paul, with a blinding light and the question of "why" he was persecuting the Lord Jesus through believers. The result of this encounter was that Paul was wonderfully saved. After his salvation, there are two notable things to remember. First, he never forgot the depths of sin from which the Lord Jesus had saved him. He had been a ruthless man who was spiritually dead in false religion. Part of his testimony was as follows: "For I am the least of the apostles, that am not meet to be called an apostle, because I persecuted the church of God" (I Corinthians 15:9). An important lesson from Paul's life is that one should not be paralyzed by a sense of unworthiness because of sin prior to, or even after, salvation. Instead, one should simply allow this reminder to fill us with a deep sense of gratitude for our salvation. Second, Paul said that God's "...grace which was bestowed upon me was not in vain; but I labored more abundantly than they all, yet not I, but the grace of God which was with me" (I Corinthians 15:10). In other words, Paul realized the supreme sacrifice Christ made on the cross, and chose to live worthy of what Christ had done for him. Thereafter, he lived for the cause of Christ in sincerity, and constant service. God's grace extended to him was to no extent "in vain."

May God's grace to you in no sense be "in vain." Be certain to live a life that is worthy of the sacrifice Christ made for you!

I DIE DAILY
I Corinthians 15:31

Mothers know the principle of selflessness. Mother birds refuse to move off their nest, even in the face of danger. Mother cats or bears will aggressively fight off males when they try to kill their young. Mothers feed their young, even to the neglect of themselves. Human mothers give birth in great pain, wake to feed their babies every two hours, and tirelessly care for their needs for many years. In a very real sense, these mothers die daily to self, so that they may live for the welfare of another.

Paul makes a short but profound statement when he wrote, "I die daily" (I Corinthians 15:31). While Paul refers to a death to self, a literal death is also in view. As God's apostle of grace, Paul endured many hardships. He lists abundant labors, stripes, imprisonments, and "deaths oft" (II Corinthians 11:23). It is this writer's conclusion that Paul literally died for the cause of Christ on more than one occasion. His stoning by unbelieving Jewish men and being left for dead is one instance (Acts 14:19). His being "caught up into the third heaven" (I Corinthians 12:2) would be another example. Throughout Paul's ministry, his life was in constant peril. He believed God had set forth the apostles to be "...appointed to death...for we are made a spectacle unto the world..." (I Corinthians 4:9) and that "...we [apostles] which live are always delivered unto death for Jesus' sake, that the life also of Jesus might be made manifest in our mortal flesh" (II Corinthians 4:11). When Paul said, "I die daily," we obviously don't believe he literally died every day. However, we believe he was in constant jeopardy of death. The secondary application of dying daily is that Paul symbolically put to death the desires and practices of the flesh each day that he might glorify Christ. Like a mother who no longer lives to please herself but lives for her child, Paul now lived, not to please himself, but His Lord. It was in this sense that Paul said he "...crucified the flesh with the affections and lusts" (Galatians 5:24), and that he was "...crucified with Christ...and the life which I now live in the flesh I live by the faith of the Son of God who loved me, and gave Himself for me" (Galatians 2:20).

It is the duty of every believer to die to self each day and live unto Christ. *In this sense, have you died today?*

159

WE ARE ALL IMPRESSIONABLE
I Corinthians 15:33

At age 16, this writer was unsaved and, admittedly, steeped in sinful behaviors, which included having some unsavory friends. When I began to date a young woman, her mother took me aside for a serious discussion. I can still almost hear her saying, "John, we cherish our daughter and want only the best for her. We are concerned about some of the friends you hang around. You need to never forget this: You are the kind of person you hang around. If you aren't like them yet, you soon will be. So be careful who you allow yourself to spend time with because they will influence you."

When believers at Corinth received Paul's first epistle, they had spent time with false teachers who had eroded their faith in the resurrection of the Lord Jesus Christ from the dead. To combat this influence, one entire chapter counteracts false doctrine with divine truth about the resurrection of our Lord, and our future resurrection. In this context the Paul wrote, "Be not deceived: evil communications corrupt good manners" (I Corinthians 15:33). The word "manners" means a moral habit. Like the mother who sought to convince this writer that those we listen to and spend time with will have an influence upon us, Paul wanted these saints to understand that they, too, were impressionable. It is highly likely that some in this church thought they were so grounded in sound doctrine that they couldn't be moved from biblically accurate understandings. However, they only fooled themselves, when they allowed others to fool them with false doctrine. Perhaps some of these saints thought they could positively influence these false teachers, but Paul warned them not to be deceived about what would happen. The "evil communications" from false teachers would indeed "corrupt" their habits, doctrine, and behavior. This is a timeless principle. Proverbs warns against "...friendship with an angry man...lest thou learn his ways..." (22:24-25). Realizing that others influence us, David surrounded himself with companions who would fear the Lord, and keep His precepts (Psalm 119:63).

Today, we believers need to take this wise counsel to heart. We must not "deceive" ourselves by thinking we won't be influenced when we listen to "evil communications." More specifically, we should not listen to people from cults who come to our door, or to anyone who does not recognize the distinctiveness of the Dispensation of Grace, and Paul's ministry.

AWAKE TO RIGHTEOUSNESS
I Corinthians 15:34

A Denver Post newspaper article, entitled, "33 Parolees Linked To 38 Murders In Colorado," cites numerous examples of inmates who committed murders within a matter of weeks after being paroled. One inmate stabbed his girlfriend to death. Another murdered a woman who was eight months pregnant. A third killed an attorney, who was found in his basement bound by duck tape.[1] When released from prison, these murderers were given a second chance at life. They needed to awake to their opportunity to live a new, lawful, and productive life in our society. Instead, they continued the same criminal behavior they knew prior to being incarcerated.

When the Apostle Paul urged the saints at Corinth to live in light of their coming resurrection to eternal life, he told them, "Awake to righteousness, and sin not; for some have not the knowledge of God; I speak this to your shame" (I Corinthians 15:34). From earlier chapters, we learn that the saints at Corinth were not acting very saintly. They were controlled by so much carnality that they could only comprehend the milk of God's Word. They commonly practiced immorality; and yet, they were puffed up over the limited spiritual knowledge they possessed. From every outward appearance, one would find it difficult to see little that demonstrated new life in Christ. They were effectively living the same kind of sinful lifestyle that they lived prior to trusting in Christ. This mattered, too. The Apostle Paul constantly taught believers to not continue in sin because God's grace was abundant toward them (Romans 6:1-3), to walk worthy of the sacrifice Christ had made for their salvation (Ephesians 4:1), and not to let the "filthiness" of sin "be once named among you" (Ephesians 5:1-5). Paul used the term, "awake to righteousness" (meaning a righteous lifestyle), warning them that many people within their sphere of influence knew nothing about receiving eternal life by Gods' grace alone. Their silence with the gospel, and their sinful lives, before lost souls was to their utter "shame."

Believer, in salvation the Lord Jesus has given you a second chance at living the way you should. *Is your speech free from profanity or impure words? Can others see in you a more righteous lifestyle, explained only by your interest in the Lord Jesus and the Bible? Do you seek to share the gospel with lost souls?* In each of these areas, we need to awake to righteousness.

PLEASE WAKE UP
I Corinthians 15:34

When my brother was about five years old, it was difficult to wake him up, when he walked in his sleep. My parents could call him by name, shake him, help him to his feet, and point him toward his bed, but he only wanted to lie back down. However, once they got him going, he'd stagger toward the bedroom. When he was within about three feet of the bed, he'd throw himself on it and drift back into deep sleep.

Similarly, most of us can identify with remaining in a sleepy stupor until we've had our morning coffee. If this sounds familiar, it may be easy to identify with I Corinthians 15:34. Here Paul wrote to believers saying, "Awake to righteousness, and sin not; for some have not the knowledge of God: I speak this to your shame." These words were given in the context of discussing a coming resurrection. Everyone, both saved and unsaved, will be resurrected after death, just not to the same place. Daniel 12:2 tells us this, "And many of them that sleep in the dust of the earth shall awake, some to everlasting life, and some to shame and everlasting contempt." Paul explained to the saints at Corinth the certainty of their resurrection to eternal life, but he scolds them for their lack of effort to rescue lost souls from being resurrected to eternal punishment.

Believers at Thessalonica had been fervently sharing Christ with others. Through their efforts in evangelism, virtually everyone in their part of the world had heard the gospel. However, the saints at Corinth had not been very diligent in sharing the good news of salvation. They were, in effect, spiritually sleepwalking in a sinful lifestyle, and calloused to the looming, eternal destruction of others. They lived next to, worked beside, and had friends and family who were still unsaved. Many did not know Christ because the believers at Corinth never shared with them the good news of eternal life by faith alone in the Lord Jesus Christ. Paul told them, "...some have not the knowledge of God: I speak this to your shame." Paul was seeking to awaken them to their need to share the gospel with others.

Through I Corinthians 15:34, the Lord is seeking to awaken us today to our need to share the gospel. *Which unsaved person can you share the gospel with today?*

A NEW BODY
I Corinthians 15:38-40

The older we get, the more our bodies wear out and are filled with aches and pains. It reminds us of our heavenly home, and it helps prepare us for the time when we step into eternity. In the fall of 2013, a dear saint in our assembly was having increasingly severe health problems. One day he stood, and said to us all: "Enjoy your aches and pains now because one day soon we will be with the Savior in heaven. There we will be given new, heavenly bodies. We will have no pain, no sorrow, and no death. A glorious future awaits us. Rejoice in this."

The above expectation is right on target. When John the Apostle explained the physical, eternal state, he wrote, "Beloved, now are we the sons of God, and it doth not yet appear what we shall be: but we know that, when He shall appear, we shall be like Him; for we shall see Him as He is" (I John 3:2). Gospel accounts of our resurrected Savior describe Him with a body similar in appearance to His previous state. We would surely expect that, as God Himself, the Savior no longer experienced any pain. Revelation 21:4 confirms this when it refers to the eternal state of the kingdom saints. He wrote, "And God shall wipe away all tears…there shall be no more death, neither sorrow, nor crying, neither shall there be any more pain; for the former things are passed away." The Apostle Paul explained that there will be vast differences in our new, eternal body. It will be a "celestial" body (I Corinthians 15:38-40), meaning it will be fitted by God to thrive in the atmosphere of the heavens. In contrast to our physical bodies that are weak, degenerating, and corruptible, our new bodies will be "raised in incorruption…glory…power…[and as] a spiritual body" (I Corinthians 15:42-44). Paul continued his explanation by saying, "…flesh and blood cannot inherit the kingdom of God…Behold I show you a mystery…we shall all be changed" (I Corinthians 15:50-51). To summarize our change, he said, "And as we have born the image of the earthy, we shall also bear the image of the heavenly" (I Corinthians 15:49).

Whenever you get weighed down with physical pain, remember that one day our Lord is going to give us new bodies without weakness or pain. Believe it, rejoice in it, and look forward to it with thanksgiving. In expectation and faithfulness, keep looking up for His return until He comes.

WHAT MOTIVATES YOU?
I Corinthians 15:31-58

Twenty years after graduating from high school, I found myself twenty pounds over weight. I was planning to attend my high school reunion, and I knew that virtually everyone from my class would be there too. Since I didn't want to be embarrassed, I was highly motivated to spend three months working hard at exercise and eating well. By the time the reunion came, I was very happy that I had taken off those twenty pounds. *What motivates you to trim away the fat of unworthy things in your life?* The Apostle Paul wanted to live for Christ out of appreciation for eternal salvation, but one of his strongest motivations was the certainty of our coming resurrection.

The theme of I Corinthians Chapter 15 is our confident expectation of being raised from the dead to live eternally with the Lord Jesus. It was because Paul kept this hope uppermost in his mind that he could say, "I die daily" (vs. 31b). Every day he died to the lure of living only for self, to being saved but only having a mediocre, lukewarm walk with Christ, and to allowing the fear of persecution to silence his efforts with the gospel. Paul chose to die each day to these temptations so that he might live in a vibrant relationship with Christ and in constant service for his Savior. It was also this expectation of the resurrection that empowered him to stand undaunted in the face of unbelievers who threatened his life because of his ministry. In verse 32, he said, "If...I have fought with beasts at Ephesus, what advantageth it me, if the dead rise not? Let us eat and drink; for to morrow we die." But Paul knew there would be the advantage of the Savior's approval and eternal reward if he remained faithful. He also wanted the saints at Corinth to remain faithful and be on fire for the Lord. Therefore, he encouraged them by writing, "...my beloved brethren, be ye steadfast, unmoveable, always abounding in the work of the Lord, forasmuch as ye know that your labour is not in vain in the Lord" (vs. 58).

There was a danger for these believers to lose the motivation that came from the resurrection because many in their day denied it, as many do today. The solution was to "Be not deceived; evil communications corrupt good manners" (vs. 33). They needed to avoid the company of those who scoffed at the resurrection. *Is there someone you should avoid?*

PROPER GIVING
I Corinthians 16:2

As a freshman in college, this writer had only been saved for one year. Coming out of a liberal church background, I had a very limited knowledge of God's Word. An older ministerial student befriended me and expressed that he did not need to give money to the Lord because he had already given his life to the Lord. At this point, I did not know the Scriptures well enough to refute his theory, but it certainly did not seem right to me.

It is easy to see that Satan attacks every major doctrine in the Bible. Sometimes, he simply distorts sound doctrine. At other times, he totally denies even basic truths. When it comes to giving back to the Lord from which He has blessed us, the principles in Scripture are clear and consistent. Paul's instructions were these, "Upon the first day of the week let every one of you lay by him in store, as God hath prospered him..." (I Corinthians 16:2). Giving should begin with each believer first giving himself to the Lord (II Corinthians 8:5), but no one is exempt from the need to give to the Lord as an act of worship. From the Garden of Eden through today, "every one" is to give. In the Dispensation of Grace, giving is to be done on "the first day of the week," which is Sunday. The implication is more than simply giving regularly. It also means to give weekly as a part of sincere worship and thanksgiving when meeting in one's local church. God always intended giving to be proportionate, or "as God hath prospered" (I Corinthians 16:2; Deuteronomy 16:17). Some may be able to give great sums, while others may sacrifice to give very little. God knows one's capability, and He is pleased when one gives with a right heart, in the right way. God has always required giving to be done "willingly" (Exodus 25:2; I Chronicles 29:9; Matthew 10:8), or as Paul describes it, "...let him give; not grudgingly, or of necessity: for God loveth a cheerful giver" (II Corinthians 9:7). One is also to give out of a dedicated heart. Paul put it this way, "...he that giveth, let him do it with simplicity..." (Romans 12:8). The word "simplicity" means in singleness, sincerity, without self-seeking, and bountifully. The Savior condemned those who gave to be seen of others. Instead, giving should be done in a quiet and private way.

Let your giving consistently model these clear principles in God's Word.

OPEN DOORS
I Corinthians 16:9

When seeking my first place of full time ministry, a pastor asked us to teach in their Christian
school. Initially, we were excited, thinking this might be an open door of
God's leading. Unfortunately, this pastor would not trust me to preach in
church until I was there for 3 to 4 years and wanted my wife and I to both to
teach for a combined annual salary of $6,100. When I told him we couldn't
make ends meet on that amount, he became indignant saying we needed to
trust God to provide for our needs. I told him we just couldn't come. Soon
after, we had a better ministry opportunity with enough pay to get by on.
We thanked the Lord for this open door and accepted the invitation.

Both the Apostle Paul and the Apostle John looked at some opportunities, or "open doors," as being from the Lord. The Apostle John wrote to
the Jewish saints in Philadelphia saying, "...behold, I have set before thee
an open door, and no man can shut it: for thou hast a little strength, and hast
kept my word, and hast not denied my name" (Revelation 3:8). Clearly, in
this instance, the Lord was working in circumstances to enhance the ability
of these saints to minister. Similarly, the Apostle Paul viewed the open door
to minister at Ephesus as an opportunity from the Lord. He wrote, "...a
great door and effectual is opened unto me..." (I Corinthians 16:9). This
meant there had been enough responsiveness to his preaching that many
were saved, and a local church was formed. So, Paul decided to stay because his ministry was being fruitful. But later, Paul decided to move on
and "...came to Troas to preach Christ's gospel, and a door was opened unto
me of the Lord" (II Corinthians 2:12). Please note that we need to use caution here. Paul had the freedom of choice to stay or to move on in ministry
to another location (vs. 13), as we see throughout the Book of Acts. Just
because an open door of opportunity is available, this doesn't mean that we
must pursue it to be in the will of God, or to be blessed by Him. Especially
in the Dispensation of Grace, open doors mean we that have an opportunity,
but God still gives us great liberty to choose where to go and what to do.

Don't see open doors as only a divine mandate. Realize that grace gives
us freedom to make wise decisions.

166

BE A BIG BOY
I Corinthians 16:13

Recently, my wife and I stood in the driveway while our grandson spent ten minutes running up and down the sidewalk and into the yard. When he rounded the corner, he stumbled and fell with both hands, sliding on the concrete. He moaned as we picked him up. We asked, *"Are you okay buddy? Do you need to put ice on your hands, or are you going to be just fine?"* He reluctantly said he was okay, so I praised him for being a tough big boy.

As the Apostle Paul closed his letter to the believers at Corinth, he instructed them, "Watch ye, stand fast in the faith, quit you like men, be strong" (I Corinthians 16:13). When Paul told them to "watch," he meant to be awake and vigilant. Like a sentinel entrusted to watch for enemy movement and alert the camp, these believers needed to watch for Satan's attack in doctrine and enticement into sin. Therefore, they were to "stand fast in the faith," like a pylon holding up a bridge. Even when the high waters of trials raged about them, they needed to remain unmovable in the sound doctrines they had learned at Paul's feet. They could, if they were moored deeply in God's Word. Telling them to "quit you like men" means to demonstrate manliness, to be bold, or brave. It's very much like us saying, "Be a big boy," or "Act like a man." Spiritual immaturity abounded at Corinth in many ways: divisions in loyalty to men (I Corinthians 1:12), carnality, envy, and strife (3:1-3), and foolishly accepting false teachers (II Corinthians 11:13). Paul feared they might be swept up into these factions, or grow so discouraged, that they might simply walk away from this local church. Instead, they must not faint. They needed to "quit you like men," or "man up," with strength and leadership. When Carl Sandburg addressed the United States Congress, he "...said that Abraham Lincoln was a man of 'velvet steel.' "[1] Likewise, believers need to exhibit a combination of strength and tenderness. Paul concluded by saying, "Be strong," which simply meant to demonstrate strength when it was needed.

Men, your family and your church need you to lead with "velvet steel." Be an example of strength, spiritual maturity, godliness, and tenderness. "Quit you like men."

ADDICTION
I Corinthians 16:15

We had someone close to us struggle with alcoholism. Once inebriated, he became obnoxious, violent and extremely abusive. It cost him relationships and his marriage when he inflicted physical injuries upon others around him. Eventually, with great hardship, he was able to remain sober for seven years. Then, a so-called friend convinced him that he had been sober long enough that he could drink again, and everything would be okay. What happened was predictable. He relapsed into binge drinking, abusiveness, and constant intoxication.

What are you addicted to: coffee, prescription drugs, nasal spray, work, television, sports, or electronic gadgets? Whether we realize it or not, most of us are addicted to something. We need to be careful about what we allow ourselves to be constantly drawn to. The Apostle Paul wrote in I Corinthians 6:12, "All things are lawful unto me, but all things are not expedient: all things are lawful for me, but I will not be brought under the power of any."

Most addictions are bad, but there is one that is very good. Paul brings this to our attention by using the addiction of one entire family as an example. In I Corinthians 16:15 he said, "I beseech you, brethren, (ye know the house of Stephanas…that they have addicted themselves to the ministry of the saints)." These believers made a conscious decision to consistently fill their lives with activity that would spiritually minister to others. We assume this meant giving encouraging words, prayer support, being there in time of need, sharing the Word of God, challenging others when their spiritual legs grew weak, and more. They followed the example of Paul, expressed in his words, "For though I be free from all men, yet have I made myself servant unto all…" (I Corinthians 9:19). Oh that all of us would become so addicted to ministry to others that we are perpetually drawn to it, can't stop it, allow it to define us, make us a different, better person, and satisfy us like nothing else. When describing this family of servants, Paul said, "…they have refreshed my spirit and yours: therefore acknowledge ye them that are such" (I Corinthians 16:18).

Do you know someone who is dedicated to the ministry of other saints? If so, acknowledge them today with cooperation, an expression of appreciation, and a greater degree of respect. Then, seek to follow their example. Get addicted to ministry for Christ.

HALITOSIS OR PEPPERMINT?
I Corinthians 16:18

An amusing commercial on television pictures a husband and wife waking up next to one another in bed in the morning. They both instantly recognize their halitosis, or bad breath, cover their mouths, and turn to get up while saying, "Good morning." We all know that after sleeping through the night, our breath has become extremely stale. That's why one of the first things we do each day is thoroughly brush our teeth. Likewise, many of us use peppermint to refresh our breath throughout the day.

When the Apostle Paul mentioned Stephanas, Fortunatus, and Achaicus, he revealed something very important about their character. He stated, "For they have refreshed my spirit and yours: therefore acknowledge ye them that are such" (I Corinthians 16:18). The Apostle Paul had been blessed to have a number of Christian friends who were a spiritual encouragement. It wasn't by accident that he companied with those who refreshed his daily walk with Christ and renewed his desire to serve the Lord Jesus Christ. Paul, like David before him (Psalm 119:63), surrounded himself with and intentionally spent time in the company of believers. The men mentioned above cared enough about Paul to travel great distances to bring him needed funds and supplies, including a supply of refreshing fellowship. Paul had previously partnered in ministry with Barnabas, traveling extensively to proclaim the Gospel of Grace. Acts 4:36 revealed the given name of Barnabas was Jose, but because his personality was one of constant encouragement, the apostles gave him the surname Barnabas "...which is, being interpreted, the son of consolation...." While others avoided or shunned Paul, Barnabas befriended, strengthened, encouraged, and partnered with him in ministry. Aquila, Priscilla, Titus, and Timothy are other examples of believers who refreshed Paul's spirit and encouraged him in his walk with the Savior. Paul's instruction to the believers at Corinth was to warmly recognize encouraging, godly people. In other words, "...acknowledge ye them that are such" (I Corinthians 16:18).

Don't allow yourself to become a complainer and discourager. Instead, choose to be like a peppermint that refreshes those around you with spiritual encouragement. Purposely remain positive in attitude, edifying in speech, encouraging in outlook, and praising those who act likewise. *Who do you know that should be acknowledged today for being one who refreshes your spirit and walk with the Lord?* Now, it's time for you to refresh the spirit of someone else.

PROPER FOCUS

Acts 1:1-7

One summer afternoon while pastoring in the Black Hills of South Dakota, I returned to the church to find a crew just finishing resurfacing the entire church blacktop. I knew we had not authorized such a project, so I asked the foreman why they were there. He had just found out from his boss that he had taken the crew to the wrong location. They were supposed to resurface another location in our subdivision. Unfortunately for them, they were focused on the wrong area.

For forty days after the resurrection of the Lord Jesus Christ, He appeared to His faithful followers, "speaking [to them] of the things pertaining to the kingdom of God" (Acts 1:3). "The kingdom of God" is a somewhat generic term relating to God's rule over all the ages, from creation to eternity future. In effect, our Lord gave them a Bible survey course to help them see how all things fit together in God's overall plan. Included in this sequence, the promised future "kingdom of heaven," or the Millennial Kingdom, was "at hand." Almost certainly, He explained about the seven years of tribulation, needed comfort to face future persecutions, and instructions to stay busy reaching lost souls. In this context, the disciples asked their Messiah, "...Lord, wilt Thou at this time restore the kingdom to Israel?" (Acts 1:6). Their question went beyond curiosity. As indicated in Matthew 19:27, they focused like a laser beam on what they would receive when the Millennial Kingdom was established. Their inquiry was wrong for two reasons. Twice before, the Lord Jesus told them that only the Father knew the exact time the Millennial Kingdom would be established (Matthew 24:36, 42). Therefore, He said, "It is not for you to know the times..." (Acts 1:7). More importantly, they had lost their focus on ministry. This answer implied that they were to continually center their focus on being faithful in His service until His return as King of kings, whenever that would be.

Sometimes we believers in the Dispensation of Grace make a similar mistake of having the wrong focus. We think primarily about family, leisure time, sports, even the study of prophecy, or expectation of heaven. We must never forget our constant focus is to be on reaching souls with the Gospel of the Grace of God, and remain faithful in His service until He calls us into the heavens. We have work to do for Christ! Stay focused on spiritual ministry above other distractions.

IN ONE ACCORD

Acts 1:14

Just recently, for much of the day, I cared for two of our grandchildren, who are siblings. Frequently, they were at each other's throats literally hitting, biting, and screaming. Then, three minutes later, they would be playing happily together with overflowing laughter and joy, or sitting side by side in a chair talking to one another in sweet voices. It occurred to me that God's children, in every age, act in much the same way.

Immediately after the final ascension of the Lord Jesus Christ into heaven, the 120 faithful followers of the Savior returned to Jerusalem. It is noteworthy that even before being endued with power from the Holy Spirit, they are described as continuing "...with one accord in prayer and supplication..." (Acts 1:14). For emphasis, and so we don't miss it, this condition of unity, which continued, is repeated for us several times. While waiting for promised miraculous power to witness to lost Israel, "...they were all with one accord in one place" (Acts 2:1). After following the unique, kingdom requirement to sell all their possessions, they continued "...daily with one accord..." (Acts 2:46). When commanded by the Jewish religious leaders to not speak to others about Christ, "they lifted up their voice to God with one accord" in prayer, asking for boldness to continue witnessing (Acts 4:23-29). As they continued in ministry, they were "...with one accord in Solomon's porch" (Acts 5:12). Simply put, those who follow Christ are to live, worship, minister, and interact with one another in blessed, harmonious unity. Paul tells the saints at Corinth, "...I beseech [beg] you, brethren, by the name of our Lord Jesus Christ, that ye all speak the same thing...that ye be perfectly joined together in the same mind and in the same judgment" (I Corinthians 1:10). Through the Word of God and indwelling Holy Spirit, the Lord is still begging believers to interact with one another in harmony. This is why we are instructed to be "endeavoring to keep the unity of the Spirit in the bond of peace" (Ephesians 4:3), and to "...be of one mind, [and] live in peace..." (II Corinthians 13:11).

Which kind of child of God are you? Are you like the ones screaming and fighting, or are you one happily speaking sweet words, making it easy to get along? You are either part of the problem or part of the solution. Decide right now that your words and conduct today are going to promote unity, not destroy it.

GOD'S WORD FULFILLED
Acts 1:15-26

In the 1660's, Robert Boyle predicted "the cure of diseases from a distance or at least by transplantation."[1] In 1865, Jules Verne predicted the moon landing in his book *From The Earth To The Moon*. He even predicted a rocket being launched from Florida, weightlessness in space, and the number of astronauts aboard.[1] While these predictions are amazing, the greatest predictions in the world are recorded in the Bible. In the Old Testament, there are hundreds of predictions that literally came true.

In Acts Chapter 1, we have an example of a divine prediction that was fulfilled, just as God promised. "Peter stood up in the midst of the disciples, and said, "...men and brethren, **this Scripture needs have been fulfilled**, which the Holy Ghost by the mouth of David spake before concerning Judas...For he was numbered with us ... Now this man purchased a field with the reward of iniquity; and falling headlong, he burst asunder..." (Acts 1:18). Peter was referring to Psalm 41:9, which says, "Yea, mine own familiar friend, in whom I trusted, which did eat of my bread, hath lifted up his heel against me." The Savior referred to this passage in John 13:18, where He specified that He chose one to be close to Him, who would betray Him, "that the Scripture may be fulfilled." We should NOT conclude that the Lord Jesus compelled Judas to betray Him. God never commandeers the free will of any man, woman, or child. Instead, God would have us understand that, in His omnipotent and omniscient power, He knows all things even before they happen. Therefore, He can predict in Scripture everything in detail, and His words will always come to pass. Isaiah 46:9-10 states it this way: "...for I am God, and there is none else; I am God, and there is none like me, Declaring the end from the beginning, and from ancient times the things that are not yet done, saying, My counsel shall stand...."

These words were intended to be a comfort to the disheartened Jewish believers of Christ who anticipated an immediate, victorious establishment of the Millennial Kingdom. They could rest in the truth that God was in control and would yet fulfill every promise the Savior made to them. We today can also rest confidently in every promise He gives to us, the Body of Christ.

FOR A PURPOSE

Acts 2:38

Kerri Walsh Jennings is an American professional beach volleyball player. She and teammate Misty May Treanor won gold medals at the 2004, 2008, and 2012 Summer Olympics. Through 2016, amazingly, Kerri lost only one match in Olympic competition. In an interview with NBC Sports, she said, "I was born to play beach volleyball and have babies." In other words, she believed these things to be the divine purposes for her life.

God always had a very specific purpose for His instructions to mankind. When Peter explained to the Jews that Christ was their Messiah and that they were responsible for His death, conviction fell on thousands of Jews on the Day of Pentecost, and they wanted to know what they should do. "Then Peter said unto them, "Repent, and be baptized every one of you in the name of Jesus Christ for the remission of sins, and ye shall receive the gift of the Holy Ghost" (Acts 2:38). This is surely not our gospel for today, or the correct instruction for how anyone is to be saved during the Dispensation of Grace. We are saved completely apart from any personal effort or merit, and through faith in God's grace alone. But Peter's instruction was correct for these Jews who were still under the Law of Moses. They could only be saved through faith in the Gospel of the Kingdom. Peter told them in Acts 2:38 that they must be baptized "for the remission [or forgiveness] of sins." This meant, unless their faith in Christ included this ceremonial cleansing, no Jew in that day could be saved eternally. When Ananias went as instructed to Saul, he gave him these same instructions: "And now…arise, and be baptized, and wash away thy sins, calling on the name of the Lord" (Acts 22:16). This message to Israel, requiring faith plus baptism for salvation, was consistent throughout the Gospel accounts. Mark 1:4 records, "John did baptize in the wilderness, and preach the baptism of repentance for the remission of sins." Water baptism was required for Israel, but it was not merely "…an outward sign of an inward change." It was for the purpose of salvation and preparing saved Jews to become a nation of priests, ready to minister to the world (Exodus 19:6).

Remember, God's primary purpose for you is to be transformed by applying biblical truths to your daily life every day. Put a Pauline truth into practice each day, and then share what you are learning with other believers!

A LIVING EXAMPLE
Acts 3:1-11

The Apostle Paul is more than a "pattern" of God's longsuffering "to them which should hereafter believe on Him to life everlasting" (I Timothy 1:16). He is more than a pattern for believers today in the unique grace doctrines we are urged to "follow" (I Corinthians 4:16; 11:1). Paul is also an example of how religious, but spiritually dead, Israel was in the past. Like Paul, however, Israel could have become vibrantly alive by trusting in the Lord Jesus Christ for eternal life.

As a nation, Israel became unnecessarily stricken with illnesses. As the Jews prepared to enter their promised land, God promised them that, "...if thou wilt diligently hearken to the voice of the LORD thy God...and wilt give ear to His commandments...I will put none of these diseases upon thee, which I have brought upon the Egyptians..." (Exodus 15:26). Had Israel been faithful to the Lord, they would have enjoyed divinely given good health. However, Israel was so repeatedly sick with the sins of false worship and spiritual adultery that many were afflicted with all kinds of illnesses. The man whom Peter and John found in the temple begging for alms is an example of Israel's spiritual condition in this day. He was "lame from his mother's womb" (vs. 2). The beggar in the temple also represented how spiritually sick and bankrupt the nation of Israel had become. As a whole, she was void of a living relationship with Jehovah. They were still very religious and active in rituals, but they were aptly described by Isaiah 29:13, when the Lord told them, "...this people draw near me with their mouth, and with their lips do honor me, but have removed their heart far from me...." However, the Lord was willing to heal them physically and spiritually if they would only fully trust in their promised Messiah, the Lord Jesus Christ. The beggar is also an example of how overjoyed Israel could become through saving faith in their Redeemer. Once healed, this beggar was literally "leaping and praising God" in overflowing joy (Acts 3:8). They could have known exuberant spiritual joy by knowing Christ.

While the beggar represents Israel's past spiritual condition in the early Acts era, he may also illustrate some believers today. If our walk is far from the Lord, we too become spiritually crippled, poor, and lacking in joy. *How is your spiritual health?* We urge you today to genuinely draw close to the Savior with dedicated worship and thankful rejoicing.

WHAT'S IN A NAME?
Acts 3:15

Ph.D student, Ahtanasios Kokkinaakis, analyzed data from a video game, the League of Legends, played by around seventy million people worldwide. He concluded, "This data is like a window on the individual players' personalities...[When a player used] anti-social expressions in their user name, they tended to adopt similar anti-social behavior in the game environment. Conversely, he found that positive in-game behavior, such as team building, or leadership, might [often] correlate both with positive usernames and positive personality traits in the real world."[1]

In early Acts, as it was in the Gospels, God used a miracle to draw unsaved Jews to Christ. When Peter was the instrument to heal a lame man, he said, "Ye men of Israel...ye denied **the Holy One** and **the Just**...And killed **the Prince of Life**" (Acts 3:12-15). The names used for God the Son are always important because they explain who Christ is and what He did for mankind. Peter described the Lord Jesus as holy and just, and therein qualified to be "an offering" for the sins of the world. He is "the Prince of Life" because a prince is a leader, or royal heir, who is worthy of subjection. The Apostle John explains, "In Him is life" (John 1:4), "And this is the record, that God hath given unto us eternal life, and this life is in [or through faith in] His Son" (I John 5:11). Elsewhere, the Lord Jesus Christ is called, "**the captain** [or the commander] **of their salvation**" (Hebrews 2:10). This is because "...there is none other name under heaven...whereby we must be saved" (Acts 4:12). Jews were also urged to continue "looking unto Jesus **the author and finisher of our faith**; who...endured the cross...and is set down at the right hand of the throne of God" (Hebrews 12:2).

From all these titles for the Lord Jesus Christ, we learn that He, and He alone, can provide eternal life to those who will come to Him in faith. Trust in Christ alone for eternal life right now. If you have trusted in Him as your only hope for the forgiveness of your sin, apart from any human merit, please do two things. Rejoice with immense gratitude in the Holy and Just One, the Prince of Life, the Captain of your salvation, the Author and Finisher of your faith. Then, share the gospel with someone before the end of the day.

BOLDNESS IN WITNESSING
Acts 4:11-19

John Knox was a 16th century preacher, famous for his evangelism and frequently used slogan, "Give me Scotland or I die." Once, however, he was arrested for "preaching the Bible outside the church," and was forced to serve many months as a slave rowing on a galley ship. With his spiritual maturity and prayer deepened by his time of slavery, he returned to boldly preach Christ, regardless of the consequences. His fearless testimony was so powerful that the corrupt Queen Mary of Scotland said, "I fear the prayers of John Knox more than all the assembled armies of Europe."[1] We need this kind of boldness and resolve in witnessing even today.

Peter and John were arrested when they proclaimed "to all the people of Israel...by the name of Jesus Christ of Nazareth" saying, "Neither is there salvation in any other: for there is none other name under heaven...whereby we must be saved" (Acts 4:10,12). When the corrupt spiritual leaders of Israel saw "the **boldness** of Peter and John, and perceived they were unlearned and ignorant men, they marvelled; and they took knowledge...they had been with Jesus" (Acts 4:13). Then Peter and John were commanded "...not to speak at all or teach in the name of Jesus" (Acts 4:18). But regardless of the consequences, they refused to stop sharing the gospel. Once released from prison, they went to fellow believers and they collectively prayed asking God to "grant unto thy servants, that with all boldness they may speak thy word" (vs. 29). Thereafter, "they spake the word with all boldness" (vs. 31). Boldness is a key element in successfully sharing the gospel with lost souls. Paul told the believers at Thessalonica, "we were bold in our God to speak unto you the gospel of God with much contention" (I Thessalonians 2:2). *But where did this boldness of these men of faith come from?* For both Peter and Paul, it came directly from prayer specifically asking for boldness. The Jewish saints asked God for boldness (Act 4:29), and Paul asked the saints at Ephesus to pray for him "that utterance may be given unto me, that I may open my mouth boldly to make known the mystery of the gospel" (Ephesians 6:19).

These examples remind us that we must not shrink from sharing the gospel, regardless of any negative consequence. When witnessing, we also need to be much in prayer for boldness on our part, and conviction in those who are lost.

CROSSING THE LINE
Acts 5:1-11

Beginning in February 2011, former Bengals cheerleader and English teacher at Dixie Heights High School, Sarah Jones (27), had an intimate affair with 17-year-old Cody York. Both parties denied the relationship for several years and lied to police, school officials, the media, and their families. After months of deception, Sarah Jones admitted to the affair, saying, "It is wrong for a teacher to have any type of relationship that crosses the line with a student, there is no gray area… What I did was wrong. And I feel guilty…that other people were hurt in this…[including] our families having to go through this."[1]

It is true that a wife should submit herself to the will of her husband, who is the head of the household. However, there are instances when a wife should not obey her husband, and we have a biblical principle that makes this clear. In Acts Chapter 5, Ananias and Sapphira sold a possession agreeing to keep a portion of it, while they told the Jewish apostles that they gave the entire amount. With a supernatural gift of knowledge, Peter rebuked the husband for lying to the Holy Ghost, and Ananias fell dead. Three hours later, Peter similarly rebuked Sapphira for agreeing with her husband to lie about this matter. Regardless of her husband's decision to lie, Sapphira should have told the truth. Instead, she lied, also crossing the line of right into wrong. We see the same principle when Abimelech took Sarah as his wife, and Abraham lied saying she was only his sister. After God intervened to stop the process, Abimelech rebuked Sarah for not speaking up to clarify their true relationship. He told her, "he is to thee a covering of the eyes… and…thus she was reproved" (Genesis 20:16). The principle that guides a wife to follow God rather than the wishes of her husband is found in Acts 4:19. Peter declared, "…Whether it be right in the sight of God to hearken unto you more than unto God, judge ye." The obvious correct answer is that every believer must always obey God, even when it is different from what any man, or husband, demands.

Ladies, if you have a boyfriend, father, or husband who pushes you to engage in any kind of sin, you must obey God rather than man. Don't cross the line from right into wrong. One's obligation to God always trumps everything and everyone else.

WHAT DOES IT TAKE?
Acts 5:1-42

Someone once said, "The test of your character is what it takes to stop you." On July 13, 1913, Adoniram and Nancy Judson were the first America missionaries to Burma. Officials told them they were not wanted in Burma so the best thing they could do was go somewhere else. But they didn't. Nancy lost her first child while sailing to their mission field. A year later she gave birth to another child who died within one year. Then, war broke out between Britain and Burma. Because Judson spoke English, he was placed in a filthy, disease-ridden death prison. While Adoniram was imprisoned, Nancy gave birth to another child; but within a year, both she and the baby had died. After seven years in Burma, Judson did not have a single convert to Christ. Nonetheless, he refused to quit. As a result, years later, Judson was called "Jesus Christ's man in Burma" because many came to trust in the Savior through his unwavering ministry.[1]

We learned in Acts 4 and 6 that the religious leaders of Israel had imprisoned Peter and John for preaching eternal life through faith in Jesus of Nazareth. At this point, these religious leaders "...took counsel to slay them" (Acts 5:33). Gamaliel, a doctor of the law, who was "held in reputation among all the people", calmed their frenzied discussion. Then, the religious leaders called the apostles back to their assembly, unlawfully beat them, and "...commanded that they should not speak in the name of Jesus, and let them go" (Acts 5:40). *Was the response of the apostle's depression or silence?* No! They left the counsel "...rejoicing that they were counted worthy to suffer shame for His name" (Acts 5:41). Then, they stood "...daily in the temple, and in every house, they ceased not to teach and preach Jesus Christ" (Acts 5:42). They would not allow even persecution to stop them from proclaiming Christ.

God placed this record in His Word to be an encouragement to believers in every age. We must not be intimidated into silence by men. Instead, we must boldly share the gospel. When any kind of opposition arises, we must learn to rejoice that we are counted worthy to suffer for Christ. We must see any hardship we face in the cause of Christ as a test of our character and faith. Refuse to stop ministering, and rely on the power of God to enable you.

178

PARTNERS IN MINISTRY
Acts 6:1-7

It has been my rich blessing to have my wife, Terri, as my helpmate in marriage and in ministry. While her role has been the less visible one of the two of us, her contributions have been immense. She is my counselor, encourager, and enabler in ministry. She continues to faithfully attend church services, teach children or women's classes, graciously hosts frequent ministry in our home, edits my writings, shares biblical truths, cleans the church buildings, and much more. In short, she has made much of our ministry possible and more effective.

When the leaders of the Jewish kingdom church were aware that it was necessary to attend to the material needs of the widows in their assembly, they looked to solid, spiritually-minded saints to fulfill these needs (Acts 6:1-3). Their ministry would be less visible than that of the apostles, but it was just as important. In fact, their fulfilling this ministry enabled the apostles to devote themselves more fully to proclaiming the Word of God. Moreover, the result of this partnership in ministry enabled "...the Word of God [to have] increased; and the number of the disciples multiplied in Jerusalem greatly..." (Acts 6:5). Likewise, having co-laborers in ministry enabled the Apostle Paul's ministry to be more productive. This principle of helpers in ministry is so important that God's Word is full of examples. Barnabas, Luke, Silas, Timothy, Epaphras, and Titus all traveled with Paul, ministering to his needs while also ministering to others. Paul recognized Phoebe as a servant, or deaconess, who had been a "succourer of many" at the church in Cenchrea. Paul also mentioned Priscilla and Aquila, calling them "my helpers in Christ Jesus:" (Romans 16:3). Notice the woman's role in ministry was just as important as that of her husband. In fact, this husband and wife are only mentioned in Scripture as a team; and in some instances, the wife's name is given first.

No matter how gifted, no one can effectively minister to every need. God's work needs men and women to teach classes, serve in the nursery, cook meals, transport others to services, clean the church building, record or mail out sermons, greet and follow up with visitors, encourage the sick, usher, deposit offerings, give counsel, lead in music, provide secretarial duties, prepare food, work with the teens, and much more. Every saved individual is greatly needed in ministry. Become a partner in ministry today; and in so doing, help your church to grow.

SATANIC OPPOSITION
Acts 6:7-13; 7:1

The people whom Satan opposes most are those who are doing the most for the cause of Christ. This was true for the Apostle Paul, who said, "...a great door...is opened unto me, and there are many adversaries" (I Corinthians 16:9). It was also true of Stephen in Acts 6:7-13. The Word of God was increasing in the lives of the Jewish saints. Miracles were being performed, and "multitudes" were professing Christ as the Son of God. To thwart this progress, Satan stirred up wicked men who "suborned [bribed] men" to raise false accusations, "stirred up the people", "and set up false witnesses" saying that Stephen had blasphemed the temple. When a ministry gains momentum in furthering the cause of Christ, you can count on Satan attacking those involved.

Paul warned the saints at Corinth about Satanic attacks, so the Devil would not gain an advantage. And he told them, "we are not ignorant of his devices." Satan has many tactics. Paul would have gone to minister at Thessalonica, but Satan hindered him (I Thessalonians 2:18). He surely hinders us today when we minister to others. Luke 8:12 tells us that Satan seeks to snatch away the seed of the gospel when it is sown in the heart of an unsaved soul. II Corinthians 4:4 confirmed that Satan "...blinded the minds of them which believe not, lest the light of the glorious gospel...should shine unto them." Acts 10:38 says many were "oppressed of the devil" with physical illnesses. This was also true of righteous Job, and it is likely true today. To fall into "the snare of the devil" (I Timothy 3:7) is to have a poor testimony before the lost; and to fall into "the condemnation of the devil" (I Timothy 3:6) is elevating a man to the position of an elder too soon, which often results in the sin of pride. Paul also warns against "seducing spirits and doctrines of devils" (I Timothy 1:4) which pull believers into such error that it is hard for them to admit their mistakes and return to sound doctrine.

Whether we realize it or not, Christians are in a constant spiritual warfare with Satan who brings the battle to us. It is unavoidable. In the power of God, we can "stand against the wiles of the devil," but we can only do so by being constantly in the Word of God, praying continually, and being equipped with the full armor of God. Satan will attack you today. Get ready.

INSUBORDINATION

Acts 7:51-54

On April 5th, 1951, a letter from General Douglas MacArthur was read aloud on the floor of the U.S. House of Representatives. This letter was strongly critical of President Truman's foreign policies, in particular, the policy that primarily focused American military resources to win the war in Europe first. MacArthur simply would not accept such a decision. He believed American armed forces should destroy communism by first taking all of Korea, and then issuing an ultimatum to China, which Truman feared would lead to World War III. While MacArthur was very popular in the states, Truman had MacArthur removed from his position as Commander of Pacific Forces for insubordination.[1]

The Pharisees and Sadducees were not military leaders, but they did have some Roman soldiers at their disposal. While assisting the spiritual leaders of Israel, the first obligation of these soldiers was to respectfully submit to the will of their Roman superiors. Similarly, it was the obligation of the religious leaders of Israel to obey all that God commanded in His Word. Yet, after the Savior's resurrection, in Acts 7:51-54, they continued to act with insubordination toward their revered Mosaic Law, Jehovah, and the Lord Jesus Christ. When Stephen presented a historical picture of the stubborn waywardness of Israel dating back to their early patriarchs, he told them, "Ye stiffnecked and uncircumcised in heart and ears, ye do always resist the Holy Ghost: as your fathers did, so do ye. Which of the prophets have not your fathers persecuted? And they have slain them which shewed before the coming of the Just One...." (vss. 51-52)? Hearing this indisputable account of Israel's sinful past, these leaders of Israel should have responded to the truth with immediate obedience, turning to the Lord Jesus in faith. Instead, they hardened their heart further. Even though "...they were cut to the heart...they gnashed on him [Stephen] with their teeth"(vs. 54). As their predecessors, they "hearkened not, nor inclined their ear" (Jeremiah 7:24). This people "make [made] their ears heavy, and shut their eyes...." (Isaiah 6:10), "Yea, they made their hearts as an adamant stone, lest they should hear...." (Zechariah 7:12).

Passages such as these should cause every soul to consider how responsive they are to the Lord and to His Word. *When the Holy Spirit convicts your heart, do you submit in immediate obedience, or do you harden your heart and walk away no different than you were before?* Allow God to transform you by putting something from God's Word into practice throughout each day.

A DIVINE APPOINTMENT
Acts 8:26-40

We have a dear elderly Christian friend who needs help with transportation. So, with some frequency, we have taken her to church, the airport, grocery shopping, and to doctor appointments. It is part of her personality that she wants to be more than punctual. She wants to arrive 30 minutes early for any appointment.

We have many appointments in life beyond social or medical appointments. There is "A time to be born, and a time to die; a time to plant, and a time to pluck up that which is planted" (Ecclesiastes 3:2). *But have you ever considered that God also gives us divine appointments to share with lost souls the Gospel of the Grace of God?* In our text, the angel of the Lord tells Philip to leave a fruitful ministry in Samaria and go south into the desert. As he obeys, Philip "coincidentally" meets an Ethiopian eunuch who is reading from the Book of Isaiah. Clearly, this was a spiritually-minded man. It also appears that he was spiritually prepared to hear a gospel message of salvation just as it was with Lydia, "...whose heart the Lord had opened..." (Acts 16:14). We are *not* suggesting God chooses only some to salvation and irresistibly draws them. We believe that God would "...have all men to be saved..." (I Timothy 2:4) and that He "...lighteth [with the conviction of the Holy Spirit] every man that cometh into the world" (John 1:9). Each soul has a free will to accept or reject salvation. We are suggesting is that it is likely that God still puts lost souls, with spiritually prepared hearts, directly in the path of saved people. Only believers can share with them the message of eternal life through faith in the Lord Jesus, and we must not remain silent when such opportunities arise.

Just think of the eternal consequences if Philip had concluded that he could not leave a thriving ministry, or he decided that he was too tired when God directed him to go into the desert. This Ethiopian may have been eternally lost, and Philip would have missed the eternal reward for sharing the gospel. When people cross our path, there is no way for us to know who is saved or lost, or how much their heart is prepared to trust in Christ alone. What we do know is that God has given ALL of us the ministry of reconciliation. Therefore, we must be looking constantly for opportunities to share the Gospel of Grace.

THE FEAR OF ME
Acts 9:10-20

In 2016, a global panic emerged over the Zika virus trans-mitted by mosquitoes. It was widely reported that pregnant women who were infected have babies with severe birth defects. Data supports a link between the virus and Guillain-Barre Syndrome, which results in varying degrees of temporary paralysis. Throughout Latin America, whenever there is an outbreak of Zika, a corresponding spike in temporary paralysis also occurs.[1]

Throughout history, true believers have experienced seasons of temporary paralysis due to the fear of men. One example is that of Ananias, whom the Lord told to go see newly converted Saul of Tarsus. Ananias' response was hesitation because he knew "…how much evil he [Saul] hath done to thy [God's] saints at Jerusalem: And here he hath authority...to bind all that call on Thy [God's] name" (Acts 9:13-14). Before Ananias would move, the Lord had to instruct him again to go, and assure him that Saul would be greatly used of the Lord to minister to Gentiles, kings, and Israel. While the fear of Ananias for his physical safety was legitimate, believers throughout history have been paralyzed into silence, fearing only the verbal, social, or emotional disfavor of men and women. Solomon wrote, "The fear of man bringeth a snare…" (Proverbs 29:25). Even great saints of the past, who were greatly used of the Lord, feared the negative response of those to whom they were sent to deliver a message from the Lord. Ezekiel was told, "thou are not sent to a people of a strange speech and of an hard language, but to the house of Israel...But the house of Israel will not hearken unto thee: for they will not hearken unto Me...Behold, I have made thy face strong... **fear them not, neither be dismayed at their looks**, though they be a rebellious house...go, get thee...unto the children of thy people, and speak unto them…Thus saith the Lord" (Ezekiel 3:3-11).

As Ezekiel of old, we believers today are often paralyzed into silence, fearing unfavorable reactions from hardened souls. We fear what they might think of us, how negatively they might respond, and we rationalize that our efforts will be unproductive. This is not the response the Lord desires from us. Cast away this temporary paralysis and fear of man. Prayerfully and intentionally take God's message of salvation to someone who needs to hear it today.

PROVE IT
Acts 9:20-22

In atheist forums, unbelievers often use what is called "Russell's Teapot."[1] They allow Christians to state claims for their faith, then basically say, "I don't believe you. Prove it." The burden of proof always lies squarely on the shoulders of the one who is making a specific claim that something is true. One can theorize, but once crossing the line from theory to stating things as a fact, one is then duty bound to prove what he says is true.

One of the exciting aspects about the record of the conversion of Saul of Tarsus is the immediate, revolutionary change in him. He went from Saul, the persecutor of Christians, to Paul, the proclaimer of salvation, solely through faith in the Lord Jesus Christ. In this, he stands as an example of the kind of immediate transformation that should exist in all who call on the name of the Lord. We too should become and remain bold witnesses, declaring eternal life exclusively through faith in our Savior. Notice how Paul witnessed. He "...increased...and confounded the Jews...proving that this is [the] very Christ" (Acts 9:22). For a Jew in this day to trust in Christ for eternal life, they had to be convinced that our Savior was the promised Messiah and Redeemer of Israel. While our text does not take the time to specify how Paul proved this to his fellow Jews, he undoubtedly showed them how the Lord Jesus Christ fulfilled many Old Testament Scriptures. The Lord Jesus was a child of Abraham, from the tribe of Judah (Genesis 22:18; 49:10). He was born in Bethlehem (Micah 5:2) at the predicted time for the Messiah (Daniel 9:25) and then fled to Egypt as predicted in Hosea 11:1. Babies were massacred in the wake of His birth (Jeremiah 31:15). A forerunner prepared His coming (Isaiah 40:3), yet Israel rejected their Messiah (Psalm 69:8). He spoke in parables (Psalm 78:2-4) and He was called a King (Zechariah 9:9). He bore the iniquities of Israel in His death (Isaiah 53:4-12) and was slain, as predicted one thousand years before the cruel practice of crucifixion began (Psalm 22:16-18).

When we witness to others about the Lord Jesus Christ being the Savior of the world, the burden is on us to prove this is so. Be prepared. Arm yourself with the Sword of the Spirit by marking your Bible with a quick reference to these fulfilled prophecies so that you too can "prove it."

COMPLETE EQUALITY
Acts 10:25-48

I once managed an apartment complex and hired a dear Puerto Rican friend, Maria, to keep my books. These apartments housed people of all races. I also hired a resident, named Kay, to collect rents. Maria would go monthly to retrieve her records before doing the books for me. On one of those occasions, Kay explained to Maria some grievance she had against a Mexican resident. Then, with a condescending attitude, she told Maria, "You know, there aren't very many smart Hispanics."

It is a sad reality that mankind has always demonstrated disdain for those who are not of their ethnic group or social status. There was a feudal system in Europe, segregation in America, and as we see in our text, the Jews considered themselves superior to Gentiles. God had chosen the Jews to be His special people. Even the Old Testament law prohibited close interaction with Gentiles, unless they turned in saving faith to Jehovah. This required separation. However, Israel was not intended to carnally feed their egos with an attitude of superiority. Because the Lord has no pleasure in the death of the wicked and is not willing that any should perish, it was always the plan of the Father to redeem anyone who looked to Him in faith. Referring to the Messiah, Isaiah 49:6 promised, "...I will also give thee for a light to the Gentiles, that Thou mayest be My salvation unto the end of the earth." Referring to the Second Coming, Isaiah 42:6-7 promises, "I the Lord have called thee in righteousness...for a light of the Gentiles; To open the blind eyes...and them that sit in darkness out of the prison house." Isaiah 60:3 continues, "And the Gentiles shall come to thy light...." God was explaining to Peter in Acts 10 that the Lord was already opening the door of salvation to all mankind. His testimony was that "...God hath shewed me that I should not call any man common or unclean" (vs. 28), ...But in every nation he that feareth Him...is accepted with Him [God]" (vs. 35).

Every believer needs to learn what Peter learned in Acts 10. It is unacceptable for any believer to look down their noses at others of different ethnicities. None of us are better than anyone else. All mankind are sinners by nature. Christ gave His life to redeem every man. Therefore, no one is to "...think of himself more highly that he ought to think..." (Romans 12:3).

SEEING THE GRACE OF GOD
Acts 11:19-24

Kirk Cameron was a child television star who was a devout atheist. He laughed at those who believed that God exists. Then one day, he accepted an invitation to church, heard the gospel, and cried out to God for forgiveness. Since that time, Kirk's life has taken an entirely new direction. As a Christian, he has chosen to play roles in *The Left Behind* series, *Fireproof*, and now hosts the *Christian Master* television series. He also travels the country to present the gospel in schools, churches, and community events. His is an example of a transformed life.

When persecuted Jewish saints fled to Antioch, they preached the Gospel of God to Gentiles, "...and a great number of them believed, and turned unto the Lord" (Acts 11:21). When the news spread, Barnabas was sent, and "...when he came, and had seen the grace of God, was glad, and exhorted them all, that with purpose of heart they would cleave unto the Lord" (vs. 23). *But how does one see the grace of God?* It is true God's grace is as invisible as the wind. But like the wind, one can witness the evidence of God's grace in many ways. Grace was evident in these new believers because they had "turned unto the Lord" (vs. 21). Antioch was a city where all the Greek, Roman, and Syrian gods were honored. It had a shrine dedicated to Daphne, whose worship included immoral practices.[1] These new believers had abandoned these kinds of false worship. Like those at Thessalonica, they had "...turned to God from idols to serve the living and true God" (I Thessalonians 1:9). Collectively, they met as a "church" (Acts 11:26), indicating a joy in salvation, a bond with others in Christ, a commitment to the study of God's Word, and a genuine desire to live for Christ. "...And the disciples [or converts] were called Christians first in Antioch" (vs. 26). Whether this title was given as a name of scornful reproach, or they gladly identified themselves as followers of Christ does not matter. What matters is that they were living a life so transformed by Christ that others could see the grace of God at work in them.

Is it your purpose to live such a transformed life that others can see the grace of God in you? Make this your goal today.

EXPECTATION IN PRAYER
Acts 12:1-17

It has been our practice at church to list prayer requests in the bulletin and to distribute a separate "Prayer Reminder" sheet. We usually divide these into categories, including one for Answers to Prayer. At the end of the year, we print an entire sheet with the answers to prayer that God has granted. While these lists are an encouragement to pray, it always seems amazing, almost shocking, how many specific answers we have seen to prayers.

When wicked King Herod killed James, then imprisoned Peter with the intent to likewise kill him after the Jewish holy week, "prayer was made without ceasing of the church unto God for him" (Acts 12:5). These believers are to be commended, not only that they prayed, asking God to intervene where they clearly could not, but also for praying fervently for an entire week, even through the night. God miraculously answered their prayers, too, by sending an angel to take Peter out of prison. However, once Peter arrived at the place of the prayer meeting, it became evident these believers had absolutely no confidence their prayers for Peter would make any difference. When Rhoda saw him knocking at the gate, she was overcome with gladness and ran to tell these prayer warriors. But their response was not joy or praise to God. They told her, "Thou art mad." When she persisted, they concluded, "It is his angel," instead of an answer to their prayers (vs. 15). When Peter was finally ushered in after persistent knocking, "they were astonished." These saints were NOT given dynamic promises of answered prayer, which were once promised only to the apostles (John 14:14; 15:7; 16:23). Miracles were lessening because Israel was being set aside in unbelief, but these saints should have possessed more faith that God would answer their prayers. Perhaps they represent the lack of faith in prayer that is often present in saints of all dispensations.

The Apostle Paul clearly believed God routinely answered the prayers of the saints. He frequently asked believers to pray for him (Romans 15:30; Colossians 4:3), and he assured them their prayers were "helping" (II Corinthians 1:11), even to the extent that he, too, would be released from prison "through your prayer" (Philippians 1:19). We must remember, it is also important how we pray. Paul wrote, "I will...that men pray everywhere... without wrath and doubting" (I Timothy 2:8). Pray regularly, and when you do, pray with the expectation that God may choose to grant your request.

YOU CAN EXPECT IT

Acts 13:1-12

Years ago, the author's favorite college football team entered a new season ranked number one in the nation, but there were many who opposed them. You could expect it. Some accused them of recruiting violations, while others criticized their ranking. Because me team had a target on their back, every team gave their best effort to defeat them. You could expect it. By the end of the season, they were still undefeated and were facing the second-ranked team in America. The opponents countered my team's every move. You could expect it. But by remaining focused and playing their best, they emerged victorious.

When we last read of Paul in Acts 9, his life had been transformed by trusting in Christ. Even with many opposing him, he was seeing many victories. Now, in Chapter 13, we see the Holy Spirit instructing the church at Antioch to ordain Paul and Barnabas for a very special "work whereunto I have called them" (vs. 2). As the church sent them out to minister, they were going to meet satanic opposition immediately, and they should have expected it. As they went out preaching "the Word of God" (vs. 5), they met an unsaved man named Sergius Paulus who "desired to hear the word of God" (vs. 7). Then, a Jewish "false prophet" named Barjesus "withstood them, seeking to turn away the deputy from the faith" (vs. 8). Here was a soul ready to be saved, and Satan sent immediate opposition. You could expect it. Paul did not cower from this attack. With the power of an apostle of God, Paul pronounced a miraculous blindness upon Barjesus. "Immediately there fell on him a mist and a darkness; and he went about seeking some to lead him by the hand" (vs. 11). *What was the result of Paul remaining in the spiritual battle of ministry for this lost soul?* "Then the deputy (Sergius Paulus), when he saw what was done, believed, being astonished at the doctrine of the Lord" (vs. 12). Praise God, another soul was eternally saved.

My fellow believer, we too are going to face satanic opposition. You can expect it. It is unavoidable. He is our "adversary" who goes about "as a roaring lion...seeking whom he may devour" (I Peter 5:8). Moreover, the more a believer seeks to be used of the Lord, particularly in winning souls to Christ, the more frequent and intense will be Satan's attacks. But don't stop sharing the gospel. Stay focused and faithful. Share the gospel with someone today!

PREPARED TO PERSUADE

Acts 13:13-44

We have a good friend who was used of the Lord to lead another friend of ours to salvation. This Bible teacher comically describes that process by using fishing as an analogy. He says, "She was a tough one. I kept baiting the hook for her soul with a simple explanation of the gospel. She would take a nibble, and then repeatedly spit it out. But I just kept giving the gospel from different angles. Once the Lord hooked her, she was hooked for good and gloriously saved."

After leading Sergius Paulus to a saving knowledge of the Lord Jesus Christ, "Paul and his company" traveled to Antioch in Pisidia. While attending the synagogue, they were given an opportunity by the leaders to say "any word of exhortation for the people" (Acts 13:15). And Paul was ready. He calmly and carefully reviewed with them the overall history of Israel. He told them that God "chose our fathers" to be His "exalted...people" (vs. 17), brought them out of Egypt and through the wilderness wanderings. He gave them judges to lead the nation and Saul as their first king. Then, from David, according to God's promise, was "raised unto Israel a Saviour, Jesus" (vs. 23). Paul also explained that their revered John the Baptist proclaimed that he was not the promised Messiah of Israel, which further identified the Lord Jesus as their Redeemer King. The explanation continued that, just as the leaders of Israel had historically not heeded the prophets, Paul's audience was responsible for wickedly demanding the unjustified death of the Lord Jesus. The good news was that the promise of a resurrection to everlasting life had been fulfilled when God raised Christ from the dead. If they would but "believe...(on the Savior ye could be) justified from all things, from which they could not be justified by the law of Moses" (vs. 39). Paul warned his hearers not to reject this message of salvation or they would "perish." To those who did respond in faith, Paul and Barnabas "persuaded them to continue in the grace of God" (vs. 43).

In Paul's presentation of the gospel, we see what appears to be a planned, prepared, practiced, polished, and progressive presentation of the gospel that was given so skillfully it was persuasive. We should follow this pattern. Even if we use references written in our Bible to assist us, we need to be prepared to give a planned, practiced, and persuasive presentation of the gospel that will lead others to saving faith. *Have you prepared?*

PENTHOUSE TO THE OUTHOUSE
Acts 14:1-22

Though I can't remember the details, a story of a professional football player has stuck in my mind. He'd just led an amazing comeback to win a game over one of his team's rivals. With the usual euphoria after a victory, the press enthusiastically interviewed the quarterback, hailing him as the hero of the game. With calmness, the quarterback said, "Boys, I've been around a long time. I've learned it isn't far from the penthouse to the outhouse." What he, and many others using a similar quote, were saying was that he's popular now, but it doesn't take long to fall from the graces of public opinion.

When Paul and Barnabas arrived in Iconium, they spoke in the synagogue and "a great multitude both of the Jews and also of the Greeks believed" (Acts 14:1). But Satan incited unbelieving Jews, making "their minds evil affected against the brethren" (vs. 2). Subsequently, the Gentiles, and "also of the Jews with their rulers" (vs. 5), sought to stone Paul. Wisely, Paul and Barnabas "fled unto Lystra and Derbe" (vs. 6). While there, Paul healed a man who had been crippled from birth. When the people saw what Paul had done, they concluded Paul was the false god Mercurius, and Barnabas was Jupiter. This frenzied mob would have sacrificed animals unto them and given them worship, but Paul strenuously convinced them to turn from such vain worship "unto the living God" (vs. 15). Subsequently, unbelieving Jews came "from Antioch and Iconium, who persuaded the people, and, having stoned Paul, drew him out of the city, supposing he had been dead" (vs. 19). Without question, the Apostle Paul knew what it meant to go quickly from the penthouse of popularity to the outhouse of public hatred. But his testimony was, "none of these things move me, neither count I my life dear unto myself, so that I might finish my course with joy, and the ministry…to testify the gospel of the grace of God" (Acts 20:24). We believe Paul did actually die in this stoning (but was raised back to life), and in other subsquent persecutions, because when describing his trials, he said he was "in prisons more frequent, in death oft" (II Corinthians 11:23).

What we want to learn from his example is neither to be enamored by the praises of men nor discouraged by their heated opposition. Like Paul, we must keep on serving the Lord faithfully and give the gospel, no matter the cost and regardless of the winds of acceptance or rejection.

LIBERTY NOT MICROMANAGING
Acts 15:34

In many ways, this author grew up in a home that seemed to be micromanaged by his father. Regardless of what was common in other families, and what seemed reasonable to us, his word was final. That meant boys never wore shorts and girls always wore dresses. We were not allowed to play organized sports, were rarely allowed leisure time with friends, and were never to question his instruction. It also meant, for us boys, that he dictated how early we started the work day, exactly what our labors were for the day, and when we were allowed to stop. But in contrast, once we left home, we had complete liberty. He never tried to tell us what to do again.

Paul explained clearly to the church at Antioch, that apart from works, God "had opened the door of faith unto the Gentiles" (Acts 14:27). However, legalistic Jews sought to impose on these Gentile converts of Paul the requirement of circumcision and keeping the Mosaic Law for salvation. These legalists just did not get the new truth that Gentiles were now being saved apart from Israel and through faith alone, but they should have understood. Paul and Barnabas vehemently disputed their efforts to impose works (Acts 15:2). They explained that Paul's gospel was different than the one given to Jewish believers that promised the Millennial Kingdom (Galatians 2:1-2). After the meeting with the Jewish apostles, Judas and Silas were commissioned to make it clear to Paul's converts that they did not agree with the legalizers-they agreed with Paul. Once their mission was finished, something very noteworthy and biblically consistent is said about Silas. Rather than return to Jerusalem, "it pleased Silas to abide there still" (Acts 15:34). Notice our text does NOT say God led him, or told him, or the Spirit guided him to stay. Instead of God micromanaging what he should do, the Lord granted him the liberty to choose with his own free will what to do and where to go. Similarly, though Paul desired Apollos to go to minister at Corinth "his will was not at all to come at this time" (I Corinthians 16:12). Likewise we read in Paul's ministry that he often determined, by God's liberty, where he would minister.

We offer these examples to the reader with a caution about thinking, or claiming, that God directs, leads, guides, or otherwise micromanages the details in our lives. Rejoice in the freedom of choice you have as a believer and use it responsibly.

SECOND CHANCES
Acts 15:36-41

Not everyone gets a second chance. "Legislation mandating the eviction of tenants whose housing units are the scene of criminal actions" was passed by the United States Congress in 1996 and signed by President Bill Clinton. In his 1996 State of the Union address, President Clinton laid the foundation for the One-Strike policy: "I challenge local housing authorities and tenant associations: Criminal gang members and drug dealers are destroying the lives of decent tenants."[1] The enforcement of this new law was an effort in good faith to protect upstanding citizens from those with a history of failing to live up to acceptable law-abiding standards.

A problem arose when Paul and Barnabas purposed to "go again and visit our brethren in every city where we have preached the word of the Lord, and see how they do" (Acts 15:36). Barnabas determined to take John Mark, but Paul simply would not have him join their ministry team. Luke describes this heated discussion by saying, "the contention was so sharp between them, that they departed asunder one from the other: and so Barnabas took Mark...and Paul chose Silas" (Acts 15:39-40). It is tragically sad, at least from our human perspective, that this great, effective team dissolved, and this strong friendship was greatly strained. *Why was it that Paul would not give John Mark a second chance?* Acts 15:38 states Mark "departed from them from Pamphylia, and went not with them to the work." Acts 13:13 reveals Mark "returned to Jerusalem." With no more information than this, we can only guess at what was truly behind John Mark's abandoning the mission with Paul and Barnabas before it was complete. He may have been homesick, immature, or frightened by the continual dangers of persecution that followed this missionary journey. But whatever the cause, Paul deemed him to be too unacceptable in character to take a second chance on him. But praise be to God, this one who had once failed became faithful and greatly used of the Lord under the encouragement of Barnabas. Paul would later say, "Take Mark, and bring him with thee: for he is profitable to me for the ministry" (II Timothy 4:11).

If you have failed the Lord, even miserably, take heart in this example. We serve a God of gracious second, and third, chances. Return to faithful service for your Savior. Also, see if there isn't someone you can encourage with a second chance in ministry opportunity.

TRUE PARENTAL RESPONSIBILITY
Acts 16:1-2

In a letter written after winning Olympic Gold in 2012, Missy Franklin gave her parents a tearful and heart-warming tribute. She publicly read to them, "This isn't just a time to tell you something I think you want to hear. This is a time to truly and honestly acknowledge you for what you've done for me. **You knew that above all else, you were my parents, and your most important job was helping me grow into the woman I was capable of becoming. You loved me!**"[1] Missy was thanking her parents for taking true parental responsibility by being her guide, and mentors.

When we are first introduced to Timothy, he is described as one who had "believed...which was well reported of by the brethren, that were at Lystra and Iconium" (Acts 16:1-2). We should realize that such an outcome of good character and testimony did not just happen. Timothy had the godly example of his "grandmother Lois, and thy mother Eunice," who had "unfeigned faith" (II Timothy 1:5). We know this walk with the Lord was passed down to Timothy because Paul tells him, "I am persuaded that [unfeigned love is] in thee also." Simply put, children imitate what they see, hear, and are taught. A commercial in 2016 shows a short excerpt of a 5-year-old boy coloring on a wall. When his father sees it, he angrily calls him "stupid." Another segment shows the boy subsequently yelling at his younger brother and calling him stupid. However, in the following segment the father calmly tells the boy we should draw on paper but not on the wall, then he lovingly invites his son to help him clean off the wall. The final segment shows the little boy calmly and lovingly interacting with his younger brother. The point in the ad is that children are like sponges. Whether for good or bad, they soak up the behavior they see and incorporate it into the their own lives. This is exactly why it is so vital for parents and grandparents to realize that they are not to strive to be the friend of their child at the expense of parenting. Instead, they must realize that, as Missy said, "... above all else, you were my parents and your most important job was helping me become the woman I was capable of becoming."

Parents, there will be time to be the friend of your child once they are grown. While they are young be their parent, mentoring and molding them into maturity.

NOT BEING OFFENSIVE
Acts 16:1-3

There is an abundance of anti-Christian attacks on-line that ridicule those who worship the Savior. Christians are justified to be offended by such disrespectfulness. However, believers also need to be sensitive about being unnecessarily offensive to lost souls, because we want to reach them for Christ. An example of callousness in this area was Fred Phelps, Sr., pastor of Westboro Baptist Church in Kansas. He led his congregation to picket the funerals of fallen soldiers while holding signs that read, "Thank God for IEDs," and "Thank God for dead soldiers."

Shortly after Timothy joined Paul in ministry, "Paul...took and circumcised him because of the Jews...for they all knew that his father was a Greek" (Acts 16:3). This seems confusing, particularly since, in the previous chapter, Paul fought legalistic Jews who sought to impose circumcision on his converts. We are indebted to C.R. Stam who shares helpful insights in his commentary on the book of Acts. Paul's actions were not a compromise of sound doctrine. The previous debate was whether Gentiles could be saved apart from being circumcised, but that was not the issue here. Paul circumcised Timothy because the Jews, with whom they wanted to share the Gospel of the Grace of God, knew that Timothy's mother was a Jew and his father was a Gentile. These Jews could rightly assume that Timothy was not circumcised. Peter explained to Cornelius that, "...it is an unlawful thing for a man that is a Jew to keep company, or come unto one of another nation..." (Acts 10:28). Jews in this day considered uncircumcised Jews to be outcasts for refusing the everlasting covenant of circumcision given to all Israel (Genesis 17:13). They also considered uncircumcised Gentiles to be offensive pagans. To remove this offensiveness and make it easier to reach lost Jews, Timothy voluntarily submitted to being circumcised by Paul. Their mindset was, "For though I be free from all men, yet have I made myself servant unto all, that I might gain the more. And unto the Jews I became as a Jew, that I might gain the Jews..." (I Corinthians 9:19-20).

We see, in this example, a proper willingness to remove what could be an offense to lost souls that would hinder reaching them with the gospel. We also see that lost souls are valuable enough for us to go to great lengths and self-sacrifice that we might reach them for Christ. May we arm ourselves with this mindset and become active in effectively sharing the gospel.

PROPER RESPONSE TO PERSECUTION

Acts 16:16-40

On July 7th, 2016, the Ark Encounter, a full scale replica of Noah's original ark built by the Christian organization Answers In Genesis, opened in Kentucky. Christians from all over the country enthusiastically gathered to see an example of biblical truth, and to rejoice in their faith. But many hostile atheists gathered to picket the opening. They even had a huge billboard with a picture of the ark, which read, "Genocide and Incest Park–celebrating 2000 years of myths." *What was the response from Eric Hovind, the host of the opening?* He thanked the protestors for the additional media exposure, urged Christians to treat the protestors respectfully, and invited those on the picket lines to come in for a free tour with complimentary refreshments.

While ministering in Philippi, Paul had a lengthy encounter with "...a certain damsel possessed with a spirit of divination..." (Acts 16:16). For "many days" she followed Paul, interrupting his efforts in ministry, until Paul cast the demonic spirit out of her. This enraged the masters of this girl, because their ability to profit from her abilities was now gone. They responded by apprehending Paul and Silas, taking them to the "magistrates," and falsely accusing them of teaching things contrary to Roman law. This unverified news incited a public multitude, causing the authorities to command Paul and Silas to be beaten severely, then cast into prison. *How did these two innocent servants of God respond?* Today, rather than continuing to speak out, the response of many Christians to any level of persecution is often surprise, a pity-party, questioning why God allowed this, depression, or even permanent silence. Thankfully, this was not how God's servants responded. Instead, "...at midnight Paul and Silas prayed, and sang praises unto God: and the prisoners heard them" (Acts 16:25). Far from being defeated in their Christian walk, they remained victorious regardless of their situation. Two things were key to their frame of mind. They prayed. Perhaps it was for strength, courage, or continued boldness. Whatever the content, they remembered to pray, and the result was a spiritual strength that maintained their victory over circumstances. They also sang praises. They chose to focus on exalting the Lord verbally, and they likely sang songs laced with biblical truths that further strengthened their souls.

It's important how we respond to any level of Christian persecution. Let your response be a testimony to the lost through godly behavior, prayer, praise to the Savior, and continuing to share the gospel.

READINESS OF MIND
Acts 17:11

Throughout our years of ministry, we have seen three basic responses to the teaching of God's Word rightly divided: rejection, indifference, and eager acceptance. One woman sat through several years of preaching, but regardless how basic the subject, she rolled her eyes and shook her head in disagreement. Another man embraced our doctrines, but attended irregularly. When I urged him to be more faithful, he plainly told me, "I'm just not that interested in church or the Bible." However, we also had many who were hungry for the Word of God, faithfully attended, asked good questions, took notes, and grew spiritually by leaps and bounds.

When Paul and Silas fled from persecution in Thessalonica, they went to Berea. Once there, they attended the synagogue. There they found Jews who "...were more noble than those in Thessalonica, in that they received the word with all readiness of mind, and searched the Scriptures daily, [to see] whether those things were so" (Acts 17:11). Particularly in those days, people of nobility were born into positions of royalty, wealth, and education. However, the word "noble" is used here in a spiritual sense, describing qualities of great character. This character included a "readiness [or willingness] of mind" to receive the truths of Scripture. We might also describe them as keenly interested, hungry to learn, and teachable. But they were not gullible or tossed to and fro with every wind of doctrine. Though open minded to what they heard from Paul, they "searched the Scriptures daily [to see] whether those things were so." We should remember that when Paul ministered to Jews in need of salvation through faith in the Lord Jesus Christ, he did so by reasoning "...with them out of the [Old Testament] Scriptures" (Acts 17:2). This included documenting that the prophesied Savior "...must needs have suffered, and risen again from the dead; and that this Jesus, whom I preach unto you, is Christ" (Acts 17:3). It was always upon this foundation that Paul proclaimed the death, burial, and resurrection of our Redeemer "according to the Scriptures" (I Corinthians 15:3-4). Those at Berea were demonstrating a spiritual nobility, or greatness, through their eagerness to learn truth from the Lord, while making the Scriptures their final authority.

How noble are you in your spiritual appetite for God's Word? How teachable are you in your spirit? How willing are you to confirm what you are taught from the rest of Scripture? It's time to begin that journey into spiritual nobility.

BURDEN FOR LOST SOULS
Acts 17:13-34

I once heard a story about a Christian woman who was burdened for the soul of her drunken, abusive husband. He would not listen to the gospel and had no use for church. However, he did agree she could invite an evangelist for dinner. As she set the table, she only set two plates, one for her husband and one for their guest. When her husband commented on this, she replied, "I am too burdened to eat. How can I eat when I know any breath might be your last and that if you die you'll go to hell?" Then she said, "I shall not eat any more food until the day you come to Christ as your Savior." Initially, her husband responded with ridicule, but he soon became broken over his sins and trusted in the Lord Jesus.

As Paul stood alone in Athens waiting for Silas and Timothy to join him, "...his spirit was stirred in him, when he saw the city wholly given to idolatry" (Acts 17:16). At this time, Athens was the most celebrated city in Greece and the cultural capital of the world. It was renown for arts, architecture, poetry, and philosophy, but it was also known for its abundance of idol worship. For all of their intellectual advances, they were utterly pagan. Historians believe this city contained more than 3,000 public idols, plus thousands of smaller idols in homes. When Paul stood looking at the bustling masses and cultural wealth, his soul was "stirred" (meaning to be moved, grieved, or burdened), for their spiritually-lost condition. This motivated him to take action. He spoke in the synagogues and "...with the devout persons...in the market daily..." (vs. 17). When given an opportunity, he spoke publicly on Mars Hill, explaining the Athenians were ignorantly worshipping every supposed god. He urged them to turn in genuine faith to the only true God, the "Lord of heaven and earth" (vs. 24), who created the world, and would one day judge the world. This judge was the Lord Jesus Christ, who had risen from the dead.

What we need to learn from this account is that Paul possessed what he called a "great heaviness and continual sorrow in my heart" over lost souls (Romans 9:2). *How long has it been since we were truly burdened for a lost soul, prayed or wept for them, or shared with them the message of God's love?* Today, may our callousness be replaced by a burden for souls.

CLEAN HANDS

Acts 18:1-6

We wash food from toddlers' hands when removing them from a highchair. We remind youngsters leaving the table to wash their hands so they don't smear food on furniture. We repeatedly ask children to wash their hands after using the bathroom. Signs in bathrooms of restaurants inform employees that they are required to wash their hands. Those in the medical field are vigorously trained to wash their hands. In all of these examples, we are reminded that dirty hands are a problem.

While in Corinth, "...Paul was pressed in the spirit, and testified to the Jews that Jesus was [the] Christ. And when they opposed themselves, and blasphemed, he shook his raiment, and said unto them, Your blood be upon your own heads; I am clean: from henceforth I will go unto the Gentiles" (Acts 18:5-6). This declaration tells us about far more than Paul beginning to take a determined step away from ministering to Jews and toward an unprecedented focus on ministering to Gentiles. Paul was also saying he was clean of any responsibility for the eternal destruction of these Jews because he had given them the gospel, and they rejected it. This concept relates back to God's words to Ezekiel. This child of God was told, "...I have made thee a watchman...hear the word at My mouth, and give them warning from Me. When I say unto the wicked, Thou shalt surely die; and thou givest him not warning, nor speakest to warn the wicked...to save his life; the same wicked man shall die in his iniquity, but his blood will I require at thine hand" (Ezekiel 3:17-18). To drive this point home, the same message is repeated in Ezekiel 33:1-9. Today, we might use the symbolic expression: "He has blood on his hands." Pilate illustrated this concept. When he could not prevail upon the Jews to release the Savior rather than crucify Him, "... he took water, and washed his hands...saying, I am innocent of the blood of this just person..." (Matthew 27:24). While Pilate was not truly innocent, Paul's hands were clean because he had warned these lost men by giving them the gospel.

It is no accident that we see the constant example of Paul proclaiming the gospel to lost souls. He knew if he did not, his hands would not be clean regarding their eternal destruction. It is also God's reminder of our responsibility to share the gospel. *Will your hands be clean regarding lost souls you will meet today?*

BURNING BRIDGES

Acts 19:19

During the Revolutionary War, it was customary to burn bridges after troops crossed over them, to prevent the enemy from slipping up behind an army, and to prevent soldiers from deserting in the heat of battle. On one occasion, General George Washington led his troops across a bridge as they were nearing a battle. One of his officers asked him whether or not to burn the bridge behind them. General Washington reportedly looked at the bridge, then to the battle, and said, "Burn the bridge, it is either victory or death."[1]

When Paul came to the city of Ephesus, God blessed him with an open door to "...speak boldly for the space of three months..." in the synagogue, "persuading them the things concerning the kingdom of God" (Acts.19:8). When many "hardened" their hearts, God opened another door "in the school of Tyrannus" where, for two years, Paul proclaimed Christ. The result was, all in Asia, both Jew and Gentile, "heard the word of the Lord Jesus" (vs. 10), and many were saved. During this time, Paul was also able to work miracles. Then, unsaved "vagabond [or traveling] Jews" sought to cast out demons, presumably for hire, "by Jesus whom Paul preacheth" (vs. 13). God did not honor lost men making merchandise of the Savior's name. Instead of being cast out, the demons beat them so severely "they fled out of the house naked and wounded" (vs. 16). Once all Ephesus heard of this event, great conviction occurred, particularly on those who had already trusted in Christ. "And many that believed came, and confessed, and showed their deeds. Many...which used curious arts [occult type practices] brought their books together, and burned them before all men..." (Acts 19:18-19). These believers had not cut their ties to previous sinful things that would greatly dishonor Christ, and hinder their daily Christian walk. When convicted of these wrongs, they had a huge bonfire, effectively burning their bridges to prevent their easy return to sinful things.

Today, serious-minded Christians likewise need to burn bridges to previous sins and get sinful things out of our lives. We need to "burn" pornography, immodest clothing, worldly beverages, and other things we know hinder our walk with Christ. Today is a good day for a bonfire. *What sinful bridge would God have you burn?*

CAUSING DIVISION
Acts 20:17-35

Terrell Owens made six Pro Bowl appearances and holds the second most receiving yards in NFL history. Yet for all his accomplishments, he was widely considered one of the most divisive players in the league. While playing for five NFL teams, he caused constant controversy through outrageous scenes, and by criticizing coaches and teammates. His presence was so disruptive, despite his abundant talents; teams ultimately traded him, and eventually would not sign him.

When the Apostle Paul called for the Elders of the Church at Ephesus, he warned them, "For I know this that after my departing shall grievous wolves enter in among you, not sparing the flock. Also of your own selves shall men arise, speaking perverse things, to draw away disciples after them" (Acts 20:29-30). It is a sad reality that Christians have often knowingly engaged in behavior that was disruptive to the unity and welfare of those in local churches. Our text refers to elders who acted as vicious wolves for self-serving purposes. Paul warned the church at Rome, "...I beseech you... [to] mark them which cause divisions and offenses contrary to the doctrine which ye have learned; and avoid them, For they that are such serve not our Lord Jesus Christ, but their own belly, and by good words and fair speeches deceive the hearts of the simple" (Romans 16:17-18). Some today enter into churches with doctrine that they know will cause a controversy. They persuade ungrounded believers to follow them while leaving the church devastated. Others intentionally send unsolicited tapes and literature with controversial content knowing it is contrary to what is taught by the pastor and elders. Doing so does not serve or honor the Savior, but it continues nonetheless. In the church at Corinth, the believers became polarized with divisions by championing either Paul, Apollos, or Peter (I Corinthians 1:12). What remained was "envying, and strife, and divisions" that caused Paul to ask, "...are ye yet carnal, and walk as (unsaved) men?" (I Corinthians 3:3).

It is gravely serious to disrupt the unity of a local church with controversial doctrine, criticism, championing one teacher over another, or having an argumentative spirit that leads to strife. God charges each one of us to "endeavor to keep the unity of the spirit in the bond of peace" (Ephesians 4:3), and warns we will "give an account" for our conduct at the Bema Seat (Romans 14:12; II Corinthians 5:10). Don't be disruptive. Work to edify and unify your church.

EMOTIONAL TIES

Acts 20:36-38

It has been my great privilege to serve in several church-es over the past forty years. It was hard each time we moved on to another ministry, but we had many good memories of sweet friendships forged, tearful farewells, and many loving embraces. While we have been blessed with close relationships in each church, we well remember one dear middle-aged brother who stood to thank us for our ministry, but he could only weep. These Christian friendships have been so precious; we've had a number who have come great distances to regularly visit us and bring rejoicing to our hearts.

As the Apostle Paul bid farewell to the elders of Ephesus, we read one of the more touching scenes in the New Testament. "And when he had thus spoken, he kneeled down, and prayed with them all. And they all wept sore, and fell on Paul's neck, and kissed him, sorrowing most of all for the words which he spake, that they should see his face no more..." (Acts 20:36-37). This obvious close relationship forged between them was so strong their parting literally brought them to tears. This kind of relationship between believers, especially between those who minister the Word and those who receive such ministry, should be the norm for all Christians. Paul experienced similar bonds with saints that were closer than biological family members. When writing to the saints at Philippi, Paul addressed them saying, "...My brethren dearly beloved and longed for, my joy and crown, so stand fast in the Lord, my dearly beloved" (Philippians 4:1). He acknowledged his dear friends Priscilla and Aquila who had housed him, worked along side him, and moved to minister with him. He described them as ones "who have for my life laid down their own necks" (Romans 16:4). Likewise, when Paul was imprisoned in Rome, Onesiphorus "... sought me out very diligently, and found me...and in how many things he ministered unto me at Ephesus, thou knowest..." (II Timothy 1:17-18). In these instances, Paul had extended his heart to believers. As he ministered, they had responded in kind, and a deeply satisfying relationship not only grew, it thrived.

Have you established an extremely close, heartfelt relationship with other believers, including those who have committed their lives to minister God's Word to you? These can be some of the sweetest and most rewarding relationships in life. Today, reach out in friendship and grateful appreciation to those who minister God's Word to you.

CORPORATE PRAYER
Acts 21:1-5

In 1857, America was riding a wave of a strong economy. As is typical in prosperity, there was a radical decrease in interest for the things of God. In September, Jeremiah Lamphier decided to call a weekly prayer meeting in NYC from noon to 1:00 p.m. The first week, six people showed up at 12:30 p.m. Attendance jumped to 20 the next week and rose in weeks to come. On October 10th, the Stock Market crashed and financial panic ensued. It wasn't long before 10,000, then 50,000, businessmen were meeting every day in NYC for prayer. By 1858, these prayer meetings, which resulted in hundreds of thousands reportedly trusting Christ, jumped to every major American city. And it all started with corporate prayer.[1]

When the Apostle Paul left the elders of Ephesus, "...he kneeled down and prayed with them all" (Acts 20:36). After coming to Tyre and finding sweet fellowship with a band of disciples, they "through the Spirit [told him] that he should not go up to Jerusalem" (Acts 21:4). This was the first of three warnings in this chapter, from God's Spirit, for Paul to avoid the trouble awaiting him in Israel's religious center. The second was from the prophet Agabus (vss. 10-11), and the third from the household of Philip and Paul's entourage (vs. 12). What we don't want to miss from these chapters in Acts is a consistent practice of corporate prayer. When the saints of Tyre realized Paul was determined to go to Jerusalem, they accompanied him to the ship, "...and we kneeled down on the shore, and prayed [together]" (vs. 5). They were committing him to Lord in prayer and asking for God's enablement. When the elders of Ephesus sorrowed, knowing they would not see Paul again, they corporately prayed together, effectively committing him to the Lord. Just prior to a demonic attack, Paul prayed with the saints in Lydia's home (Acts 16:14-16). When the saints at Antioch ordained Paul and Barnabas for their unique ministry, they did so while collectively practicing prayer for their ministry. Similarly, the Jewish kingdom church practiced corporate prayer for their needs, and God richly blessed with divine intervention (Acts 13:1-3).

The repeated listing of these practices of prayer is placed here "for our learning" (Romans 15:4). The Lord would have us learn the importance of constantly practicing corporate prayer, in all circumstances, and in all places. Join with another believer in prayer today.

RISKING OFFENSE
Acts 22:1-23

While in college preparing for the ministry, I encountered another student from the Deep South. He was a boisterous individual who made condescending racial remarks while thinking he was superior to those of color. He was wrong. His comments were very offensive to me. I knew three perspective changing biblical principles. All mankind were sinners, and that God loved everyone in the world enough to send His Son to die for all. Peter had been taught, "…What God hath cleansed, that call not thou common [unclean or inferior] (Acts 11:9). Romans 12:3 also tells believers "…not to think of himself more highly than he ought to think…." Whether or not this fellow student became offended, I decided to share with him a more biblical perspective.

After an angry mob of Jews sought to kill Paul in the temple, Roman authorities apprehended him. As he was being taken away, he asked to speak to his attackers. His approach was to tell them three things they needed to hear, even if it further offended them. As he gave his testimony of being saved on the road to Damascus, he specified that a heavenly voice spoke to him identified itself by saying, "I am Jesus of Nazareth, whom thou persecutest" (Acts 22:8). This would be an unwelcome reference to these Jews who considered Christ a blasphemous imposter. Paul continued. He said that, when he later went to Jerusalem to minister in the name of the Lord Jesus, he was divinely warned to "make haste, and get thee quickly out of Jerusalem, for they will not receive thy testimony concerning Me" (vs. 18). This spoke not only to the hard-heartedness of the Jews in the past it implied their present and persistent condition. Finally, Paul shared that, since the Jews were rejecting faith in their Messiah, the Lord Jesus told him, "Depart, for I will send thee far hence unto the Gentiles" (vs. 21). This reference to ministering to the Gentiles so offended these bigoted Jews that it sent them into a frenzy, further calling for Paul's death. But each of these things were true, and they needed to hear it.

It should never be our goal to offend people, and we should be wise in seeking to avoid offensive behavior or speech. But, even if it offends the lost, we must share with them that meritorious works won't save them. Only faith in Jesus Christ apart from all works will. Don't let the fear of offending the lost silence you. Speak up!

NOTHING SURPRISES ME
Acts 23

When this author was growing up, it was a different era. Men wore short hair and didn't wear earrings. Women typically tried to be modest and were embarrassed if even their slip was showing. On the Dick Van Dyke Show, Rob and Laura were shown sleeping in separate beds, not naked or having sex. In the media, profanity was not used, people of Christian faith were portrayed in a good light, morality was extolled, and homosexuality was not constantly promoted. Over the years, our nation has deviated far from godly principles. This was evidenced during a 2004 Super Bowl appearance, when Janet Jackson had her breast exposed at halftime. Things have become so wicked that most of us can say, "Nothing surprises me any more."

When Paul was arrested in Jerusalem for proclaiming Christ, he had to be put into protective custody by Roman officials. The chief priests and elders, who were supposed to lead the people into godliness, bound themselves with a curse to eat or drink nothing until they had slain Paul (Acts 23:14). Worse yet, they conspired to lie to the Roman guard by asking to question Paul for clarity-but they intended to take him by force (vss. 15-21). Nothing should surprise us about how low unsaved men would go to thwart Paul from proclaiming eternal life through the Lord Jesus Christ. There had been a long pattern of outrageous sinful behavior everywhere Paul went. Contrary to the law, the high priest commanded his men to smite Paul on the mouth (Acts 23:1-3). The Jews falsely accused Paul of teaching against Israel, the Mosaic Law, the temple, and polluting the temple by bringing in a Gentile (21:26-30). The Jews "spake evil" of Paul's discourse when he documented for them in Scripture God's overall plan of bringing a divine rule to the world through His promised Messiah (19:8-9). While in Thessalonica, when Paul proclaimed that Scripture specified "...Christ must needs have suffered, and risen again....the Jews which believed not, moved with envy, took unto them certain lewd fellows of the baser sort...and set all the city on an uproar" (17:2-5). Paul had seen it all: lies, misrepresentations, threats, conspiracies, refusal to listen to Scripture, and multiple attempts on his life.

Dear believer, nothing should surprise you when Satan opposes your efforts to share salvation as a pure gift of God's grace through faith alone. Expect it. No matter what, don't be discouraged or silenced. As Paul did, keep on giving out the gospel. Some will still believe.

A CLEAN CONSCIENCE
Acts 24:16

Citizens in America know that there is enormous corruption by many in public office. In stings, Senators have been caught selling their votes for bribes. Our congress passed the Universal Healthcare Law while exempting themselves from it. Many leave office as multi-millionaires because they practice what amounts to insider trading-investing based on knowledge of contracts soon to be awarded. One group has had enough and is calling on all public officials to take a "Clean Conscience Pledge." It includes the promise to limit outside income to enable better focus on the needs of constituents, limiting contributions from special interest groups, and the transparent disclosure all discretionary spending and conflicts of interest.[1]

One official that did not need this pledge was Paul, the Apostle of the Gentiles. He could honestly tell Governor Felix, "...herein do I exercise myself, to have always a conscience void of offense toward God, and toward men"(Acts 24:16). This certainly did not mean others did not wrongly take offense when Paul proclaimed the promise of eternal life through faith in Christ. But he did not allow himself to do anything he knew was wrong, whether before God or men. This was the high standard to which he always held himself. When sharing his heavy burden for the lost souls of Israel, he said, "I say the truth in Christ, I lie not, my conscience also bearing me witness in the Holy Ghost, That I have a great heaviness...in my heart" (Romans 9:1-2). Because guilt over wrongdoing did not plague him, he wrote, "For our rejoicing is this, the testimony of our conscience, that in simplicity and godly sincerity...by the grace of God, we have had our conversation [or manner of life] in the world, and more abundantly to you-ward" (II Corinthians 1:12). To sum up the importance of a clean conscience, he wrote, "Now the end of the commandment is charity out of a pure heart, and of a good conscience, and of faith unfeigned" (I Timothy 1:5).

Scripture repeats this principle of the importance of a clean conscience a number of times because it is vital for all believers. When God pricks your heart that something you are doing, saying, looking at, or planning to do, is wrong, do not violate your conscience. You will be able to sleep better, look people in the eye, and have greater confidence at the Bema Seat.

A LAW ABIDING CITIZEN
Acts 25

It has been my lot in life to minister to a number of believers, who have a clear testimony of salvation and who also have strong anti-government sentiments. They speak often of governmental conspiracies. One of these believers specified that NASA knowingly causes huge weather swings, including droughts and hurricanes, by launching the space shuttle. These saints are vocal in criticism of the corruption and over-reaching hand of government. Their extreme response has often been to refuse to pay any income tax, apply for a driver's license, or otherwise recognize any authority of the government in their lives.

When the Apostle Paul defended himself against false accusations during questioning by Festus, he said, "Neither against the law of the Jews, neither against the temple, nor yet against Caesar, have I offended any thing at all" (Acts 25:8). Paul specified these things because, to strengthen their efforts to kill the apostle of grace, Jews who opposed his preaching of the Lord Jesus Christ frequently accused Paul of promoting an insurrection against Roman tyranny. In this text, and elsewhere, he strongly and specifically denied ever doing anything of this sort. In fact, even though there were terrible injustices, such as the common practice of slavery, oppressive taxation, and cruel Roman treatment, Paul never spoke out against these social issues. Instead, Paul stayed focused on spiritual ministry, and he actually taught believers to demonstrate respectful compliance to those in authority. He told the believers at Rome, "Let every soul be subject unto the higher powers. For there is no power but of God; the powers that be are ordained of God...Wherefore ye must needs be subject, not only for wrath, but also for conscience sake..." (Romans 13:1-6). Peter also followed the same principle, writing, "Submit yourselves to every ordinance of man for the Lord's sake: whether it be to the king, as supreme, or unto governors... For so is the will of God..." (I Peter 2:13-15 – see also vss. 16-17).

For the sake of the testimony of the Lord Jesus Christ, every believer should earnestly seek to be a law-abiding citizen. Regardless of any frustration with government officials, we need to be very measured in our criticisms. We represent Christ to a lost world and to other believers. How we do so will either enhance our ability to have spiritual ministry, or it will effectively neutralize it. Be conscious of this as your go through this day and be careful to exalt Christ.

HOW TO PLANT THE GOSPEL
Acts 26

This author's father was proud to be a farmer. On many occasions he told me, "Farmers are the most important people in the world. Without farmers, the world would starve to death." There is some truth to his concept. Many people wouldn't know how to plant a crop, what seeds to use, or when to plant them. Success requires proper information and skill in application. The same is true when planting the seed of the gospel in the hearts of lost souls.

There is something valuable for us to glean by carefully studying the methods used by the Apostle Paul, in different instances, when he planted the gospel seed. When defending himself before King Agrippa, he carefully gave his testimony of trusting in Christ for eternal life (Acts 26:1-23). When people won't listen to Scripture, they will often listen to a testimonial from a "satisfied customer" of God's grace. Paul explained that Christ had to suffer and rise from the dead (vs. 23), which is the heart of the gospel. Emphasizing Christ, that He died for our sins and triumphantly rose again, is essential because, "...there is none other name under heaven whereby we must be saved" (Acts 4:12). Those who win souls to Christ look for open doors of opportunity and immediately share the gospel when they find one. Paul used this opportunity with Agrippa, as Philip did when he found the Ethiopian Eunuch reading Scripture. When Paul was given an opportunity to speak in synagogues, he "reasoned" with the Jews out of the Scriptures (Acts 17:2; 18:4, 19; 24:25). It is always ideal to use the authority and power of God's Word to penetrate hardened hearts and to document what the Lord says about salvation. Paul also defended his reputation before Agrippa because, in order for his witness is to have credibility before the lost, he needed to be "...blameless and harmless, the sons of God, without rebuke... among whom ye shine as lights in the world" (Philippians 2:15). An invitation needs to be given to lost souls who need "to open their [spiritual] eyes, and to turn from darkness to light" (Acts 26:18). Ask your listener to trust in Christ when they understand the basics of salvation by grace alone.

We ought not to be discouraged when we witness and see no immediate results. Paul said, "I have planted, Apollos watered; but God gave the increase" (I Corinthians 3:6). Just plant the gospel seed and leave the rest to God. Some seeds don't germinate immediately.

CHILD–LIKE FAITH
Acts 27:1-25

When I was a youngster, my parents told me stories about Santa Claus, the Easter Bunny, and the Tooth Fairy. I believed them implicitly because they were my authority figures that I believed would always act with complete honesty and integrity. I vividly remember feeling devastated when I learned they had lied to me and, for whatever reasons, betrayed my trust. This experience led my wife and I to not repeat the same mistake. After all, we wanted our children to believe what we were teaching them about salvation through the Lord Jesus Christ, the trustworthiness of the Bible, and everything else we told them.

While the Apostle Paul was aboard a ship in route to Rome as a prisoner, winter was setting in. Paul recommended that they remain in Crete until spring, but the captain and centurion paid him no mind. When a violent and persistent storm threatened all life on board, an angel appeared to Paul assuring him that he, and all aboard, would be spared. Indeed, he would appear before Caesar in Rome. With child-like faith, Paul believed everything this messenger from God told him. Then he announced this event to everyone on board, saying, "Wherefore, sirs, be of good cheer: for I believe God, that it shall be even as it was told me" (Acts 27:25). The Lord always honors those who choose to believe Him. In this instance, Paul's influence was enhanced: passengers ate as he suggested, they abided in the ship when he counseled them to do so, and the centurion took measures to protect Paul when the ship broke apart. There are Old Testament examples of note too. When Abraham was promised a child and a vast number of descendants, "…he believed the Lord, and He counted it to him for righteousness" (Genesis 15:6). Daniel was taken out of the lion's den, "…and no manner of hurt was found upon him, because he believed in God" (Daniel 6:23). When Jonah predicted that Nineveh would be violently overthrown, "…the people of Nineveh believed God, and proclaimed a fast" (Jonah 3:5). They turned to the Lord in faith, and Jehovah stayed their downfall.

Believers today must believe God too. We need to believe God will work all things for our good (Romans 8:28), that rather than sin, we can always find a way to escape it (I Corinthians 10:13), and that we are always accepted by God in Christ (Ephesians 1:6). Whatever God says, choose to believe it!

ENCOURAGING OTHER SAINTS
Acts 28

It has been a rich blessing to have a number of wonderful saints become close friends. When the wife of one close couple had a life-saving kidney transplant in Nashville, I traveled from Rapid City, South Dakota, to be with them until she was stable. In turn, when I faced a possible life-threatening surgery in Jacksonville, Florida, the husband drove from Illinois to spend several days with us until I was stable. When another friend broke his leg and struggled in recovery, I flew from Orlando to Detroit to spend four days encouraging him. In turn, when I recently had consecutive surgeries on my back, this couple made two trips to Tampa to be with my wife and me. I believe hearts are greatly comforted by acts of love, friendship, and encouragement. I know these dear friends greatly encouraged my heart.

When Paul landed in Italy for his trial, he was then required to travel some 132 miles to Rome, possibly on foot. "And...when the brethren heard of us, they came to meet us as far as Appiforum, and the Three Taverns: whom when Paul saw, <u>he thanked God, and took courage</u>" (Acts 28:15). Just think of this. Some of these saints traveled 38 miles, and others 45 miles, all to encourage Paul as he faced a trial in Rome that could have cost him his life. This wasn't an easy air-conditioned car ride on an interstate. Whether by foot or riding on horseback, this would have taken a good deal of time, sacrifice, and effort. While Paul was a brave and courageous man, he also seemed to have some measure of anxiety about what lay ahead for him. While conflict followed him everywhere, it was not something he enjoyed. It was just unavoidable as a soldier of Christ. Perhaps he had this on his mind when he wrote, "Yea, and all that will live godly in Christ Jesus shall suffer persecution" (II Timothy 3:12). But how wonderful that, in this instance, on his difficult road to Rome, Christians came to bolster him with love and encouragement. It is also of note that Paul felt discouragement later when "...no man stood with me, but all men forsook me" (II Timothy 4:16).

You, too, may one day travel a difficult road on which you would greatly benefit by other believers coming to stand by your side. Until then, "pay it forward" by being ready to be there when someone needs you.

A CAUSE FOR REJOICING
II Corinthians 1:14

When I recently arrived to pick up our two-and-a-half-year-old twin granddaughters, I got quite the welcome. They called my name, gave me a big unsolicited hug, and sat on my lap. Then they took Grandpa by the hand and led me to the door. These little girls, to whom we gave life through our daughter, caused me great rejoicing of heart.

When the Apostle Paul addressed the saints at Corinth that he led to Christ, he told them: "…we are your rejoicing, even as ye also are ours in the day of the Lord Jesus" (II Corinthians 1:14b). It is amazing how often the Scriptures urge saints to serve the Lord in this life so they have the joy of reward in the hereafter. The Savior urged Israel: "…lay up for yourselves treasure in heaven, where neither moth nor rust doth corrupt, and where thieves do not break through nor steal" (Matthew 6:20). When these Jewish saints had only a "lukewarm" walk that did little to prepare for eternal reward, a rebuke was given. The Savior said: "…thou sayest, I am rich, and increased with goods…and knowest not that thou art wretched, and miserable, and poor…I counsel thee to buy of me gold tried in the fire, that thou mayest be rich, and (have) white raiment, that thou mayest be clothed…" (Revelation 3:17-18). While these Jewish saints had an earthly kingdom hope, the principle of serving the Lord with a view of eternal reward is the same for us today in the Body of Christ. The Apostle Paul told Timothy to "charge them that are rich in this world…that they do good, that they be rich in good works…laying up in store…a good foundation against the time to come" (I Timothy 6:17-19). All believers need to be serving Christ so they have reward reserved in eternity. This is what Paul was referring to when he told the Corinthians they would be his rejoicing in the Day of Christ. Likewise, he told the Thessalonians: "For what is our hope, or joy, or crown of rejoicing? Are not even ye in the presence of our Lord Jesus Christ at His coming" (I Thessalonians 2:19)? These saints that Paul led to Christ represented the certainty of eternal reward and future rejoicing for him.

Will you have rejoicing over rich reward in heaven because you served the Savior and led others to salvation? Riches in eternity are far more important than riches on earth. Let's get busy working for the Lord today.

SPIRITUAL DICTATORSHIP
II Corinthians 1:23-24

While preparing for the ministry, I attended a very strict legalistic Christian college. While there, I agreed to work as a security guard in their extensive art gallery. When I was hired, I requested Sundays off, stating that it was my understanding from Scripture that I should not work on Sundays. The art gallery was the pet project of the chancellor. When he heard about my request, he became extremely angry and nearly had me kicked out of school. I could hardly believe this treatment from fellow Christians, especially since I was respectful, up-front in my request and complied with what at the time I believed was biblically correct.

The Apostle Paul's usual approach was to reason, instruct, and even beg believers to rise to a standard worthy of their Savior. Even though he had exclusive, unique apostolic authority, he normally dealt with the saints in tenderness. Because he did not view himself as a spiritual dictator, he stated his perspective this way: "Not for that we have dominion over your faith, but are helpers of your joy: for by faith ye stand" (II Corinthians 1:24). He dealt with them in humility, equality, tenderness, and liberty. What a contrast to the false teachers who were being abusive toward the believers in the church at Corinth. Paul told them: "For ye suffer fools gladly ... For ye suffer, if a man bring you into bondage, if a man devour you, if a man take of you, if a man exalt himself, if a man smite you on the face" (II Corinthians 11:19-20). These believers were allowing others to enslave them with legalism, consume their assets, steal their liberty in Christ, lord a false authority over them, and be physically abusive. The conduct of these false teachers resembles the incorrect approach of denominations, synods, and the pope, who seek to establish spiritual dominion over people today. It is one thing to lead, encourage, or help others in their Christian lives, but it is simply wrong to abusively lord one's authority over another. Doing so leads to error, pride, gullible compliance, and a host of other things that do not honor the Lord.

If you are a leader in the Lord's work, we urge you to be careful to deal with others in humility and seek to be a helper of other believers' joy. We encourage all others to stand fast in our liberty from any abusive religious hierarchy.

I HAVE CONFIDENCE IN YOU
II Corinthians 2:3-11

Several years ago a college football program was chasing their first national championship. The team had one extremely good player at a highly skilled position. In his junior year, this player engaged in bar fights, and continued in the week leading up to the national championship game. In many colleges around the country, the coach would have kicked such a player off the team, or suspended him for the game by sending him home. However, this player never got more than a slap on the wrist, at most. The rationale was that he was needed to win the big game.

When the Apostle Paul wrote to believers in II Corinthians 2:3, he tells them he had "...confidence in you all." *Why?* While we justifiably think of this church as the most carnal of all Paul's converts, they were still spiritually-minded enough to follow his instruction in church discipline. In I Corinthians 5:9-13, Paul gives them a list of specific sins by believers that are never to be tolerated in a local grace assembly. Since some of these were present at Corinth, he tells them to withdraw complete fellowship from believers living in these sins, and they did. It seems today, few, if any churches or believers, practice church discipline. It is rationalized away with excuses about not being loving or needing them in the church. Perhaps we should ponder how spiritual we really are when the church at Corinth was more spiritually mature in this area than most believers are today.

Because of their previous obedience in discipline, in II Corinthians 2:3-11, Paul expressed confidence that they would now embrace the one from whom they previously withdrew fellowship. He had benefited from their discipline, repented, and now needed to be restored to the church. Paul tells them his "...punishment, which was inflicted of many" was "sufficient" (vs. 6). It was now time to "forgive him, and comfort him, lest...[he] be swallowed up with overmuch sorrow" (vs. 7). Because he had repented, now was the time to "...confirm your love toward him...lest Satan should get an advantage of us; for we are not ignorant of his devices" (vss. 8,11). While many believers find it almost impossible to restore relationships once they have been severed, Paul was confident these believers would obey.

Could others justifiably have confidence in us that we would obey difficult instructions from God's Word? What area is lacking obedience in your life today?

SATAN'S ADVANTAGE
II Corinthians 2:5-11

In a 2015 NBC episode of Chicago PD, a police candidate who had been working at the police station was brutally murdered. Officers in the precinct wanted the city to pay for a gravestone and a plaque to honor this comrade. But a city official refused to release the funds. However, Sargent Hank Voight had an advantage over this official. He brought an incriminating file on this official to his attention and threatened to make it public unless he signed off on this funding. With this powerful leverage, the official quickly changed his mind.

Prior to Paul writing his second epistle to the Corinthians, one of the believers in this assembly had been practicing flagrant and gross immorality. Appropriately, and with Paul's instructions, many in the church had inflicted this individual with the punishment of withdrawing their fellowship and putting him out of the church (II Corinthians 2:6). Thankfully, their positive peer pressure had reaped a good spiritual harvest. This believer had repented, changed his behavior, and proven his change was genuine. Now Paul writes, urging the entire church to "…forgive him, and comfort him, lest perhaps such a one should be swallowed up in overmuch sorrow" (vs. 7). It would serve no positive purpose to continue to punish this believer who had changed his ways. Instead, they were to follow Paul's example when he tells them: "…for your sakes forgave I it in the person of Christ" (vs. 10). They were to confirm their love to this saint by receiving him back into the fellowship of the church (vs. 8). Paul tells them to do so: "Lest Satan should get an advantage of us: for we are not ignorant of his devices" (vs. 11). We might normally think of Satan's devices being lies, spiritual deceit, immorality, addiction, apathy, or blinding the eyes of the lost to the gospel. While all of these are in Satan's toolbox, one of his most effective tools is to influence Christians to refuse to forgive fellow believers. When this happens, it robs the unforgiving one of peace, joy, spiritual growth, and a proper testimony for Christ. Seldom does it hurt the wrongdoer as much as the one wronged. But the lack of forgiveness by believers can drive a sinning saint into deep sorrow and further into a worldly way of living.

Dear believer, don't let Satan get an advantage over you by refusing to forgive a fellow blood-bought believer. Instead, "…Be ye kind…forgiving one another, even as God for Christ's sake hath forgiven you" (Ephesians 4:32).

CAUSING US TO TRIUMPH
II Corinthians 2:14

At our grandson's bowling party, the attendants set up bumpers in the alleys and a stand to roll the balls down toward the pins. We needed to help the children position the stand, carry their bowling ball, and help them roll it down. Whenever their ball knocked down pins, we praised them for doing a good job, and they would squeal with happy excitement. In reality, they had little to do with this accomplishment because they needed assistance from someone bigger, stronger, and more knowledgeable than they were. Still, the children participated, and we were pleased to see them so happy.

Despite the persecution Paul endured, he was rejoicing in spiritual victories. He rejoiced that God used him to lead many to Christ at Corinth (II Corinthians 1:14). He rejoiced in their obedience in exercising needed church discipline (2:3). He rejoiced in the repentance of the one disciplined (2:6-7), and in open doors to proclaim "Christ's gospel" (2:12). In this context, Paul says: "Now thanks be unto God, which always causeth us to triumph in Christ, and maketh manifest the savor of His knowledge in every place" (2:14). Paul was picturing the Roman Triumph, when a victorious general returned to Rome in a chariot pulled by white horses, parading those he had conquered to demonstrate his glorious victory. Often the general's son would walk behind his chariot, therein sharing in the glory of victory. During this procession, Romans priests would burn incense that wafted a distinctive odor. For the captives, this fragrance meant slavery and, often, death in the arena. To the general, it meant a victorious homecoming. While Paul "laboured more abundantly" (I Corinthians 15:10) than all the apostles, he always attributed his victories to "the grace of God which was with me." He acknowledged that his every triumph was due to his strong, omniscient Savior who sovereignly worked through him. As a son of God, Paul followed behind the Savior who allowed Himself to be the sacrifice for our sins and then triumphed over death. Every time Paul proclaimed the gospel to a lost soul, giving them the knowledge of salvation by grace alone, it was like a beautiful fragrance, or "savour," being offered to the Lord.

We, too, can offer thanks for the triumphs in ministry that are given to us by the hand of God. Today, let's make the gospel known to a lost soul and allow the fragrance of our ministry to be pleasing to our Savior.

I CAN READ YOU LIKE A BOOK
II Corinthians 3:2

My wife's parents had an interesting dog named Feller. Whenever he did something wrong, he'd lower his head and show his teeth in a grin. If he'd dug a hole in the yard or gotten on the furniture, he'd show that grin. You could read him like a book. People are that way too. We have good Christian friends from San Diego. The wife recently told us she knows when her husband is trying to pull a trick on her because he gets this gleam in his eye. She can read him like a book.

God often uses His children to be read like a book! The Lord told Isaiah: "…Go and loose the sackcloth from off, thy loins, and put off thy shoe from thy foot. And he did so, walking naked and barefoot" (Isaiah 20:2). As an illustration of the kind of impending divine judgment God was going to send upon the Egyptians, God's man Isaiah walked completely naked for three years. *How would you have liked that job?* It was difficult and unusual, but it was an effective message. The Lord said to Hosea, "…Go, take…a wife of whoredoms and children of whoredoms: for the land [or the people of Israel] hath committed great whoredom, departing from the Lord" (Hosea 1:2). *Men, how would have liked this job?* This, too, was difficult and unusual, but it was likewise an effective tool in sending a message to Israel about their wretched spiritual condition. The Apostle Paul said: "For I think that God hath set forth us the apostles last, as it were appointed to death: for we are made a spectacle unto the world, and to angels, and to men" (I Corinthians 4:9). Paul felt like he lived in a glass house where everyone, including angels, could see every aspect of his life, including his impending death from persecution.

Did you know that God is similarly using every believer today? Paul says: "Ye are our epistle …known and read of all men" (II Corinthians 3:2). We are the only message from God that many people will ever read. Lost souls are reading our lives every day even when we don't realize it. That makes how we talk, react, treat people, act at work, and live very important. *What kind of living epistle are you choosing to be?* Make your life a good book for others to read that will draw them to the Author of The Good Book.

NOT GIVING UP

II Corinthians 4:1-2

The three years before this writer entered high school, we had so little rain we had virtually no crops to harvest. Banks were repossessing many farms that had been in families for generations. But my father did not give up. He got the best job he could find. He would work all night, come home to sleep for about four hours, then work the farm until time to leave for his night job. I often wondered where he found the strength and resolve, but he just kept plugging away.

When the Apostle Paul wrote his second epistle to the believers at Corinth, he had already experienced many severe trials. But he didn't give up his ministry for the Lord. He could say, "We are troubled on every side, yet not distressed; we are perplexed, but not in despair; persecuted, but not forsaken; cast down, but not destroyed" (II Corinthians 4:8-9). He told the saints that while "...our outward man perish, yet the inward man is renewed day by day" (II Corinthians 4:16). As he spent time each day in God's Word, he was "changed...even as by the Spirit of the Lord" (II Corinthians 3:18). It was this time of daily spiritual renewal that kept the Apostle Paul from giving up in discouragement and able to just keep plugging away in the cause of Christ. But there were three things that motivated Paul to be faithful. He wrote, "Therefore, seeing we have this ministry, as we have received mercy, we faint not..." (II Corinthians 4:1-2). He saw the ministry the Lord gave him as a real privilege and responsibility. People were counting on him, and the Lord was counting on him. So he needed to keep plugging away regardless of hardships. Paul also never forgot that God had bestowed His divine mercy upon him. He was a guilty sinner deserving only God's wrath. But in mercy, the Lord saved him and entrusted him with ministry. Therefore, it was his reasonable service to remain faithful. Third, Paul had cultivated a genuine burden for lost souls (Romans 9:1-3; 10:1), because he realized the gravity of eternal punishment, even if the lost did not. So, he never gave up trying to reach people with the gospel.

Have you grown weary in faithfulness, ministry, or trying to reach the lost? Don't give up. Allow these three things to motivate you to remain faithful and renew your strength through a daily quiet time.

GROWING FAINT?
II Corinthians 4:2

Have you ever grown "faint" [to be weak or to fail in heart] in efforts to minister to others? I have two grace pastor friends who suffered such poor treatment from their churches that they permanently got out of the ministry. When I called to encourage them, they were hurt and completely drained spiritually. Most pastors know how they feel too. Christians can be unresponsive, unappreciative, overly critical, petty, and simply cruel.

Paul knew others in his day had similar struggles with being "faint" in the ministry and their daily walk with Christ. When a heavy load of legalism discouraged many in Galatia, Paul taught them to stand fast in their liberty, and he encouraged them by saying: "...Let us not be wearying in well doing: for in due season we shall reap, if we faint not" (Galatians 6:9). Paul, too, resisted the urge to faint in discouragement. But several things sustained him. He said: "Therefore, seeing we have this ministry, as we have received mercy, we faint not" (II Corinthians 4:1). God's great mercy given in forgiveness and eternal life, rather than eternal punishment, caused Paul to see ministry for the Lord as only his reasonable service. But beyond this, he viewed ministry as a great responsibility. He did not faint because it was a privilege to serve the Lord. Eternal souls hung in the balance, as they needed the gospel, and those already saved needed ministry. With this in mind, he pressed on in faithful ministry "...commending ourselves to every man's conscience in the sight of God" (II Corinthians 4:2). Paul also saw the influence and impact he could have on the saints as a motivator to keep him going in ministry. He wrote: "For all things are for your sakes, that the abundant grace might through the thanksgiving of many redound to the glory of God. For which cause we faint not..." (II Corinthians 4:15-16). Paul had a strong desire to see the God of all mercy glorified. This would be done through other saints if he would only "faint not" and remain faithful in ministry.

If you've grown faint in ministering to others, you're not alone. But we must remember that we will reap rewards in eternity if we faint not. "Therefore, my beloved brethren, be ye steadfast, unmovable, always abounding in the work of the Lord, forasmuch as ye know that your labor is not in vain in the Lord" (I Corinthians 15:58). If you've stopped ministering to others, please start again.

OUR HIDDEN GOSPEL
II Corinthians 4:3-4

I'm sure this will seem almost impossible for most women to believe, but men have a hard time finding things. Countless times, I've looked in utter frustration for things in the refrigerator, or for my keys. When I ask my wife or girls to help me, more often than not, they are able to find what I'm looking for right way. I have an excuse: not being able to find things is in the "Men's Manual," and it's our way of helping the ladies know they are needed. As the saying goes: "That's my story and I'm sticking to it."

Many of us are burdened for lost loved ones to trust in Christ alone for eternal life, before it is eternally too late. The gospel is easy to see, or understand, yet it seems as if the simplicity of "our gospel is hid...to them that are lost" (II Corinthians 4:3), because they stubbornly cling to their unbelief. *Why do they respond this way?* The Lord Jesus explained, "men loved darkness rather than light, because their deeds were evil" (John 3:19). Some stubbornly refuse the free gift of salvation, purchased on Calvary, out of love for their practice of sins. Regardless of the eternal consequences, they choose to hold on to sin rather than trust in Christ. Those who receive eternal life must do so willingly, because God will not force His love on those who do not want it. Satan dupes others into believing that faith in Christ is utter nonsense. Paul explained, "for the preaching of the cross is to them that perish foolishness, but unto us which are saved it is the power of God" (I Corinthians 1:18). The god of this world, Satan, has hundreds of thousands constantly proclaiming an anti-God message: secular professors, the media of television and movies, literature, and the common man or woman. Through this bombardment of false information, they convince the lost that everything about our faith is only fiction for fools. "The god of this world hath blinded the minds of them which believe not, lest the light of the glorious gospel of Christ, who is the image of God, should shine unto them" (II Corinthians 4:4). We must never forget that Satan is waging a constant battle against every living soul.

Don't be discouraged. Keep on sharing the clear gospel of salvation by faith in Christ apart from all works. It is "the power of God unto salvation" (Romans 1:16). Some will believe this good news.

CHOOSING WHAT TO FOCUS ON
II Corinthians 4:16-18

On November 14th, 2008, I awoke to a house on fire. A contractor working on the home we built cut a corner on the fireplace. He was supposed to install a triple lined stainless steel pipe, but he only did so until he reached the attic. The result was a fire that burned almost everything we had accumulated over thirty years of marriage. My wife and I stood there and watched it all burn. Rather than focus on all we lost, together we made a conscious decision to fill our minds with all God had given us and continually praise Him for these things. This gave us victory.

Just because we know the Lord Jesus as Savior doesn't mean He is going to spare us trials and hardships. Even the great Apostle Paul's life was filled with problems. He said, "We are troubled on every side, yet not distressed...perplexed, but not in despair; persecuted, but not forsaken; cast down, but not destroyed; always bearing about in the body the dying of the Lord Jesus..." (II Corinthians 6:4-10). Paul tells us he was beaten five different times with "forty stripes save one, thrice was I beaten with rods, once was I stoned." He was also shipwrecked, in constant peril and "in weariness and pain" (II Corinthians 11:23-27). Such a list makes most of us wonder how he could remain faithful and keep from being crushed under the weight of discouragement.

The answer is found in II Corinthians 4:16-18. His victory began with being continually in God's Word so "...the inward man is renewed day by day" (vs. 16). Then, being spiritually strengthened by the power of the Scriptures, he made a conscious decision to look at every trial from a proper perspective. He chose to view all the negative things that had happened to him as only "light affliction, which is but for a moment" (vs. 17a). He didn't magnify the hurt. He minimized it, remembering that, in light of eternity, it only lasted a short while and his faithfulness through it all would bring him eternal reward. Finally, he did not constantly dwell on his trials. He chose to "...look not at the things which are seen...but at the things which are...eternal" (vs. 18). His victory was a matter of proper focus.

You too can have victory even when severe trial comes your way. But, it will depend on what you choose to focus on. Focus on God, His Word, and eternity.

August 2

AN UNAVOIDABLE APPOINTMENT
II Corinthians 5:10-11

When I was in high school, I was stopped by the police and issued a ticket for…inappropriate driving. The ticket came with a scheduled appointment to appear before the local judge. What made matters worse was I had visited this judge's house two years earlier, on Halloween, to do mischief. Unfortunately, he caught me in the act and he was very unhappy. This judge had known me since I was little so I was wishing I had behaved better in both instances.

Everyone who knows the Lord Jesus as Savior has an unavoidable appointment in the future. The Apostle Paul tells us: "For we must all appear before the judgment seat of Christ…" (II Corinthians 5:10). Notice it's not optional. We "must appear." A Bible teacher I know likes to say, "Words mean things." God does not call this a celebration or an awards banquet. He calls this the judgment seat of Christ. Our initial time before the Lord will be one of judging everything we have chosen in life after salvation, "whether it be good or bad" (II Corinthians 5:10). This will not be a time of punishment. Instead it will be a time to reveal how we chose to live after salvation. Whether we choose sinful paths or Christ-honoring ones, this will be revealed. It will be a time of accountability. We live in a society where few seem to assume responsibility for poor decisions. But God tells us: "So every one of us shall give an account of himself to God" (Romans 14:12). Whatever this means, this is not God giving us an accounting but us giving God an account of our life. This can be a time of shame or commendation. II Timothy 2:15 talks about the need to rightly divide the Word of God that one need not "be ashamed." Or perhaps for some, it will be like the parable when the master says, "…well done, thou good and faithful servant" (Matthew 25:21). It will be a time of eternal reward or realization of possible reward lost. All our life after salvation will be tried by fire. Only things worthy of reward will remain (I Corinthians 3:13-15). Don't fixate on only one aspect of this future time. All are in view.

This future sobering appointment should motivate all believers to good choices after salvation. Paul said, "Knowing…the terror of the Lord, we persuade men…" (II Corinthians 5:11). Let's make good choices today.

WHOM DO YOU LIVE FOR?
II Corinthians 5:14-15

We have friends who have an autistic son whom they love from the depths of their souls. Once embracing the reality of his handicap, the mother left her lucrative job to stay at home to work with this son. They sought every avenue imaginable to help their son: doctors, therapies, and trips to the state capital to lobby for special education funds. The mother even became her son's teacher at a public school that offered classes for those with special needs. For all practical purposes, this mother has been living for this son with extraordinary dedication. Her son is her top priority.

The truth is, all of us are living for someone or something. We may be living primarily for a mate, children, work, wealth, status, recognition, or simply to please ourselves. While some of these things are worthy of a measure of dedication, the Lord desires for us to know that there is something for which we should be living with total, unreserved dedication. Using himself as an example, the Apostle Paul said, "For the love of Christ constraineth us, because we thus judge, that if one died for all, then we were all dead [in trespasses and sins]: and that he died for all that they which live should not henceforth live unto themselves, but unto Him which died for them, and rose again" (II Corinthians 5:14-15). Notice, the Savior did not only die that He might save you and me from eternal punishment, nor even that we might live for all eternity in heaven. He also died that we might choose to "live...unto him which died" for us. After salvation, God's will for each of us is that we live to please Him, serve Him, and further His cause. We are to be utterly sold out to living for this higher calling. The reason why the Apostle Paul had such an impact on so many was because he embraced this calling. That is why he said, "I am crucified with Christ: nevertheless I live; yet not I, but Christ liveth in me; and the life which I now live in the flesh I live by the faith of the Son of God, who loved me, and gave Himself for me" (Galatians 2:20).

What is your top priority or, said another way, who are you living for? Let's have a family discussion today about this subject and, as a family, put living for Christ at the top of our list of priorities.

WHAT A WASTE
II Corinthians 6:1

When singer Whitney Houston died of an overdose, a number of people said, "What a waste." She had an incredible voice, rare opportunities with such talent, great riches, and a full life. Yet, tragically, she ended her life far to soon. It was such a waste.

Believers sometimes waste the riches of God's grace after receiving the gift of salvation. *How?* By not rejoicing in the great riches we have in Christ, not using the opportunities we have to serve the Lord and by choosing selfish pursuits, or a sinful lifestyle, rather than living for the Savior who died for us. Many effectively suppress their spiritual life by a tragically wayward walk far from the will of God. Because this was happening within the church at Corinth, the Apostle Paul writes them saying, "We, then, as workers together with Him, beseech you also that ye receive not the grace of God in vain" (II Corinthians 6:1). There was a way for these believers to not waste the grace of God extended to them. Paul urged the Corinthians to be careful to live in a way they were "giving no offence [to the lost] in any thing, that the ministry be not blamed" (vs. 3). He did not want their testimony to bring reproach on the name of Christ and enable lost souls to use them as an excuse to remain unsaved. Instead, they were to live so purely that "...in all things [we are] approving ourselves as the ministers of God..." (vs. 4a). Just as an ambassador for the United States must represent our country well through good conduct, we who know Christ must do the same. This must be so no matter what our circumstances: "...in afflictions, in necessities, in distresses, in stripes [meaning beatings during persecution], in imprisonments, in tumults, in labours, in watchings, [or] in fastings" (vss. 4b-5). Paul was urging them to draw upon the strength of God's daily grace and represent God's grace well. This would mean demonstrating "patience," "pureness," "longsuffering," "kindness," "love," "rejoicing," and service to the Lord (vss. 4-10). If these believers would proclaim "the Word of truth, by the power of God" (vs. 7), the grace of God would be a divine investment that was not wasted, or received "in vain" (vs. 1b).

Don't let God's grace be wasted on you by not allowing it to produce the kind of dedicated life to Christ that He desires. Represent your Savior well today by demonstrating the godly qualities listed above.

GIVING NO OFFENCE
II Corinthians 6:3-7

My wife and I have become friends with one of the ladies in our neighborhood. She is quite outgoing and gregarious. While she was at the grocery store, she saw a woman whom she concluded was pregnant. She went up to the woman, put her hands on the woman's stomach literally, then asked, "When is your baby due sister?" In disgust, this lady told our neighbor, "Excuse me. I'm not pregnant!" This neighbor told us, "Talk about putting my foot in my mouth, there was absolutely no way to get out of that situation gracefully."

In the context of realizing he represented the Lord Jesus Christ, the Apostle Paul gave his testimony about how he sought to live each day. He wrote, "Giving no offence in any thing, that the ministry be not blamed: but in all things approving ourselves as the ministers of God, in much patience…by pureness…by longsuffering, by kindness…by love unfeigned, by the Word of truth, by the power of God…(II Corinthians 6:3-7). Since every believer is an ambassador of Christ, we too should adopt these same goals for how we live before others. If we are to be effective in our spiritual influence, near the top of our list must be to seek to give "no offence in any thing." Most of us have probably heard someone say, "If that is what being a Christian is like, then I don't want anything to do with it." Like Paul, we need to be consciously careful not to offend others. He said, "It is good neither to eat flesh, nor to drink wine, nor any thing whereby thy brother stumbleth, or is offended, or is made weak" (Romans 14:21). Since this is to be our standard in how we conduct ourselves before other believers, our conduct before the lost must rise to an even higher level of carefulness. I Corinthians 10:32-33 confirms this: "Give none offence, neither to the Jews, nor to the Gentiles, nor to the church of God: even as I please all men in all things, not seeking mine own profit, but the profit of many, that they might be saved."

Right now would be a good time to pause to consider if there is currently anything in your life that could offend others, and push lost souls away from the Lord Jesus. If the Holy Spirit convicts you about anything, through His power, change that conduct immediately.

REMAIN SEPARATE
II Corinthians 6:14-17

My wife and I once visited the world famous San Diego Zoo. It was immense and incredibly diverse. While viewing these animals, it occurred to us that the zoo operates on a biblical principle. When the Lord created the world, He created the animals "after their kind" and told them to "multiply," and they did so "after their kind" (Genesis 1:20-25). With few exceptions, these animals in the zoo are kept separate from one another to maintain tranquility.

Most of the Apostle Paul's letters address problems in the lives of the believers to whom he wrote. For instance, the Corinthians needed correction about being divided, reveling in heinous immorality, being unloving, and lacking in giving to the work of the Lord. Paul continued his correction by telling them, "Be not unequally yoked together with unbelievers," (II Corinthians 6:14). Those who genuinely knew the Lord Jesus Christ as Savior were willingly being joined in marriage with those who did not know Christ. This was a formula for spiritual and marital disaster. Although some animals in zoos may live in somewhat close proximity, those who keep these animals do not indiscriminately put them together. Cats were not meant to live with birds, nor lions with lambs, nor foxes with chickens. It doesn't take a lot of foresight to realize most of them are completely incompatible, and some would be readily devoured. The same is true regarding believers who join in marriage with unbelievers. The Lord has never intended for these two to live together in the bond of marriage. The two are simply incompatible with different goals, standards, philosophies, and especially with different spiritual responses. Paul explains, "What fellowship hath righteousness with unrighteousness...[or] light with darkness...or he that believeth with an infidel?" (6:14-15). Yet, far too many believers have knowingly ignored Paul's warning by entering into an unequal spiritual yoke in marriage with an unbeliever. Usually, the result is that the spiritual walk of the Christian is devoured by the non-Christian, or the marriage falls apart because they are not even close to being compatible.

Are you contemplating marriage? You can save yourself a great deal of heartache by not dating anyone, even one time, who is not saved, does not embrace right division, or is not serious minded about living for the Lord. Don't let your life and spiritual walk be devoured by joining in an unequal yoke. Find joy and compatibility with a fellow believer of like precious faith.

August
8

"IT'S TO DIE FOR"
II Corinthians 7:8-9

We have a friend who seems to always be using the phrase: "It's to die for." She says things like: "Have you been to the new restaurant? The food there is to die for." "Have you gotten the new iPhone? It's to die for." This saying never made sense to me. Few things in life are really worth dying for, and if you died for this thing, you would never enjoy it or anything else again. There certainly are some things worth dying for but it would have to be something far more important than a meal or object that would not soon be remembered anyway.

However trite the above saying might be, Paul said something similar to the saints at Corinth: "...ye are in our hearts to die and live with you" (II Corinthians 7:3b). There actually are things and people worth living and dying for. Paul was willing to die for the cause of Christ. Persecutors had tried unsuccessfully to silence him when he preached Christ and a new dispensation of grace available to Jew and Gentile alike. But the Apostle Paul would not be silenced because he did not live for himself. His attitude was, "For me to live is Christ" (Philippians 1:21). Paul had embraced the truth that Christ "died for all that they which live should not henceforth live unto themselves but unto Him which died for them and rose again." In other words, the Savior was worth living for and he was doing just that. But he also thought ministry to other saints, like those at Corinth, was worth dying for. He told the saints in II Corinthians 7:3, "ye are in our hearts to die... with you." In other words, he was willing to die for their spiritual benefit. That's why he told the saints at Philippi the same thing: "if I be offered upon the sacrifice and service of your faith, I joy, and rejoice with you all" (Philippians 2:17). He also accepted the possibility of dying for Christ and those he ministered by seeing it as "gain" or "far better" (Philippians 1:21-23). Going home to his Savior would only be a joyous reunion.

Have you come to the place spiritually where you are willing to truly live for Christ and others, or even to die for Him and other believers? Today is the day you need to mentally pack for this journey, surrender to Christ, and report for duty. HE is to live or to die for.

225

GODLY SORROW
II Corinthians 7:8-11

When Alejandro Avila was convicted of kidnapping and murdering five-year-old Samantha Runnion, her mother, Erin spoke at his sentencing. In part, she told him: "You have absolutely no concept of how heinous, how egregious your crimes are...But you just don't care...our lives were shattered...And you should be sorry...Not sorry you got caught; not sorry your wasted life will be taken...but sorry that you took a life, the life of a very special little girl."[1]

It is a sad reality that, far too often, people are sorry for getting caught, but not sorry for the wrong they have done. Believers are not immune to this callousness either. We have personally witnessed this when Christians gossip, lie, destroy reputations, steal, cause church splits, and more. The Apostle Paul saw it in his day too. He warned the saints at Corinth, "...when I come again...I shall bewail many which have sinned already, and not repented of the uncleanness and fornication and lasciviousness which they have committed" (II Corinthians 12:21). This defiant practice of ongoing sin must break the heart of God. Instead, He desires the response of Psalm 51:17, "The sacrifices of God are a broken spirit: a broken and contrite heart, O God, thou wilt not despise." Thankfully, this is exactly how the sinning saint, described in I Corinthians 5, reacted when rebuked and disciplined by the church. He had "...sorrowed to repentance: for ye were made sorry after a godly manner...For godly sorrow worketh repentance to salvation [deliverance from sinful practices] not to be repented of...what carefulness it wrought in you, yea, what clearing of yourselves...what vehement desire [to do right]...in all things ye have approved yourselves to be clear in this matter (II Corinthians 7:9-11). He allowed his heart to be broken over his wrongdoing, and sought to genuinely correct his behavior.

Dear believer, how do you respond when you know you have sinned or wronged someone else? Do you defiantly rationalize it, ignore it, excuse it, continue in it, or do you demonstrate the kind of godly sorrow described above? Are you only sorry if you get caught and suffer consequences, or are you sorry because your conduct was wrong, hurtful, and offensive to the Lord? May we allow the Lord to speak to our hearts about developing a pattern of true godly sorrow.

ARE YOU DISCIPLINED?
II Corinthians 8:6

For several decades I was pretty disciplined with exercise. For about two years I ran about five miles nearly every day. After a knee operation, I decided rollerblading would put less stress on the joints. For about a dozen years, I "bladed" between ten to twenty miles per day. It helped my eating habits, waistline, and blood pressure. Then, I started walking. For the nearly twelve years I walked three to five miles almost every day. But I haven't been nearly as disciplined with exercise as I once was. I'm still walking, but it seems harder to get this old body in motion than it used to be.

How disciplined are you? Many show great discipline in exercise, diet, work ethic, or other needed things. But, *did you know God expects us to be very disciplined in the matter of giving?* Three times in II Corinthians Chapter 8 God refers to giving as a "grace" we are to grow in. A year earlier Paul had shared his burden for the Jewish saints in Jerusalem who were in desperate poverty. Paul taught that giving to them would be giving to the Lord, and they had promised to do so. Now Paul sends Titus to gather their offering and "...finish in you the same grace also" (II Corinthians 8:6). As some of the more financially affluent saints, such giving would not have been a hardship. Paul told them: "...ye abound in every thing, in faith, and utterance, and knowledge, and in all diligence, and in your love to us, see that ye abound in this grace also" (II Corinthians 8:7). Paul wanted them to see that giving to the Lord was just as important as any other area in their spiritual life. It was also, in effect, a test as to how spiritual they really were. Would their walk be one of only talking the talk, or truly walking their talk as a believer? How they gave, or would not give, would be a gauge. Paul also took special measures to insure the integrity of how these funds would be handled. Only trustworthy men would carry these funds to Jerusalem, and he explained they would "...travel with us with this grace" (II Corinthians 8:19).

The definition of "grace" is more than "unmerited favor." In II Corinthians Chapter 8, Paul uses it to mean a discipline in giving. Whether for the first time, or to begin anew, now is the time to become disciplined in giving.

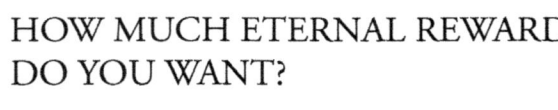

HOW MUCH ETERNAL REWARD DO YOU WANT?

II Corinthians 9:6

When my grandfather planted corn it was the norm to plant in rows forty-two inches apart and then every forty-two inches down the row. It yielded about forty to fifty bushels per acre. It was called "check corn" because of the checkerboard pattern. Planting corn today has evolved to planting in twenty inch rows, kernels nine inches apart, with yields often far greater than two hundred bushels per acre. If your goal is to reap as little crop reward as possible, you could still plant the old fashion way, or plant nothing at all. But, if you want a reward of the highest yield possible, it is necessary to plant a higher corn population.

As the Apostle Paul addresses the subject of proper Christian giving one last time in this epistle, he writes, "He which soweth sparingly shall reap also sparingly; and he which soweth bountifully shall reap also bountifully" (II Corinthians 9:6). Here, Paul is using the same example shared above about planting corn and volumes of yield. As he does, he adds three basic principles. First, when giving is done to the Lord it should be proportional with what God has given, but it must only be done willingly or "not grudgingly," but as a "cheerful giver" (vs. 7). If one cannot give willingly and cheerfully, one may as well not give as far as reaping an eternal reward. Therefore, we should seek to have the proper heart attitude when we give. Remembering the supreme loving sacrifice on the part of our Savior should help. Second, Paul tells us God is able to work in our circumstances that, even when we have less after giving, God can enable us to still have "...all sufficiency in all things" (vs. 8). Some view this as the Lord working to keep expenses down through making things last longer. Others view this explanation as the Lord working within to make us simply satisfied with less. Either way, God supplies. Third, when we do give to the Lord, we leave for ourselves a reward that will last "for ever" (vs. 9). First Timothy 6:19 describes it as: "Laying up in store a good foundation against the time to come...."

This principle of sowing and reaping is true no matter what we do for the Lord. *How much eternal reward do you want?* Someone once said, "Only one life will soon be past, only what's done for Christ will last." Consistently plant seed for eternal reward through proper giving.

OUR WEAPONS
II Corinthians 10:4

I have a cousin who, during the Vietnam War, was a special operations soldier. What he did was classified information, so he seldom talked about it and even then not in any detail. We do know he was dropped behind enemy lines to accomplish his missions, and we suspect that included Cambodia. When sent on missions, he had a number of weapons that were essential to his survival. He had a long-range rifle, utility-type knife, grenades and perhaps others that we still don't know about.

Whether we realize it or not, each of us who have trusted in the finished work of the Lord Jesus Christ as our only hope for eternal life are in a serious spiritual battle every day. Satan is "...the god of this world..." (II Corinthians 4:4). This world is Satan's present domain. We have, in effect, been dropped behind enemy lines to "wrestle...against...principalities, against powers, against the rulers of the darkness of this world, against spiritual wickedness in high places" (Ephesians 6:12). Thankfully, we are not left to engage in this warfare in our own strength. We have the indwelling Holy Spirit, and weapons to enable us to survive and win this battle. The Apostle Paul tells us: "For the weapons of our warfare are not carnal, but mighty through God to the pulling down of strongholds; casting down imaginations, and every high thing...against the knowledge of God, and bringing into captivity every thought to the obedience of Christ" (II Corinthians 10:4-5). *What could these weapons be?* They are the Word of God and prayer. Scripture is a "powerful" weapon (Hebrews 4:12) that has the miraculous ability to cleanse our thinking (Ephesians 5:26), renew our mind (Colossians3:10), and transform our lives (Romans 12:1-2). When we read it with a yielded heart, it can bring every thought into obedience to the Savior. We also have the weapon of instant access to the Lord in prayer. God helped Paul in his deep distress through the prayers of the saints (II Corinthians 1:8-11). He will help us too if we avail ourselves to this weapon.

You are behind enemy lines today. Don't leave home without the weapons of God's Word in your mind and prayer in your soul. If you already left home without being properly equipped, put on the armor of prayer right now. Then, spend time in the Word when you get home. Tomorrow, be sure not to leave the door without being fully equipped with both of these weapons.

MINISTRY ENVY
II Corinthians 10:10-13

I was saved in a large church whose pastor was dynamic in preaching and personality. When my heart was burdened to go into the ministry, I hesitated, thinking I would never be a man as capable as this pastor. While in college, it was my privilege to listen to a number of preachers who were extraordinary in their preaching skills, and again I thought I could never become what they were. During my years of ministry, I have met several outstanding preachers and prolific writers. This could have caused me to be discouraged, if not envious, unless I, like the Apostle Paul, embraced two important lessons.

Though Paul led the believers at Corinth to a saving knowledge of Christ, many were being disrespectfully rebellious toward him as God's Apostle of Grace. "For his letters, say they, are weighty and powerful; but his bodily presence is weak, and his speech contemptible" (II Corinthians 10:10). Perhaps they were comparing him to Apollos, "an eloquent man and mighty in the Scriptures" (Acts 18:24). At the very least, Paul had to rebuke the Corinthians for divided loyalties to men. He wrote them, saying, "Now this I say, that every one of you saith, I am of Paul, and I of Apollos, and I of Cephas, and I of Christ. Is Christ divided" (I Corinthians 1:12)? The reality was, Paul was not an eloquent man and few would have wanted him as their pastor. He admitted, "I be rude in speech" (II Corinthians 11:6) and that when with these believers, he "came not with excellency of speech" (I Corinthians 2:1). But two truths kept him faithful in ministry. He knew, "God hath distributed to us" the capabilities each of us have (II Corinthians 10:13). Therefore, all God expects us to do is our best, rather than being as successful as someone else. Then he embraced the principle: "For we dare not make ourselves of the number, or compare ourselves with some that commend themselves: but they measuring themselves by themselves, and comparing themselves among themselves, are not wise" (II Corinthians 10:12).

It is time for each of us to stop comparing ourselves with others, which only leads to envy and discouragement. God only expects you to do the best you can with the capabilities He has "distributed" to you. Simply be faithful with the time, abilities, and opportunities the Lord has entrusted to you, and choose to be content with these God-given blessings. Embrace this and simply be faithful.

FALLING AWAY
II Corinthians 11:3-4

A young man from my youth group came from a solid Christian family. His parents were very active in this doctrinally fundamental church and sacrificially sent all their children to a Christian school to bolster their faith. For four years, this young man attended a Christian college that stood for "fundamental doctrine." He heard a pure gospel hundreds, if not thousands, of times. While I never considered this young man to be very genuine or spiritually minded, I was surprised to learn from his father that he had become an Episcopal priest. When I asked, "How can this be? That church does not preach a gospel that will save anyone," his father just shrugged his shoulders.

When the Apostle Paul addressed the saints at Corinth, he expressed concern that they too might become spiritual casualties. He told them, "I fear, lest by any means, as the serpent beguiled Eve through subtlety, so your minds should be corrupted from the simplicity that is in Christ" (II Corinthians 11:3). As they do today, false teachers abounded at Corinth. Paul told them that he feared they "might well bear with him" [or them] (vs. 4). So he warns them of three doctrinal dangers. They must not accept "another Jesus, whom we have not preached" (vs. 4). Through fulfilled prophecies and dynamic miracles, the Lord Jesus Christ proved He is the Messiah of Israel and the only Savior of the world. The Corinthians must not listen to those denying Christ or promising another Jesus. Paul warned them not to receive "another spirit" (vs. 4). The word "spirit" can mean a principle, mental disposition, an angel, or the Holy Spirit. These believers had already received the indwelling Holy Spirit to seal them in Christ, to comfort and to guide into spiritual truth. There was an ongoing danger of accepting false teaching from demonic influences delivered by human false teachers. They must stand firm in Paul's teaching. Paul also feared they might endorse "another gospel, which ye have not received" (vs. 4). False teachers were promoting a false gospel of grace mixed with the Mosaic Law, or works, as they do today. The Corinthians, having trusted in Paul's gospel of grace apart from all works, were not to waver from this pure gospel, which is the only one that saves lost souls today.

Don't become a spiritual casualty by listening to false teachers, who proclaim a different gospel, savior or spirit of influence. Stay grounded in the doctrines delivered to us by the Apostle Paul.

CHRISTIANS ROBBING CHRISTIANS

II Corinthians 11:7-10

I once worked as a carpenter. When we decided to move out of state, I notified my boss of my last day at work. I had hoped he would have a check waiting for me at the job site, but he did not. Instead, he told me he would mail the check for my last week of wages. When I left that day, I had the sense I would never see that money, and I didn't. For all practical purposes, he knowingly and intentionally stole money from me that was properly due because I had worked for it.

I have known preachers who faithfully pastored their churches for decades while working both in ministry and in secular jobs simply to support their family. These jobs have included sales, carpentry, painting, printing, janitorial, window washing, self-employment, and more. These men have continued in ministry, often receiving little or nearly nothing, because they are serving the Lord and willingly serving the Lord's people. It is a great wrong when those receiving ministry fail to do their utmost to financially support those who invest their time, abilities, and faithfulness to minister to them. The Apostle Paul told the believers at Corinth that he had "preached to you the gospel of God freely" (II Corinthians 11:7). But he still had to eat, so he said, "I robbed other churches, taking wages of them, to do you service" (vs. 8). Paul did not literally rob other believers, but he did in the sense that he allowed dedicated believers from other locations to support him while those at Corinth, whom he was ministering to, did not. We wouldn't expect a mechanic, doctor, repairman, or painter to work on our behalf, without paying them. To do so would essentially be stealing from them. Yet, all too often, believers do not do all they can to pay those who minister to them. Paul asked, "If we have sown unto you spiritual things, is it a great thing if we shall reap your carnal things" (I Corinthians 9:11)? From Melchisedec to present day preachers of divine truth, God's design has always been for those receiving ministry to adequately financially support those who minister to them (I Corinthians 9:7-14).

Are you following God's design by doing the best you can to financially support those who minister to you? If not, now is the time to correct this wrong. If you have been paying them adequately, keep doing the right thing.

I LOVE YOU
II Corinthians 11:11

When I first met the lady who was to become my wife, within a few weeks I knew she was "the one." One day after a date, I took the coward's way out. I wrote to her thanking her for the time together and signed my letter: "Love, John." By this time, I knew I loved her and I longed to hear her confirm her love for me. But I had not yet worked up the courage to say that to her, so I signed my affection in a letter. I didn't expect much of a response, but the next day she boldly said, "I love you too."

In many grace circles and relationships, we often talk about love as a Christian standard and study about it. But it is somewhat uncommon for believers to personally and specifically communicate their love for one another. In contrast, it is noteworthy how many times the Apostle Paul boldly declares his love for the saints among whom he fellowshipped. He explained his motive for writing his first stern letter to the Corinthians by saying, "For out of much affliction and anguish of heart I wrote unto you with many tears; not that ye should be grieved, but that ye might know the love which I have more abundantly unto you" (II Corinthians 2:4). Our Apostle thought it was important that they knew he loved them and that any action taken related to them was based on that genuine love. Paul went on to explain the reason why he ministered to them without accepting any financial support. He asks: "Wherefore? Because I love you not? God knoweth" (II Corinthians 11:11). He ministered to them without any pay for two reasons: he loved them, and he wanted to remove further reasons for any offense. Later, he poured out his heart to them saying, "And I will very gladly spend and be spent for you, though the more abundantly I love you, the less I be loved" (II Corinthians 12:15). Though these believers often behaved poorly, Paul wanted them to know, no matter how they acted or reacted, it would not ill affect his love and sacrificial attitude toward them. He didn't want there to be any question in their minds that they were loved unconditionally and without ceasing.

Perhaps there would be greater harmony between believers if we too confirmed our love for one another. Surely someone needs to hear from you that they are loved. Tell them today.

A GAG ORDER
II Corinthians 12:1-4

We in America enjoy two important freedoms guaranteed to us by amendments to our constitution: the freedom of speech and freedom of the press. While these are vital to our way of life, it is not uncommon for a judge in a courtroom to order a "gag order" about a pending case. When so specified by the court, defendants, lawyers, victims, family members of victims, court officials, and even the press are absolutely forbidden from disseminating any information about the case. This is done to better insure a fair trial from an impartial jury.

The Apostle Paul refers to someone, presumably himself, who had been given, what amounts to, a divine gag order from the Lord. He states, "I knew a man in Christ…caught up to the third heaven…how that he was caught up into paradise, and heard unspeakable words, which it is not lawful for a man to utter" (II Corinthians 12:2-4). The word "paradise" means a park, garden, or place of future happiness. It is referred to here as the third heaven, above earth's atmosphere and outer space. It is the dwelling place of God. *Have you ever wondered why the Lord would not allow a vivid and detailed description of this place?* We already know our eternal dwelling place will be in "heavenly places" (Ephesians 2:6; 1:3). Once taken to heaven, we will have the utter joy to "ever be with the Lord" (Jesus, who ransomed us, I Thessalonians 4:17). We will be "raised [with] a spiritual body" (I Corinthians 15:44). We assume, like the kingdom saints in eternity, "there shall be no more death, neither sorrow, nor crying, neither shall there be any more pain: for the former things are passed away" (Revelation 21:4). I Corinthians 6:9 states plainly that sinners will not be present in heaven. Therefore, we conclude every child of God in heaven will experience freedom from the old nature and will finally be enabled to live apart from sin. We will be able to view the power, majesty, and indescribable beauty of God's throne (Revelation 4:1-6). Yet, all this information appears to be only the proverbial tip of the iceberg regarding how wonderful heaven will be.

Why are we not permitted to know more? Perhaps it is because we might lose focus on our earthly mission of serving Christ, hasten our departure, or to hinder Satan perverting our concepts of eternity. But we know enough to rejoice in these future riches, even today.

234

TITLES ARE IMPORTANT
II Corinthians 12:12

According to an Internet article in 2009,[1] Enrique Vela-Lopez and his wife, Ute Marquez, were arrested in Polk county Florida for practicing medicine without a license. Undercover detectives witnessed this couple using a device called an Asyra machine, far beyond it's authorized use, to diagnosis patients and prescribe treatment. They made far-reaching claims, including being able to cure cancer, all of which were simply exercises in fraud. These two perpetrators were fined, the public warned of their activities, and anyone learning of the use of an Asyra device was asked to contact law enforcement immediately.

If you use the title of M.D. after your name and claim to be a doctor, you better be qualified and capable to practice medicine with great skill. Likewise, one must be very careful about the kind of titles used under the umbrella of "ministry." We have a church in our town where the sign boasts their leader is both "Pastor and Apostle." In II Corinthians 12:12, Paul the apostle writes, "Truly the signs of an apostle were wrought among you in all patience, in signs, and wonders, and mighty deeds." The word "apostle" literally means "a sent one." It implies unmistakable divine direction and enablement from the Lord to go to a specific place for ministry. Examples would be when Paul was sent by God into Damascus by God's voice from heaven, (Acts 9), or when he was sent to Macedonia (Acts 16:9). For good reason, God uses this word on a very limited basis in Scripture. No one today is an apostle, and no one can properly claim such direction from the Lord today. Miraculous displays like these have ceased with the completion of God's Word, just as promised in I Corinthians 13:8-10. Moreover, today no one can properly claim "the signs of an apostle." When bitten by a venomous snake, Paul suffered no harm, and he was able to pray over the handkerchief of one very ill and have that person restored to full health instantaneously (Acts 19:11-12).

Beware of preachers who use titles other than "pastor," "preacher," "Bible teacher," or "elder." Likewise, beware of any who make claims of miracles. God wants our attention, confidence, and awe to be in His Word, not in men or some supposed emotional or miraculous experience. Satan will deceive us and lead us astray if our focus is not on His Word.

CHRIST LIVING INSIDE
II Corinthians 13:5

When I was six years old, my mother was pregnant with my youngest brother. I was told, "You're going to have a baby brother or sister, and that baby is inside mother's tummy." That was a difficult concept for me to grasp. It also generated a number of questions about how, when, and why all of this was going to take place. But I did understand it was an important event that was going to change our family dynamic.

Throughout the letters of the Apostle Paul, he expresses a somewhat parallel concept. In II Corinthians, he asks the question: "Know ye not your own selves, how that Jesus Christ is in you..." (13:5). When first declared to these saints, they too may well have been confused and had many questions. They had been taught the Lord Jesus Christ had died for their sins and rose again to ascend into heaven where He is presently seated on the right hand of the Father until He returns to rapture us into the heavens. *How then could He be within these often sinful believers at Corinth?*

Several passages further explain how Christ lives in believers today. Paul's description is, "that Christ may dwell in your hearts by faith..." (Ephesians 3:17). Christ lives within us *in a figurative sense* the moment we trust in Him alone for eternal salvation. He is still seated in the heavens but, as omnipresent God, He also lives within the heart of His children of faith. The moment we trust in Him, we are instantly "baptized into his death..." (Romans 6:3-4), His burial, and resurrection (8:9-11). Baptism by the Holy Spirit is an identification with His sacrifice for our sins and a new standing in His righteousness. So, we are in Him, identified with His righteousness, and He in our hearts by faith. But Christ is also in every believer through the person of the Holy Spirit. Paul explains, "But ye are not in the flesh, but in the Spirit, if so be that the Spirit of God dwelleth in you...and if Christ be in you...the Spirit is life because of righteousness" (Romans 8:9-10).

It is a marvelous truth that Christ, the Creator of the entire universe, lives in us today. We have the presence of God the Son within us everywhere we go. We are never alone. This truth gives us cause for rejoicing, holiness, constant fellowship with Christ, and service for His cause.

EXAMINE YOURSELF
II Corinthians 13:5

Author, Warren W. Wiersbe wrote about a teenager in a church he pastored, who frequently caused problems. When this teen went to a church youth camp, the leaders agreed to pray for him every day. At one of the meetings, this teen announced he had just gotten saved. Though he had been a member of the church and a participating musician, his profession of Christ had been a counterfeit. Thankfully, he trusted Christ at this camp and went on to serve the Lord faithfully.[1]

The Apostle Paul urged the Corinthians: "Examine yourselves, whether ye be the faith; prove your own selves" (II Corinthians 13:5). While perhaps the most carnal of the churches to which Paul wrote, he never questioned their collective salvation. Instead, he addressed them as "the church of God which is at Corinth, to them that are sanctified in Christ Jesus, called to be saints..." (I Corinthians 1:2). Their outward conduct was certainly not holy or set apart from sin. There was carnality, stunted spiritual growth, a lack of unity, boasting in horrendous immorality, and abuse of the Lord's Supper. Also, there was a persistent lack of love and a lack of support for those who ministered to them. But since God's program of grace for today is not a performance system, none of these dreadful descriptions meant that these believers were not truly saved. The Apostle Paul did not make that assumption about any professing believer on the basis of sinful behavior. Christians aren't perfect, they are just forgiven and in need of daily transformation through the power of the Holy Spirit and God's Word.

Nonetheless, Paul did urge them to "examine yourselves, whether ye be in the faith." One may be exposed to the gospel, regular messages from God's Word, good Christian influences, even be involved in ministry activity, and not be truly saved. Only the Lord and that individual truly know. Consistently causing problems may be an indication one has only a profession of Christ, but not a possession of salvation. Because eternal punishment is so grave, and eternal life so important, Paul urged each one to be certain they are truly saved. Dear reader, if you only been going through the motions of Christian activity without having genuinely trusting in Christ alone for eternal life, we urge you to do so right now. It is not worth risking eternal punishment by delaying even one more day. Other Christians will rejoice when they learn of your newfound faith in the Savior.

THE SON OF GOD
Hebrews 1:2-12

A pastor's son from a very large church lived in the dorm room adjacent to me during my sophomore college year. At the time he was a junior, so one would think maturity would have begun to set in, especially as a preachers kid. To my disappointment, this young man was quite aloof, condescending, and acted like he was better than everyone else. He largely epitomized the attitude of arrogance demonstrated in recent movies by children of the President of the United States, problem children who did not represent their father well.

The exact opposite is true of the Son of God, the Lord Jesus Christ. He always represented His Father well by conducting Himself as the supreme good example. God the Father's testimony of His Son was this: "Thou has loved righteousness, and hated iniquity; therefore God, even Thy God, hath anointed Thee with the oil of gladness above Thy fellows" (Hebrews 1:9). It is important for all to fully understand that the Lord Jesus Christ is the Son of God, or the second Person of the Trinity. Therefore, the Father says He "...hath in these last days spoken unto us by His Son, whom He appointed heir of all things" (1:2). He is "...the brightness of His [the Father's] glory, and the express image of His person..." (1:3). Because He is God, He is the one who is "...upholding [or maintaining] all things by the word of His power..." (1:3). After He "...by Himself purged our sins, [He] sat down on the right hand of the Majesty on high" (1:3). No mere mortal has this honor, only God the Son. When brought into the world in human form to redeem mankind, the Son of God was made "...so much better than the angels..." (1:4). Therefore, the Father instructed His holy angels saying, "...let all the angels of God worship Him" (1:6b). Further substantiating Christ's deity is Hebrews 1:8 which states, "But unto the Son he saith, Thy throne, O God, is for ever and ever; a scepter of righteousness is the scepter of Thy kingdom."

We who are mere mortal "sons of God" (Romans 8:19) must choose to love righteousness and hate evil as THE Son of God does. We must worship Him, not as "the man upstairs," but as God, and rejoice that He loved us enough to suffer and die for us. *As you go about your day, will it be your purpose to represent your Heavenly Father well?*

DON'T LET THEM SLIP
Hebrews 2:1

In her later years, my beloved mother took a long trip with me to a Christian family camp where I was speaking. On the way home she confided in me that one of her worst fears was that, as her health declined, she might not even remember her children or their names. Four years later, Alzheimer's had gradually stolen her independence, dignity, and memory. One of the last times I saw her, I sat across the table from her for some time. Then a caregiver introduced me to her, giving her my name. She looked at me so puzzled and confused that it was heartbreaking. Those things she held most dear had slipped away from her memory.

When the writer of Hebrews addressed Jewish believers who were waiting for the Lord Jesus Christ to return to establish His Millennial Kingdom, he warned them about one of his greatest fears. He said, "Therefore, we ought to give the more earnest heed to the things which we have heard, lest at any time we should let them slip..." (meaning to slip away from us, Hebrews 2:1). It is very likely this writer had in mind Israel's persistent history of forgetting Jehovah. The Lord repeatedly warned His people, that in times of blessing in the promised land of plenty, they must "...beware lest thou forget the Lord, which brought thee forth out of the land of Egypt, from the house of bondage" (Deuteronomy 6:12). Despite these warnings and God's instructions to "...take heed to thyself, and to keep thy soul diligently, lest thou forget the things which thine eyes have seen, and lest they depart from thy heart..." (Deuteronomy 4:9), they repeatedly forgot the Lord anyway. Isaiah told Israel, "...forgettest the Lord thy maker..." (Isaiah 51:13). Jeremiah described them as having "...perverted their way, and they have forgotten the Lord their God" (Jeremiah 3:21). The writer of Hebrews was concerned those in his day would likewise buckle under the pressures of persecution and turn away from their faith in the Lord Jesus as their Messiah. Therefore, he urged them not to let the truths they had embraced "slip" away from them.

Believers today need to likewise "hold fast the form of sound words" (II Timothy 1:13). A book could be written about those in our day who were once faithful but have let precious fundamental truths slip away by listening to errant teachers. Don't be one of them. Guard and cling to the dispensational truths taught by the Apostle Paul.

FEAR OF DEATH
Hebrews 2:14-15

Most people are simply afraid to die. But we know one stellar exception. When a godly Christian woman we knew was diagnosed with terminal cancer, her family was devastated. However, she told her loved ones: "Don't cry for me. I have no fear of dying and am ready to go. I know I'll be going to be with the Lord Jesus and saved family members who have gone before me. I'll be far better off, and I will see each of you again, so I welcome this time." When she passed away a few weeks later, it was a peaceful experience for her.

Those who know the Lord Jesus Christ as Savior and the confident assurance of eternal life beyond the grave have a comfort that can remove the fear of death. But those who have not trusted in Christ for forgiveness of sins and eternal life are chained to the bondage of fear in death. The writer of Hebrews explained that God the Son, the Lord Jesus Christ, came in the flesh "...that through death he might destroy him that had the power of death, that is, the devil; And deliver them who through fear of death were all their lifetime subject to bondage" (Hebrews 2:14-15). For those who know Christ as Savior, there need be no fear in death. But for those with no assurance of being spared God's eternal wrath over their sins, the fear of death is universal. Job 24:17 refers to the ungodly as being "...in the terrors of the shadow of death." David wrote of the wicked who often "prosper in the world; they increase in riches" (Psalm 73:12), while rejecting "the most High" (vs.11). David grew discouraged, knowing he had cleansed his heart before the Lord, yet his life was filled with troubles. But when he went to worship the Lord, he wrote, "...then understood I their end. Surely thou didst set them in slippery places; thou castest them down to destruction... in a moment! they are utterly consumed with terrors" (of death and eternal punishment–Psalm 73:17-19). Some who deny Christ describe death as "the great unknown" or say it is only to "rest in peace." In reality, even if they deny it, they fear death, the eternal wrath of God, and punishment for their sins.

Believer, you have been delivered from the bondage of fearing death. Look with comfort and confidence to being forever in the presence of the Savior once your earthly life is over.

SPIRITUALLY HARDENED
Hebrews 3:13

We once mentored a young man who was intelligent, articulate, and demonstrated a zeal for the things of the Lord. We provided him with teaching materials, teaching opportunities, many discussions in the Scriptures, and even took him to a national Bible conference. Then he began to dabble in sinful practices, eventually plunging into a variety of sins. While doing so, his interest in spiritual things first waned, until he completely fell away from the things of the Lord. When we tried to salvage him spiritually, it was already too late because his heart had been hardened by the practice of sin.

Like warning lights flashing on a railroad crossing bar, Hebrews 3:12-13 warns: "Take heed, brethren, lest there be in you an evil heart of unbelief, in departing from the living God. But exhort one another daily, while it is called Today; lest any of you be hardened through the deceitfulness of sin." It is noteworthy that this verse describes sin as being deceitful. The world, the flesh, and the devil all try to convince every heart, even in believers, that one will be better off living in sin. This deceit whispers in our hearts things like: "everyone else is doing it," "you won't get caught," "it will make you happier," "you deserve it," and "it will be worth it." But none of these are true. While one may experience "...the pleasures of sin for a season" (Hebrews 11:25), there will always be a high cost to sin. The practice of sin leaves one feeling empty, guilty, ashamed, and spiritually hardened, if persisted in. The deceitfulness of sin lures people without revealing to them that some sins lead to addiction, bankruptcy, or physical ruin. The deceitfulness of any sin robs the participant of spiritual peace, joy, satisfaction, and tenderness toward the Lord. The practice of sin replaces all of these good things with a spiritual hardness that wears on the soul and can often be seen on the face of those who walk apart from the Lord. The writer of Hebrews was instructing these Jewish believers to regularly band together, not only for worship, but also for exhorting one another to resist both the deceitfulness of sin and departing from walking "with the living God."

Dear believer, are you struggling with the deceitfulness of sin? Has your heart begun to be hardened to the importance of a close walk with the Lord and the standards of God's Word? Turn back to the Lord and away from your besetting sin.

REST FOR THE WEARY
Hebrews 4:3

There are two basic concepts about how to obtain eternal life. One is to work hard throughout life with good religious works to try to "tip the scales in your favor." But one can never rest in confidence that eternal life is yours. The other concept is to trust the risen, nail-scarred Savior, who purchased eternal life with His blood and offers it to us freely apart from all works, by trusting in Him alone. Those who trust in Christ find a confidence in their redemption based on the truths in Scripture.

In Hebrews 4:3, the writer stated a simple, but profound, truth: "For we which have believed enter into rest..." These words refer to the rest of eternal salvation. Verse 2 specifies, "the gospel [had been] preached," but with some it was not received "with faith in them that heard it." Verse 11 urged the readers to "enter into that rest, lest any man fall after the same example of unbelief." The gospel referred to here was the Gospel of the Kingdom, not today's Gospel of the Grace of God. Those who believed this gospel by faith had to believe that the Lord Jesus was the promised Messiah of Israel (John 1:49; 6:69; 11:27), confess their sins (Matthew 3:6), repent of their sins (Matthew 3:2), and be water baptized for the remission of sins (Matthew 3:6; Mark 1:4; Acts 2:38). Yes, these were "works" that God required to demonstrate their faith, just as described in James 2:21 and 24. Here the Jews were told, "Was not Abraham our father justified by works, when he had offered Isaac his son upon the altar?" "Ye see then how by works a man is justified and not by faith only." But even with these works, Jews still under the Law of Moses were given salvation on the basis of faith, as implied in Hebrews 4:2. Hebrews 4:10 described those who believed this gospel as having "...entered into His rest, he also hath ceased from his own works, as God did from His."

Our Gospel of Grace for today offers eternal life, through faith alone, apart from all works. Once received, we likewise enter into a rest from attempts to work our way to heaven. We also rest in the assurance of eternal life, God's love, and all spiritual blessings in Christ. But out of appreciation for salvation received, we are not to rest from serving Christ until He comes to take us to heaven.

GOD'S LIE DETECTOR
Hebrews 4:12-13

When two of our grandchildren were playing, the youngest started crying loudly and holding his head. When adults came to investigate, the oldest was asked, "Did you hit your brother?" The expected answer was, "No." But the proof of a crying child rubbing his head was right in front of us. So, a second question was asked of the oldest child: "Where did you hit your brother?" This time the sheepish answer was: "On the head." We learned that when you ask the right questions, in the right way, it can serve like a Lie-Detector machine that reveals the heart of the matter.

There is something far more powerful than a man-made machine, or even a mother's austere stare, to get to the truth of what lies within the heart of children of all ages. It is the Word of God. Hebrews 4:12-13 puts it this way: "For the Word of God is quick, and powerful, and sharper than any two edged sword, piercing even to the dividing asunder of soul and spirit, and of the joints and marrow, and is a discerner of the thoughts and intents of the heart. Neither is there any creature that is not manifest in his sight: but all things are naked and opened unto the eyes of him with whom we have to do." Our Bible is a miraculous book in the way God gave it, preserved it, and in how effectively it works within the heart. The above verses describe it as being "quick," meaning it is alive with divine ability to work in any soul. It is "powerful," or mighty, in its ability to convict or empower us to victory. It is "sharp," like a surgical instrument that can easily cut or penetrate hardened souls. It cuts away foolish rebellion better than logic, our testimony, or tears. The Scriptures are able to pierce the soul (the seat of our emotions), spirit (the mind or intellect), and even tough joints and marrow. It can get to the inner man of the unsaved who stubbornly resists salvation, or to the saved not in a proper spiritual place. God's Word discerns and reveals our thoughts and motives, and exposes everyone, as if naked, before the Lord, who is the author of this miraculous book.

These truths enable believers to place confidence in God's Word, use it generously when ministering to the unsaved, and respond when it speaks to our hearts. We encourage you to read God's Word every day.

COME BOLDLY
Hebrews 4:16

Ancient subjects of kings did not presume to come before him, unless they were summoned. This was true even of Esther, the wife of a king. When her people, the Jews, were in danger of being exterminated, Esther's uncle tried to convince her to take this matter before the king. Her response was, "All the king's servants, and the people...do know, that whosoever, whether man or woman, shall come unto the king into the inner court, who is not called, there is one law of his to put him to death, except such to whom the king shall hold out the golden scepter, that he may live: but I have not been called to come into the king..." (Esther 4:11).

The nation of Israel had an even graver fear of coming before the Lord. They had witnessed His power and glory. When given the Ten Commandments, "...the people saw the thunderings, and the lightenings, and...the mountain smoking...they removed, and stood afar off. And they said unto Moses, Speak thou with us, and we will hear, but let not God speak with us, lest we die...And Moses drew near unto the thick darkness where God was" (Exodus 20:18-21). They knew they were sinful, unworthy to be in the presence of their holy God, and that He could smite them with death in an instant. Therefore, they were extremely hesitant to come before the Lord even in worship. It is with this background that the writer of Hebrews tells his fellow Jews about their permanent "high priest," the Lord Jesus Christ, who has "passed into the heavens" (Hebrews 4:14), who "...ever liveth to make intercession for them" (Hebrews 7:25). It is with this in mind that they were given the invitation: "Let us therefore come boldly unto the throne of grace, that we may obtain mercy, and find grace to help in time of need" (Hebrews 4:16). Because of Christ, they could now come before the presence of God in prayer in the bold confidence they would find divine mercy and help in all areas of life. What a contrast, what a privilege, and what an encouragement.

While the above verses were written to Jews still under the Law of Moses, the same principle is true for us today under grace. We too "...have boldness and access with confidence by the faith of Him" (Ephesians 3:12). Don't fear taking your needs to the Lord, nor deprive yourself of His help. Take advantage of prayer constantly!

UNSKILLFUL IN GOD'S WORD
Hebrews 5:11-14

When our oldest grandchild was two years old, within a short time, he could operate our iPad far better than I could. It was just amazing to watch him flip through the screens from one application to another, master different children's games, and access the pictures of the family. In short order, he was able to show some of the adults how to make this electronic gadget work. We were amazed at how adept he became with all this. I, on the other, am so unskilled in such things that I can only fumble around in frustration.

The book of Hebrews was written several years after the resurrection and ascension of the Lord Jesus Christ. There had been an ample amount of time for these believers to grow in their capabilities with the Scriptures that applied directly to them. Unfortunately, they had not grown beyond a very elementary understanding. In fact, they were still not grounded in even basic and essential doctrines. Therefore, Hebrews 5:12-13 states, "For when for the time ye ought to be teachers, ye have need that one teach you again which be the first principles of the oracles of God; and are become such as have need of milk, and not of strong meat. For everyone that useth milk is unskillful in the word of righteousness: for he is a babe." There were three things that caused such a lack of spiritual growth. Verse 11 says that they were "dull of hearing." They simply *did not have enough interest* in the things of the Lord to want to be under the teaching of God's Word. This is why they needed to be urged to "not (continue) forsaking the assembling of ourselves together, as the manner of some is…" (Hebrews 10:25). Just as we do today, believers were meeting weekly, and in many cases daily, to study, worship, and be encouraged in the Lord. But, *apathy* was keeping them from this needed time. They were also *not spending adequate time* in the Scriptures themselves. They could only digest the milk of God's Word, because "strong meat belongeth to them…who by reason of use have their [spiritual] senses exercised to discern both good and evil" (Hebrews 5:14).

Don't let these verses describe you. Cast away apathy. Make time to study God's Word yourself every day. Then faithfully place yourself under the sound teaching of God's Word at a local church that proclaims a clear gospel and the right division of the Scriptures.

GATHERED TO BE BURNED

Hebrews 6:8

As a youngster, one of my jobs in the summer was to gather thistles out of the pasture. These weeds are very thorny, so you couldn't just easily pull them. Instead, I dug them up by the root with a spade, loaded them into the pickup with a pitchfork, took them far away, doused them with gasoline, and burned them. With so many thistles in a large pile, it was quite a sight to see them burn as the black smoke billowed upward.

The book of Hebrews was written as a warning to the Jews in the Acts era about "eternal judgment" (Hebrews 6:2). As the author appealed to his fellow Jews to fully embrace faith in Christ and to remain faithful, he uses an illustration of the earth drinking in rain to produce herbs that are profitable. Then he says, "But that which beareth thorns and briers is rejected, and is nigh unto cursing; whose end is to be burned" (Hebrews 6:8). These words are a direct reference to what will happen to all lost souls in eternal judgment. In Matthew 13:37-43, the Lord Jesus Christ described lost souls as "the tares," or weeds, a coming harvest at "the end of the world; and the reapers are the angels." "The tares are [or will be] gathered and burned in the fire...And shall cast them into a furnace of fire: there shall be weeping and gnashing of teeth." Matthew 13:49-50 confirms this process by saying, "So shall it be at the end of the world: the angels shall come forth, and sever the wicked from among the just. And shall cast them into the furnace of fire; there shall be wailing and gnashing of teeth." There will never be any reprieve for those who suffer eternal punishment. The Savior warned that, in hell, "the fire is not [or will never be] quenched" (Mark 9:48), and those there are described as being in constant "torment" (Luke 16:23-24). All lost souls will be "tormented with fire and brimstone...And the smoke of their torment ascendeth up for ever...and they have no rest day or night" (Revelation 14:10-11).

These descriptive warnings are intended to prompt lost souls to trust in Christ alone and to motivate the saved to urgently share the gospel that can spare others this dreadful fate. If you've never trusted in Christ apart from all works, please do so right now. If you know Christ as Savior, please share the gospel with someone today.

WHAT GOD CANNOT DO
Hebrews 6:18

Why is it that witnesses in a court proceeding are always sworn in with the words: "Do you solemnly swear that the testimony you are about to give will be the truth, the whole truth, and nothing but the truth so help you God?" It is because all mankind has the tendency to be devious and to outright lie. We simply cannot be trusted to always tell the truth. Therefore, under threat of imprisonment for perjury, it is a necessity for witnesses to agree to a solemn oath of truthfulness.

As the author of Hebrews refers to the promise of eternal life, he too refers to "an oath" (Hebrews 6:17). He was reminding his fellow Jews: "God made [a] promise to Abraham" (vs. 13). Specifically, God promised Abraham that He would make of him "a great nation," bless him, "make thy name great; and thou shalt be a blessing; And I will bless them that bless thee, and curse him that curseth thee; and in thee shall all families of the earth be blessed" (Genesis 12:2-3). It is important for us to realize that inherent in the above promise was also the promise of eternal life. We learn from Titus 1:2 that the "hope of eternal life...[was given] before the world began." Paul explained to the Jews that God had promised a resurrection from the dead "unto [all] the fathers" (of Israel–Acts 13:28-34). It was primarily this promise of a resurrection to eternal life that the author of Hebrews referred to when he pointed back to Abraham as an example of God always fulfilling all of His promises. This promise of eternal life served as "an anchor of the soul, both sure and steadfast" (Hebrews 6:19). But the rock into which the anchor of confidence rested was God's oath. *What was this oath?* It was His steadfast promise that "it was impossible for God to lie" (Hebrews 6:18). Man can and does lie. In contrast, because God is righteous and holy, He gave us His oath that He cannot lie. That means His promise of resurrection to eternal life, to those who receive it by faith alone, is steadfast and sure. Moses wrote saying, Jehovah is a "God of truth." David sang to God: "thy words be true" and the Lord "keepeth truth forever" (II Samuel 7:28; Psalm 146:6).

If you've trusted in Christ alone, never waver in your confidence of eternal life. "God, that cannot lie" promised it (Titus 1:2).

KING OF PEACE
Hebrews 7:1-3

As I approached my senior year in high school, the Vietnam War was raging with American soldiers dying there every day. I knew within a year, I could be on the battlefield myself. This brought to the forefront of my thinking the question: *"Where I would spend eternity?"* I had no peace about the answer. As I began to search for someone who could give me assurance of eternal life, I found a fundamental church. They explained that Christ died for my sins, and I could have eternal life as a free gift by trusting in Christ alone, apart from all works. The day I trusted in this simple message, I had the flood of peace and joy that I had been searching for.

Hebrews Chapter 7 refers to Melchisedec, King of Salem, to whom Abraham "gave a tenth part of all" as an offering in worship (vs. 1-2). Although Melchisedec was a human king, he was a type of Christ because the Scriptures offer no record of his father or mother, his "beginning of days" (when he was born), nor a record of his "end of days" (vs. 3). Therefore, in these ways, he was "made like unto the Son of God" (vs. 3b). It is in this context that Hebrews 7:2 refers to Melchisedec as "King of peace" (vs. 3). Abraham found peace when he worshipped Jehovah by giving Melchisedec a tithe in worship. Peace with God has always been the pressing need of man. We learn from Psalm 7:11 that "God is angry with the wicked every day." Sinners, who have not yet received justification from their sins by faith, are in constant danger of being ushered into eternity where they will experience the wrath of God through eternal punishment. The only way to escape eternal punishment is through faith in Christ, who bore our sins on Calvary. Isaiah promised peace to Israel through their Messiah when he foretold the following: "He was wounded for our transgressions...the chastisement of our peace was upon Him." Peter went to Israel "preaching peace by Jesus Christ" to any Jew who would trust in their Redeemer (Acts 10:37). Now in our new Dispensation of Grace, Paul assures all who trust in Christ alone are "justified by faith, we have peace with God through our Lord Jesus Christ" (Romans 5:1).

The Lord Jesus "made peace [with God on our behalf] through the blood of His cross" (Colossians 1:20). Trust in Christ alone and you too can have peace with God.

248

LEVITICAL PRIESTHOOD CHANGED
Hebrews 7:11-24

We have a very close friend who was raised with a strong loyalty to the Catholic Church. Everyday she faithfully prayed the rosary, made the sign of the cross, and went to mass. She also "religiously" confessed her sins to a priest each week. All this was her devoted pattern for decades until someone shared the gospel of grace with her and she was wonderfully saved. Subsequently, she learned and embraced the grace message, seeing the difference between instructions to Israel and the Body of Christ. These truths brought a radical change, from the previous bondage of religious rituals, to the freedom of following Christ under the liberating principles of grace.

In Hebrews Chapter Seven, the author explained a dynamic change in proper worship for Israel even while still under the Law of Moses. Because the "...Levitical priesthood..." was not perfect, there was a "...need...that another priest should arise after the order of Melchisedec, and not after the order of Aaron" (Hebrews 7:11). In other words, the priesthood ministering to Israel had been "...changed, (and) there is made of necessity a change also of the law" (vs. 12). The change that took placed replaced the priesthood of the tribe of Levi with the priesthood of the Lord Jesus Christ. The weakness of the Levitical priesthood was not only that mere human priests inherently practiced sin, but also their ministry was eventually limited by physical death. However, God the Father ordained the new priesthood of Christ "after the power of an endless life" (vs. 16). Those in the Levitical priesthood could not continue in ministry "...by reason of death" (vs. 23), but the Lord Jesus "continueth [for]ever" having "an unchangeable priesthood" because "...He ever liveth to make intercession for them" (vss. 24-25). This information about a new priesthood in Christ was intended to move saved Jews to worship Jehovah in a new way. Instead of worshipping through the Levitical priesthood, they now were to worship God directly through the priesthood of the Lord Jesus Christ. Moreover, they were to do so in the confidence that the Savior was "...able to save them to the uttermost..." (vs. 25).

Likewise, Christians today no longer need any human priesthood to worship the Lord. We are to worship God directly through the person of the Lord Jesus and are free from all religious rituals. We are also to live changed lives of godliness, devotion, and consistency as we expect His return at the Rapture. *Are you changing in these ways?*

FAR BETTER
Hebrews 8:6-13

Dealerships used to lure customers with advertisements of trade-in values for old vehicles. If you could "push, pull, or tow" your car onto their property, you were "guaranteed" a good value toward the purchase of a new car. We once literally towed an old worn-out car into a dealership, and we left with a new car that was, without question, far better than the one we traded in.

Hebrews Chapters 7 and 8 refer to things that are far "better." Because the Levitical priesthood was not perfect, Jehovah established a *better eternal priesthood* in the person of the Lord Jesus Christ (Hebrews 7:14-17, 22-23, 26-28). The priesthood of the Savior is able to save anyone "to the uttermost that come to God by Him" (Hebrews 7:25). Israel was also given *"a better covenant"* (Hebrews 8:6). The word "covenant" means a contract that God made with Israel. Early in the Old Testament, God made a covenant with the Jews that if they would faithfully follow His commands, He would greatly bless them. But if they refused to obey and walked in waywardness, He would curse them with divine judgment that would make their lives miserable (Deuteronomy 11:26-28). Hebrews 8:6 explained God had given Israel a "better covenant" which is identified as "a new covenant with the house of Israel" (vs. 8). Because the Jewish people had been so consistently disobedient and wayward, they were not experiencing God's blessings and joy. There was nothing wrong with their old covenant. The problem was with constantly failing human beings in Israel. Therefore, God promised He would one day make a new covenant, wherein Israel will be supernaturally enabled to walk in godliness because He would write His "...law in their inward parts...[and] in their hearts..." (Jeremiah 31:31-33; Hebrews 8:10-12). This will ultimately happen in the Millennial Kingdom, but Hebrews 8:13 was explaining they already had a taste of this in early Acts. Their old covenant was "<u>ready</u> to vanish away." They were to anticipate the new covenant, wherein they would be supernaturally enabled to live apart from sin.

The Apostle Paul tells us we are "...able ministers of the new testament [or covenant]; not of the letter [given to Israel], but of the spirit..." (II Corinthians 3:6). We are to joyously live in expectation of living completely apart from sin in eternity. This will be "far better" than our daily experience now. In the mean time, *are you to genuinely seeking to live apart from sin?*

A BOTHERED CONSCIENCE
Hebrews 9:9-16

In 2002, Reese Witherspoon starred in the movie *Sweet Home Alabama*. It was a romantic comedy about a married couple that had split up but eventually got back together. Within the lyrics of the theme song are the words: "Now Watergate does not bother me. Does your conscience bother you?" Through the ages, many have been greatly bothered by their conscience when they know they have committed sin.

Under the Law of Moses, each year the high priest went into the Holy of Holies to offer the blood of an animal sacrifice for the sins of the nation of Israel. This system was "imposed on them until the time of reformation" (Hebrews 9:10). The Lord required this system of worship until something far better would eventually replace it. Beyond this annual shedding of blood, there were also individual regular sin offerings required that literally kept the fire upon the altar going continually. We learn from Hebrews 9:9 that these "...gifts and sacrifices...could not make him that did the service perfect, as pertaining to the conscience." *Why?* It was because "...in those sacrifices there is a remembrance again made of sins every year" (Hebrews 10:3). These sacrifices became a nagging reminder to their conscience of how constantly sinful they were. Knowing this, Jehovah always intended to reform this system with a better one. When the Lord Jesus Christ died for the sins of all mankind, "...by His own blood He entered in once into the holy place [in the heavenly tabernacle], having obtained eternal redemption for us" (Hebrews 9:12,23-24). God told Israel, Christ's "once for all" (Hebrews 10:10) sacrifice was able to "...purge your conscience from dead works to serve the living God" (Hebrews 9:14). These Hebrew believers were being encouraged to know that Jehovah was permanently satisfied with the blood of His Son as the covering for their sins. Therefore, their conscience need not bother them with ongoing accusations of guilt.

This principle is even clearer in Paul's letters: "...We have redemption through His blood, the forgiveness of sins..." making us "accepted in the Beloved" (Ephesians 1:6-7). Therefore, our conscience need not continually condemn us. However, God still uses our conscience to convict us if we are callously indulging in sinful behavior. *Does your conscience bother you?* When it does, embrace permanent acceptance in Christ, but immediately stop sinful behavior.

THE NECESSITY OF A BLOOD SACRIFICE

Hebrews 9:22

On April 15th, 2013, Dzhokhar Tsarnaev and his brother perpetrated a devastating bombing attack during the running of the Boston Marathon. Three people were killed and 264 people were seriously injured. Once captured, Tsranaev was easily proven guilty. For many of the families of those terrorized or killed, the only just punishment would be a death for such a heinous, heartless, and unprovoked crime.

Hebrews 9:22 defines the just consequences for sins required for Jews under the Law of Moses: "And almost all things are by the law purged with blood; and without [the] shedding of blood is no remission [of sin]." There were two exceptions. When Aaron symbolically placed the sins of Israel on the "scapegoat" and released it into the wilderness, he had to thoroughly wash, or cleanse, his body before reentering the camp (Leviticus16:21-26). By association with sin, he was unclean. When Israel returned with spoils from battle, they had to purify their bounty of gold and silver with fire, then wash themselves and women captives "with the water of separation" before reentering the camp (Numbers 31:13-24). Here too, contact with sin required cleansing. In all other instances, a perfect animal sacrifice had to suffer and die. Then its blood had to be offered before one's sins would be covered and the individual made acceptable to God. This blood shed on behalf of the guilty party was "...sprinkled both [on] the book [of the law], and all the people...and all the vessels of the ministry" (Hebrews 9:19-21). Ultimately, these animal sacrifices represented and looked forward to the Lord Jesus, whose blood would permanently cover sins. *But why did God require the death and blood of an innocent victim to atone for sin?* This writer believes it is in part, to convey to everyone the wretchedness of sin before THE Holy God and the seriousness of sin's consequences.

Those who have been "justified by His blood" (Romans 5:9), and have received "...the forgiveness of sins, according to the riches of His grace" (Ephesians 1:7), should be forever grateful for the supreme sacrifice of our Savior. Moreover, we should always remember: "...Ye are bought with a price: therefore glorify God in your body, and in your spirit, which are God's" (I Corinthians 6:20). We must never allow ourselves to callously practice the wretchedness of any sinful behavior. Instead, by God's grace, we must seek to live apart from sin and unto the one who died for us and rose again.

WHAT'S GOING TO HAPPEN NEXT?
Hebrews 9:27

Years ago, with three painful, degenerating disks in my lower back, I took a bad fall which made it much worse. Subsequently, I had the flu, which developed into pneumonia. Then I was diagnosed with a progressive cornea disease that caused a considerable reduction in vision. Finally, in frustration, I exclaimed to my wife, "What's going to happen next?"

In God's timetable of human events two things are absolutely certain. Hebrews 9:27 tells us: "...It is appointed unto men once to die, but after this the judgment." Every human soul will experience death. The only exception may be those taken in the Rapture. Believers and unbelievers who die prior to the Rapture will all experience the usual painful departure of death. Then, for every soul, their judgment before God will follow. Chronologically, believers in the Body of Christ will be the first to experience judgment by the Lord Jesus Christ. "...We shall all stand [in respect and soberness] before the judgment seat of Christ," where every believer will "give account...to God" (Romans 14:10,12). There will be no punishment here, but there will be accountability, resulting in reward and loss of reward. The next in sequence will be kingdom saints who will be resurrected at the close of the seven years of Tribulation. They will come before Christ, after His second coming to rule on earth, "When the Son of Man shall...sit upon the throne of His glory" (Matthew 25:31). These saints with an earthly hope (from Abraham through mid-Acts and the Tribulation) will be resurrected and ushered into the Millennial Kingdom. However, they will first be judged to determine their rewarded positions. Finally, after the final rebellion of man at the close of the Millennial reign of Christ, all lost souls of all time will be assembled at the Great White Throne of Judgment. There, Christ as Judge will sentence these lost souls to the unending torment of the Lake of Fire (Revelation 20:10-15). Their persistence in sin and refusal to receive the righteousness by faith in Christ will result in eternal punishment.

Those who are wise will prepare for a time of future judgment. If you have never placed your trust in the payment Christ made for your sins, apart from all works, we urge you to trust in Christ today. If you already know Christ as Savior, we urge you to live each day with the Judgment Seat of Christ in view: in faithfulness, purity, sincerity, and service for the cause of Christ. Be prepared.

FORSAKING THE LOCAL CHURCH
Hebrews 10:23-25

Nearly every preacher has heard dozens of times: "I don't need to go to church to worship God." The truth is, those who refrain from attending any local church seldom worship the Lord in any form. Moreover, it is highly significant that sincere believers, from both the Jewish Kingdom program and the Body of Christ, inherently gathered together for regular worship. Additionally, every letter written by the Apostle Paul was written either to a local church or the leader of a local church. This emphasizes that it is God's design for His children to regularly link themselves to a sound local church, if at all possible.

Nonetheless, it was necessary for the author of Hebrews to write to the Kingdom saints, urging them "Not [to be among them who are] forsaking the assembling of ourselves together, as the manner of some is; but exhorting one another: and so much the more, as ye see the day approaching" (Hebrews 10:25). *Why was it then, and why is it now, important to have regular fellowship, partnership, and ministry in a local church?* Verse 25 describes the local church as a place of exhortation. The word "exhorting" means to call one near, comfort, entreat, or pray. Every one of us needs a place to belong with others. We all need comfort, understanding, and support in times of hardship or sorrow. God's design is to help meet these needs through a regular partnership in a local church. These Jewish believers were urged to be even more faithful to the local church as they saw "the day approaching." For them, this meant the hardships of the tribulations prior to the return of Christ in His Second Coming. We in the Body of Christ will be raptured out of this world before the Tribulation begins. As we see world events paving the way for the coming of the Anti-Christ, we too should be more faithful to the encouragements found in the local church. It is God's plan to use the interaction within the local church to "provoke [or encourage one another] unto love and to good works" (Hebrews 10:24). It is also this constant contact with sincere believers, and time together in God's Word that encourages us to "hold fast the profession of our faith without wavering…" (vs. 23).

All of us need these positive benefits of the local church. If you've stopped attending, now is the time to begin again and become an example in faithfulness.

AN ENDURING SUBSTANCE
Hebrews 10:34

A couple years ago we purchased a new vehicle. To us, it looked so pretty and had that great new car smell. We were careful to keep it garaged, washed, and waxed. Most of the time we parked further from the store to minimize damage by others. But it wasn't long before we saw a huge ding where someone had opened their door into our car. Soon after, there was a large scrape from a shopping cart. Then a chip appeared in the front of the car from gravel. In short order, that thing we had highly prized didn't look sharp anymore. *Does this sound familiar?*

As the author of Hebrews wrote to encourage Jewish saints to remain faithful to the Lord in their daily walk; he pointed out something to highly motivate them. He said: "...ye have in heaven a better and an enduring substance" (Hebrews 10:34). The word "substance" means an existing property, wealth, or goods. The connotation is that these believers had a tangible eternal reward that they should highly prize. Moreover, unlike our earthly treasures, eternal reward endures without tarnish, blemish, or decay. Peter described it as "...an inheritance incorruptible, and undefiled, and that fadeth not away, reserved in heaven for you" (I Peter 1:4). These encouragements came after the Lord Jesus Christ urged His Kingdom followers to not be concerned with amassing earthly treasure. He told them: "...lay up for yourselves treasures in heaven, where neither moth nor rust doth corrupt, and where thieves do not break through nor steal" (Matthew 6:20). *How were they to lay up these eternal enduring rewards?* The Savior told them: "Blessed are ye, when men shall revile you, and persecute you, and shall say all manner of evil against you falsely, for My sake. Rejoice, and be exceeding glad: for great is your reward in heaven..." (Matthew 5:11-12). We in the Dispensation of Grace are to be similarly motivated to faithfulness by eternal reward. We are urged to not build our lives after salvation with perishable things that will be burned at the Bema Seat (I Corinthians 3:12-15). Instead, we are to build with gold, silver, and precious stones in the sense of living for the cause of Christ, and to set our affections now on "things above, not on things on the earth" (Colossians 3:1-2).

My fellow believer, we need to be purposely earning eternal reward by doing something specific to further the cause of Christ. *What will you do today?*

ASHAMED OF YOU
Hebrews 11:10-16

One of the most devastating things in my childhood was something my parents told me. After very poor behavior on my part, they scolded me sternly. Then they said: "I'm ashamed of you. You know better than to act like that." Like any other child, I wanted to hear their praises and wanted them to be proud of me. Hearing those words crushed my spirit, but those words also motivated me toward better behavior.

There is a profound statement in Hebrews 11:16: "...God is not ashamed to be called their God...." The author is referring to several of the Old Testament saints of Israel. Righteous Able is the first to be mentioned (vs. 4). God had revealed to Adam and his sons that the true way to worship Jehovah was through the blood sacrifice of a perfect, yet innocent, animal. By faith, Able offered the correct sacrifice, and it cost him his life as his brother angrily slew him in jealousy because God accepted his worship. Enoch "pleased God" (vs. 5) by having a daily personal walk in fellowship with the Lord. Consequently, he grew in his faith and God rewarded him by translating him to heaven without seeing death. Noah became "...heir of the righteousness which is by faith..." when he obediently built an ark. II Peter 2:5 refers to Noah as "a preacher of righteousness," because while building that ark for over a hundred years, he proclaimed faith in Jehovah to an unbelieving and scoffing world. Hebrews 11:16-17 refers to Abraham as one about whom the Lord was not ashamed. God promised him a son from whom the Lord would make a great nation. Abraham had to wait over 25 years to see God's promise of a son fulfilled. Nonetheless, Abraham obeyed and left his native land, though he didn't know where God was leading him. He did not know how God would fulfill His promise of a son because Abraham and Sarah were past childbearing years. But he still believed God's promise by faith (Romans 4:13-25). Even though he did not understand why, Abraham obeyed years later when God told him to sacrifice his son, who was a miraculous provision.

All these saints demonstrated genuine faith in God's promises and obedience to His instruction. It is no surprise that God was not ashamed to be called their God. Likewise, if you seek to demonstrate faith, godliness, and obedience to the Lord, He will not be ashamed to be called your God.

A BETTER RESURRECTION
Hebrews 11:24-35

When I was a young man with children still at home, a wise retired couple gave me some valuable advice. In order to provide for their present needs and future retirement, the two of them had worked for many years at Boeing. Through all those years, they followed a simple financial rule. They told me: "Always pay yourself (into a retirement investment) first, before you take anything out of your pay check. If you don't do it first, it will likely never get done." They wisely sacrificed some indulgences they wanted as they went through life in order to be able to enjoy a better retirement.

God gives us a number of examples of saints who lived in dedicated ways that "...they might obtain a better resurrection" (Hebrews 11:35). Moses was raised in the palace of Egypt with all the privileges, pleasures, and power anyone could desire. Yet "...when he was come to years, [he] refused to be called the son of Pharaoh's daughter...esteeming the reproach of Christ greater riches than the treasures of Egypt..." (vss. 24-26). After hearing how Jehovah miraculously protected and prospered the nation of Israel, the harlot Rahab demonstrated the righteousness of faith. She "received the [Jewish] spies with peace," rather than siding with her spiritually rebellious people (vss. 31). With fearful reservations (about God using him to deliver Israel from their enemies), Gideon obeyed the Lord's instructions to lead his people in battle, thereby stepping into harm's way (vs. 32). David refused to do wrong by defending himself against murderous King Saul. Then he went on to walk closely with the Lord, continually read the Scriptures, surrounded himself with godly people, and influenced his nation for Jehovah. Samuel was God's fearless and dedicated prophet, boldly proclaiming the Lord's message to king and commoner alike, at great personal sacrifice (vs. 32). Others are referred to, "who through faith...wrought righteousness... quenched the violence of fire...out of weakness were made strong...were tortured, not accepting deliverance; that they might obtain a better resurrection" (vss. 33-35).

We often hear believers resolve to being "a street sweeper" or "cleaning out stables" in eternity. While this won't be the condition of any in the heavens, we must not have such meager aspirations. Follow the example of those before us who so lived to obtain a better resurrection. By the grace of God, seek to be all that you should be now for Christ.

LAY ASIDE THE WEIGHT
Hebrews 12:1-3

While training for athletic competition in high school, the coach had us strap weights to our ankles. Then we ran laps, ran the bleachers in the gym, and even wrestled one another. The extra weight made our legs feel much heavier and slowed us down. But when we were allowed to take the weights off, it was amazing how light our legs felt and how much faster we could move!

Hebrews 12:1-2 urged the Jewish believers: "...let us lay aside every weight, and the sin which doth so easily beset us, and let us run with patience the race that is set before us, looking unto Jesus the author and finisher of our faith...." *What kinds of things were weighing down these Jewish believers?* Some had become "dull of hearing" when it came to listening to the teaching of God's Word (Hebrews 5:11). Some had lost their interest in spiritual things. Their salvation had lost its luster, and, perhaps, like Demas, the lure of worldly things had stolen their affections. They were being urged to lay these things aside and get on track with walking with the Lord. Others may have been ill influenced by too much contact with "scoffers" (II Peter 3:3), who walked "after their own lust," denied divine creation, and ridiculed the promises of eternal life. In any age, it is foolishness to spend very much time with those who reject a genuine interest in the Lord or ridicule the fundamentals of our faith. They will slowly choke the spiritual life out of sincere believers. Apparently, some were once bold in their witness but had grown discouraged when persecutions came. They were told: "...think it not strange concerning the fiery trial...as though some strange thing happened unto you" (I Peter 4:12). Clearly, there were also those practicing sin that had dulled their spiritual senses and chilled their heart to Christ. All these people were urged to strip off their particular weight that they too "might obtain a better resurrection" (Hebrews 11:35). They, as we, were to be motivated to a higher walk by remembering how much Christ had "endured" for them (Hebrews 12:3), and be empowered by "...looking unto Jesus..." for their strength (vs. 2).

Dear believer, do you have a sinful weight that is making it harder for you to run the daily race of life for Christ in a way that honors Him? Whatever it is, lay it aside today "...lest ye be wearied and faint in your minds" (vs. 3).

RESPECT AND OBEDIENCE
Hebrews 12:7,17

This writer grew up in an era where respect for others was taught and demanded. We never addressed our parents by their first name. We were taught to always use the title "Aunt" or "Uncle" preceding a relative's first name. A teacher was always referred to as "Mr.," "Mrs.," or "Miss" preceding their last name. A doctor or pastor was never referred to without his title. In the 1960's, Aretha Franklin had a hit song with lyrics that said: "R-E-S-P-E-C-T, find out what it means to me." The Lord instructs us to show respect to church leaders, and it is important for each of us to find out what that means to Him.

Just as we are privileged to have elders and pastors lead our local assemblies today, the Jewish churches in the Acts era did too. They were instructed: "Remember them which have the rule over you, who have spoken unto you the Word of God: whose faith follow, considering the end of their conversation" (Hebrews 13:7). It may surprise many, but God's work was never intended to be a democracy! Citizens in the U.S. exercise limited voting rights, but congregational voting is an inherent mistake in the local church. God's design for every assembly has always been to use multiple men who are "apt to teach" (I Timothy 3:2), and skilled enough in the Scriptures to "...have their senses exercised to discern both good and evil" (Hebrews 5:14). With the demonstration of spiritual strength, biblical wisdom, and godliness, leaders are to "rule over" (Hebrews 12:7; I Thessalonians 5:12) the local assembly with a humble servant's attitude. But the people are to "obey them that have the rule over you [in the church], and submit yourselves, for they watch for your souls..." (Hebrews 13:17). Paul states the same principle, saying, we are to "...esteem them very highly in love for their work's sake..." (I Thessalonians 5:13). Hebrews 13:7 states believers are also to observe their godly "conversation," or manner of life, and follow their example. In the context of a church, God's definition of respect is to embrace the rule of elders and pastors, appreciate their ministry with the Word, obey, or submit, to their leadership, and imitate their godliness. Nothing less is acceptable.

One test of our spirituality is whether or not we will obey difficult instructions from the Lord. *Will you choose to embrace biblical church government and demonstrate proper respect to church leaders?*

WRITTEN IN HEAVEN
Hebrews 12:23

Every organized local church has a Church Constitution and By-Laws. This document must be registered with state and federal governments to receive a tax-exempt status. These documents also the adopted rules that govern the function of that assembly. While well-intentioned men usually write these documents, at best, each is only a man-made document that is often unbiblical in function. Unfortunately, in many assemblies, this document is fiercely defended and followed even when it is evident that it is contrary to Scripture. Changes are often refused, and it is frequently given priority over clear instructions in God's Word. For some, it is viewed as if this document in their local church had been written in heaven itself.

The Jewish believers in the Acts era were being encouraged in the Book of Hebrews to not grow weary in the face of intense persecution. A reason for encouragement was the assurance that their names were "written in heaven" (Hebrews 12:23). This was not a new concept for Jews familiar with the Old Testament. Exodus 32:33 explained: "the Lord said unto Moses, Whosoever hath sinned against Me, him will I blot out of my book." Apparently, by virtue of being God's chosen people, Jews were automatically recorded in God's book, that listed all who had been given eternal life. But Jews could be blotted out of that book through sin and unbelief. Daniel 12:1 promised those who will go through the Tribulation, if their name "shall be found written in the book," God would deliver them. The Lord Jesus instructed His disciples to rejoice, "because your names are written in heaven" (Luke 10:20). The Apostle John warned of the time in eternity, when all unbelievers will be assembled, then "the book of life" will be opened, and other books with a record of their sins, and they will be judged accordingly (Revelation 20:12). Looking into eternity future, John also described the New Jerusalem, where Christ will dwell, and he said, only "they which are written in the Lamb's book of life" may enter (Revelation 21:27). Even the Apostle Paul referred to "my fellowlabourers, whose names are in the book of life" (Philippians 4:3). From all these references, it is clear that those from all dispensations who have eternal life are recorded in our Savior's "book of life."

If your name is "written in heaven," rejoice in this wonderful gift of grace. If your name is not recorded in the Lamb's book of life, trust in Him alone today.

UNPROFITABLE FOR YOU
Hebrews 13:17

In 1955, the movie *Rebel Without a Cause*, starring James Dean and Natalie Woods, portrayed moral decay in American youth. Three teens, disenchanted with their circumstances, rebel against authorities and their parents. Sadly, this film and its title has become something of a cultural rallying point for rebels of varying ages.

The book of Hebrews concludes with sobering warnings. Like today, rebellious tendencies had emerged among believers toward their churches and leaders within the church. Some were callously forsaking attendance (Hebrews 10:25), while others chafed against the authority of the leadership. Elsewhere, God addressed the need for church elders to have a proper attitude of humility (I Peter 5:3). However, the focus in Hebrews 13 is on the proper attitude and conduct of believers in local assemblies. God's instruction was to "*remember them* which have the rule over you" (vs. 17). Many become immediately rebellious when it is suggested anyone is to rule over them, even in a godly way. Nonetheless, Gods' divine instruction is to "remember" the valuable ministry of elders by showing respect and appreciation. Each believer was also to "*obey them*" and "*submit yourselves*" (vs. 17). *Why should any adult believer submit to any church leader?* There are several reasons. Beyond appreciation for their ministry of the Scriptures, we must remember, "God is not the author of confusion" (I Corinthians 14:33). To avoid chaos and aimlessness, the Lord ordained that order be provided through biblically-qualified, proven, and godly men. This was true in Jewish kingdom churches, and it is true for grace churches today. Further, these elders who are to be well grounded and capable in the Scriptures are to "... *watch for your souls*" (Hebrews 13:17). Sound teachers who are good leaders help protect believers from being tossed to and fro with every wind of doctrine. Finally, *if we rebel against their authority, "that is unprofitable for you"* (vs. 17). God views rebellion as heinously wrong as the sin of practicing witchcraft (I Samuel 15:23), and He hates the practice of sowing discord among the brethren (Proverbs 6:16-19). To defiantly rebel against church leaders is unprofitable because it can't be done with a clean conscience, we rob ourselves of joy and peace now, and we will ultimately answer for such conduct with loss of eternal reward. That makes rebellion unprofitable.

Have you been rebelling against church leadership? Let God's instruction, that doing so is "unprofitable for you," be an impetus to abandon rebellion and fully cooperate with leaders in your church.

SO SOON REMOVED
Galatians 1:6-9

About a year after I trusted Christ, my parents called to say they, too, had trusted in Christ. In the months that followed, they grew in their faith through attending church and participating in several Bible study groups. On a visit home, I attended one of their Bible study groups. A good deal of the content was sound, but not all of it. When the teacher advocated water baptism for salvation, I objected and went through the biblical plan of salvation. The response of the teacher was: "Oh yes, we believe that, but just to be sure, one needs to be water baptized." Tragically, this Bible teacher was feeding my parents doctrine not intended for the Dispensation of Grace.

When Paul writes to the believers in Galatia, he scolds them saying: "I marvel that ye are so soon removed from Him that called you into the grace of Christ unto another gospel, which is not another; but there be some that trouble you, and would pervert the gospel of Christ" (Galatians 1:6-7). Like wolves in sheep's clothing, false teachers had swept in upon these new believers before they were well grounded. They convinced them that a legalistic religious act was necessary for salvation. They had fallen into the same satanic trap Paul warned about in II Corinthians 11:3-4: "But I fear…as the serpent beguiled Eve through his subtilty, so your minds should be corrupted from the simplicity that is in Christ. For if he that cometh preacheth another Jesus…another spirit…or another gospel…ye might well bear with him." In secondary doctrines, believers ought to demonstrate grace and grant liberty to others to see things differently. However, there are key doctrines that are so critical that no believer should listen to any incorrect teaching, not for a minute. The most important of these is salvation by grace alone. Therefore, Paul charges the saints at Galatia to let any teacher be "accursed" who teaches any works for salvation (Galatians 1:8). This concept relates back to Deuteronomy 7:26 when God forbade Israel to bring any object of idol worship into their home. These were an "abomination… a cursed thing…thou shalt utterly detest…and…abhor [avoid] it, for it is a cursed thing." This principle was so important Paul immediately repeats this command in Galatians 1:9.

Any of us can be swept away from the truth of salvation by grace alone. When it comes to the clarity of the gospel, never put up with what you should put away from you.

262

TRUE SERVANTS OF GOD?
Galatians 1:10

An elder and pastor once struggled with a faction within a local church over an important doctrinal issue. A believer from out of state, who presented himself as being a leader, inserted himself, further inflaming the controversy. When the elder and pastor explained their biblical position, he said: "I know that is what Scripture says, but that is not what the people want. You have to give the people what they want. I'm siding with them."

When the saints in Galatia were being swept away with a false gospel, it may have been easier for the Apostle Paul to simply go with the flow. But instead, the Apostle Paul took a firm stand against this unsound gospel. He did so not because he was just being stubborn or hard to get along with, or wanted to exert his power as a Christian leader. He did so based on two primary principles. First, any gospel message proclaiming salvation through anything other than pure grace apart from all individual human works, is one that leads to eternal punishment. This is so important, there is simply no room for error or compromise. So appropriately, Paul denounced this error in the strongest terms while urging believers to stand with him. Second, Paul would not compromise on key doctrines, because true servants of God don't cooperate with error. His explanation was: "For do I now persuade men, or God? Or do I seek to please men? for if I yet pleased men, I should not be the servant of Christ" (Galatians 1:10). Paul warned that in the last days before the Rapture, many "will not endure sound doctrine; but after their own lusts shall they heap to themselves teachers" (II Timothy 4:3) who will only tell them want they want to hear instead of what God wants them to embrace. But those who compromise like this are not God's true servants. Paul explained that his standard was: "we labour, that...we may be accepted of Him [the Lord Jesus Christ] (II Corinthians 5:9). He refused to adulterate biblical truth to be accepted by man. If that meant others would not approve, he could say: "with me it is a very small thing that I should be judged of you ...He that judgeth me is the Lord" (I Corinthians 4:3-4).

Dear believer, don't stand on the sinking sand of current popular opinions. Choose to be a true servant of God, who stands unwaveringly on the truth found in God's Word.

STANDING FOR TRUTH
Hebrews 8:6-13

While studying the book of Romans, Martin Luther learned that salvation was completely on the basis of faith and not through religious works. On October 31, 1517, in protest of "indulgences" from Pope X to further extract money from the people, Martin Luther nailed his famous 95 theses to the chapel door at the University of Wittenberg. Within two weeks, copies of this theses spread throughout Germany, then within months, throughout Europe. When pressured by the Catholic Church to renounce his theses, he refused unless he could be disproved from Scripture. Going further, he renounced the authority of the papacy to interpret Scripture. This stand for truth brought persecution, but Martin Luther persevered because he was a man of principle who would not compromise truth.

The Apostle Paul likewise took a stand for doctrinal truths. When false teachers sought to impose legalism on his converts he said: "...we gave place by subjection, no, not for an hour, that the truth of the gospel might continue with you" (Galatians 2:5). Had he not spoken out to prevent these falsehoods from gaining a foothold, the only true message of salvation and millions of eternal souls may have been lost. Later, when Peter came to Antioch, he had already learned from the Lord and Paul that God had opened the door of faith to the Gentiles (Acts 14:27). Peter ate and fellowshipped with Paul's Gentile converts. But when Jews who still kept the Law came, Peter was influenced to withdraw and separate himself from the company of Gentile converts. The implication was that they did not believe Gentiles were worthy of salvation, and they did not endorse Paul's Gospel of Grace to all. This was a crucial time when ministry to millions of Gentiles could have been lost. But, referring to Peter, Paul said: "I withstood him to the face, because he was to be blamed" (Galatians 2:11). Paul wasn't being unloving or difficult. He was taking a stand for "...the truth of the gospel" (Galatians 2:14), so it would not be lost but rather flourish with it's life giving message.

We who know Christ as Savior today owe much to men like the Apostle Paul and Martin Luther. Had it not been for their stand for truth, we would be still eternally lost. God still needs you to stand for truth in your local assembly and to stand with those who stand for sound doctrine. *Will your history read that you stood for truth?*

IT DOESN'T WORK ANYMORE
Galatians 3:23-25

Months ago we bought a new desktop computer for my office. Unfortunately, it didn't work well for very long. Somehow, a corrupted file with a virus must have been downloaded, because my computer developed problems. It would lock up, delete work, and refuse to respond to commands. Even though it had been dependable and worked great in the past, it just wouldn't work anymore.

The Book of Galatians was written in an attempt to rescue truly saved individuals that were being drawn back into keeping the Mosaic Law. False teachers were convincing them that works were needed for eternal salvation. Paul told them they should still be standing fast in the position "Knowing that a man is not justified by the works of the law" (Galatians 2:16). The laws given to Israel were an elaborate system that the Lord used for millenniums. But God never intended it to be a permanent program to govern His people. Paul explained to the church at Corinth that God always intended for the Law of Moses to be "done away" and "abolished" (II Corinthians 3:7-13). Today, God has a new system of grace to govern man. It works far better than the Law, which was only an "[ad]ministration of "death" and "condemnation" (II Corinthians 3:7,9). Something better was needed, something new, that could give life rather than death. "For if there had been a law given which could have given life, verily [or truly] righteousness should have been by the law. But the Scripture hath concluded all under sin, that the promise by faith of Jesus Christ might be given to them that believe" (Galatians 3:21-22). Before setting Israel and the Law aside in mid-Acts, those who sought the Lord were "…kept under the law, shut up unto the faith which should afterward be revealed. Wherefore the law was our schoolmaster to bring us unto Christ, that we might be justified by faith. But after that faith is come, we are no longer under a schoolmaster" (Galatians 3:23-25). The Law given to Moses simply does not work any more. One might refuse to move on to a better system of grace, but this is an effort in futility. Like the antiquated floppy disk system, God has discontinued His program of the Law and replaced it with a new program of grace.

Share the good news, that a new, and far better, program of grace has replaced the Mosaic Law. Then rejoice and stand fast in grace.

AN ORPHAN FINDS A FAMILY
Galatians 4:6

August Rush is a movie about a young boy without a family. His mother was told her newborn son had died, but, in reality, he was given to an orphanage. He waited and longed for his real parents to come get him so he could have his true family, love, and a place to belong. As a young teen, he even ran away from the orphanage searching for his parents. Through an amazing series of events, both his biological mother and father found him, and were joyously united as a family.

The Apostle Paul informs us: "...ye are sons" (Galatians 4:6). This is amazing because, as Gentiles, we were once alienated from the family of God, His chosen people Israel. We were "...aliens from the commonwealth of Israel, and strangers from the covenants of promise, having no hope, and without God in the world" (Ephesians 2:12). But in this new Dispensation of Grace, the Heavenly Father has invited us into the family of God by faith in Christ alone. Our condition and position has radically changed. "And because ye are sons, God hath sent forth the Spirit of His Son into your hearts..." (Galatians 4:6). God sought us out in salvation through the sacrifice of His Son and wooed us by the conviction of the Holy Spirit. Then, as sons, He has given us the Holy Spirit to dwell inside us every day. Never again will we be alone. The Holy Spirit is constantly inside us to comfort, guide, strengthen, and direct. We also now have an intimate relationship with God that enables us to speak to Him calling Him "Abba [meaning father] Father" (Galatians 4:6). From the heart, with the deep emotion of gratitude and love, we can call Him our Father and relate to Him all our needs. We have also received "the adoption of sons" (Galatians 4:5). This means that He deals with us, not as small children, but as adult sons with great freedom of choice and standing in grace. He also promises that we are now "an heir of God through Christ" (Galatians 4:7). Not only are we given the riches of grace in salvation, but also great spiritual riches to enjoy now and in eternity.

Dear previously orphaned saint, count it a real privilege, honor, and blessing to be a "son of God," or one of God's children. Rejoice in this today and live in such a godly way that it honors the family name of Christ.

HOW DO YOU TREAT GOD'S SERVANTS

Galatians 4:16

We have friends with an adolescent in the late teens. The mother and father have been experiencing heart-wrenching rebellion from this young person. The teen has been moody, mouthy, disobedient, unappreciative, defiant, and far more. The father often takes the side of the misbehaving child, likewise railing on the mother. As a result, the teen is living in sin, the relationship of the parents is broken relationship, and the mother is heartbroken.

While this real life example depicts a broken family, far too often a similar situation exists in the family of God within local churches. Even the Apostle Paul experienced the rebellion of the saints and the heartbreak of strained or broken relationships. The believers in the region of Galatia had been ill influenced by false teachers who had been successful in pulling them back into the bondage of trying to keep the Mosaic Law. They were even compromising a clear gospel of grace alone. So, Paul instructed them to stand fast in salvation by grace, in their liberty in grace, and in the doctrines of grace. Sadly, they did not want to hear sound doctrine and responded poorly. Paul had to ask them: "Am I therefore become your enemy, because I tell you the truth" (Galatians 4:16). The Corinthians were also carnal in their treatment of Paul. When he sought to bring them out of sinful conduct, he was actually "despised" by those he sought to help (I Corinthians 4:10). *How?* Certainly they despised him in attitude, but there were other ways too. Even after He led them to Christ, Paul said they questioned his apostleship, demanding further "proof of Christ speaking in me" (II Corinthians 13:3). Even through all this, Paul told them that he was willing to sacrificially "spend and be spent for you; though the more abundantly I love you, the less I be loved" (II Corinthians 12:15). It seemed like the more he did for them, the less they appreciated it, and their treatment of him deteriorated more and more. How sad!

How do you treat God's servants, especially those who regularly minister to you? Do you angrily resist the truth they teach when it stands contrary to how you want to do things? Do you question their authority as a leader God has graciously provided? Do you allow yourself to despise them? Or do you appreciate their work and sacrifice on your behalf? Let today mark a positive change in the way you treat God's Servants.

NEVERTHELESS
Galatians 4:30

My father mispronounced a number of words: "crick" instead of "creek," "choirpractor," instead of "chiropractor," and "warsh" instead of "wash." It wasn't until my teen years that I learned, to my embarrassment, that I too had been mispronouncing these words. My father and I would have been well served to have checked the right pronunciation with an authoritative source, such as a dictionary. Correcting an error is always better and wiser than stubbornly persisting down an errant path.

The Bible is not just a source of suggestions. It is to be our supreme and final authority in what we believe, teach, and practice. Our testimony is to be: "...I will keep Thy precepts with my whole heart" (Psalm 119:69). It is important for us to recognize that dangers exist when we resist the revealed will of God. We tend to do this when it runs contrary to what we want, or what someone has taught us. Today, believers quite often persist in practices that conflict with biblical standards. In error, some ignore the biblical qualifications for elders and deacons (I Timothy 3:1-3; Titus 1:5-11) just to keep a quota in a church constitution. Even though the Bible consistently condemns the practices of homosexuality (Romans 1:27-28), and practicing sex outside of marriage (I Corinthians 6:18; Hebrews 13:4), many Christians have come to accept both. Though nature and Scripture tell us it is a shame for men to wear long hair (I Corinthians 11:14), it has become commonplace today. Many believers continue to use vulgar language after salvation when God tells us "these things ought not so to be" (James 3:10). When we persist in unbiblical beliefs and practices, we are, in effect, rejecting God's Word and God's will. This greatly displeases the Lord and robs us of His richest blessing. Proverbs 19:20-21 says: "Hear counsel, and receive instruction...The counsel of the Lord, that shall stand." We must not become those who "...have set at nought My [God's] counsel..." (Proverbs 1:25). As Christians, we need to return to the standard stated by David in Psalm 119:128: "I esteem all Thy precepts concerning all things to be right; and I hate every false way."

Regardless of tradition, or what is accepted by society, we must examine all things by one question: "Nevertheless what saith the Scriptures?" (Galatians 4:30). Whatever God's Word says, we must bring our thinking, voting, and practice into conformity. Whether or not anyone else stands with you, choose to stand for what God says in Scripture.

MISUSING LIBERTY
Galatians 5:13

During my high school years, I knew many who were allowed to freely attend school functions or simply hang out with friends multiple times per week. But in our household, teenagers were allowed only one evening out per week, with no exceptions. One of the problems with being so restricted was, once granted that weekly evening liberty, my brother and I went to extremes to make the most of the limited time we had. We were abusing our liberty with very poor conduct.

A similar problem existed throughout most of the churches founded by the Apostle Paul. Many who had been freed from the exacting bondage of the Mosaic Law were misusing their new found liberty. Paul wanted them to "Stand fast therefore in the liberty wherewith Christ hath made us free, and be not entangled again with the yoke of bondage" (Galatians 5:1). But some were taking their liberty to extremes of sinful conduct. This is why Paul's letters warn about immorality, lying, theft, drunkenness, a lack of giving, and more. Paul tells them: "...brethren, ye have been called to liberty, only use not liberty for an occasion to the flesh, but by love serve one another" (Galatians 5:13). God had given them great liberty through grace, but they were not to misuse that liberty. These abuses were offending new believers, and bringing shame on the testimony of Christ. So Paul addressed this problem, saying: "But take heed lest by any means this liberty of yours become a stumbling block to them that are weak" (I Corinthians 8:9). In addition to sinful conduct or offending others, there are two standards to judge the proper use of liberty. Paul said: "All things are lawful unto me, but all things are not expedient...I will not be brought under the power of any" (I Corinthians 6:12). If your choices are causing you to lose self-control that restrains you from sinful practices, they are wrong. First Corinthians 10:23 counsels: "All things are lawful for me...but all things edify not." If your choices do not build up other believers in Christ, they, too become a misuse of liberty.

Liberty in Christ can be misused today too. We have liberty in our choices of clothing, a marriage partner, length of hair, beverages consumed, frequency in the Scriptures, and church participation. But we must not use our liberty "for an occasion to the flesh." Purpose today that your liberty will only be used to honor Christ.

RESTORED
Galatians 6:1

In 2009, my mother went home to be with the Lord. One of the things I got from her house was an old beat up dresser that my siblings just wanted to throw away. I brought it home because my daughter wanted it as a keepsake. Together, we spent a week restoring it. When we stripped and sanded away layers of old paint that had been on it for decades, we discovered beautiful marbled wood. Then we stained it and added three new ornate handles matching the other ones. When it was all finished, we had a surprisingly beautiful and cherished family heirloom.

In Galatians 6:1, Paul tells the saints: "Brethren, if a man be overtaken in a fault, ye which are spiritual, restore such an one in the spirit of meekness; considering thyself, lest thou also be tempted." The simple truth is that this is not the way most believers act. Instead, we seem very quick to just throw such a brother or sister onto the junk heap of discarded relationships. Instead, the Apostle of Grace instructs us to demonstrate grace toward an erring brother. By way of illustration, we are to see all who have trusted in Christ alone for salvation as members of our own body. When we do, we realize: "...the eye cannot say unto the hand, I have no need of thee. Nay...those members of the body, which seem to be more feeble, are necessary" (I Corinthians 12:21-22). When one part of our body is injured, we don't just lop it off and throw it away. Instead, we attend to it and nurse it back to health. In Galatians, Chapter 6, Paul, in effect, is saying we are only truly "spiritual" if we treat other erring saints with the same care that we use to treat ourselves. Moreover, we are to help them correct their error in a "spirit of meekness" (Galatians 6:1), rather than lambasting or avoiding them. In so doing, we seek to "bear...one another's burdens" fulfilling the law of love (6:2), and we will do so without being easily "weary in well doing" (6:9). If we won't seek to restore others, even if we "think...[ourselves] to be something...[we are] nothing" (6:3) when it comes to being truly spiritual.

Is there someone in your life or your church that needs you to demonstrate the kind of grace that will restore a relationship with them? Let the Lord speak to your heart and take action today.

September 23

REAPING WHAT YOU SOW
Galatians 6:7-8

Growing up on our farm in the 50's and 60's meant that we had a great deal of very labor-intensive work. We shoveled grain, lifted bales of hay, and much more. The only job I ever really hated was walking the fields to pull weeds. In that day, at least on our farm, we did not use spray to control weeds. Instead, Dad had us all help walk the fields to pull weeds by hand. We had two different fields that, year after year, were always just loaded with weeds. I jokingly accused Dad of sowing weed seeds in the fields so we would have to spend over a month pulling them. Had he sown weed seeds, we knew with certainty we would've gotten weeds, because you reap what you sow.

This principle is true throughout life. This is why the Apostle Paul wrote: "Be not deceived; God is not mocked: for whatsoever a man soweth, that shall he also reap. For he that soweth to his flesh shall of the flesh reap corruption; but he that soweth to the Spirit shall reap life everlasting" (Galatians 6:7-8). When Cain sowed the seeds of stubborn rebellion by refusing to bring the proper sacrifice, God rejected his offering. When he jealously killed his brother, God judged him by making him "a fugitive and a vagabond...in the earth" (Genesis 4:12). He was also told that the ground would no longer yield fruit to him. Cain responded by saying: "My punishment is greater than I can bear" (vs. 13). Particularly as a farmer, he should have known that you reap what you sow. When Solomon made the political and spiritual decision to marry multiple wives who worshipped false gods, it was not surprising that "his wives turned away his heart [from worshipping Jehovah]" (I Kings 11:1-4). After all, we reap what we sow. When Paul described saints who chose to live in gross sin like the world, it was predictable that their hearts would have spiritual "blindness" and become "past feeling" (Ephesians 4:18-19). We reap what we sow. When Paul warned about the Bema Seat, he said: "Some men's sins are open beforehand, going before to judgment; and some men they follow after" (I Timothy 5:24). In eternity, we'll reap giving an account for whatever we sow now.

This principle is timeless, and we can benefit by it. Let's choose today to sow a life of godliness and service so that what we reap in eternity will be joyous.

"FAITHFUL"

Ephesians 1:1

In the 1980's, my wife and I served in a church in Illinois. One of the people we came to love there was Jack. He was, and still is, a likeable man who can keep you in stitches with his humor. He was saved in his thirties out of a rough background, and he immediately allowed God to completely change his life. He became active in children's ministry, taught an adult Bible study, became a consistent soul-winner, lead singing, read his Bible, regularly attended church, and much more. Today, even after serious heart problems and all these years, Jack remains faithful.

As the Apostle Paul opens his letter to the Ephesians, he refers to them as: "the faithful in Christ Jesus" (1:1). That description is high praise. The word "faithful" means to be "trust-worthy, sure, or true." It has never been easy to find people who allow the Lord to raise them to this standard. David wrote: "Help, Lord; for the godly man ceaseth; for the faithful fail from among the children of men" (Psalm 12:1). Solomon agreed. Under inspiration, he wrote: "Most men will proclaim every one his own goodness; but a faithful man who can find" (Proverbs 20:6). Even though faithful men were scarce, God found a few. The Lord actually called a number the saints "faithful." "My servant Moses is …faithful in all Mine house" (Numbers 12:7). Abimelech asked: "And who is so faithful among all thy servants as David…" (I Samuel 22:14). In Nehemiah, it was said that God chose Abraham "And…foundest his heart faithful before Thee"(Nehemiah 9:7-8). The Apostle Paul wrote: "I thank Christ Jesus our Lord, who hath…counted me faithful, putting me into the ministry" (I Timothy 1:12).

In the Book of Ephesians, Paul referred to the saints as "faithful." This implies that they were faithful in doctrine, in service, in conduct, in the local church, and more. From the Old Testament to the New Testament, even today, some chose to be truly faithful to the Lord. *How important is this?* Just as it is important for us to be faithful to our marriage partner, The ONE who died for us deserves nothing less than our total faithfulness. With God's help, let's decide to be, as the definition describes, trustful, worthy, sure, and true. The Savior wants you to be faithful. *Will you stop right now to ask Christ to enable you to become faithful to Him, like the faithful men referred to above?*

SHOWERS OF BLESSING
Ephesians 1:3

We have an elderly loved one who has suffered a series of strokes. Her last stroke robbed her of virtually all sight on her left side. Consequently, particularly with previous diminished capacity in her right eye, she has a difficult time seeing things in her surroundings. To her, it is a real blessing when family comes to see her. She also loves to have many sentimental family antiques. Yet often when these, and other, blessings are right in front of her, she either can't see them at all, or she fails to recognize what they are.

It is often the case that Christians fail to see, or to recognize in their minds and hearts, all the ways in which God has so richly blessed us. We learn from Ephesians 1:3 that "...the God and Father of our Lord Jesus Christ...hath blessed us with all spiritual blessings in heavenly places in Christ." *What kind of spiritual blessing do we have based on our salvation in the Lord Jesus Christ?* "The middle wall of partition" (Ephesians 2:14) separating us from God, has been broken down. We have been "quickened [made spiritually alive] together with Him, having forgiven you all trespasses" (Colossians 2:13). Believers are now "the righteousness of God" in Christ (II Corinthians 5:21). We are sealed with eternal security, justified, given access to God through prayer, and given hundreds of other spiritual blessing. But we must not be shortsighted. God has also showered us with many blessing that would not be characterized as those "in heavenly places" (Ephesians 1:3). Paul taught that we are to give God thanks for food (Romans 14:6). This implies that the Lord ultimately provides our food, the money to buy it, the health to earn it, and the employment to make it possible. Saints of old saw children (or family), rain, God's written Word, friends, homes, wealth, open doors to serve the Lord, safety in travel, protection from wrongdoers, and much more, all as blessings from God. We need to see that "every good gift and every perfect gift is from above, and cometh down from the Father of lights" (James 1:17).

If we fail to look beyond our spiritual blessing in Christ to also see the daily blessings provided by the hand of God, we will miss the joy of comprehending all His blessings. Be alert to all of God's blessed provisions and make a written list for which you can give Him thanks.

ACCEPTED BY THE FATHER
Ephesians 1:6

A family we once knew had a very unruly son. The father loved this son and was always doting on him. When he became a teenager, even though they couldn't really afford it, the father bought him a new car. When others tried to discretely tell the father that his son was driving recklessly within city limits, he would not believe them. He wouldn't believe it even after he wrecked that new car, and two more, by driving too fast. In the eyes of this father, his son could do no wrong, and this father continued to lavish great gifts on his son.

God tells us He hath "...made us accepted in the Beloved [Son] (Ephesians 1:6). The word "accepted" means more than to receive willingly or respond favorably. It is the same Greek word used when Mary was told she was "highly favored" before the Lord (Luke 1:28). When Paul told the Ephesians that they were "accepted" by God the Father, it meant more than that God was receiving them favorably. He was explaining that they were highly favored. But Paul was not referring here to individuals. He was referring to the corporate Body of Christ. Collectively, we were "chosen" to be "holy and without blame...[and] predestinated...unto the adoption [declared to be an adult son] of children by Jesus Christ" (Ephesians 1:4-5). God the Father no longer sees the Body of Christ in the guilt of sin. In His eyes, we stand in the righteousness of His sinless Son, the Lord Jesus Christ. As a body of believers, we have been forgiven all trespasses. Our Heavenly Father will not listen to any accusation of Satan that would alter our collective standing before Him. Regardless of poor conduct, He also continues to heap great "spiritual blessings" (or riches) upon the Body of Christ (Ephesians 1:3). What is true of the collective Body of Christ (a righteous standing in the Lamb of God, and blessed with great spiritual riches) is also true of each individual who knows the Lord Jesus as Savior. No one is individually predestined to eternal life, but those who choose to trust in Christ are chosen to stand in the acceptance and the spiritual riches of the Savior.

Our response to these blessings should be to "...walk worthy of the vocation wherewith ye are called" (Ephesians 4:1). Evaluate all you say and do today by the standard of being worthy of the love of your Father who has given you so much.

SECURITY IN CHRIST
Ephesians 1:13

From nearly the instant my wife and I first walked into the house we currently live in, we knew "this was home." We liked the layout, special features, and location. So, we immediately made an offer, put down a adequate amount of earnest money to "seal the deal," and specified a move-in date. We were thrilled when our offer was accepted. Our new home had been secured.

Every individual in the Dispensation of Grace who has trusted in the finished work of Christ for eternal salvation has the assurance from God's Word that a home for us in heaven is eternally secure. We have *a new resident* guaranteeing our salvation. Ephesians 1:13 promises that, when we "trusted...the gospel of your salvation...ye were sealed with the Holy Spirit of promise." The moment we trusted in Christ alone for eternal life, God the Father gave us God the Holy Spirit to dwell inside us. Ephesians 1:14 calls this "the earnest [or down-payment] of our [eternal] inheritance." Like earnest money given to secure the buyer of home will follow through with the purchase, the indwelling Holy Spirit is God's guarantee that He will bring us, His purchased possession, to the heavens at the right time. His constant presence seals this irrevocable promise of eternal life as a gift of complete grace. We are also given a *new condition* of being made "the righteousness of God in Him [or in Christ]" (II Corinthians 5:21). God the Father now only sees us in the imputed holiness of His Son. Through grace, this positional standing with God will never change, even when our practice is sinful. This gives us *a new acceptance*. Ephesians 1:6 states that the Father "hath made us accepted in the Beloved [Son]." We no longer approach God in our own merits, hoping He will accept us. We are accepted because we are able to approach Him in the merit of His righteous Son, the Lord Jesus Christ. All this is compatible with our *new position*. Galatians 4:6 explains: "And because ye are sons, God hath sent forth the Spirit of His Son into your hearts, crying, Abba, Father." We have received the "adoption of sons," (Galatians 4:5) making us part of the family of God and capable of having a living relationship with the Lord every day.

Our new condition gives us wonderful spiritual and eternal security in Christ. Sharing the truth of these spiritual riches with someone today may increase their joy, and yours.

DEAD AND ALIVE
Ephesians 2:1-10

Tony Yable's family found him not breathing and without a pulse. They preformed CPR on him until paramedics arrived. They were, likewise, unable to revive him. He was taken to *Kettering Medical Center* in Columbus, Ohio, after being unresponsive for 45 minutes with no vital signs. Only when his son Lawrence screamed: "Dad, you're not going to die today" did his heart begin to beat once again. Doctors cannot explain his recovery. He was dead, but now he is alive.[1]

Tony's physical condition, in many ways, mirrors our spiritual condition before trusting in Christ. The Apostle Paul describes us as being "... dead in trespasses and sins" (Ephesians 2:1). He confirms our condition prior to salvation by repeating that "...you, being dead in your sins...hath He quickened... (and) forgiven..." (Colossians 2:13). Regardless of how religious we might be, until we place our trust in the sacrifice of the Lord Jesus as our only hope for eternal life, we remain dead in our sins with no spiritual heartbeat. We are nothing more before the Lord than "...by nature the children of wrath" (Ephesians 2:3). Only at the moment we respond in faith to the call of God's Son, through the Gospel of Grace, are we granted forgiveness and eternal life. It is only then we are "quickened" or made alive (Ephesians 2:1) by one miraculous instantaneous act of God.

When most people have a near-death experience, they conclude God intervened and they were spared for a reason. In the spiritual realm of our salvation, this is certainly true. God intervened through His Son to bring us life. We are now to "...walk in newness of life" (Romans 6:4), "... walk honestly..." (Romans 13:13), and "walk in the Spirit (or control of the Holy Spirit–Galatians 5:16). We were "created (or saved) in Christ Jesus unto good works, which God hath...ordained that we should walk in them" (Ephesians 2:10). *Are you seeking to walk in the path God intended for you when He saved you?* If not, let's begin that journey today. If you have been walking on the biblical path for which God saves you, keep walking.

AT A LOSS
Ephesians 3:14-21

A Christian woman who was having marital problems came to me for counsel. From her perspective, the husband was completely wrong and making her life miserable. She told me I was to say nothing to anyone. Every time I suggested a course of action, she said that they had tried it or that he wouldn't be willing. I felt badly for her, but with no foreseeable action toward a solution, it left me at a loss about how I could be of help.

If you've ever felt at a loss about how to pray for yourself or others, there is an excellent pattern to follow in Ephesians 3:14-21. Paul said he started by bowing his knees in reverent submission to the Lord asking for the "riches" of His glory, or grace, to be given (vss. 14-16). He asked for others to be "strengthened with might by His Spirit in the inner man" (vs. 16). God strengthens us internally, primarily through the reading and counsel of His written Word. So, in effect, Paul was praying for others to be drawn into Scripture to find the spiritual life they needed. Next, he asked for others to grow in "faith" and to be "rooted and grounded in love" (vs. 17). These believers already had saving faith. What they needed was a growing faith to meet the trials of each day and growth in Christ to exhibit real love. The latter would produce greater peace, joy, compatibly with others, and a good testimony for their Savior. Then he prays they will better "comprehend" with other saints a deeper experiential realization of how much God loves them. He tells them this was far greater than "knowledge." Sound doctrine is essential to pleasing the Lord, but it is not, as many saints conclude, God's primary goal for them in life or Bible study. God's primary goal for us is to grow spiritually, become more like Christ in holiness, and know Him intimately each day. Only then will we be "filled with all the fullness of God" (vs. 19). Paul closes his prayer by committing them to "Him that is able to do exceeding abundantly above all that we ask or think according to the power [of God] that worketh in us" (vs. 20). *Aren't these kinds of specific requests to the Lord far better than a generic, non-specific "God be with this person"?*

Let's make this kind of meaningful and mature prayer our pattern and follow it regularly, especially when we can't really do anything but pray.

ACTING LIKE A CHILD OR AN ADULT?

Ephesians 4:3

When our five young grandchildren get together, things change. They greet each other with smiles and hugs. Then you can hear their soft sweet voices asking each other to go play. But things soon deteriorate. Before you know it, they are fighting over the same toy. It can quickly escalate to screaming, crying, hitting, or even biting. Usually, they won't stop until an adult intervenes. As annoying as this may be, they are simply acting like children.

The truth is, there is often little difference with the bigger kids, from age 20-80, who are brothers and sisters in the Body of Christ. We often meet and greet one another with a smile, hug, or happy words. But it doesn't seem to take very long before we, too, are fighting, backbiting, and refusing to get along. This is exactly why the Apostle Paul begs the believers at Ephesus to rise to the level where each one is: "Endeavoring to keep the unity of the Spirit in the bond of peace" (Ephesians 4:3). This passage tells us God has given all believers a natural state of "unity" by virtue of mutually knowing the Lord Jesus Christ as Savior. The word "unity" means a state of oneness, harmony, agreement, or accord. We all have the responsibility to "endeavor," (meaning to try hard or make an earnest attempt), to "keep," or maintain, this precious unity. Throughout Scripture, the Lord repeats this principle. In I Corinthians 1:10, Paul writes: "Now I beseech you, brethren, by the name of our Lord Jesus Christ, that ye all speak the same thing, and that there be no divisions among you; but that ye be perfectly joined together in the same...judgment." To make this possible, the saints are told that the "...strong [or mature] ought to bear the infirmities of the weak, and not to please ourselves. Let every one of us please his neighbor for his good to edification" (Romans 15:1-2). When we act to keep this harmony between believers, Paul says. "For he that in these things serveth Christ is acceptable to God, and approved of men" (Romans 14:18).

When conflict arises between believers, it is because someone is serving self rather than serving Christ. Someone is acting like a child, and someone needs to act like an adult. *Which one are you going to be?* Let's choose right now to act like a mature, Christ-like adult.

278

WHAT WE HAVE
Ephesians 4:12

When I was 10 years old, we had a huge snowstorm that left a snowdrift in front of our house. A week later, it had repeatedly thawed and frozen again, been driven on, walked on, and compacted to a sheet of ice. My mother instructed me to take a shovel and clean off the steps and sidewalk by chipping this ice away. I'd had to do this before. It was a hard, time-consuming job, and I didn't want to do it. But she persisted. Angrily, I began my task, muttering to myself: "I wish I was John Biles, (a rich friend my age). I bet he doesn't have to do a job like this." When my mother overheard this, she scolded me thoroughly, saying: "You should be ashamed. You have a good family, a nice home, plenty of food, and everything you need. You should appreciate all you have."

Believers often are miserable because they focus on what they don't have instead of being thankful for all we have in Christ. Many churches and individuals are also weak and defeated because they do not understand all we have in this new Dispensation of Grace. To equip and encourage the saints, Paul listed some of our spiritual riches: "...we have boldness and access [to God] with confidence..." (Ephesians 3:12). Old Testament saints did not have boldness to approach God's presence. When the holiness and majesty of God were displayed through "...the thunderings, and the lightenings... and the mountain smoking: and when the people saw it, they removed, and stood afar off" (Exodus 20:18). They were afraid God might strike them dead. So they asked Moses to speak on their behalf. In contrast, in Christ, we now have boldness and access to God. In ancient times, as in the days of Esther, even the queen had to have permission to see the king. If a person entered without permission, it usually meant death. But today, we have access to God any hour of the day. We also have the strengthening of the Spirit of God within our inner man (Ephesians 3:16), the ability to fully "comprehend with all saints" the breadth and depth of the love of Christ (vss. 17-18), and God's working on our behalf "...exceedingly abundantly above all that we ask or think..." (vs. 20). We have many great spiritual blessings.

Don't make the mistake of focusing on things you don't have. Thank God for these spiritual riches that you do have, and rejoice with a grateful heart.

A HIGHER STANDARD
Ephesians 5:3-16

The *Today Show* has a daily segment called "What's trending." By definition, a trend is a general tendency of events or opinions. It can be dangerous if we allow ourselves to be influenced by these fickle trends. In different incidents, over twenty years ago, I had a young professing Christian woman, then a young Christian man tell me, without embarrassment, they were living with someone outside of marriage. Then, only a few years ago, two Christian couples in their 70's told me the same thing. Regardless of the trends or rational of our day, this is still unacceptable for a Christian.

Paul states: "But fornication, and all uncleanness, or covetousness, let it not be once named among you, as becometh saints; neither filthiness, nor foolish talking...but rather giving of thanks" (Ephesians 5:3-4). While any form of immorality is wrong even once, it is far worse to plunge knowingly into a lifestyle of immoral behavior. In verses 4-6, Paul described a range of associated sins among the unsaved and reminded the saints that this is how a lost soul acts. Unless the individual trusts in Christ, they will experience God's eternal wrath. Paul went on to urge believers to live a higher standard of conduct, saying: "Be not...partakers with them" (vs. 7). He continued by urging them to prove what is "acceptable unto the Lord" (vs.10), and to live like "children of light" (vs. 8) rather than like the children of darkness and destruction. His instructions were, "it is a shame even to speak [approvingly] of those things which are done of them in secret" (vs. 12), and obviously far worse to intentionally practice them. Instead, we who know Christ are to live in such purity that we become a light that points lost souls to the Savior (vss. 13-14). Paul concluded by urging those sinning saints to understand "what the will of the Lord is" (vs. 17), to redeem the time given them, and "walk circumspectly, not as fools, but as wise" (vs. 15-16).

Our purpose here is not to beat up someone who has temporarily fallen into the temptation of immorality. Instead, it is to caution all to not embrace the ungodly trends of our time or continue to live in sin for even another day. Let's be careful not to fall into these traps of Satan. Living in sin is not only wrong, it dulls our spiritual senses, ruins our testimony, and numbs us to a relationship with Christ. Instead may we seek to rescue those who are so ensnared.

SEIZE THE OPPORTUNITY
Ephesians 6:19-20

While looking for a house, my wife and I became instant friends with the realtor. We all enjoyed our time together and met regularly. We even gave her the gospel while we looked at houses. We had purposed at our next meeting to share the gospel with our Bibles in hand. Then we got a phone call from her colleague telling us she had gruesomely committed suicide, leaving behind a husband and beautiful 5-year-old daughter. The news hit us like a ton of bricks. While looking for the right house was important and giving the gospel to her verbally was a start, we miserably failed this lost soul, and there will be no second chance.

Paul asks for prayer "…that utterance may be given unto me, that I may open my mouth boldly, to make known the mystery of the gospel…that therein I may speak boldly, as I ought to speak" (Ephesians 6:19-20). We might think of an apostle or pastor, as always having the boldness to speak to anyone anywhere or anytime. But this passage shows we all lack boldness at times. Like Paul, *we should pray for adequate boldness.* Then we should pray for several other things. In Colossians 4:3, Paul asks the saints to continue "…praying also for us, that God would open unto us a door of utterance, to speak the mystery of Christ…" Sometimes it is appropriate to begin a conversation about eternal matters. But it is wonderful when God so works in the heart of a lost soul that they open the door, allowing you to present God's plan of salvation. An example would by Lydia, in Acts 16:14, "…whose heart the Lord opened…" when Paul shared the gospel with her. So pray for open doors. *Pray that the Lord would powerfully convict,* through the Holy Spirit, before and during your time of sharing the gospel. In II Thessalonians 3:1, Paul asked for prayer that, when he ministered the Word, "…the word of the Lord may have free course…." So it is appropriate for us to pray that the power and effectiveness of God's Word in the gospel will lodge in the heart unhindered.

Surely there is someone in your path that is lost and headed for eternal punishment. Learn from our mistake. Seize the opportunity now. Don't delay in sharing the gospel, because they may not have much time left. Pray for prepared hearts, then go share the gospel today.

DOING IT BY THE BOOK
James 1:22-24

When NASA launched the space shuttles, our family drove over to the Cape to observe several times. Thousands lined the coast to watch and feel the shock waves from the engines that were miles away. Before the lift off, the flight controller went through a launch check, polling many officials who were monitoring thousands of gauges and screens. Each department had to give a verbal "Go to launch" or the mission would be scrubbed. They were careful to "do it by the book" because doing otherwise could bring disaster.

It is extremely important for believers to live according to the dictates of God's Word and to do so "strictly by the Book." This principle was true for saints in the Old Testament, those awaiting Christ's return to establish the Millennial Kingdom, and for us today who live in the Dispensation of Grace. We are reminded in James 1:22-24: "But be ye doers of the word, and not hearers only, deceiving your own selves. For if any be a hearer of the word, and not a doer, he is like unto a man beholding his natural face in a glass: for he beholdeth himself, and goeth his way, and straightway forgetteth what manner of man he was." It would be foolish for us to see ourselves in a mirror with unkept hair, a dirty face, and soiled clothing, and then do nothing to correct these problems. Likewise it is foolish when, through His Word, the Lord shows us a problem in our lives, and we choose to do nothing about it. We are actually worse off than before, because doing nothing is an act of defiance, or indifference, that spiritually hardens our hearts. Every day we should be looking for something in God's Word to put into practice immediately. When our heart is convicted about a needed area of change, we must become a "doer of the word." Just as parents expect compliance when they give their children important instructions, and it greatly displeases them if these instructions are disobeyed, so it is with the Lord. He expects our compliance to His Word; it displeases Him when we ignore His instructions, but He is greatly pleased and honored IF we respond in obedience.

How do you respond when you read something in God's Word that points to a needed change in your life? Establish a pattern of acknowledging it to the Lord, asking for His help, and consciously taking steps to comply that very day.

FAITH WITHOUT WORKS
James 2:14-26

A young man with a clear testimony of faith in Christ and knowledge of dispensational truth was at one time excited about the Lord. He even taught at church. Then he stopped serving and drifted away from the Lord into a destructive pattern. His spiritual life in Christ lay dormant inside and was stifled. Finally, he hit a low that brought him back to a daily walk with Christ. Today he is actively serving Christ and experiencing a joy within that he lacked for a number of years.

The Apostle James told the kingdom saints something unique to Israel's program when he wrote: "Even so faith, if it hath not works is dead, being alone" (James 2:17). James was talking to fellow Jews about being justified from sin and given eternal life. He asked: "Was not Abraham our father justified by works, when he had offered Isaac his son upon the altar" (vs. 21). James made this statement because the Jews he addressed were still under the Law of Moses. They could only be saved through faith in the Lord Jesus as their Messiah and obedience to the Gospel of the Kingdom. This gospel required circumcision (Genesis 17:7-14; Acts 15:1), confession of sin (Matthew 3:6; Romans 10:10), repentance, and water baptism for forgiveness and eternal life (Acts 2:38; Mark 1:4). This was why James used the examples of Abraham and Rahab, who demonstrated their faith by works and therein received justification from the Lord. Under Israel's program, which has now been set aside, James was correct to say: "Ye see then how that by works a man is justified, and not by faith only" (2:24). All this stands in stark contrast to God's present program of grace. Today we are saved 100% apart from works by faith in the work of Christ alone (Ephesians 2:8-9; Romans 11:6). No works can be added. God will accept no works to merit eternal life. Salvation today is wholly a gift of God's grace.

There is something for us to learn as a secondary application from the words of James about faith and works. In any dispensation, there is a certain spiritual deadness, dormancy, or void that creeps in if we fail to work for the cause of Christ after salvation. Serving Christ brings spiritual joy, purpose, satisfaction, and fulfillment. It breathes a life and vitality into our faith that cannot be experienced without it. Don't miss out. See your faith come alive by regularly working for your Savior.

DIFFICULT TO TAME

James 3:2-13

A story was related to me about a young man from an affluent family. He told his father that he wanted-ed a particular new car as a graduation present. When that day arrived, his father presented him with a new Bible. Angrily the son said insulting things and told his father that was not what he wanted, nor what he asked for. He was so angry that he had nothing to do with his father for years. At the reading of the will, he learned the car he had asked for was purchased before his graduation and parked in the father's garage. The key was in the Bible he had been given. In his deep regret, he wished he had not spoken so poorly to his father and had maintained that relationship.

The problem of saying foul things is a consistent part of human nature that exists in every dispensation. James describes it this way: "But the tongue can no man tame, it is an unruly evil, full of deadly poison" (James 3:8). In truth, there is often little difference in the way believers and unbelievers talk. But there should be! James addressed the misuse of our tongues saying: "Therewith bless we God, even the Father; and therewith curse we men...Out of the same mouth proceedeth blessing and cursing. My brethren, these things ought not so to be" (James 2:9-10). We instinctively know that we should clean up our language after salvation for testimony sake and out of gratitude for eternal life. Our standard should be: "Let no corrupt communication proceed out of your mouth, but that which is good to...edifying" (Ephesians 4:29). James adds: "If any man among you seem to be religious, and bridleth not his tongue, but deceiveth his own heart, this man's religion is vain" (James 1:26). The word "vain" means empty. If our language as a believer is corrupt, it demonstrates emptiness in our walk with the Lord. We need to consciously seek the Lord's strength to control what we say. Beyond gratitude to the Lord, and for testimony sake, one further motivation to maintain wholesome speech is to avoid unnecessary problems. Peter stated: "For he that will love life, and see good days, let him refrain his tongue from evil, and his lips that they speak no guile" (I Peter 3:10).

We should all allow God to speak to our hearts about this matter and pray as David did: "Set a watch, O Lord, before my mouth..." (Psalm 141:3).

YE HAVE NOT

James 4:2

A dear believer once told us God does not answer prayer today. His belief was that God's intervention was a thing of the past for Israel and that "prayer today is primarily to make us feel better." The outworking of that thinking was predictable in his life. He acknowledged he seldom prayed and said: "My prayer time is my Bible study."

This concept of prayer discourages us from spending time in prayer and causes us to miss out on a great deal of blessing the Lord intends for our life. Throughout Paul's letters, he repeatedly shared his testimony that he never ceased to offer prayer for his needs and the needs of those he led to the Lord (i.e. Colossians 1:9; Ephesians 1:16-19). He even instructed those he sought to ground in sound doctrine to likewise: "Pray without ceasing" (I Thessalonians 5:17). Moreover, prayer was not to be seen as Bible study. When Paul prayed, he said: "...I bow my knees unto the Father of our Lord Jesus Christ" (Ephesians 3:14). His prayer was an oral communication to the Lord whether spoken or silently offered. Prayer was then, and is now, important as an act of worship. The Lord instructs us to come to Him in prayer that we have the benefit of His intervention in our needs. If we fail to avail ourselves to the Lord in prayer, we only hurt ourselves. James 4:2 puts it this way: "...ye have not because ye ask not." It is abundantly clear in a number of Scriptures that God does answer prayer and intervene in our lives in the Dispensation of Grace. When Paul despaired for his life due to persecution, he told the saints they were "...helping together by prayer for us" (II Corinthians 1:11). Paul assured the Philippians: "For I know that this shall turn to my salvation [deliverance from prison] through your prayer" (Philippians 1:19). Paul instructed believers to pray for governmental authorities "...that we may lead a quiet and peaceable life...(I Timothy 2:2). This implied, circumstantial peace could be achieved by invoking God's intervention. Paul offered prayer because he believed God "...is able to do exceeding abundantly above all we ask or think..." (Ephesians 3:20). This included intervening in mercy in the life of Epaphroditus when he was "sick nigh unto death" (Philippians 2:27).

Believer, don't "have not because ye ask not." God may intervene in your circumstances when you pray. Beginning today, make prayer your first response to problems and your constant practice.

HE GIVETH MORE GRACE
James 4:6

The hymn "He Giveth More Grace," by Annie J. Flint, has potent words of encouragement that minister to all of us: "He giveth more grace as our burdens grow greater, He sendeth more strength as our labors increase; To added afflictions He addeth His mercy; to multiplied trials He multiplies peace. When...our strength has failed ere the day is half done, when we reach the end of our hoarded resources, our Father's full giving has only begun. His love has no limits, His grace has no measure, His power has no boundary known unto men: For out of His infinite riches in Jesus, He giveth, and giveth, and giveth again."

This hymn is based on the truth from one short phrase in James 4:6: "But He giveth more grace." The believing Jews, to whom James wrote these words, were facing great difficulties. They were under persecution from unbelieving Jews who hated them for their faith in the Lord Jesus. These believers also anticipated seven years of far greater persecution prior to their Savior's return to vanquish their enemies before the Millennial Kingdom. Added to all this, they struggled, as do we today, with a fallen old nature that made living godly very difficult. In the preceding verses, James rebuked them for internal fighting within their churches (vs. 1), a lack of prayer (vs. 2), prayer with wrong motives (vs. 3), improper worldliness (vs. 4), and the acknowledgment that "...the spirit that dwelleth in us lusteth to envy" (vs. 5). *What was the answer to defeat these sinful tendencies?* James told them that, in the midst of all their struggles, God giveth more grace. They needed to rely on that. Similarly, when the Apostle Paul was exhausted from persecution and the work of the ministry, he came to the end of his human resources when a painful "thorn in the flesh" (II Corinthians 12:7) persisted. Three times he asked the Lord to remove this physical infirmity. The Lord's answer to him was: "...My grace is sufficient for thee" (II Corinthians 12:9).

In every dispensation, in every situation, and for every saint, God's strengthening grace is our greatest need in our most difficult times. If you're going through a divorce, difficulty at work, wearisome illness, emotional distress, or other difficulties, remember, "...He giveth more grace." Spend sufficient time in God's Word, in prayer, and in fellowship with God's people. Specifically ask God for His strengthening grace. He may not remove your trial, but He will give you more grace.

DRAW NIGH UNTO GOD
James 4:8

An old joke refers to an elderly Grandpa and Grandma driving down the road in the car. Grandma turns and says, "Do you remember when we used to take drives every Sunday?" "Yep," says Grandpa. "Do you remember when we used to sit so close you couldn't put a piece of paper between us?" "Yep," says Grandpa. "Why don't we sit close like that anymore?" Grandpa turns to Grandma and says, "I haven't moved."

If you feel like God is far off, just remember that God hasn't moved. He created mankind for close, regular fellowship, as we see by God's voice when walking in the Garden with Adam and Eve (Genesis 3:8). It was their choice to experience sin that caused Adam and Eve to hide from His presence. Sin brought a fear of God, distanced them from the Lord, brought neglect to a relationship with Him, and spiritually deadened their hearts. The good news is that God's forgiveness renews our love for Him and our desire to be in His presence. Especially in the Dispensation of Grace, forgiveness is a constant state for us, whether it feels this way or not (Colossians 2:13). **He does not distance Himself from us** when we sin, because His grace and Christ's blood covers our sins. He remains near desiring our close fellowship. Moreover, the Scriptures abound with encouragements for us to: "Draw nigh to God, and He will draw nigh to you" (James 4:8). In fact "…He…(is) not far from every one of us…"(Acts 17:27). Likewise, Jeremiah 23:23 asks: "Am I a God at hand, saith the Lord, and not a God afar off?" The happy answer is: "Yes." He is near. All we need to do is thank Him for His mercy and forgiveness, continue in prayer, get back into the Scriptures, and seek consistent daily fellowship with Him. As we draw nigh to Him, He will always draw nigh unto us. Our walk with the Lord can be as sweet and close as it was when we were at our strongest spiritually. The Psalmist promised: "The Lord is nigh unto all that call upon Him, to all that call upon Him in truth" (Psalm 145:18).

If your daily walk has drifted away from the Lord into a cold or barren spiritual climate, it does not have to remain that way. Right now, draw nigh unto God, and He will draw nigh unto you. He is waiting for you.

KNOWING TO DO GOOD
James 4:17

One night, I happened upon a head on collision between a compact car and a heavy, full-size pickup. This accident was on a two-lane highway at dusk, and the vehicles were in the middle of the road just around a curve. As I approached the compact car, one of the teens in great pain begged me for help. Resisting the urge to simply go home to rest after a tiring day, I called 911, directed traffic until authorities arrived, and tried to comfort those who were injured. *Would it have been wrong for me to just drive home without rendering assistance?*

A timeless principle is recorded through a simple statement in James 4:17: "Therefore to him that knoweth to do good, and doeth it not, to him it is sin." The context does not imply any specific act. The Apostle James was recording a general standard Jewish believers needed to live by. However, there were previous teachings about sinful omissions for Jewish believers. God used the responsibility of the "watchman" to illustrate to Ezekiel that if he failed to warn Israel of divine judgment: "his blood will I require at thine hand" (Ezekiel 33:6-9). The Savior rebuked the hypocritical Pharisees who strained over compliance to their traditions while omitting the "... the weightier matters of the law, judgment, mercy, and faith: these ought ye to have done, and not to leave the other undone" (Matthew 23:23). Christ taught that unsaved Jews who refuse to engage in acts of kindness to persecuted saints during the Tribulation will be denied entrance into the Millennial Kingdom. He explained, "...inasmuch as ye did it not to one of the least of these, ye did it not to Me" (Matthew 25:45). Similarly, the Apostle Paul taught: "As we have therefore opportunity, let us do good unto all men, especially unto them who are of the household of faith" (Galatians 6:10). Notice the instruction here remains general. Paul does not limit our ministry in helping others. Seizing opportunities to do good things needs to become a way of life for believers of all dispensations.

While the instruction from James about the sin of knowing to do good but doing it not was given to Israel, it is surely a principle applicable to us today. As I learned in the car wreck mentioned earlier, it would be easier to ignore the needs of others, but it would be wrong. Today, take action when you have the opportunity to do good.

THE EFFECTIVENESS OF PRAYER
James 5:16

A Christian couple had their saved daughter go through a very rebellious time in her teen years. This young lady witnessed discouraging examples of ungodliness from multiple professing Christians. This, coupled with wrong influences and wrong friends, prompted her to leave her walk with the Lord, and rebel against her family. Understandably, her parents were heartbroken. But they continued to fervently pray for her. To God's glory, and in answer to prayer, the Lord worked in the young woman's heart and circumstances to bring her back to a proper daily walk. Today she is once again a sweet vibrant example of what a Christian should be. Ask this family if they believe God still answers prayer, and you will hear a resounding: "Yes, absolutely!"

A verse that must stay prominent in our thinking is James 5:16, which says: "The effectual fervent prayer of a righteous man availeth much." The Apostle James sought to encourage his fellow Jews, who were still under the Law, with this promise about the effectiveness of prayer while facing very difficult times. But God's promise about answering prayer is just as relevant for believers today in the Dispensation of Grace. Paul believed in answered prayer when he asked the saints to pray that he "…may be delivered from them that do not believe in Judea; and…that I may come unto you with joy by the will of God…" (Romans 15:31-32). He believed in prayer when he asked the Lord to give him a "…prosperous journey…" to see the saints in Rome that he might minister to them (Romans 1:10). When the believers at Philippi prayed that Paul would be spared death and be released from prison, he was so confident that God would answer their prayers that he told them: "And having this confidence, I know that I shall abide and continue with you all for your furtherance and joy of faith" (Philippians 1:25).

Even Paul did not receive all things that he prayed for and neither will we. But God does often answer the fervent prayers of His children, especially those who are seeking to walk in a righteous path of regular godly fellowship with Him. In fact, just as parents take joy in granting some of the wishes of their children, Almighty God is pleased to grant many of our requests. Believe this is true and constantly take your needs before the Throne of Grace. *Why?* Because in every dispensation, "the effectual fervent prayer of a righteous man availeth much."

October 12

GIRD UP YOUR MIND
I Peter 1:13-15

Imagine being a police officer preparing for a shift in a dangerous part of a metropolitan city. You would check in at headquarters for the latest information. After dressing in uniform, you would put on your radio that connects you with headquarters. Next, you would put on your belt equipped with mace, a baton, flashlight, gun, and bullets. After girding yourself with all these, you would gird your mind with an alertness to danger, a willingness to serve and protect, and a purpose to come home safely at the end of your shift.

As Peter addressed Kingdom saints who were awaiting the Tribulation and ultimate Second Coming of the Lord Jesus, he told them: "Wherefore gird up the loins of your mind, be sober, and hope [meaning to expectantly wait for His coming in faithfulness] to the end for the grace that is to be brought unto you at the revelation [or revealing] of Jesus Christ" (I Peter 1:13). Peter realized his fellow believers were in hostile territory, whether in metropolitan cities or rural areas. Therefore, they needed a sober, or serious, spiritual mindset as they faced many dangers. In order to keep from becoming weary in their faith and remain faithful, they needed to maintain a focus on the return of Christ. Peter continued his instruction, urging them to not revert back to the sinful lifestyle prior to their salvation (vs. 14). Instead, they must strive to be "holy in all manner of conversation [or lifestyle] (vs. 15), because "…He which called you is holy…" (vs. 15). While the people, program, and promises are different in I Peter, Paul told believers in the Dispensation of Grace essentially the same thing. We too are to be "sober" minded while "…putting on the breastplate of faith and love; and for an helmet, the hope of salvation" (I Thessalonians 5:8). Each day we are to put off our old man, be renewed in the spirit of our minds (Ephesians 4:22-23), and expectantly wait for our "blessed hope" of Christ's return (Titus 2:13). While there are many distinctives only for Israel in the Hebrew epistles, there are also many parallels to encourage us in our daily walk, if we're willing to look for them.

Believer, you too are in hostile territory. Be alert to spiritual dangers, stay in touch with your heavenly headquarters, arm yourself with God's Word, remain willing to protect and serve the saints, and purpose to go home safely to Christ as a good example.

DESIRING GOD'S WORD
I Peter 2:1-3

The honest truth is that I have a strong aversion to vegetables. On the positive side, I love chocolate, ice cream, and pastry. However, my family tells me the sweets I gravitate toward are actually very bad for my health. Therefore, I recently armed myself with the mindset of a new, healthier diet, finding inventive ways to cook vegetables so that they actually taste good, and I'm eating them every day. I've even been juicing vegetables. My family thinks this change is something like a miracle. But in reality, it is a choice of a willing mindset.

When Peter addressed Kingdom saints, he wrote: "As newborn babes, desire the sincere milk of the word, that ye may grow thereby" (I Peter 2:2). He knew the only way they would be able to find consistent spiritual victory, or to grow spiritually, was through consistent time in God's Word. The Lord intended for their faith to be demonstrated in a vibrant, transformed, and satisfying daily walk. In the previous chapter, Peter instructed them not to revert back to sinful habits consistent with life before their salvation. Instead, they were to demonstrate a newness of life by "...laying aside all malice, and all guile, and hypocrisies, and envies, and all evil speakings" (I Peter 2:1). Only time in God's Word and a surrendered spirit would empower them to do so. Therefore, Peter urged them to "desire" God's Word. This would be a choice to willingly embrace a mindset to want to consume the Scriptures as one consumes food. Perhaps Peter had in mind the words of Jeremiah 15:16, which says: "Thy words were found, and I did eat them; and Thy word was unto me the joy and rejoicing of mine heart..." Peter wanted these saints to crave the Word of God and experience the joy of being spiritually fed in the Scriptures. He also appealed to them to embrace this mindset because "...ye have tasted that the Lord is gracious" (I Peter 2:3). If they wouldn't choose to love the Scriptures to find victory, perhaps they would by remembering how gracious God had been in giving them eternal salvation, freeing them from eternal punishment.

Dear believer, have you consciously embraced the mindset that you will choose to desire God's Word and consume it for yourself each day? It's beneficial, it will taste good to your soul, and it is the only realistic way for you to live a vibrantly transformed life for Christ.

SILENCING OUR CRITICS
I Peter 2:13-15

When a new girl was hired into the office where my wife, Terri, worked, she reported to a co-worker that Terri had used profanity in front of one of her patients. Without a second of hesitation, the coworker told her: "Oh no she did not. Terri would not say something like that. You must have misunderstood what she said." That ended the controversy. My wife had demonstrated such a consistent godly testimony before all of the workers in the office that every one of them knew she would not talk or act sinfully.

When Peter wrote to Kingdom believers, they were often under attack by unbelieving Jews. These unsaved men were looking for any opportunity they could find to discredit the lives of Christians and their proclamation of the Lord Jesus Christ. To preserve their testimony, Peter told them: "Submit yourselves to every ordinance of man for the Lord's sake, whether it be to the king, as supreme; or unto governors..." (I Peter 2:13-14). Then he added: "For so is the will of God, that with well doing ye may put to silence the ignorance of foolish men" (vs. 15). Refusing to pay taxes or being disrespectful of those in authority would have turned detractors off to listening about Christ. In contrast, if they conducted themselves in real godliness it would silence their critics and give credibility to their faith. Perhaps Peter was even thinking of the example of Daniel. When those who hated him "...sought to find an occasion against Daniel... they could find none occasion nor fault..." (Daniel 6:4). His godliness and "excellent spirit" echoed his faith. Peter wanted his fellow believing Jews to not use their "...liberty as a cloke for maliciousness, but as the servants of God, [to] honor all men" (I Peter 2:16-17). The Apostle Paul was on the exact same page when he urged believers in the Dispensation of Grace to live out their faith in genuine godliness. He instructed young men to maintain "...sound speech, that cannot be condemned; that he that is of the contrary part may be ashamed, having no evil thing to say of you" (Titus 2:8). A godly life gives unbelievers no ammunition to fire against our testimony or against the truth that eternal life is found in Christ alone, by faith alone. It simply silences the critics.

Dear believer, the lost may reject the gospel when you share it, but they cannot ignore a life transformed into genuine godliness. Silence your critics.

A GODLY WIFE
I Peter 3:1-6

My best friend throughout college had a remarkably godly mother. She had a quiet inner strength that exuded a spiritual influence and stability that positively influenced her family. She was a "guide [to] the house" (I Timothy 5:14) as she gently encouraged family devotions, gave godly biblical counsel, and constantly prayed for her family. "She [also] opened her mouth with wisdom, and in her tongue is the law of kindness" (Proverbs 31:26). She was married to a man who was certainly saved, yet he had strangely stubborn, foolish, and often ungodly tendencies. Nonetheless, this woman remained a constant godly woman and submissive wife. Given that her circumstances were far from ideal, it must have often been difficult. But she submitted to her husband's leadership in the home while softly encouraging him to be a man of God.

The Apostle Peter left timeless principles about the role of women in marriage. He wrote by inspiration: "...ye wives, be in subjection to your own husbands; that, if any obey not the Word, they also may without the Word be won by the conversation [or manner of life] of the wives" (I Peter 3:1). The word "subjection" means to subordinate or obey. A married couple should be a team, giving mutual respect and working in harmony. Yet it is God's design for a wife to submit to her husband's leadership in the home. This doesn't mean she is weak. To the contrary, it takes great inner strength for a capable and intelligent woman to take a step back to allow her husband to be the head of the home. Doing so gives her man room to grow and encourages him to be all he can be. Her outer adornments are wonderful IF secondary to adorning herself with the inner qualities of "a meek and quiet spirit, which is in the sight of God of great price" (vss. 3-4). The combination of submission to her husband with a quiet spirit, and cultivating genuine inner spiritual strength, makes any woman a real beauty. Moreover, such godliness can win even a stubborn lost mate to Christ as he sees virtues he needs (vs. 2).

Ladies who seek to follow this divine design for marriage are worthy of great respect and admiration. They will find this is the path for maximum marital harmony and godly influence to everyone in their home. If you are a married woman, ask for God's so strength that your life can be described by these principles.

HONOR YOUR WIFE
I Peter 3:7

It is with great thankfulness that I can say one of the greatest examples of a husband honoring his wife is my son-in-law, Justin. With great consistency, he is sensitive to his wife's well-being, considerate of her wishes, loving in how he treats her, respectful of her opinions, and wise enough to regularly seek her counsel. He involves her as an equal in all aspects of family decisions and frequently puts her wishes above his own interests. Though married for years, he still takes her on date nights, and leaves her complimentary notes confirming his love. In short, he treats her like a queen. Justin is a real answer to prayer. My wife and I are very happy our daughter has this man to partner with in life.

When Peter wrote timeless principles about how a man is to treat his wife, he said: "Likewise, ye husbands, dwell with them according to knowledge, giving honour unto the wife, as unto the weaker vessel, and as being heirs together of the grace of life..." (I Peter 3:7). The word "honour" means to value, esteem to be of the highest degree, or count precious. A man who is treating his wife properly will demonstrate that he views her as the greatest blessing in his life, after his eternal salvation. He will protect her, make her his priority, show her great respect, and cultivate a good relationship with her. In order to dwell with her "according to knowledge," he will seek to find out what pleases her and what displeases her, then act accordingly to provide an environment where she is happy and content. This will mean more than providing material things; it will mean providing spiritual encouragement and cooperation coupled with love, consideration, and tenderness. He will seek to shoulder the bulk of the stresses of life, knowing she is "the weaker vessel." That does not mean she is lesser than the man, only that God enables men to bear these burdens better. It is the proper role of the man to shield her when possible. This is how "real men" treat their wives. Beyond peace, harmony, and a stable relationship, treating one's wife this way also insures that their "...prayers [will] be not hindered" (vs. 7b).

Men, we encourage you to act like a gentleman toward your wife, demonstrate to her that she is your most valued blessing from God, and honor her with great respect. Doing so will pay high dividends here and in eternity.

FERVENT BROTHERLY LOVE
I Peter 4:8

It was my joy to be the pastor of man who was a tremendous example in fervent brotherly love. Newton frequently came to see me, constantly told me how much he loved me, showered us with gifts to demonstrate his affection, promoted our ministry, prayed for us, and overlooked our faults to see only the positive. He always acted in a way that enabled us to feel completely safe and confident in his love.

We learn from the Book of Acts and the early chapters of Revelation that Jewish believers with a Kingdom hope gathered regularly, as do we today, in local assemblies. These saints had the hope of eternal life and many things in common, but this did not mean they always peacefully coexisted. Therefore, Peter instructed these saints: "And above all things have fervent charity [or love] among yourselves; for charity shall cover the multitude of sins" (I Peter 4:8). These saints needed to realize that, as they interacted with one another, there would be nothing more important than demonstrating love toward each other. This by no means minimized the importance of sound doctrine that taught them what God expected in their daily walk. But towering even above sound doctrine was their need to demonstrate love. The Savior had told them: "By this shall all men know that ye are My disciples, if ye have love one to another" (John 13:35). Without love, their testimony, and their doctrines, would be worthless before the unsaved. But when genuine love prevailed, it gave a powerful testimony that attracted others to their message. Moreover, they were not to demonstrate a shallow, "on again, off again" sort of love. They were to love one another with a "fervent" love, meaning a love that is intense and without ceasing. The Lord wanted strong, bonded relationships demonstrated by keen affection and kindness. Here's where the rubber meets the road. When others hurt, disappointed, or angered them: "…charity shall cover the multitude of sins" (vs. 8). That simply means their love for others would overlook the offence while continuing to love the wrongdoer and demonstrate love. If they would obey these instructions, their assemblies would experience harmony and effectiveness.

The Apostle Paul likewise taught that love is the paramount thing needed in our assemblies. Without it, even with doctrinal correctness and busy activity, we are nothing and our work for Christ profits us nothing (I Corinthians 13:1-3). Today, raise God's standard of love as the highest priority in your church.

GIVING GOD GLORY IN SUFFERING
I Peter 4:16

As a teenager, my girlfriend, her parents, and I trusted Christ within days of one another. In short order, we began attending a Bible-teaching church fifty miles away. My childhood church background had been in a liberal, modernistic denomination where attendees never heard a true gospel. When my former pastor learned that I was attending a church out of town with my girlfriend's parents, he went to their place of work, railed on them, and tried to get them fired. These were difficult times for them, but they trusted Christ, and kept attending the new church where they were growing.

When Peter wrote his first epistle to Kingdom saints, they too were enduring persecution for their growing faith. Peter encouraged them with these words: "But let none of you suffer as a murderer, or as a thief, or as an evil-doer, or as a busybody...Yet if any man suffer as a Christian, let him not be ashamed; but let him glorify God on this behalf" (I Peter 4:15-16). The saints to whom Peter was writing had been "scattered abroad," throughout the known world, by persecution over their faith in the Lord Jesus as their promised Messiah (James 1:1). Unbelieving Jews, like Saul before he became the Apostle Paul, pursued them wherever they went, seeking to imprison and torture them until they renounced their faith in Christ. If they would not recant Christ, many were murdered. It was in this context that Peter instructed these saints about suffering. They were to be careful to never engage in sinful activities that would bring negative consequences. If they suffered for the sake of Christ, they were to not "be ashamed," or shrink from their stand for our Lord. Instead, they were to respond with verbal praise, sing praises, and remain steadfast, therein bringing glory to God. Peter himself had done so when beaten and commanded to no longer speak in Christ's name. He responded with "...rejoicing that they were counted worthy to suffer shame for His name" (Acts 5:41). Likewise, Paul and Silas "...prayed, and sang praises" (Acts 16:25). Responding with angry words or threats would not glorify Christ, but demonstrating godliness would do so and enhance their testimony.

In every dispensation "...all that will live godly in Christ Jesus shall suffer persecution" (II Timothy 3:12). Be bold in sharing Christ in a wise and godly way. When persecution comes, respond in a way that will "glorify God" (I Peter 4:16).

RESISTING GOD
I Peter 5:5

When I was twelve years old, I drove our pickup into a field and parked on a hill. While I was walking away, the pickup started moving. I quickly ran to the front hood and pushed against it with all my might. I was resisting its forward movement, but the power of gravity, with all that weight, made my effort futile. In the end, the pickup rolled to the bottom of the hill. Thankfully, it didn't hit anything, and I was able to get out of the way without being injured.

As Peter wrote to Kingdom saints, he addressed proper conduct in their local assemblies. He addresses the elders who led the churches, urging them to minister willingly as good examples (I Peter 5:1-3). Then he directed his instructions to younger saints saying: "...submit yourselves unto the elder. Yea, all of you be subject one to another, and be clothed with humility: for God resisteth the proud, and giveth grace to the humble" (vs. 5). In these words, we have an extremely important principle. It is noteworthy that when Solomon listed seven things that God hates and that are an abomination, at the very top is "a proud look" (Proverbs 6:16-19). God hates pride because it hardens one's heart toward Him and leads to further sinful behavior contrary to His will. Peter was implying that, when any refuse to submit themselves to church leadership, the real reason would be pride, causing God to resist their efforts. To "resist" means to oppose or set oneself against. What a futile condition when believers put themselves in a position where the power of God, like a weighty object, is working against their efforts. Furthermore, they miss out on the grace, meaning God's divine influence on the heart, which would otherwise be given to them. The Apostle James likewise wrote: "...God resisteth the proud, but giveth grace unto the humble" (James 4:6). The context reveals that James was addressing "... fightings among you" in local churches, improper prayer, and worldliness (vss. 1-5). Here again, these saints are warned that God will resist the proud conduct of those who harden themselves to the Lord's work in their hearts that produces proper conduct.

In I Thessalonians 5:12-14, Paul addresses this same subject with similar instructions. Compare them for yourself. *In your circumstance, are you humbly submitting to God or proudly refusing to submit, bringing God's resistance?* Choose the path of humility.

BE VIGILANT
I Peter 5:8

Our family used to enjoy watching the small prairie dogs in the Black Hills of South Dakota. These animals live in underground communities connected by a series of tunnels and surface holes. For safety reasons, when they come outside for food, they stay very close to a means of escape. They frequently stand up on their back legs looking, with great vigilance, for any predator. They aren't the smartest of God's creation. Hunters often shoot one of the prairie dogs and another standing right beside it simply looks in bewilderment at its dead companion. But if a human gets anywhere close, they quickly vanish into the safety of their den.

In Peter's parting words in his first epistle, he warns: "Be sober, be vigilant, because your adversary the devil, as a roaring lion, walketh about, seeking whom he may devour" (I Peter 5:8). The intended word picture is one of a powerful, hungry, and mature lion on the prowl looking for prey. Its victim may not even be aware it is being stalked with stealth until fatally within the lion's unmerciful clutches. As a spiritual being, Satan is an unseen enemy who constantly prowls searching for any he can attack, particularly believers in the Lord Jesus Christ. Satan can use false teachers, appeal to our flesh to pursue sinful paths, or even use other believers to "devour" us in discouragement. The Lord wanted Peter to inform the saints of this constant danger and specifically warn them to be "vigilant." Being vigilant means to be awake, watchful, or alert. Believers must not become careless or indifferent to the attacks of our enemy. If we do not choose to be consistently alert to our ever-present danger, we will make ourselves easy prey for our enemy. Therefore, believers are to be "sober," or serious minded, about this threat. This means to not only look for Satan's attacks, but to "resist," or stand against them, in the power of the Lord. James gave the encouraging promise, "Resist the devil, and he will flee from you" (James 4:7). Satan cannot overpower a believer, nor can he be successful, unless one is careless, unprepared, or facing Satan in one's own strength.

The Apostle Paul likewise warns about our constant struggle against satanic forces (Ephesians 6:11-13). To be prepared for this danger, we are instructed to put on the "whole armour of God" that we might be able "to stand" victorious in His power. *Are you dressing for this battle daily?*

NEVER BARREN OR UNFRUITFUL
II Peter 1:5-9

We have Christian friends in Canada who own a fruit orchard. A few years ago, they had an unusually warm and early spring. All of the trees grew beautiful new blooms in preparation to produce a hefty harvest. Then a severe cold snap with snow swept in, killing all those new blooms and any hope for a good harvest. It didn't matter how deeply rooted the trees were, or how beautiful the trees looked in summer. Those trees were going to remain barren and unfruitful for one whole year.

In Peter's second epistle, he gave a meaningful promise to his fellow Kingdom saints about spiritual growth. After discussing their "precious faith" (II Peter 1:1) unto salvation, and their "precious promises" (vs. 4) of a new nature and eternal hope, he told them to give "all diligence" to add six things to their faith. First, he told them to add "virtue," which means manliness, valor, or excellence (vs. 5). Believers needed courage and toughness to face trials, rather than being too soft. Paul urged the same mindset when he told us to "quit you like men, be strong" (I Corinthians 16:13). Second, they needed to add "knowledge," which refers to an assimilation of basic doctrinal facts to know what the Lord expected of them. Third was "temperance," meaning self-control. They would never be spiritually stable if they exercised no restraint in sinful tendencies. Fourth was "patience," referring to endurance. They must not establish a pattern of crumbling every time hardship came. Instead they must draw on God's grace, endure, and remember this victory for future strength. Fifth was "brotherly kindness," or brotherly love. Just as one is incomplete without being loved, one is incomplete without demonstrating a kind love for other saints. Sixth was "charity," which refers to an unconditional love for others. This quality is the needed icing on the cake of Christianity. Peter promised "if these things be in you, and abound...ye shall neither be barren nor unfruitful." To be barren of spiritual fruit would indicate a barrenness, emptiness, and lack of spiritual life within the soul. Instead, allowing the Lord to produce these qualities would bring real spiritual life and inner joy.

Peter's list is mirrored by two references from Paul. Romans 5:3-4 refers to maturing through tribulation, patience, experience, and hope. Then, in Galatians 5:22-26, he specifies the fruit of the Spirit. If you want to never be barren or unfruitful, allow God to grow these qualities in you.

CONSTANT REMINDERS
II Peter 1:12-15

My wife and I have a large 3D-type painting of the face of the Lord Jesus Christ on the cross. When you look closely, a detailed account of the crucifixion emerges from the hidden details within the picture. We have a plaque which reads: "A soft answer turneth away wrath," taken from Proverbs 15:1, emphasizing a key to harmony in our home. Another plaque reads: "Love one another," based on I Thessalonians 4:9 and Romans 13:8. This highlights the glue that holds families together. We've intentionally placed these constant reminders of our faith on the walls so their truth will become deeply imbedded into our souls.

After instructing the Jewish saints to add a list of virtues to their faith (II Peter 1:5-8), Peter goes on to say three different times that he will continue to remind them of these truths. He says: "...I will not be negligent to put you always in remembrance of these things, though ye know them, and be established in the present truth" (vs. 12). Peter knew that even saints who are well grounded in truth tend to forget the truths of Scripture, or can even be swayed by false teaching. Peter was well aware of our Lord's parable about the sower sowing the Word of God and the "wicked one" coming to snatch that seed away (Matthew 13:19-20). So he told his readers he would be intent on constantly reminding them of the virtues they needed to add to their faith. Peter put it this way: "Yea, I think it meet [or appropriate], as long as I am in this tabernacle, to stir you up by putting you in remembrance" (vs. 13). It may have sounded like a broken record to some. To others his reminders would be like the saints in the hymn "hungering and thirsting to hear it like the rest." As long as he was alive, Peter intended to sing this same tune to remind them of needed truths. Finally, Peter told them another reason for his persistence: "I will endeavour that ye may be able after my decease to have these things always in remembrance" (vs. 15). My father had over a dozen memorable quotes about wisdom in life that he repeated over and over. This repetition has branded these saying into my mind. So, I am certain Peter's repetition of truth was effective.

Believer, we suggest you constantly review the truths, and even basic doctrines of God's Word with your family. Doing so will assure they won't be easily forgotten.

DELIVERED FROM TEMPTATIONS
II Peter 2:1-10

Without having been there, we can try to imagine a little of what it must have been like on 9/11 after the planes hit the towers. The buildings were shaken, as were the people. Fire and smoke filled many rooms. We know many fire fighters were dispatched and entered the buildings to rescue those in peril. *Could it have been, at least on the lower floors, that firemen went into smoke-filled rooms with flashlights calling out to those in need?* If so, the victims could have reached safety by listening to the calls, following the flashlights, and heeding instructions that would lead to safety.

Peter's second epistle reveals that the Jewish Kingdom saints were in spiritual peril. Evil men whom he called "false prophets" (II Peter 2:1) had entered the safety of their churches with dangerous lies. These men "were even denying the Lord that bought them..." (vs. 1). Unfortunately, as they called out this bad doctrine, Peter said: "And many shall follow their pernicious ways..." (vs. 2). No doubt the hearers thought they were following the light of truth to safety when, in fact, they were being led the wrong way. It was in this context that Peter told his fellow saints: "The Lord knoweth how to deliver the godly out of temptations, and to reserve the unjust unto the day of judgment to be punished" (vs. 9). This verse sounds quite similar to I Corinthians 10:13, which says: "There hath no temptation taken you but such as is common to man: but God is faithful, who will not suffer you to be tempted above that ye are able; but will with the temptation also make a way to escape, that ye may be able to bear it." *How does God deliver believers from temptations?* The answer is essentially the same in every dispensation. The Lord does not commandeer our will. We must choose to allow Him to lead us to victory by listening to the right voices of influence, following the light of God's truth into paths of safety, and yielding in obedience to the Holy Spirit who always leads us away from the perils of sin.

The Jews in Peter's day needed to stop listening to the confusing false teachers and to simply heed the truths they had heard from sound teachers. Similarly, today, we need to choose to yield to the Holy Spirit, who always leads away from sin, and listen only to teachers who are consistent with truth taught by Paul.

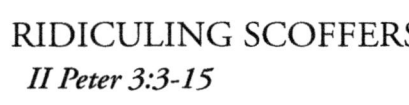

RIDICULING SCOFFERS
II Peter 3:3-15

We have a close friend who has three daughters. The oldest daughter is an aggressive, outspoken, avowed atheist. She goes out of her way to disrespectfully ridicule her mother's faith in Christ, calling her stupid, ignorant, and crazy for believing all her religious garbage. Recently, her mother posted a picture of a Bible and the book *Fifty Shades of Gray* on her Facebook page, suggesting the Bible was a better influence. As expected, the verbal attack was vicious and demeaning. The youngest of the sisters once had a faithful walk with Christ. However, she has chosen to draw closer to the older sister and, as expected, the influence has been spiritually devastating.

It isn't anything new for people to ridicule and demean true faith in Christ, along with other key truths recorded in the inspired Scriptures. It's been going on for thousands of years. Peter warned his fellow believing Jews: "Knowing this first, that there shall come in the last days scoffers, walking after their own lusts, and saying, Where is the promise of His coming? for since the fathers fell asleep, all things continue as they were from the beginning of the creation" (II Peter 3:3-4). Both Peter and Paul referred to "last days," but in a different context. When Paul referred to the "last days" (II Timothy 3:1-9), or "latter times" (I Timothy 4:1), he was talking about the last days in the Dispensation of Grace just prior to the Rapture. In contrast, Peter's "last days" refer to the days in the Tribulation leading to the Second Coming of Christ. In both instances, mankind in general will be largely proud, fiercely arrogant, void of doctrinal truth, and ridiculing the faith of true believers. Even though there is more obvious evidence to support divine creation than the false theory of evolution, Peter said unbelievers would be "willingly...ignorant" (II Peter 3:5), or stubbornly refusing to consider, that God created all the order we see, just as described in Scripture. Peter urged his readers not to allow their faith to be shaken by these evil mockers. He reminded them that God will keep His promises of coming judgment on the unsaved (vss. 7-10). In the meantime, believers are to hold fast biblical truths, live godly, and continue to be motivated by the promise of eternity in the "new heavens and new earth" (vss. 13).

Today, believers can likewise benefit from these same encouragements in faithfulness. We should also minimized contact with people who ridicule truths we hold dear.

HE NEVER GIVES UP ON YOU
Philippians 1:6

We knew a pastor's son named Tim. Being a preacher's kid is like living in a fishbowl of constant criticism and high expectations. Added to this hardship, his mother died of cancer when he was 15. Depressed and confused, Tim became rebellious. It was never anything severe. It was mostly falling short of his father's expectations. When the father remarried shortly thereafter, he threw Tim out of the house. His father said he had done all he could with Tim, and he'd given up on his son. We can only imagine how hopeless and alone Tim must have felt.

God will never throw us out of His family, nor will He ever give up on us. Ephesians 4:30 promises, when we trust in Christ alone for the forgiveness of our sins, we are "sealed unto the day of redemption." The indwelling Holy Spirit is our assurance from God that our salvation and sonship will remain constant forever. Just as we are saved by grace, we are kept by grace. Romans 8:35-39 promises that absolutely nothing can "...separate us from the love of Christ...." We are secure in the family of God and are always welcome in the presence of God the Father. Our standing with Him never changes, and He continues to work with us through all our ups and downs. Paul was so certain of this, he tells the saints at Philippi that he was "...confident of this very thing, that He which hath begun a good work in you will perform it until the day of Jesus Christ" (Philippians 1:6). To be "confident" is to be fully persuaded. The "good work" Paul refers to is the entire process of salvation and sanctification. At the moment we trust in Christ, we are set apart from the penalty of sin and into identification with the righteousness of Christ. Thereafter, we are permanently set apart from the world as we grow in our faith. Paul was convinced this process never ends until we go home to be with the Lord. God will never give up on us, even when we are inconsistent or rebel into a wayward path. God still loves us and seeks to draw us back to Himself. He keeps working within, through the Holy Spirit, and without, through circumstances, to grow us into a mature child of God.

Share the news today that, regardless of ups and downs in our faithfulness, God never gives up on us.

MURMURING
Philippians 2:14

After high school, I worked in a huge plant that employed thousands. Four gals from my high school worked there also, so we began sharing lunch breaks. However, one of them was constantly negative. Nearly everything out of her mouth was a complaint about something or someone, and it had a negative effect on the others in the group. It was depressing just listening to it all. After nearly a week, I decided I simply wouldn't be around them any more.

God's children of faith are not immune to a complaining spirit. When Moses was sent back to Egypt to deliver Israel out of cruel slavery, the Israelites repeatedly complained. Even a chance at freedom should have brought appreciation. But after finally being miraculously released, Israel murmured (meaning "to grumble") against Moses when Pharaoh's armies pursued them. Later "the people murmured against Moses" over a lack of water (Exodus 15:24). Then while in "the wilderness of Sin," they murmured over a lack of food (16:1-4). **It had become a pattern of life.** When God promised victory over the inhabitants in Canaan, they once again murmured in disbelief that God would give the victory (Numbers 14). God's anger was so kindled that an entire generation, except for Joshua and Caleb, perished without seeing the Promised Land. Paul refers to this in I Corinthians 10:10 warning the believers: "Neither murmur ye, as some of them also murmured, and were destroyed of the destroyer." Complaining is a dangerous, negative habit. It embitters the soul, sours the spirit, ignores the rich blessings of God, and robs one of the joy of life. It also unnecessarily makes life miserable for those around us, becomes a poor testimony to the lost, and poisons our outlook on life. Perhaps, worst of all, it spreads like an outbreak of the flu to others, who, in turn, mirror this negativity.

Simply put, God hates a complaining spirit. Paul warns the saints at Philippi saying: "Do all things without murmurings and disputings: that ye may be blameless and harmless, the sons of God, without rebuke, in the midst of a crooked...nation, among whom ye shine as lights in the world" (Philippians 2:14-15). It is not possible for us to be blameless before the Lord or man if we have a complaining spirit. Ask someone today to hold you accountable any time you are being negative, then purposely practice being positive in your speech and outlook.

THE NECESSITY OF REPEATING
Philippians 3:1

Most of our purchases are with a credit card. There is a convenience because we don't need to carry large amounts of cash, but we also do it to accumulate points to use for free airline tickets. Recently, I scheduled a doctor's appointment over the phone, and they required a deposit with a credit card to secure my appointment. After reading off the card number, I repeated it again for clarity. Sure enough, the listener had recorded it incorrectly. I anticipated this possibility. That's why I repeated the number just to be sure they got it right. It was the safe thing to do.

As we read through Scriptures, it is easy to see that God often repeats the same instructions over and over. *Why does He do so?* Paul tells us why in Philippians 3:1: "To write the same things [again] to you, to me indeed is not grievous, but for you it is safe." It didn't bother Paul to repeat important doctrine. He knew believers easily forget, and that the truth doesn't always register the first time. Three subjects were often repeated to Paul's converts: circumcision, baptism, and forgiveness. Freedom from the Mosaic Law was hard for many to embrace. In part, this was because false teachers constantly sought to impose this legalism on those Paul led to Christ. They also had not fully grasped the principle of rightly dividing between instructions to Israel and to the Body of Christ. So, Paul warned the Galatians that circumcision avails nothing. They needed to stand fast in liberty (5:1-2). Then he explained to the Colossian believers that they had a far superior spiritual circumcision (Colossians 2:10-11). Water baptism was confusing for many, because God once required this to accompany faith in order for Jews to be saved (Mark 1:4; Acts 2:38). In our new Dispensation of Grace, Paul explained we have salvation by faith alone. Water baptism would detract from the cross, and today we have a superior spiritual baptism (Ephesians 4:5; I Corinthians 1:14-18; I Corinthians 12:13). Many are also confused about forgiveness. God required Israelites to confess their sins for forgiveness (Matthew 3:6, Mark 1:5). But believers today are given full forgiveness of all sins at the moment of salvation (Colossians 2:13; Ephesians 1:7).

Paul knew forgetfulness and lack of comprehension made repeating key doctrines the safe thing to do. When we read these verses, may we be, as a hymn describes: "hungering and thirsting to hear it like the rest."

WHERE IS YOUR LIFE?
Philippians 3:20

We have a very close friend who moved to Florida from Puerto Rico twenty-six years ago. Understandably, she is still proud of her native country, misses family there, and occasionally longs to see her hometown. However, during a recent visit, she realized that her old home simply isn't home any more. So much has changed in Puerto Rico over the years that it barely resembles how she remembers it. Moreover, she has built a new life here with current relationships and has a grace church that she loves. Her epiphany has been that her new life is really home. Her former home could never really be home again.

Philippians 3:20 says: "For our conversation [or citizenship] is in heaven; from whence also we look for the Savior, the Lord Jesus Christ." In a real sense, every true child of God today has had a transfer of citizenship. Prior to salvation, we all "...walked according to the course of this world, according to the prince of the power of the air, the spirit that now worketh in the children of disobedience" (Ephesians 2:2). We were at home, or comfortable, with the sinful characteristics of our day. But that changes within when we trust in Christ alone for salvation. "...If any man be in Christ, he is a new creature [or creation]: old things are passed away; behold, all things are become new" (II Corinthians 5:17). This certainly does not mean believers never fail in sin or never again desire sinful activities. It does mean that God changes us within spiritually. Now, when we knowingly sin, the Holy Spirit strikes our conscience and gives us a deep desire to live for Christ instead of simply for self. Like Moses, who refused the "pleasures of sin" in Egypt so that he might walk with the Lord (Hebrews 11:24-27), believers are drawn in the new nature, by God, to walk with Him. We realize, as the chorus says: "This world is not my home, I'm just a-passing through, my treasures are laid up somewhere beyond the blue..." Our real home is heaven.

Talk about your new heavenly home, think about it, and long to see it. Never again allow yourself to become "at home" in this world. Our life should now be spent setting our affections on things above (Colossians 3:1-6) and living for Christ. We must be looking for the Savior who may return for us soon. Remember, you are now a citizen of heaven.

REJOICE IN THE LORD

Philippians 4:4

My wife's father and I are both real football fans. We can joyfully talk about football for long periods of time. We anticipate every recruiting class, season, and game. When our teams played for, and won, the national championship, we talked about it extensively, replayed the game, and rejoiced in the victory. With a sense of reverence, it occurs to me that we believers should be even more enthusiastic fans of God and be constantly rejoicing in Him.

In Philippians 4:4, Paul tells us to: "Rejoice in the Lord always, and again I say, rejoice." Notice that the emphasis, and focus, of rejoicing is not in our circumstances, but in the Lord Himself. A study of the Scriptures reveals there are many aspects of the Lord that should produce rejoicing in us. Jeremiah wrote about how mercifully God deals with sinful man. He said: "It is of the Lord's mercies that we are not consumed, because His compassions fail not, they are new every morning..." (Lamentations 3:22-23). David wrote: "The Lord is merciful and gracious, slow to anger, and plenteous in mercy" (Psalm 103:8). He added: "Great is the Lord, and greatly to be praised...I will speak of the glorious honor of Thy majesty... the Lord is gracious, and full of compassion, slow to anger, and of great mercy" (Psalm 145:3-8). Likewise, Moses said: "The Lord is longsuffering, and of great mercy, forgiving iniquity and transgression, and by no means clearing the guilty..." (Numbers 14:18). Even in the face of Israel's blatant rebellion, Nehemiah proclaimed: "...but Thou art a God ready to pardon, gracious and merciful, slow to anger, and of great kindness, and forsookest them not" (Nehemiah 9:17). But even when, in righteousness, God will judge the sins of mankind, we have the assurance: "Shall not the Judge of all the earth do right?" (Genesis 18:25). Many passages describe God's holiness, righteousness, power, omniscience, and love. For example: "...God commendeth His love toward us, in that, while we were yet sinners, Christ died for us" (Romans 5:8). After we trust in Christ, we have the assurance of eternal security, and on our behalf, He "...is able to do exceeding abundantly above all that we ask or think..." (Ephesians 3:20).

Throughout today, we should exalt the Lord in songs of praise and rejoice in His greatness. Doing so will not only glorify God, but it will also draw us closer to Him and give us a greater appreciation for our salvation.

October 30

PRAYING ALWAYS FOR YOU
Colossians 1:3

In 1985, my vision became seriously impaired. I could only read with great concentration, and then only with my Bible very close to my eyes. The specialist diagnosed me with keratoconus. This is a disease that thins the normally round cornea, bulges it into a cone shape and, in my case, leaving ripples in the cornea. This progressive disease causes distorted vision, depth perception problems, and light sensitivity. When this disease began and intensified, I feared I would become incapacitated, unable to minister or support my young family. Once word spread about my difficulty, believers from around the country began to call me with the encouraging words: "I'm praying for you." It's hard to express how much that meant to me and how thankful I am that God answered their prayers.

When the Apostle Paul opened his letter to the believers at Colossae, he encouraged them by saying he was: "praying always" for them (Colossians 1:3). Paul was, what we call today, "a prayer warrior." He prayed regularly for the needs of other saints. He assured the believers at Ephesus that he would "cease not to give thanks for you, making mention of you in my prayers" (Ephesians 1:16). Paul reminds them again of his prayers over his concern that they would be discouraged by his persecutions. He writes: "For this cause I bow my knees unto the Father…that He would grant you, according to the riches of His glory…" (Ephesians 3:14,16). When Paul was aware of a need in the life of other believers, his response was to hold them up to the throne of grace, asking God to intervene on their behalf. Knowing there were questions and concerns among new believers at Thessalonica about what happened to saints when they died before the Rapture, Paul again assures them of his prayers. He tells them he planned to come see them soon, and that he was "night and day praying exceedingly that we might see your face…" (I Thessalonians 3:10). It must have been an encouragement to the believers at Colossae to know Paul was praying for them, and that he would "not cease to pray" for their needs (Colossians 1:9).

You, too, have likely been greatly encouraged by the assurance of someone praying for you in a time of real need. Now it is time for you to "pay it forward." Spend some time now lifting up someone in prayer, and seek to become a real prayer warrior.

SATAN'S FOUR STRATEGIES
Colossians 2:4

When John Lennon was at the height of popularity, he put out a song saying: "Imagine there is no heaven. It's easy if you try. No hell below us, above us only sky…I'm not the only one (who thinks this way)…I hope some day you'll join us, and the world will be as one." John Lennon didn't realize it, but he was being used of Satan to spiritually lead many astray.

Colossians Chapter Two reveals four sinister, but effective, strategies of Satan to pull people in the wrong spiritual direction. The first is to "beguile you with enticing words" (Colossians 2:4). The word "beguile" means to entice with a deceitful parallel logic. It is somewhat like two sets of train tracks running side by side that seem to be going in the same direction. However, somewhere down the line those tracks separate, taking participants to different places. In the spiritual realm, Satan seeks to get us to board the wrong train of doctrinal beliefs that will lead ultimately to ruin. Satan's messengers are often great orators whose words sound good but are designed to lead you astray. Their strategy is man's "philosophy" (vs. 8). Once individuals are derailed onto the wrong path, *where will Satan take them*? He wants them to follow man's sinful way of thinking instead of God's way. If that strategy doesn't work, Satan attempts to use what may be scripturally, but not dispensationally, correct. In verses 16-17, Paul corrects the believers at Colossae for returning to a practice of being under the bondage of the Mosaic Law. We are to understand those things given to Israel were only a "shadow," or illustration, of all we now have in Christ without the Law. We're not to place ourselves under Israel's previously-required legalism. We are to live in the new truths and liberty of grace. When the previous strategies don't work, Satan seeks to use the most extreme of all tactics. He seeks to place us under the influence of extra-biblical, so-called revelations. Some at Colossae were influenced to voluntarily practice the worshipping of angels, doing so from their "fleshly [or carnal] mind" (Colossians 2:8). More common examples today would be to follow the Apocrypha, Book of Mormon, New Age practices, or Scientology literature, which may satisfy the flesh, but do not satisfy God.

It is important for us to be alert to these four strategies of Satan. Look today for songs and conversations with these tactics, but stay focused on the truths in Paul's letters.

ESTABLISHED IN THE FAITH
Colossians 2:8

Six months after I trusted in the Lord Jesus Christ alone for eternal life, I had a major trial. When I came home one Saturday night, a friend of my parents, a Jehovah's Witness, was waiting for me. He'd heard about a spiritual awakening within me, and he had come with the mission to pull me into the fold of their teaching. For well over an hour, we talked about doctrine. Even though I was still a babe in Christ, I had quickly learned many key doctrines and was able to refute many of the things he was teaching by quoting Scripture. Had I not been established in the faith to the extent I was, my life would have likely taken a far different spiritual path.

Satan often sends his human messengers to derail and recruit unsuspecting souls. This is exactly what was happening at Colossae and the reason Paul wrote to them. He warned: "Beware lest any man spoil you through philosophy and vain deceit, after the tradition of men, after the rudiments of the world, and not after Christ" (Colossians 2:8). After beginning to correct false doctrine they had already embraced, Paul warns: "Let no man beguile you of your reward..." (2:18) by following errant teaching. *What were some of the errors they had been convinced to believe?* False teachers had convinced them that they had to keep the Mosaic Law to have a proper standing before God. But Paul shared good news saying: "And ye are complete in Him, which is the head of all principality and power" (2:10). The moment we trust in Christ, we have His complete righteousness and complete forgiveness of all our sins (2:13). This makes us entirely complete apart from all religious rituals. Some at Colossae were "intruding" into areas they ought not, such as the "worshipping of angels" (2:18). This meant they were no longer properly esteeming, or were "not holding the Head" of our faith, the Lord Jesus Christ, as their exclusive focus of worship (2:19). Believers can be truly saved by Christ and yet become so confused by false doctrine that they even turn from their Savior. These confused saints were also embracing many legalistic "ordinances" (2:20-23), which did nothing to enhance true spiritual growth.

How established are you in sound doctrine? If you're not, you're vulnerable to Satan's deceptive attacks with false doctrine. Begin a daily time of Bible study, and sit regularly under the sound teaching of someone who feeds you the Word of truth rightly divided.

WHOLEHEARTEDLY
Colossians 3:23

The NFL Pro Bowl is a one game competition between the elite players from both leagues. NFL players, coaches, and fans vote for who they consider to be the best four or five at every position. These players play one semi-competitive game. Those chosen consider it a great honor to be so recognized by their peers. However, by comparison to the players' usual salary, the financial compensation is not great enough to risk an injury that may end their career. Consequently, the participants only halfheartedly play the game. In 2015, the play was so lackluster that some of the fans attending began to boo the players.

The Apostle Paul gave a number of instructions to the saints in Colossians 3: seek things above, put to death sinful habits, put on the new man, let God's Word dwell in you richly, and submit to proper authority. However, Paul seems to have anticipated only a half-hearted response because he concludes by saying: "And whatsoever ye do, do it heartily, as to the Lord, and not unto men" (3:23). As a Jew, Paul was keenly aware of the constant promptings in the Old Testament to not simply follow the Lord half-heartedly. Israel's pattern was to be wayward, then return to the Lord only after being chastened. But it was often with little commitment. So, the Lord warned them to "...return unto the Lord thy God...with all thine heart, and with all thy soul..." (Deuteronomy 30:2). What the Lord really wanted from Israel was for them to follow Him whole-heartedly. The Old Testament often repeats God's commandments for them to love, follow, and serve Him with all their hearts. Among the best verses that demonstrates this is Joshua 22:5, which says: "But take diligent heed to do the commandment and the law...to love the Lord your God, and to walk in all His ways, and...to cleave unto Him, and serve Him with all your heart, and with all your soul." Similarly, the Apostle Paul did not want to see only a half-hearted effort on the part of the saints at Colossae. He wanted to see them apply the instructions in God's Word "heartily," or with all their heart and might.

As we read this, may the Lord speak to our hearts about how fervently we are following Him. He would have us read His Word, follow Scripture, attend church, pray, and serve Him with all our hearts. Decide today that this is how you will follow Christ.

REDEEMING THE TIME

Colossians 4:5

Harry Chapin's 1974 number one song "Cat's In the Cradle" sends a message to fathers about redeeming the time. The lyrics describe a father too busy for his son when he was born and when he learned to play, because there were planes to catch and bills to pay. As the father grew much older, he wanted time with his grown son and with his son's family. But his son declines, as his father had, because he was too busy. After it was too late, the father realized he'd raised a son just like him, foolishly hurrying through life without taking time for what is really important.

As Paul closes his letter to the Colossians, he urges them to: redeem the time (Colossians 4:5). The word "redeem" means to buy up, or purchase. People used to receive green stamps with purchases, then later use them to redeem, or purchase, products. The time God gives us needs to be used to purchase what He thinks is valuable. This principle is so important that it frequently occurs in Scripture. In Colossian 4:5-6, Paul tells the saints to redeem their time by walking "in wisdom toward them that are without [outside salvation]...Let your speech be always with grace..." The time to guard our testimony and seek to have a positive impact for Christ on lost souls is now, not some future day. Redeem the time. In Ephesians 5:16, Paul tells the saints to be "redeeming the time, because the days are evil." The very fact that we live in spiritually dark days is intended to motivate us with a sense of urgency in living for Christ and reaching the lost with the Gospel of Grace. The context tells us how: "not as fools, but as wise" (vs. 15), "...understanding what the will of the Lord is" (vs. 17), and "giving thanks always for all things" (vs. 20). Solomon likewise urged the young to redeem the time. He told them: "Remember now thy Creator in the days of thy youth..." before you arrive at old age having never done so (Ecclesiastes 12:1).

Most of us live as though we have all the time in the world to waste before getting serious about living fervently for the Lord. But we don't. Our time will soon be all gone. Redeem your time now by getting serious about a close, living relationship with Christ that is being transformed day by day. Redeem the time.

CONFESSING DAILY SINS
I John 1:9

Imagine growing up in a strict home where forgiveness was only granted after performing a required legalistic protocol. Now grown, you cling to the same mindset. When you offended a friend, you beg for their forgiveness, and they graciously accept your apology. Then, every time you see your friend, you plead for them to forgive you. Over and over this is repeated. Each time your friend assures you that they forgave you long ago and put it behind them. They also ask you to please stop begging for forgiveness. *Should you still continue to plead with your friend to forgive you?*

One of the most misunderstood verses in the entire Bible is I John 1:9, "If we confess our sins, He is faithful and just to forgive us our sins, and to cleanse us from all unrighteousness." John was writing this instruction to Israel, not the Body of Christ! In order to experience God's mercy, Jews were required by God to confess their sins (Proverbs 28:13). They were also required to (and frequently did) confess their national sins to obtain God's mercy (i.e. Nehemiah 1:6; 9:3-38; Ezra 10:11; Jeremiah 3:13). The context of I John 1:9 reveals John was urging <u>lost Jews</u> to confess their national sins of rejecting Christ, so that they could likewise have "fellowship" (vs. 3) with God and be cleansed from all sins (vss. 7, 9). This was consistent with the conduct required of Jews for eternal life prior to our present Dispensation of Grace, as explained in Matthew 3:6 and Romans 10:10. However, <u>confessing daily sins has nothing to do with believers today</u>. Knowledgeable saints do not attempt to keep the Sabbath which required restricting travel and forbidding work. Nor do they practice circumcision as a religious requirement or keep Jewish feast days. *Why?* It is because all of these rituals belonged exclusively to Israel while under the Law of Moses. The practice of confessing sins also belongs to that same program and has been set aside.

When Paul wrote to Gentile believers in our present Dispensation of Grace, he explained we have already been "...forgiven you all trespasses" (Colossians 2:13), whether past, present, or future. Not one verse from Paul suggests we should continue to confess daily sins for forgiveness. It is appropriate to tell the Lord you are sorry for sin and ask for His strength to find victory. But rest and rejoice in your total forgiveness of all sins without asking Him to forgive what is already forgiven.

RIGHTLY DIVIDE JEWISH EPISTLES
I John 2:3-6

We have a Christian friend with a clear testimony of salvation. At one point, she was really struggling spiritually and failing in a besetting sin. For weeks she listened to a popular preacher on the radio who repeatedly said: "If Jesus isn't Lord of all in your life, He isn't your Lord at all." What he meant was that truly saved individuals will not sin. He was preaching the doctrine of sinless perfection, basing it on passages written to Jews who were still under the Mosaic Law with an earthly eternal hope. Though our friend was an established grace believer, she became so confused, convicted, and discouraged that she nearly took her own life.

It is of the utmost importance, when reading the books written to Israel, that we rightly divide the Word of truth. Paul tells us all Scripture is "profitable" (II Timothy 3:16) for grace believers and is provided for "our learning" (Romans 15:4). Therefore, we should also study the books of our Bible not written by the Apostle Paul. However, we must always compare Jewish doctrine with Paul's letters and only make a direct application to our lives when we can verify similar principles found in Paul's epistles. With this in mind, we know we will find a number of applications in Jewish books that can only be properly applied to Jews and should not applied to ourselves. The following are some examples from the Book of I John. The Apostle John told his readers they could know saving faith in Christ "if" they kept his commandment. If they did not obey, they did not know Christ (I John 2:3-6). This does not apply to us today. Even though the Corinthians were extremely carnal, Paul did not question their salvation. In fact, he called them "saints" (I Corinthians 1:2). John continued, "if any man love the world, the love of the Father is not in him" (I John 2:15). Yet when Demas quit ministering with Paul because he "...loved this present world" (II Timothy 4:10), Paul never questioned his salvation, because grace is not a performance system. We are saved by grace, kept by grace, and God deals with us every day by grace.

We can glean many edifying examples and principles out of books written to Jewish saints still under the Law (I Corinthians 10:1-11). So don't avoid these books. However, be careful to apply only what is consistent with our primary instructions for today from the Apostle Paul.

SPIRITUALLY STRONG YOUNG MEN
I John 2:14

Every parent knows the frustration of not being able to make wise decisions for their children. Especially as they grow into teens. I remember one teen boy who was continually rebellious and totally disinterested in the spiritual influence of his Christian parents and church. One day his mother excused these tendencies by blaming struggles in school and bad experiences. I remember thinking that a parent is only going to get as much spiritual responsiveness and maturity out of their children as they expect from them. Therefore, expecting more spiritual responsiveness from this young man, rather than making excuses, could have made a difference.

When John wrote to Jewish believers anticipating the Tribulation days, he said something significant about young people; "I have written unto you, young men, because ye are strong, and the Word of God abideth in you, and ye have overcome the wicked one" (I John 2:14). John's reference to these young men being strong had nothing to do with their physical capabilities. He was describing their strong spiritual interest and walk with the Lord. Like Joseph, who as a youth, demonstrated godly strength before Potiphar's wife and Pharaoh, like Daniel, before a nation of idol worshippers, or like Timothy when he dedicated himself to minister with Paul, these young Jewish men were strong spiritually. The source of their spiritual strength was spending ample time in the Word of God and allowing it to dwell within them in abundance. We can find this to likewise be true of Joseph, Daniel, and Timothy when we study their lives in Scripture. The result of being strong students of God's Word and being spiritually strong generally produces the power of God to "overcome the wicked one." Apparently, due to their faith in Christ and time in God's Word, these young men had not been deterred by the ridicule and threats of unbelieving Jews. They were standing strong in their faith. For that, the Apostle John acknowledged and praised them.

High spiritual expectations for ones teen doesn't insure success because they can choose to rebel. But it does appear to be true from Scripture that one gets a better outcome from young people when they know genuine spirituality is expected of them. This is exactly why Paul wrote to Timothy: "Let no man despise thy youth; but be thou an example of the believers, in word, in conversation, in spirit, in faith, in purity" (I Timothy 4:12). Parents, let your children know you expect spiritual interest and responsiveness.

SONS OF GOD
I John 3:1-3

We know a Christian family where the wife was previously married and had two small boys. The father of these boys passed away, and like all children, they needed the love, acceptance, and nurturing of a father. When the mother remarried, her new husband adopted these boys, giving them his name. However, he frequently physically and verbally abused these boys. When new children were added to the family, the husband, in particular, showed blatantly obvious favoritism to his own children. One can only imagine the unfulfilled longing these boys had throughout the years. A boy needs more than a man's name to feel loved and accepted. He needs constant demonstrations of love.

The Apostle John gave a beautiful description of what it is like to be a child of God. He wrote: "Behold, what manner of love the Father hath bestowed upon us, that we should be called the sons of God..." (I John 3:1). Notice that John emphasized a new relationship with the Lord for these Jews. No longer did he refer to them as "the children of Israel" as in the Old Testament. Instead, he referred to them as "sons of God." This title implies a genuine acceptance, and inclusion into, a family and a more mature standing. Moreover, each member is reassured that God the Father loves them in a deeper sense than can be put into human words. He emphatically proved this when "God commendeth [or demonstrated] His love toward us, in that, while we were yet sinners, Christ died for us" (Romans 5:8). A proper father yearns for an ongoing and growing relationship with his children. He will also constantly stand ready to help when needed. The Lord confirmed to these saints that He is always accessible and invited them to "...come boldly unto the throne of grace, that we may obtain mercy, and find grace to help in time of need" (Hebrews 4:16). A confidence this kind of healthy relationship with God encourages each saint to "purifieth himself" (vs. 3), in order that one might be more "like Him" (vs. 2) even prior to eternity.

Believers today are also blessed to have a similar, loving relationship with God that gives us a satisfying sense of security. Galatians 4:6 states: "And because ye are sons, God hath set forth the Spirit of His Son into your hearts, crying, Abba, Father." Rejoice in your relationship with God, that He loves, accepts, and is always ready to help you.

DON'T BE GULLIBLE
I John 4:1-3

A family we know has two children as different as night and day. When someone would tell a tall tale, the son would look at them with a surprised, believing expression, and say: "Really?" It was comical and amazing how gullible he could be. In contrast, when an even more convincing story was woven and presented, almost instantly the younger daughter would make a face and say: "Oh yah, right!" It was hard to pull one over on her. She was pretty savvy to detect something that wasn't true.

The Apostle John wrote to fellow Kingdom saints, saying: "Beloved, believe not every spirit [referring to the true motives and message of human teachers], but try the spirits whether they are of God: because many false prophets are gone out into the world" (I John 4:1). John was concerned that these Jewish believers were too gullible. They had been warned about false teachers who would deny "...that Jesus Christ is come in the flesh..." (vs. 2). He told them "...even now already is it in the world (vs. 3). Unless they were very careful, they would be "...tossed to and fro, and carried about with every wind of doctrine, by the sleight of men, and cunning craftiness, whereby they lie in wait to deceive" (Ephesians 4:14). So John told them to "try the spirits," of those who taught them. This has always been God's instruction to His children. We, the Body of Christ, are to "prove all things, [and] hold fast that which is good" (I Thessalonians 5:21) and to be continually "proving what is acceptable unto the Lord" (Ephesians 5:10). *But how are saints to try the spirits, prove all things, and prove what is acceptable?* The simple answer is to compare anything taught with the truth of God's Word. Our "gold standard" by which we are to measure all things is "...what saith the Scriptures?" (Galatians 4:30). The saints at Berea were exemplary as they "received the Word with all readiness of mind, and searched the Scriptures daily, [to see] whether these things were so" (Acts 17:11). Just like inspecting meat with possible contamination, "if there is any doubt, throw it out."

As we see in the above references from Paul, the danger of false teachers is real for us today too. Be careful not to be gullible to swallow any doctrine until checking to see if it is consistent with the writings of the Apostle Paul.

November 9

THIS IS THE RECORD
I John 5:11-13

It was revealed in 2015 that NBC news anchor Brian Williams, fabricated a story about being in a helicopter that was hit with enemy fire. Military personnel who had been with him publicly objected that such a false claim because it detracted from the heroism of our service men and women. Video records were scoured to document that the helicopter Williams rode in had, in fact, not been hit and to prove Mr. Williams' repeated claims were a falsehood. These records were so compelling that Mr. Williams was permanently removed as the anchor of NBC news. He learned that records, video or otherwise, are important.

The Apostle John told his readers the purpose for his first epistle: "These things have I written unto you that believe on the name of the Son of God; that ye may know that ye have eternal life" (I John 5:13). John previously heard the Lord Jesus teach: "...He that heareth my word, and believeth on Him that sent Me, hath everlasting life, and shall not come into condemnation, but is passed from death unto life" (John 5:24). The Savior was promising eternal life to any who put their complete trust in the message that eternal life is only found through a trusting faith in God the Son. In clear wording, Christ taught: "I am the resurrection, and the life: he that believeth in Me, though he were dead, yet shall he live (John 11:25). Similarly, He taught: "I am the way, the truth, and the life; no man cometh unto the Father, but by Me" (John 14:6). It was in this overall context that John continues in his first epistle by saying: "this [Scripture] is the record, that God hath given to us eternal life, and this life is in His Son. He that hath [through a trusting faith in] the Son hath life; and he that hath not the Son of God hath not life" (I John 5:11-12). Prior chapters indicated other qualities that would be present in the life of a true kingdom believer. John was confident his readers had true saving faith in Christ. His epistle was intended to serve as a divine record of proof these believers could count on so that they would "know" they possessed eternal life.

There are many dispensational distinctions in John's letter that apply only to Israel. However, we today, likewise, have a written record in Ephesians 1:13 assuring us of eternal life. Confidently stand fast in this assurance!

NOT IN MY HOUSE
II John 1-10

Lydia Cladek owned a car dealership in St. Augustine, Florida. She offered 15% interest to investors, promising their money would be backed with vehicles as collateral. Many invested sums totaling in the millions of dollars. When the checks stopped coming, investors and authorities eventually learned this was only an elaborate pyramid scheme. *Knowing this, would you invite Lydia into your home, especially if anyone would conclude you were endorsing her sales pitch?*

The epistle of II John was written primarily to warn a Jewish woman, who had believed on Christ as her promised Messiah, from extending hospitality to an abundance of spiritual "deceivers" (vs. 7). The nature of their deceit was rooted in denying "that Jesus Christ is come in the flesh" (vs. 7). All three of John's short epistles were likely written within twenty years of the Savior's resurrection. Yet, in that short time, Satan had been busy promoting a key doctrinal error about the Lord Jesus. Unbelieving Jews believed our Lord to have been an impostor instead of, as He claimed, the promised Redeemer who came as the ultimate King of Israel who would die for their sins. They taught the Lord Jesus was only a wicked man and an imposter deserving of death. A philosophical group, called "Gnostics," were also beginning to gain a foothold. They taught that all matter is evil. Therefore, the true Messiah could not have come in the flesh, but only in the form of an angel or spirit. Many cults and unbelievers today teach that the Lord Jesus Christ was only a prophet, teacher, good man, or a fictional individual. Any of these views nullify the sinless substitutionary death of our Lord, who bore our sins and punishment that we might have eternal life through faith in Him. This is why the denial that Christ had come in the flesh was such an insidious doctrine so vigorously promoted by deceivers (I John 4:2-3; II John 7). In so doing, they were "an Anti-Christ" (I John 4:3) meaning over or against the real Christ. John's instruction was not to receive anyone who teaches this false doctrine "into your house" (II John 10), to avoid the danger of being swayed from "the truth" (vss. 1-4) and lose one's "full reward" (vs. 8) for proper faith in Christ.

We still have people teaching different perversions about who Christ is. They come to our doors or within our homes via television or literature. Beware and "receive him [or them] not into your house (vs. 10)."

OUR HAPPIEST EXPERIENCES
II John 4

We usually think of the happiest experiences in life being our wedding day, the birth of a child, or maybe the day we retire. Among the happiest occasions for my wife and I have been returning to churches where we used to minister, finding many of the saints still faithfully walking with the Lord and serving Christ. In particular, when we returned after two decades to our first church, it was exciting to see some we led to Christ still actively functioning as productive members of the Body of Christ. We rejoiced for them, but we also rejoiced that our ministry had not been in vain. It was still bearing fruit.

The Apostle John expressed this same sentiment when he wrote: "I rejoiced greatly that I found of thy children walking in truth, as we have received a commandment from the Father" (II John 4). The encouragement of faithful saints was so meaningful to John, and so important to the inspiring Holy Spirit, that this principle is again mentioned even more clearly. In III John 4, we read: "I have no greater joy than to hear that my children walk in truth." John wasn't the only one with a deep interest in whether or not those being ministered to were responsive and living what they had been taught by dedicated ministers of God's Word. The prophet Isaiah recorded that he knew: "The Lord hath called me from the womb…And…made my mouth a sharp sword…And [God] said unto me, Thou art My servant, O Israel, in whom I will be glorified" (Isaiah 49:1-3). Yet, out of discouragement, because of the waywardness of those who heard him, Isaiah wrote: "Then I said, I have laboured in vain, I have spent my strength for nought… my work with my God" (vs. 4). He was not only discouraged by how unfruitful his people had been, he appears to have been contemplating getting out of the ministry. Likewise, the Apostle Paul wrote saying: "I am afraid of you, lest I have bestowed upon you labor in vain" (Galatians 4:11). He also urged the saints at Philippi to hold forth the Word of God "…that I have not run in vain, neither laboured in vain" (Philippians 2:16).

Beloved, those who minister to you usually do so with great dedication and often out of great sacrifice. Don't allow yourself to be a discouragement to them. Let them know you appreciate their ministry and encourage them by being responsive to their teaching.

MALICIOUS WORDS
III John

I have a pastor friend who once shared his heartache. It was his assessment of one glaring problem in so many who understand the distinctiveness of the Apostle Paul's ministry. This pastor had endured savage treatment by a local church and witnessed repeated viciousness among believers from across the country. He said, "I know we have the right message, but there is something fundamentally wrong when our sound doctrine does not demonstrate itself by genuine consistent love between believers. As a group, we seem to be often missing what doctrine is intended to produce: love, godliness, and harmony between believers."

In III John, the Apostle John wrote to Gaius, a Jewish believer in a church who was awaiting the Second Coming of Christ to establish the Millennial Kingdom. This epistle informs us that one from this assembly, Diotrephes, was strongly opposing the ministry of John the Apostle. He was doing so by "...prating against us with malicious words" (vs. 10). The word "malicious" means "to be hurtful in effect or influence." Apparently, this man was knowingly saying derogatory and untrue things about a spiritual leader, John, whom he should have been humbly following, supporting, and promoting. His motive was transparent too. John said he was one "...who loveth to have the preeminence among them [in his sphere of influence]" (vs. 9). Spiritually-rebellious bullies, backbiters, gossips, and slanderers seem to frequently find their way into "Christian" circles. So aggressive was this man's evil activity that when others did not comply with the venom he was spewing, he would aggressively cast "them out of the church" (vs. 10). The Lord Jesus had taught His disciples: "By this shall all men know that ye are my disciples, if ye have love one to another" (John 13:35). The words and actions of Diotrephes demonstrated a glaring lack of love, humility, and harmony that was surely a very negative testimony to the lost that would hear of these things. John told Gaius not to be swept up in this carnality when he said: "Beloved, follow not that which is evil, but that which is good..." (vs. 11).

Dear Christian, Satanic and carnal influences have many times repeated "malicious words" in Christian churches and organizations. Don't be a participant by listening to or repeating hurtful things about others. We must uphold the standard of Ephesians 4:29: "Let no corrupt communication proceed out of your mouth, but that which is good to the use of edifying, that it may ministry grace unto the hearers."

A GOOD EXAMPLE
I Thessalonians 1:7

As the first one to trust Christ in my family at the age of seventeen, I was blessed to have a good spiritual example to follow. A dedicated Christian man attended the church where I was saved. He was a skilled mechanic who used his ability to keep six buses going for church bus routes. He put his three teenagers in a Christian school a hundred miles away. He attended every church service, read, and talked about Scripture, and encouraged me to be faithful. I've often wondered if I would have grown in the Lord and sought to be faithful without his encouragement and example.

The Apostle Paul recognized the powerful impact of good spiritual examples. He seemed to always be conscious of being a pattern for others to follow. In II Thessalonians 3:7-9 he explains that he, and all who traveled with him, sought "...to make ourselves an example unto you to follow us." He instructs Timothy: "...be thou an example of the believers, in word, in conversation, in charity, in spirit, in faith, in purity," (I Timothy 4:12). Similarly, he tells Titus to be "a pattern" in godliness (Titus 2:7). Then, when writing to the saints at Thessalonica, he praises them saying: "...ye were ensamples to all that believe in Macedonia and Achaia" (I Thessalonians 1:7). We are not left to wonder why they were so praised or how they were so exemplary. They were examples in sharing the gospel: "For from you sounded out the word of the Lord...in every place" (vs. 8). They were examples in changed lives after salvation. Paul praised them for having "... turned to God from idols to serve the living and true God..." (vs. 9). Paul told them he remembered "without ceasing your work of faith, and labor of love, and patience of hope in our Lord Jesus Christ" (vs. 3). They "received the Word in much affliction" while still living "with joy in the Holy Ghost" and were faithful "followers" of Paul's doctrines of grace (vs. 6). With anticipation, they had also begun to watch and "...wait for His Son from heaven" (vs. 10). All of these qualities were important examples for other saints to follow.

Whether you realize it or not, someone in your life needs you to be an example in godliness and dedication to Christ. Right now would be a good time to stop and pray for God's strength to be the kind of example that makes a powerful, positive, spiritual impact for your Savior.

ARE YOU STILL THE SAME?
I Thessalonians 1:9

William Ashley "Billy" Sunday was an outfielder for the Chicago White Stockings in 1887. After a night of drinking with teammates, he attended a Bible service at the Pacific Garden Mission. It was there that his life was changed when he accepted Jesus Christ as his Savior. He left his professional baseball career to preach "fire and brimstone" evangelistic messages over much of America. These meetings were usually held in tents with sawdust in the aisles. Many "walked the saw dust trail" to trust in Christ. This writer heard the gospel for the first time in a church that formed after one of those evangelistic campaigns. Billy Sunday's life had an obvious, marked change when he got saved, and it should be the same for us too.

When many in Thessalonica heard and trusted in Paul's Gospel of Grace, there was a radical change in their lives that produced godliness. In I Thessalonians 1:9-10, the Apostle Paul praises them saying: "...ye turned to God from idols to serve the living and true God; and to wait for His Son from heaven..." They were never the same again. Other than forgiveness unto salvation, *what kind of changes took place in their lives?* There were at least four major changes. Paul told them: "...ye were ensamples [or examples to all that believe in Macedonia and Achaia" (I Thessalonians 1:7). Paul pointed to them as examples of transformed lives that all believers should emulate. He praised them, saying: "from you sounded out the Word of the Lord...in every place..."

(1:8). They chose to be consistent and aggressive in their evangelism. In this and other ways, they were willing to "...serve the living God..." (1:9). They did not just sit on their salvation doing nothing. They intentionally served their Savior. Paul said they expectantly continued to "wait for His Son from heaven" (1:10). Perhaps it was this latter anticipation of our Lord's return that produced such dynamic, godly changes in their lives.

As we read about testimonies of dynamic change in the saints from biblical times, or in accounts in our present day, it should cause us to examine if there has been a dynamic change in our life. Surely when you stand before Christ in eternity you'll want Him to read a record of godly change in your life. Let today be the start of incorporating all four of these life-changing principles into your life. Choose to live a transformed life.

November
15

IS IT MAKING A DIFFERENCE?
I Thessalonians 2:13

Historically, I've had a weak immune system and frequent illness. In recent years, we've been regularly taking a range of specific supplements. Over the Christmas holidays, all of our immediate family, including grandchildren, were quite sick. We still saw them for Christmas and church and even babysat. Then we had good friends from out of state stay with us for a week. One of them becoming quite sick. Through it all, my wife and I escaped the "bugs" they had. We were careful, not only to take the vitamins, but to do so with food. For vitamins to work properly, you must have food in your stomach so the supplements can absorb into your system.

As we read Paul's letter to the saints at Thessalonica, he tells them: "For this cause also thank we God without ceasing, because, when ye received the Word of God which ye heard of us, ye received it...as it is in truth, the Word of God, which effectually worketh also in you that believe" (I Thessalonians 2:13). Paul was writing to believers who had allowed the Scriptures to make a real difference in their lives. They allowed God's Word to convict their hearts and empower their walk. That's why they "turned from God to idols to serve the living and true God" (1:9) and urgently "sounded out the word of the Lord" reaching many with the gospel (1:8). That's why, with expectation, they were waiting for the Rapture (1:10) and why they abounded toward each other in love (4:9-10).

God's Word is intended to make a difference in the way we live every time we read it! If we read it like the noble Bereans in Acts 17:11, we will absorb it "with all readiness of mind." That means we will allow it to encourage, convict, instruct in paths of righteousness, and break old patterns that do not exalt our Savior. But just as vitamins need food to do their proper work, the Scriptures need a yielded heart and a mind that is looking for the right things. *Is God's Word "effectually working in you"? Or, is Bible study only an academic exercise?* As you listen to or study the Scripture, embrace the deep doctrines. But don't forget to look for things to transform the way you live. When the Holy Spirit convicts about a needed change, allow God's Word to "effectually worketh also in you" by applying truth to yourself with a yielded heart.

A SUPPLEMENT NOT A SUBSTITUTE
I Thessalonians 3:6

I got a call from an eighty-eight year old woman who had found one of our church tracts with my phone number on the back. She had come to grasp the basics of right division. She saw distinctions between the Body of Christ in Paul's letters in contrast to the rest of Scripture written to and about Israel. However, she was adamant that she did not want to attend church, establish relationships with other believers, or have any expectations placed upon her. After a forty minute conversation, she asked: "Am I wrong to not want those things, and to only want to do my own thing separate from everybody else?" I said: "Since you asked me the question, the answer is: 'Yes, that is wrong.'"

It is a blessed thing for us to have so much good Bible teaching available in our day through books, videos, and, in some cases, even on television. Thank God for these good avenues of ministry. However, we should never lose sight of the fact that every single letter written by the Apostle Paul was written to a local church, or the leader of a local church. God's primary method of building up the believer, grounding them in sound doctrine, giving them regular encouragement and prayer support, having a place to regularly serve Christ, and a place to point others led to Christ, is through the local church. God never intended for believers of any dispensation to be isolated from these local and regular means of edification. This was true even with believers in Israel's program. Those with a kingdom hope in the Book of Acts always gathered in groups and developed close bonds with one another (Acts 2:44-47; 4:23-33; Hebrews 10:25). The Apostle John likewise addressed seven different kingdom churches in Revelation 1:19-3:22. Notice also when Paul addresses the saints in I Thessalonians 3:6, he rejoices in their mutual love for one another, saying: "...that ye have good remembrance of us always, desiring greatly to see us, as we also to see you." These kinds of close bonds between believers should be our experience too as we interact in a local grace church.

Bible study on television is no substitute for the loving, encouraging relationships found in a local church. It should only be a supplement. Especially if you have a grace church within driving distance, you should make the decision to end your isolation and consistently attend. Fully commit to that assembly without delay.

GOD CARES
I Thessalonians 4:8

Several years ago, while boarding a plane, a family asked me if I would switch seats so they could sit together. I gladly gave them my seat and took one directly in front of them. Before the plane left the ground, the eight-year-old boy began kicking and pushing on my seat with his feet. This continued throughout the three-hour flight. The mother was sitting right next to her son, but she just sat there as if she did not care whether or not he behaved. But it mattered to me....

Some have concluded that since God has already forgiven believers all their sins, past, present, and future, that He doesn't care how they live after salvation. However, Scripture informs us that He cares very much how believers live after salvation! He has repeatedly instructed us that we are to live apart from sin. In Romans 6:1-2, the Apostle Paul asks: "What shall we say then? Shall we continue in sin, that grace may abound? God forbid. How shall we, that are dead to sin, live any longer therein?" Apparently, believers at Rome were confused about whether living in sin mattered because some had misrepresented what Paul taught about the grace of God. In Romans 3:8 he responded: "And not rather, (as we be slanderously reported, and as some affirm that we say,) Let us do evil, that good may come?" Paul wanted them to know it simply was not true that he taught that it didn't matter to God if we continued to live in sin. He told the saints at Thessalonica: "For God hath not called us unto uncleanness, but unto holiness. He therefore that despiseth [this instruction], despiseth not man, but God, who hath given unto us His Holy Spirit" (I Thessalonians 4:7-8). They needed to know he was speaking with divine authority when he instructed all believers to live apart from sin. The saints at Corinth had fared no better. Even though they were saved, the two letters to this church describe a lifestyle of horrendous sin. So, Paul wrote them, saying: "Having therefore these promises, dearly beloved, let us cleanse ourselves from all filthiness of the flesh and spirit [our minds], perfecting holiness in the fear of God" (II Corinthians 7:1).

God cares how we live after salvation. If you're allowing known sin in your life, make a decision right now, while God is speaking to your heart, to turn to a higher standard of holiness.

THE WILL OF GOD
I Thessalonians 5:18

A Christian man lamented to me how his life had turned out. Through alcohol and poor decisions, he had lost his job, his family, and many of his friends. He blamed his father for inattentiveness, he blamed other Christians for offenses, and then he blamed God. Among other things, he said: "I just wish I knew what God's will was for my life. All of my friends knew exactly what God wanted them to do with their lives, but God never showed me." He was failing to take personal responsibility for his decisions and failing to understand God's will.

Webster's dictionary defines *"mysticism"* as *"any doctrine that asserts the knowledge of spiritual truths through intuition or meditation, vague thinking or belief, of occult character or meaning."* Without realizing it, many believers embrace the concept of mysticism as they seek God's will in their lives. God has a better idea. Galatians 4:1-7 explains that God deals with us, not as children, but as adult sons. Galatians 5:1 tells us we have great liberty to make decisions in life without God micromanaging every detail. That means He gives us the freedom to choose who we will marry (I Corinthians 7:39), what work we pursue (I Timothy 3:1), even where we go (I Corinthians 16:12). This means God gives us wide latitude to decide our direction in life, yet He will work within us every day regardless of which path we choose. But God has also plainly told us we can understand His will today (Colossians 1:9; Ephesians 5:17). It is God's "...will [to] have all men to be saved and to come unto the knowledge of the truth" (I Timothy 2:4), and to "...deliver us from this present evil world..." (Galatians 1:4). "This is the will of God...that ye should abstain from fornication: that every one of you should know how to possess his vessel in sanctification and honor..." (I Thessalonians 4:3-4). Then, "In everything give thanks: for this is the will of God in Christ Jesus concerning you" (I Thessalonians 5:18). Beyond this, all the obvious instructions in Paul's letters are God's will: being transformed (Romans 12:2), walking in newness of life (Romans 6:4), renewing our minds through Scripture (Ephesians 4:23; 3:16), and much more relating to growth in godliness.

Have you been searching to understand God's will for your life? You don't need a mystic experience, or a seminar. Understand your liberty in Christ and the principles in Paul's epistles that clearly define God's will.

COUNTED WORTHY

II Thessalonians 1:5

It is well publicized that the United States military academies have a stringent "honor code." This is a set written standard that governs integrity in academics and prohibits such activities as lying, cheating, or stealing. Men and women who aspire to serve their country are held to a higher standard than the general public. This "honor code" is deemed necessary to develop character, and it also makes one worthy of public trust. Conduct falling short of these standards is considered conduct unbecoming to an officer and unworthy of the branch of service it represents.

The Scriptures likewise imply a high code of conduct for every believer. We represent the Lord Jesus Christ and His message of grace. To be worthy of public trust, it is essential that we live worthy of our Savior. In Ephesians 4:1, Paul begs the saints to "...walk worthy of the vocation wherewith ye are called." In Colossians 1:10, Paul prays for the saints: "that ye might walk worthy of the Lord unto all pleasing, being fruitful in every good work, and increasing in the knowledge of God." In I Thessalonians 2:12 he implores the believers: "that ye would walk worthy of God..." These passages make it is clear that a worthy walk of godly conduct is extremely important. When the Apostle Paul wrote the saints in II Thessalonians 1:4, he praised them for their "patience and faith in all your persecutions and tribulations that ye endure." He further states their godly conduct was "...a manifest token of the righteous judgment of God, that ye might be counted worthy of the kingdom of God, for which ye also suffer" (vs. 5). The fact that these believers were, through the grace of God, able to maintain such godliness with unwavering faith and endurance, no matter how severe the persecution, was a demonstration to the lost. It proved their message of salvation through Christ alone was real. Their testimony pointed to eternal life for those who trust in Christ, and to the looming divine punishment for those rejecting faith in the Lord Jesus. Paul assured them that this kind of daily walk made them worthy of the Savior they served. This certainly does not mean any kind of merit leading to eternal life. It simply means they represented the Savior so well that they were worthy to be considered genuine soldiers of Christ.

How about you, beloved? Are you seeking to be a worthy soldier of Christ by living a godly life worthy of His name?

RESTRAINING EVIL
II Thessalonians 2:6-7

When my wife worked as a dental hygienist, everyone in the office knew she was a Christian. She had witnessed to most of them, and she worked hard to maintain a testimony for Christ. One day at break time, the conversation became sordid. Out of respect, one gal turned to my wife and said: "Cover your ears Terri, you're not going to want to hear this." My wife's presence did not prevent all sinful conversations, but her presence was unmistakably a deterrent holding back what would have otherwise been far worse.

If you've been in a situation with unsaved people, and they say something like: "We need to watch our language because…is here," then you are doing your job as a Christian. That means your testimony is, at least in part, being a deterrent to the Satanic influence in your arena of influence. When Paul wrote to the believers in II Thessalonians 2, these saints were concerned that they had missed the Rapture of the Body of Christ. Their present persecutions caused them to wonder if they were in the midst of the seven years of Tribulation. But Paul assured them "the day of Christ" (vs. 2), meaning the Rapture, had not yet occurred. Their persecution for their faith was a normal experience for spiritually-dark perilous times. All who live godly in Christ Jesus will suffer some level of opposition. Satan's momentum to pave the way for the coming of the Anti-Christ is growing. The job of every Christian is to live a godly life that serves as a restraining element to Satan's onslaught of evil. This was Paul's message when he told the saints: "…ye know what withholdeth…only He who now letteth will let, until He be taken out of the way" (2:6-7). The words "withholdeth" and "letteth" refer to the restraint of evil by the Holy Spirit as He works within believers. Like the heaps of waters in the Red Sea restrained by the power of God, when Israel passed through on dry land, believers in the Dispensation of Grace are to be God's agents restraining the evil tide of Satan's march toward ushering in the Anti-Christ. *How?* We are to win the lost, live godly testimonies, vote for those who most uphold biblical standards, and seek to influence others with biblical truth.

Christians have a job to do until Christ takes us home. As you start your day, make it your prayerful goal to be a godly restraining influence on others.

WORK IS COMMANDED
II Thessalonians 3:10

We know a young Christian adult, with no ambition to find regular employment, still living at home with parents. Instead there is a complete contentment to live off others. When we carefully encouraged this Christian to join a sibling working at Walmart, this individual told us plainly: "I don't need money." We explained that everyone needs money for food, transportation, housing, clothing, and simply to follow the instructions in Scripture. However, this one remained undeterred and became angry that we would suggest the need to work.

The Scriptures are abundantly clear and consistent in the instruction that every able-bodied believer should be industrious in the area of gainful employment. When some believers at Thessalonica stopped working, Paul told them they should "study to be quiet...and to work with your own hands, as we commanded you" (I Thessalonians 4:11). When they did not heed this instruction, he repeated it, saying: "For even when we were with you, this we commanded you, that if any would not work, neither should he eat" (II Thessalonians 3:10). Notice, in both instances, Paul's instruction for everyone to work was not just a suggestion. It was "commanded." *Why is this so important?* Work is God's design to responsibly provide for one's own needs. These verses clearly state that those who shirk the responsibility to work should not be allowed to eat. Providing them with food only enables their wrong behavior. Another purpose of God is revealed in Ephesians 4:28 "...let him labour, working with his hands the thing which is good, that he may have to give to him that needeth." Whether giving to further the work of the Lord or to help believers in genuine need, God instructs us to work. Even young widows are required to work lest "...they learn to be idle, wandering about from house to house; and not only idle, but tattlers also and busybodies, speaking things which they ought not" (I Timothy 5:13). Work helps to prevent other wrong patterns of behavior by filling one's time with wholesome activity. The Scriptures are also full of instructions clearly explaining how wrong it is to be "slothful," or lazy (consider Proverbs 18:9; 24:30; Ecclesiastes 10:18, and many more).

If you are responsibly working, you are to be praised. Keep it up. If you are not, it's time to demonstrate real spirituality and maturity by getting to work. If you are enabling someone who won't work, withdraw that enablement today. God "commanded" it through Paul's letters.

VIOLATING ONE'S CONSCIENCE
I Timothy 1:5

When our daughters were still school age, my wife and I had very restrictive finances. Years earlier we had made a decision to make a particular provision for our daughters that we thought essential to their spiritual well-being. However, it had become increasingly more expensive and difficult to follow through with that decision. So, with great reluctance, we stopped that provision. For the next three weeks, I could not sleep at night, nor concentrate during the day, as I agonized over the impact our recent decision might have on our daughters. Then, not knowing how we were going to pay for it, we recommitted to the original provision for our girls. We simply could not violate our conscience any longer. By the way, God provided.

Twice in I Timothy 1, the Apostle Paul wrote to his son in the faith, Timothy, about the importance of not violating one's conscience. Our God-given conscience is that inner judge that accuses us when we have done something wrong. Romans 2:15 describes the work of our conscience as a standard "…written in our hearts, their conscience also bearing witness, and their thoughts the mean while accusing or else excusing one another." When Paul gave Timothy firm directives about ministry, he wrote: "Now the end of the commandment is charity [or love] out of a good conscience, and of faith unfeigned" (I Timothy 1:5). In order for Timothy to be effective in ministry and unhindered in his relationship with the Lord, one of the top three things he needed to maintain was a conscience that did not accuse him of wrong doing. The maintenance of his conscience was a directive so important that he referred to it not as good advice or mere instruction. Instead, he called it a "commandment." Then, in verse 19, Paul continues by saying Timothy must also continue: "Holding faith, and a good conscience; which some having put away concerning faith have made shipwreck." Paul was essentially saying that to violate one's conscience is a slippery spiritual slope that had made others slide downward into error, and become unprofitable in the cause of Christ. At all costs, Timothy must never violate his inner conscience.

Dear believer, never violate your conscience. If you are doing something that your mind accuses as wrongdoing, cease immediately. If you are pondering a path you know will violate your conscience, don't go there. Choose another path. It is extremely important to maintain a clear conscience before the Lord.

FOUR KINDS OF PRAYER
I Timothy 2:1

A woman raised in a Christian home has maintained a rebellious and bitter spirit for decades. Her parents trusted in Christ when she was eleven. From that point on, the parents immersed themselves and their children in a Bible-teaching local church. Each of the children made professions of faith, but this woman was always the spiritually-rebellious one. She pushed the boundaries, made it clear she did not want to attend church, and resisted spiritual input. For decades after college, she seldom contacted her parents unless she wanted, or needed, something from them. Hers was not a loving relation or interaction, it was more a "what can you do for me now" attitude.

A believer does not need to have a rebellious or bitter spirit to interact with the Lord in prayer almost exclusively on the level of wanting things. We can drift into an imbalanced practice of prayer, only asking God to give us things or do things for us. But the Apostle Paul gives us a more mature picture of prayer when he writes: "I exhort therefore, that, first of all, supplications, prayers, intercessions, and giving of thanks be made for all men" (I Timothy 2:1). Notice there are four different kinds of prayer listed in this passage. "Supplications" literally means to petition, make a request, or beg. Paul's instruction in verse two reveals he believed, and wanted Timothy to believe, God sometimes intervenes in our circumstances in response to our prayers. Verse three explains that bringing our needs to the Lord in prayer "is good and acceptable in the sight of God our Saviour." But Paul teaches that our interaction with the Lord should also include "prayers." Specifically, this is a communication of worship. Our prayers should contain a balanced amount of acknowledging the greatness of our Lord's attributes, such as His mercy, longsuffering, power, love, wisdom, and more. "Intercessions" refer to making requests, not for ourself, but for others. Paul's letters are full of examples of him praying for the spiritual growth and well being of other believers. Finally, prayer should include "giving of thanks." We live in times when gratitude and giving thanks to humans, and to the Lord, is becoming more uncommon. But for the believer, large portions of prayer time should include giving God thanks for all He has done and will do on our behalf. It's part of a grateful, mature, and appreciative heart.

When you pause to pray, include all four of these aspects of prayer.

WORDS MEAN THINGS
I Timothy 3:1-13

S omeone we know often uses the phrase: "Words mean things." As a Bible teacher, he goes through a passage emphasizing key words, and aids the understanding of those he teaches, by defining words. Particularly when coming to instruction that some of us may resist because it challenges previously held positions, or that simply speaks to the heart about a needed change, he uses his phrase. With a wry smile, he'll say: "Words mean things." Then he'll let the truth of that Scripture sink into the soul. His point is that God says what He means, and we have the obligation to conform to His written Word.

When Paul wrote to Timothy about elders and deacons, in I Timothy 3:1-13, he uses key words to describe the qualifications for any who might serve in these offices. Before we even begin to look at God's instructions, let's remind ourselves that the local church is God's work. He, and only He, has the right and authority to mandate who is to lead and serve in His local work. Regardless of what any church constitution may say or require, the requirements in God's Word trump any man-made document. Now, lets look with an open heart into the words that describe these offices. God says a man must "desire" the office of an elder. One should not be coerced into serving. Instead, he must have a desire, not for power or prestige, but only to serve the Lord by providing wise scriptural leadership. He must be "blameless." This does not mean he must be totally without sin. It means he must have a good testimony of godliness with no major areas in which he could be accused of wrongdoing. Paul says he "must." That means what follows is not an optional suggestion. It is an unwavering standard, regardless of public opinion, even within the church. An elder must "be apt [given to, able, or ready] to teach." Leaders in God's work must "have their senses exercised to discerned both good and evil" (Hebrews 5:14). The only way for a man to have the depth of knowledge needed to properly function as a leader in the local church is to be in the Word as a teacher. This is God's requirement for God's work.

These, and other requirements for leaders in the local church, are often ignored because they are not popular today. But words mean things. *Can God count on you to stand for these standards in your local church?*

333

LIVING GOD'S WORD
I Timothy 4:12

The most godly example I've known was my Grandma Fredericksen. She was exceptional. She was hard not to like, but, more importantly, she was an extremely godly woman with a vibrant testimony for Christ. She faced many difficulties in life: marrying a widowed man with two children, a house fire, a lawless rebellious son, mistreatment by family members, and much more. Yet through it all, she had a sweet spirit and unwavering faith.

In Paul's first epistle to Timothy, he urges him to become a powerful example in godliness that everyone in the church could follow. God's leaders have always been held to a higher standard of godliness. Ezra had learned three things that made him effective. "For Ezra had prepared his heart to seek the law of the Lord, and to do it, and to teach in Israel statutes and judgments" (Ezra 7:10). Notice the sequence: an open heart seeking to obey the Lord, living what God taught him, and then not merely lecturing with cold, hypothetical facts, but sharing an overflow of what God had done in his life. Similarly, Paul told Timothy: "...be thou an example of the believers, in word, in conversation, in charity, in spirit, in faith, in purity" (I Timothy 4:12). The words spoken by Timothy needed to be pure and Christ-worthy. His "conversation," or manner of life, must be godly, and Christ honoring. His "charity," or love, needed to be genuine as he exhibited a godly affection for all saints and the Lord. His "spirit," meaning his thinking and attitude, needed to demonstrate the sweetness of close communion with Christ. His "faith," or confidence, in all he believed needed to be unwavering as he lived what he learned from the doctrines of grace, and he needed to live in moral "purity." If Timothy did all this, then he would be prepared to be a leader in the local church and to teach the saints God's Word with effectiveness.

While this is the standard for leaders in the church, this is God's standard for every believer. Being an effective spiritual influence on others is more than accumulating doctrinal facts and rightly dividing the Scriptures. Our lives must be undergirded by godliness to give us credibility when we share these truths. *Are we seeking to live what we learn in God's Word and to be "an example of the believers" in these six areas? Starting right now, which one aspect do you need to ask God to transform?*

THEY DON'T KNOW THEY'RE DEAD
I Timothy 5:6

Some childhood memories are more vivid than others. As a child, I remember my father bringing home 500 rooster chicks. They grew quickly, and we began butchering those chickens to provide food for our family. It freaked me out every time but, the first time I saw my father remove the heads of several chickens, it scared me to death. Without a head, those chickens ran around frantically for several minutes, as if they were trying to find their heads. When I asked how that was possible, my brother told me: "They're dead, they just don't know it yet."

In the spiritual realm, the same can be true even for a believer. We can be dead spiritually and not even know it. In I Timothy 5:6, the Apostle Paul explained the proper care for godly widows. Then he wrote about widows who are not dedicated believers, saying: "But she that liveth in pleasure is dead while she liveth." It is possible, perhaps even common, for believers to be running around like chickens with their heads cut off in a frantic effort to pursue the things of the world, to the neglect of their walk with the Lord. It's a matter of focus and priority.

When each of us are saved, we are made "...a new creature; old things are passed away; behold, all things are become new" (II Corinthians 5:17). Our hearts are filled with joy over receiving eternal life as an unmerited gift of grace. Our minds develop a sense of gratitude over having escaped eternal punishment. Our soul yearns to live apart from sin and "...unto Him which died for them and rose again" (II Corinthians 5:15). But the flesh is weak. It is easy for the cares of this world to dull our spiritual senses. It is natural to drift toward a focus on worldly things and away from a close walk with Christ. Particularly in America, where we have so much abundance, our affections for things often crowd out our love for the Lord. God tries to draw us back to Him every day. But if we are not diligent in our quiet time with Him and looking always for truth to transform our lives, we can become spiritually dead, and not even know it.

Take your spiritual heartbeat. If it's not as strong as it once was, it's time to "awake...and arise from the dead" (Ephesians 5:14).

FOLLOWING HARD
I Timothy 6:11-12

While I was growing up on the farm, we had dog that loved to chase rabbits. Many times I saw him running for all he was worth after a rabbit that was trying to elude him. The rabbit would swerve back and forth, change directions on a dime, and sometimes go deep into a hole burrowed in the field. Undeterred, our dog relentlessly dug until he could reach in and get his prey. No matter how difficult, he was single-minded on obtaining his objective.

Paul's instructions to Timothy were to both flee and follow. He wrote: "But thou, O man of God, flee these [carnal] things; and follow after righteousness, godliness, faith, love, patience, meekness. Fight the good fight of faith, lay hold on eternal life…" (I Timothy 6:11-12). A man or woman of God, doing what they should do, will flee, like a frightened rabbit, from "the love of money" (vs. 10). Paul reminded Timothy that he brought nothing into this world and will take nothing material out when he dies. As long as he has food, clothing, and the pursuit of godliness, he is to be content (vss. 6-9). But a man or woman of God also must follow hard after several things. We must pursue "righteousness" (vs. 11). This word means an equity of character, or doing right. "Godliness" refers to devoutness, seeking to be holy, or like God in conduct. "Faith" means a persuasion, conviction, or constancy of belief. We should be like a dog pursuing a rabbit in seeking to obtain these qualities as a consistent part of our character. But we also need more. We must pursue an agape "love," meaning an unconditional affection, for others. Paul told the Thessalonians they were "taught of God to love one another," but they must seek to "abound" in this love and do so "toward all men" (I Thessalonians 4:9; 3:12). We need "patience," meaning endurance, rather than fainting in our seriousness about living for the Lord. The servant of the Lord also needs "meekness," which means gentleness in all situations. If we have these qualities, we can then "fight the good fight of faith" (I Timothy 6:12) in truly living for Christ, and lay hold on the importance of eternal life given to us.

We pursue many things in life: fun, a mate, monetary gain, friendships, security, and more. However, as a child of God, we must be as relentless as a dog chasing a rabbit in our pursuit of these godly qualities.

HOLD FAST
II Timothy 1:13

As a younger man, I worked for a year in a huge meat packing plant. My job was to trim sections of beef to be ground into hamburger. I worked eight hours a day, six days a week. I had to hold the knife so tightly and for so long, it took a toll. Each morning I awoke with a clinched fist in the hand that I held the knife. I could only open that hand by holding it under warm water and painfully prying it open with the other hand. It was as if I was still holding tightly to that knife.

Paul implored Timothy to "Hold fast the form sound words, which thou hast heard of me, in faith and love which is in Christ Jesus" (II Timothy 1:13). For two years, Timothy companied with Paul as he proclaimed new doctrines of grace. Timothy frequently heard Paul's doctrines as he taught in the synagogues, the school of Tyrannus, and in local churches formed in places like Ephesus. But Ephesus was a dangerous and difficult place for Timothy to minister in Paul's absence. It was notorious for their avid worship of Diana (Acts 19:19-35). A riot broke out over Paul's teaching, forcing him to leave the city. It appears that some of the Gentiles who came to Christ were also seeking to integrate false teaching about Diana with the new doctrines of grace, because Paul warns about fables being taught in the church. Some of the saved Jews were also seeking to teach the necessity of observing the Mosaic Law in this grace assembly (I Timothy 1:5-10). It was in this setting Timothy is charged to hold fast to the doctrines he had learned at the feet of Paul. In fact, he was to charge others that they "teach no other doctrine" (I Timothy 1:3). Paul was counting on Timothy to be the guardian of the truth so that truth would not be compromised or lost. He would have to do so in the face of opposition, perhaps even alone. But he must stand for the truth, the whole truth, and nothing but the truth, so help him God.

We, too, live in perilous times when unsound doctrine finds it's way into our assemblies. Like one refusing to lose his grip, God is counting on you to hold fast to the exclusive doctrines of grace and insist that all Paul's teachings are followed. Even if you stand alone, hold on to the truth.

A GOOD SOLDIER
II Timothy 2:4

In 2015, the movie, *American Sniper,* portrayed the life of Navy Seal Chris Kyle. Volunteering for service in the Iraq war, Chris became the most effective sniper in American history. He and a small team would be dropped behind enemy lines. They would position themselves in strategic areas and shoot those who posed a threat to American soldiers, thus protecting countless lives. Chris served with distinction and a deep sense of duty to his country and fellow soldiers. He also repeatedly put himself in harms way by volunteering for four tours of duty before returning home.

When Paul sought to encourage young Timothy as he ministered in Ephesus, he urged him to "...endure hardness, as a good soldier of Jesus Christ" (II Timothy 2:3). Everyone around the Mediterranean in Paul's day was acutely aware of Roman soldiers who conquered territories and enforced the tyranny of the Roman Empire. Roman soldiers were extremely tough individuals. They were expert fighters with swords, spears, shields, and more. They also had to carry over sixty pounds of equipment, plus three days of rations, while they frequently marched 15 to 20 miles per day. These soldiers were often in peril as they served at the pleasure of their Caesar. It was with this example in mind that Paul urged Timothy to be a good soldier of Jesus Christ. Neither Timothy, nor we, should expect the Christian walk to be one of ease nor one without sacrifice and dangers. Timothy was to see himself as a soldier of the greatest leader ever, the Lord Jesus Christ. He was to serve at His pleasure, fight for His cause, and seek to conquer others with His Gospel of Grace. This would mean vigilantly carrying the weight of ministry over the span of years, being burdened for lost souls, and helping believers to grow in their faith. Timothy needed a mindset to voluntarily endure hardships without ever deserting the battle. This would mean facing opposition with "the sword of the Spirit, which is the Word of God (Ephesians 6:17), and being careful to not unduly "entangleth himself with the affairs of this life; that he may please Him who hath chosen him to be a soldier" (I Timothy 2:4).

Dear believer, do you think of yourself as a soldier of Christ? Have you armed yourself with a mindset of toughness and sacrifice? The moment you trusted Christ as Savior, you were enlisted in His army. Serve with distinction and honor as a good soldier.

WHAT DO YOU LOOK FOR?
II Timothy 3:16-17

When some men look for a wife, they often look only for physical beauty. Everything else seems to be incidental. When I was looking for the right woman to be my wife, I was looking for a combination of very important things. Yes, I wanted her to be pretty. But I needed her to know Christ as Savior, be seriously spiritually minded, be willing to serve in the ministry, have a sweet spirit, and share the same philosophies of life. I knew that every one of these aspects were vitally important for us to be a good match.

What do you look for when you study the Scriptures, whether in personal study or while sitting under a good Bible teacher? Sadly, many only seem to be looking for one thing: academic doctrine. Please don't misunderstand. Every believer needs a firm foundation in grace doctrine to know how to live a pleasing life to the Lord and to be stable enough in the Scriptures not to be swept away into error. We need doctrine, but also we need to look for more than doctrinal information when we study God's Word. Paul told Timothy what God intends for us to look for in Scripture when he wrote: "All Scripture is given by inspiration of God, and is profitable for doctrine, for reproof, for correction, for instruction in righteousness: that the man of God may be perfect [meaning complete or mature], throughly furnished unto all good works" (II Timothy 3:16-17). Think carefully about this content. While being established in sound doctrine, every believer needs to allow the Scripture to reprove wrong behavior and attitudes. Without this, we will not grow in godliness but will remain ever hardened in sinful habits. Once reproved, we must allow God to correct wrong behaviors or attitudes. God's goal for us is to become "conformed to the image of His Son" (Romans 8:29), or more Christ-like. As we yield to the Lord in this process, He continually gives us "instruction in righteousness" (II Timothy 3:16), if we will only look for this in His Word. Without this process of spiritual growth, we are not truly "perfect" mature, or complete, no matter how much doctrine we know. Finally, doctrinal correctness alone does not qualify us for ministry. Growth in godliness makes us "furnished unto all good works" (II Timothy 3:17).

If this combination hasn't been what you've been looking for when you study Scripture, let this journey begin today and continue every day hereafter.

RECEPTIVE TO ALL TRUTH
II Timothy 4:3-4

We have known some individuals who claim to stand for the distinctive doctrines of Paul but reject the clear words of Scripture. One said, "I think Paul's instructions on that subject are outdated. We don't need to follow them." Another said, "I know that's what the Scriptures say, but you'll never convince me my way is not better." A Bible teacher said, "Yes, that is the biblical pattern, but that's not what the people want. You have to give people what they want." A fourth individual shoved the Bible back across the table and said, "I don't care what the Bible says." I could hardly believe what I was hearing, especially from Christians.

The Apostle Paul warned Timothy: "For the time will come when they will not endure sound doctrine; but after their own lusts shall they heap to themselves teachers, having itching ears; and they shall turn away from the truth, and shall be turned unto fables" (II Timothy 4:3-4). While Paul was specifically writing to Timothy about the conditions at Ephesus, this writer believes our apostle had divine insight into the last days of grace before the Rapture. In I Timothy 4:1, he warned about characteristics of "the latter times," when "...some shall depart from the faith, giving heed to seducing spirits, and doctrines of devils." In II Timothy 4:3-4, we believe Paul is readdressing the mindset in the last days. He warns of satanic efforts to draw believers away from following the doctrines and instructions for the local church laid out by our apostle of grace under the inspiration of God. Instead of following Scripture, some will gravitate to man-made doctrines, stubbornly clinging to them. When Paul warned the time would come when some "will not endure sound doctrine," he was referring to believers not willing to put up with, or embrace, God's instructions. *How did Paul say this would manifest itself?* They will resist truth, argue against it, become angry when it is taught, spread discontent in other believers, and try to find anyone who will teach what they want to hear. But it doesn't have to be this way. We can, and must, make the decision that we will consistently follow the instructions in the letters of the Apostle Paul.

If the Lord returned today, would He find you standing for His truth, or promoting error? Our Scripture reading today is a reminder to sincerely ask God to help us be loyal to following His Word in every area.

HOW TOLERANT?

Titus 1:10-11

A believer new to an assembly had a clear testimony of salvation, embraced the grace message, and was regular in attendance. The elders didn't give it much thought when he set up a table promoting tapes and literature from other teachers. After a year, the elders realized he had been promoting several devisive errors contrary to sound doctrine and the church constitution. Moreover, he had won several converts within the assembly. When the elders kindly asked him to discontinue promoting these doctrines, he defiantly refused in a publicly, argumentative way. *What should the elders have done next?*

Paul's instruction in the pastoral epistles is abundantly clear that when bad doctrine is being promoted, it must not be tolerated. Titus was instructed to "rebuke them sharply, that they may be sound in the faith" (Titus 1:13). *Why?* Because even those who know Christ sometimes deceive others with empty, incorrect doctrines that often "subvert whole houses," leading entire families into error (Titus 1:10-11). Bad doctrine is like a cancer. It grows, spreads, and overtakes its victims. Paul tells Titus he must not be tolerant of error in major doctrines. Instead, it is appropriate to give "sharp" rebuke when those in error refuse to listen to sound doctrine or follow the leadership God has placed within the church. God will hold the elders of each church accountable at the Bema Seat to assure their church is always "the pillar and ground of the truth" (I Timothy 3:15; Revelation 2:14-15, 20). Every assembly should be a safe haven of grace for everyone, where only truth is promoted. When error is introduced into the assembly, elders are to reason from the Scriptures with the one in error (Titus 1:9). Should the errant one defiantly continue to promote bad doctrine, Paul says, "a man that is an heretick after the first and second admonition reject" (Titus 3:10). To "reject" means "to put out, or not have alongside." Romans 16:17 says it clearly: "…mark them which cause divisions and offenses contrary to the doctrine which ye have learned; and avoid them." Everyone is to obey this command.

It isn't wiser to tolerate bad doctrine to maintain numbers in a local church. It isn't loving to continue to befriend one in error. Both are disobedience that bolsters their defiance. If your church leaders deem it necessary to take strong action against error, come down on the right side of the issue, God's side, by standing with those who stand against error.

ARE YOU SOBER?

Titus 2:1-4

When in high school, from the first day I went out for a sport, I made up my mind I was going to give it my absolute best effort. It didn't matter if some on the team slacked off when doing conditioning drills or practicing for competition. I was going to take a sober-minded approach to give it my all every step of the way.

In Paul's instructions for Titus about how to live a dedicated Christian life, four times in Chapter Two he mentioned being "sober." The word "sober" means "to be sound minded, serious minded, or vigilant." The first thing Titus was to tell the "aged men" was to be "sober" (vs. 2). Perhaps this is needed because in older years we tend to let down our spiritual guard. We grow weary, no longer have children in the house to properly influence, and perhaps think more than we should about living to please self in our closing years. But even aged men need encouragement to be vigilant, or sober, in their thinking about living for Christ and serving Him. Titus was to teach the aged women to teach "young women to be sober…" (vs. 3-4). It is often the case that younger girls and women are overly focused on fun social activities, clothing, and fads. These young ladies needed instruction to be more serious-minded, vigilant, or sober, with the mindset of growing to be a godly wife and mother. Titus was to speak to "young men likewise exhort [them] to be sober minded…" (vs. 6). The temptation is strong for young men to be preoccupied with worldly entertainments, ambition for riches, or pursuing women. Paul wanted Titus to challenge the young men in his sphere of influence to be serious-minded about being a pattern of good works for the cause of Christ, sound in doctrine, sincerity, and wholesome speech. These qualities would produce a godliness that would eliminate criticism from lost souls. Then Paul told Titus that God's grace has "appeared to all men, teaching us…we should live soberly, righteously, and godly…" (vss. 11-12). Every believer, regardless of age or gender, has an urgent need to be armed with a soberness, or serious mindedness, about living a godly life before the Lord and others.

These four reminders should cause each of us to evaluate how sober-minded our walk with the Lord is presently. May the Lord find us to be more serious about living for Him than anything else and seeking to be transformed by His grace daily.

BE GENTLE AND MEEK

Titus 3:3

One member of a family is often outspoken and bombastic. She goes out of her way to be offensive, rude, disrespectful, and defiant. She is constantly posting what even she calls "controversial" things on Facebook. Then she verbally attacks anyone with whom she disagrees in a degrading manner. Perhaps you have encountered someone like this. *How are Christians supposed to respond to such frequent mistreatment?*

We learn from Ecclesiastes 3:1: "To every thing there is a season, and a time to every purpose under heaven." This passage goes on to explain there are times to "...keep silence, and a time to speak..." or "...to break down, and a time to build up" (vss. 7,3). God does not demand that we simply take every wrong, be everyone's doormat, or suffer in silence regardless of what abusive behavior is heaped upon us. Sometimes we must stand up to abusive behavior. However, this should not be our first or regular response. In Titus 3:2, Paul gives us a general rule to guide our conduct when he says: "To speak evil of no man, to be no brawlers, but gentle, shewing all meekness unto all men." We are to seek to avoid conflict when we can. Treating others with gentleness will often avert problems. Having humility with strength under pressure is a good testimony to all. Even when grossly mistreated, we are to "recompense to no man evil for evil" but instead seek to "...live peaceably with all men" (Romans 12:17-18). If it isn't possible to live peaceably with an individual, it is appropriate to object to their wrong behavior, insist they stop, distance ourself from them, or seek the help of others to stop the abuse. However, we must always be careful in our attitude, reaction, and motives. It would be very easy to allow our flesh to take control and our actions degrade to the level of the abuser. Our ardent goal must be to maintain a good testimony for Christ. It may be easier to do so if we keep in mind how foolish we once were before being saved, and purpose to live for Christ. Paul tells us: "For we ourselves also were sometimes foolish, disobedient, serving divers lusts and pleasures, living in malice and envy, hateful, and hating one another" (Titus 3:3).

Abusers are often unhappy people with a void without Christ in their lives. They need to see Christ in us. Pray that Christ will enable you to demonstrate Him to the wrongdoer.

I'M SO BLESSED
Revelation 1:3

It is more prevalent than one might think to hear people say, "I'm so blessed." By looking at the volume of instances in social media, it seems that even lost people are using this phrase. However, there are many instances when Christians post these words as a way to thank God for providentially providing health, a loving spouse, children, a dream job, a good church, friends, and more. It is appropriate for us to have a thankful heart and give God praise for His many blessings. But let's remember one other thing that makes us richly blessed.

When the Apostle John wrote the Book of Revelation under inspiration, he told the reader, "Blessed is he that readeth, and they that hear the words of this prophecy, and keep those things which are written therein: for the time is at hand" (Revelation 1:3). John wrote this book to seven Jewish kingdom churches under intense persecution during the Acts era, prior to Paul's last epistle (see Colossians 1:25). John specifically promised them God's blessing if they read, believed, heeded, and took encouragement from the content of Revelation. These churches were instructed to correct specific failures, expect specific persecutions, find courage in knowing that Christ ultimately will return to vanquish His enemies and reward the faithful. While not ignoring this context, we should remember believers in every dispensation are always greatly blessed when they read and obey God's written Word. For a believer, the Scriptures rejoice the heart while enlightening the eyes (Psalm 19:8), become a light to our path (Psalm 119:105), give understanding to the simple (Psalm 119:130), and give reproof that directs into the proper way of life (Proverbs 6:23). As the sword of the Spirit, God's Word equips for spiritual warfare (Ephesians 6:17) and thoroughly furnishes us unto all good works with a balance of doctrine and correction (II Timothy 3:16-17). It is, therefore, a great blessing to those who will take the time to read it, and even more so to those who will really study and live it. Jeremiah said God's Word was unto him the rejoicing of his heart (Jeremiah 15:16). And David said time in Scripture was more to be desired than gold, even fine gold (Psalm 19:10).

How blessed do you want to be? Beyond physical or tangible blessings, every believer needs earnestly to desire the blessings of learning spiritual truths in God's Word, then put them into practice in everyday life. Right now, purpose in heart to do both regularly.

THE MAN UPSTAIRS?
Revelation 1:9-20

In his song entitled "Unanswered Prayers," country singer Garth Brooks refers to God as "the Man upstairs." Similar phrases referring to Almighty God include: the Big Man, my Co-pilot, my Homeboy, my Golf-buddy, or simply JC. The user may not intend it this way, but such references are highly disrespectful, and reveal a lack of understanding about who and what our Great High God really is.

When the Apostle John encountered the Lord Jesus Christ who was instructing him to write what would be revealed to him, he said, "I fell at his feet as dead" (Revelation 1:17). Notice there was nothing casual in John's response. *Why?* When the Lord Jesus Christ spoke, it was with "a great voice, as of a trumpet" (vs. 10). "His eyes were as a flame of fire" (vs. 14), and "His countenance was as the sun" (vs. 16). This brief picture, and the reaction of a mere man in the presence of God, is consistent with the rest of Scripture. Isaiah says he saw "the Lord...high and lifted up" with dynamic angelic hosts attending Him crying, "Holy, holy, holy, is the Lord of Hosts" (Isaiah 6:1-3). Isaiah's response was not casual or irreverent. He said, "Woe is me! For I am undone; because I am a man of unclean lips, and I dwell in the midst of a people of unclean lips" (vs. 5). People of old had a far greater reverence for the Lord. King David described his great God by saying, "The Lord reigneth, He is clothed with majesty; the Lord is clothed with strength...Thy throne is established of old: Thou art from everlasting" (Psalm 93:1-2). He continued, "God sitteth upon the throne of His holiness" as He reigns over all men (Psalm 47:8). He's not just a co-pilot or a buddy. Balak declared, "God is not a man, that He should lie" (Numbers 23:19). The Lord tells us this is because, "...My thoughts are not your thoughts, neither are your ways My ways...For as the heavens are higher than the earth, so are My ways higher than your ways, and My thoughts than your thoughts" (Isaiah 55:8-9). In the context of all this information, the Lord Jesus said of the Father, "Hallowed [meaning holy or sacred] be Thy name" (Matthew 6:9).

It would be appropriate to lovingly share articles such as this with lost souls who lack understanding of God's holiness and magnificence. More importantly, in humility, we believers need always to show great reverence to the Lord and to His name.

FIRST LOVE
Revelation 2:1-7

My wife and I once knew a couple who were deeply in love during their days of courtship. They had "that look" that communicated they had found true love. Each thought the other was great, and they were happy to be together. However, after several years, that love began to cool. They spent less time together. He fixed up the garage as his man cave, and she began to go out more at night with her friends. Before long, their love was barely a dying ember, and then it was completely dead. They had lost that first love they had for one another.

When John wrote to "the church of Ephesus" (Revelation 2:1), he was not writing to a future tribulation church, but to a Jewish Kingdom church existing in the early Acts era. Revelation 1:19 gives us an outline for the book. "The things which thou hast seen" (meaning the vision in Chapter One), "and the things which are" (referring to the kingdom churches existing in early Acts and addressed in Chapters 2-3), "and the things which shall be hereafter" (meaning the remainder of Revelation that describes the seven years of Tribulation). This church at Ephesus was to be praised for many things. They had "labour," (Revelation 2:2) indicating that they were busy seeking to further the cause of Christ. They had "patience," indicating they endured persecution in faithfulness for the name of Christ (vs. 3). They also would not "bear them which are evil," referring to false apostles seeking to corrupt their doctrine (vs. 2). Yet for all this activity, the Lord says, "I have somewhat against thee, because thou has left thy first love" (vs. 4). In all their busyness, they were only going through the motions of a spiritual walk with the Lord without the zeal, excitement, or the genuine love for the Lord Jesus that they once possessed. That love had become a dying ember while their hearts were gradually becoming more distant from the Savior whom they once loved with such a pure passion. Busyness for the cause of the Lord, faithfulness while enduring hardship, and intolerance for errant doctrine are good things. But these are not substitutes for a healthy, living, daily, personal, interactive relationship with the Savior.

We believers today can lose the fire of our first love for Christ. Our relationship with Him will become stale and dead unless we give Him priority time, intimately interacting with Him in prayer and His Word. Rekindle your first love with the Lord today.

YOU'RE A RICH MAN
Revelation 2:8-11

An adult Christian couple I know has a clear testimony of knowing Christ as their Savior. They devotedly embrace the distinctives of grace proclaimed by Paul, and they also attend a grace church. They have beautiful, happy, healthy children that delight the soul. Though they are of modest means, I told the husband, "You are a wealthy man." By that I meant, they know the riches of salvation and dispensational truth, and God has blessed them with riches in these young lives entrusted to their care. That makes them rich. They knew exactly what I meant and nodded in agreement.

The message of the Savior to the church at Smyrna was, "I know thy works, and tribulation, and poverty, (but thou art rich) and I know the blasphemy of them which say they are Jews, and are not, but are the synagogue of Satan" (Revelation 2:9). Notice there is no rebuke here, only acknowledgment of their faithfulness. Their "works" were no doubt remaining faithful to proclaim salvation through the Lord Jesus as the prophesied Messiah of Israel. The mission of the Jewish kingdom church was to "go ye into all the world, and preach the gospel [of the kingdom] to every creature" (Mark 16:15). Their "tribulation" assuredly included persecution from unbelieving Jews who vehemently opposed faith in the Savior and those who proclaimed Him. Those who opposed were willing to "say they are Jews" (Revelation 2:8), or boast of their heritage as God's chosen people as if this merited eternal life (Matthew 3:9). Even though attending the temple, as unbelievers they were of "the synagogue of Satan" in their opposition to Christ. The "poverty" of these Jewish saints was due to their obedience to the Lord's commands to "take...no thought for the morrow" (Matthew 6:34). Jewish believers were to abandon earthly "treasure," and trust the Lord to provide for them supernaturally, as He will in the Millennial Kingdom. This is not our instruction for today, but it was taught by Christ, practiced and proclaimed by the apostles (Mathew 19:27), then carried on by Jewish believers in early Acts (2:41-47). Their faithfulness to the Lord made them "rich" in the potential for eternal reward.

While the program and requirements are different for us today, we too can be either rich or poor regarding God's approval and eternal reward. We must choose to be sold out to the Lord, no matter the hardship, and view this as being "rich."

EXPOSURE TO ERROR
Revelation 2:12-17

There has been a justifiable outcry of criticism over Joel Osteen's doctrinal views revealed in an interview with Larry King. When asked whether people of other faiths go to heaven, he replied, "You know, I'm very careful about saying who would go to heaven, and wouldn't go to heaven. I don't know...." When asked about atheists going to heaven, he said, "I'm going to let God be the judge...." Then he recounted a trip to India, saying he did not believe the people there were going to hell if they were sincere in their hearts.[1] Osteen believes his ministry is only to help people to be their best selves. Don't mistake objections to this kind of false doctrine as "sour grapes from jealous preachers." God's truth and salvation through Jesus Christ alone is the key issue.

The church at Pergamos had made the foolish mistake of allowing people to infiltrate who were mixing truth with error, and they tolerated it. They were told, "thou hast there them that hold the doctrine of Balaam... [and] also the...doctrine of the Nicolaitanes, which thing I hate" (Revelation 2:14-15). Balaam was a true prophet of God who prostituted his gifts to gain money from King Balak (Numbers 22-25). The king hired him to put a divine curse on Israel. God prevented Balaam from doing so, but Balaam advised the king to befriend the Jews by inviting them to worship and feast at pagan altars. Israel cooperated in this compromise, and even committed fornication as part of these pagan rites. God so hated this compromise that He slew twenty-four thousand guilty participants (Numbers 25:1-9). This example paralleled what was happening in Pergamos. This city had the first temple dedicated to the worship of Caesar and a temple to Aesculapius, whose symbol was a serpent coiled on a pole. These false services were so vile, they are referred to as "Satan's seat" and "where Satan dwelleth" (Revelation 2:13). The name "Nicolaitanes" means "to rule the people, or lord it over"[2] others, while leading them astray. Not only were believers tolerating error, they were allowing others to pressure them into accepting it.

The Lord sternly told them to get rid of this error. We today must not fall into the same trap of tolerating false doctrine. Once exposed it must be expelled. "He that hath an ear, let him hear" (vs. 17).

A SEDUCTIVE MESSENGER
Revelation 2:18-29

A Christian friend sent us a link to a website warning about dangerous doctrines promoted by televangelist Joyce Meyer. She teaches that Jesus stopped being the Son of God on the Cross, yet went to hell to pay for our sins, and was the first to be born again. She claims that she receives direct revelations from God, that she is no longer a sinner, and that Christians are little gods.[1] The truth is far different. The Lord Jesus Christ remained God, had no sin, and did not need to be born again. Sin was atoned on the Cross when He said, "It is finished" (John 19:30). No one receives direct revelation today, because the revelation of Scripture is complete. Paul's letters prove Christians still sin and certainly are not gods.

When the Savior addressed the church at Thyatira, He strongly rebuked them "because thou sufferest that woman Jezebel, which calleth herself a prophetess, to teach and to seduce my servants to commit fornication, and to eat things sacrificed unto idols" (Revelation 2:20). While having a parallel during the Tribulation, this Jewish kingdom church existing in Acts was allowing an evil woman, symbolized by the name Jezebel, to entice true believers into false worship. Jezebel is used as an example because she was an evil Gentile queen married to the king of Israel. She lead both the king and the Israelites into the worship of Baal. This was a particularly seductive influence because the Jews were being drawn to Baal by temple prostitutes but still retained some fashion of worship to Jehovah (I Kings 18:21). Essentially the same thing was happening in the church at Thyatira. A brazen, evil woman was claiming to be God's servant, a prophetess, and luring Jewish believers into the spiritual fornication of false worship to Apollo. Unbelievably, the church was allowing this wicked woman in its midst without rebuking her soul-damning doctrines or eliminating her platform of influence. The Lord gave a unique warning to her and those following her. If they did not repent and turn to the Lord, they would be "cast…into a bed [of]…great tribulation" (Revelation 2:22). This referred to them going through severe trials during the time of Jacob's trouble, and ultimately, into eternal punishment.

Believer, don't allow false teachers an opportunity to deceive you with false doctrines in your home or church. Avoid them, even if they give some truth or have large a following. They are still dangerous.

SPIRITUALLY DEAD
Revelation 3:1-6

This author attended a liberal denominational church until his late teens. The minister wore a robe, we participated in responsive congregational readings, used candles in some services, and were required to go through a confirmation process. There was a lot of religious activity. Apparently others there did not see it, but I realized early on there was no real spiritual life in this church, or within me. What I needed was to be delivered from this influence that was keeping me spiritually dead.

The message from the Lord Jesus to the church at Sardis was, "I know thy works, that thou hast a name that thou livest, and art dead" (Revelation 3:1). Obviously, this is not a reference to them being like zombies pictured in movies today. But many of them were spiritually dead while still physically alive. Notice there is no rebuke for doctrinal error (vs. 4), nor is there a reference to being persecuted for boldly proclaiming Christ. Apparently, neither was present. Sardis had once been a great city of commerce but was in economic decline while largely focusing on the worship of Artemis, one of the nature cults.[1] We believe this was a real Jewish church with an earthly kingdom hope existing about A.D. 50. The problems they exhibited will resurface among believers in the tribulation, and mirror many believers and churches today (compare Ephesians 4:18-19). They had once been spiritually vibrant but were now nearly spiritually dead. Perhaps they were resting on past laurels of spiritual vitality or had lingered in apathy after losing a real love for the Lord. Like the church at Ephesus (Revelation 2:4), their spiritual life was effectively on life-support. Thankfully, there was still hope, particularly for some. The Lord Jesus tells them, "Be watchful, and strengthen the things which remain" (Revelation 3:2). To be "watchful" means to WAKE UP with alertness and take appropriate action. There was still time to come back to life spiritually and be awarded white robes in eternity (vs. 5) indicating salvation and implying spotlessness in their eternal record.

In every dispensation, including today, it is possible to be sound doctrinally yet susceptible to becoming spiritually dead. If you have lost the robust life for the Lord you once had, do what the Savior instructed here: "remember" past zeal once possessed, "hold fast" to truth, "watch" or awake spiritually, and "strengthen" the life of Christ remaining inside (vss. 2-3). Don't delay, do it today.

GOOD JOB
Revelation 3:7-13

Parents everywhere encourage their little ones with the words "good job." When they first learn to walk, become potty trained, start to repeat words, throw a ball, or begin to read, we seem to say to them instinctively, "good job." Our purpose is to give positive reinforcement, or acknowledgment, of doing a good thing, or doing something well. It is our hope our words will help to motivate them to continue down the right path.

Regardless of any lack of secular history to document Jewish churches in each of the cities addressed in Revelation during the early years in Acts, we believe they existed because of this sacred record. Their Jewish identity is seen in the phrases: "the key of David" (vs. 7), "synagogue" (vs. 9), and "new Jerusalem" (vs. 12).[1] The Savior's words to the church at Philadelphia were, "I know thy works...thou hast a little strength, and hast kept My Word, and hast not denied My name" (Revelation 3:8). Unlike the Savior's messages to previous churches, for these believers there were no words of rebuke, only praise, positive acknowledgment of faithfulness, and implication of genuine spiritual life. In effect, the Lord Jesus was saying, "good job." Local Jews, pictured in the words "the synagogue of Satan" (vs. 9), were described this way because of their efforts to thwart the Jewish believers from proclaiming the Gospel of the Kingdom. However, the Savior promises His faithful ones, "I have set before thee an open door, and no man can shut it" (vs. 8). An open door in Scripture is frequently used to describe an opportunity for ministry (Acts 14:27). The Lord Jesus was promising He would continue to give them opportunities to share their message of eternal life. He further promises "I also will keep thee from the hour of temptation" (vs. 10), indicating divine protection from persecution. He also acknowledges that they had "a little strength" (vs. 8), implying they could effectively complete their ministry if they relied on His strength given to them by a close continual walk with Him. If they were faithful, great eternal reward lay ahead (vss. 12-13).

There are many parallel applications in this text for believers today. In our present Dispensation of Grace, we are to be praised if we have kept the truths of God's Word and not defiled God's name with a sinful lifestyle. Good job. Now use God's open door to share the gospel. If you will, eternal reward will be yours.

NEITHER HOT NOR COLD
Revelation 3:14-22

Our grandkids beg for hot chocolate, and we adults like a good hot cup, especially when the day is cold. On one occasion my wife made hot chocolate for everyone. I was distracted and didn't get around to drinking mine for over an hour. When I found the cup that had been made for me, without thinking it through, I took a big gulp. It was terrible. It was neither cold, like chocolate milk out of the refrigerator, nor hot like hot chocolate is supposed to be. It was lukewarm and putrid to my palate.

When the Lord Jesus addresses "the church of the Laodiceans," He tells them, "I know thy works, that thou art neither cold nor hot: I would that thou wert cold or hot. So then because thou are lukewarm...I will spue thee out of My mouth" (Revelation 3:15-16). This was a vivid illustration of the indifferent spiritual condition of these believers and how distasteful it was to the One who had died for them, risen again, and offered them "life... more abundantly" (John 10:10). Sadly, like King Saul before them who did not even realize when his power from the Lord was gone, these Christians did not realize their sickening spiritual condition nor that their power was gone. Their attitude was, "I am rich, and increased in goods, and have need of nothing" (Revelation 3:17). While they may have basked in monetary wealth and had an abundance of things, the Lord viewed them as spiritually "wretched, and miserable, and poor, and blind, and naked" [without eternal rewards, vs. 17]. He describes their lack of service for Christ as "the shame of thy nakedness" (vs. 18). The Savior's counsel to them was "anoint thine eyes with eyesalve, that thou mayest see." They had become so cold and calloused, they could not see their real spiritual condition nor did they seem to care. But our Lord instructs them to "buy of Me gold tried in the fire [symbolizing service tried in the fire of persecution], that thou mayest be rich, and...clothed" (vs. 18). It was to believers Christ said He was standing at the door and knocking to be let in so that a hot spiritual zeal would return (vs. 20).

It is unclear from the record in Revelation whether or not these believers responded. But, *if this account describes your spiritual temperature, will you respond right now?* The Lord is knocking at the door of your heart seeking a relationship that is hot with zeal.

WHAT WILL ETERNITY BE LIKE?
Revelation 4

On March 26, 1997, police discovered 39 souls in California who had committed suicide. They were members of Heavens Gate, a cult taught to put aside earthly things to prepare for heaven. When the Hale-Bopp Comet neared, in preparation for a trip to heaven, they packed their bags, ate a poisonous meal, and lay down to die. Author Mark Moring thought this was foolish, then realized, whether in truth or error, we all long for heaven.[1]

Revelation Four moves from references to the days in which Apostle John lived (Revelation 1:19), and when Jewish kingdom churches were established after being dispersed through persecution (Acts 8:3-4; 11:19-20), to the future. "A door was opened in heaven," and John was told, "Come up hither, and I will shew thee things which must be hereafter" (Revelation 4:1). While the Apostle Paul may have also been temporarily taken to heaven during one of the times he experienced death (II Corinthians 11:23), his reference to knowing a man "caught up to the third heaven" (II Corinthians 12:2) may have also referred to John. But, before details about the future tribulation were revealed, the Apostle John witnessed an amazing view of the Lord Jesus Christ sitting on His heavenly throne (Revelation 4:2). His deity is reflected in the description of Him ornamented with precious stones and a rainbow (vs. 3). His Omnipotence is represented by the presence of great lightning, thunder, voices, and the seven Spirits of God (vs. 5). To amplify His worthiness of all praise and honor, before His throne is "a sea of glass like unto crystal" and "four [imposing angelic] beasts" declaring night and day, "Holy, holy, holy, Lord God Almighty" (vs. 6-8). These angels "give glory and honour and thanks" to the Savior, then 24 martyred elders followed suit with "worship" and praise (vss. 9-10). We know Jewish saints will ultimately experience eternal life as they inherit the earth, but this quick peek into life after death for kingdom saints reveals part of what eternity will be like for them. It will include the joy of being in the presence of the Savior and giving Him humble, sincere worship with praise.

While the eternal hope for the Body of Christ is heavenly, there is quite possibly a parallel. We, too, will be united with Christ, and surely worshiping the Savior with thankful appreciation and praise. *But why wait?* Start that practice of thanksgiving and praise right now.

December 15

WORTHY IS THE LAMB
Revelation 5

A Mormon leader asked a twenty-one-year-old man if he was considering going on a two-year missionary commitment. This man said, "I wanted to go, but I am not worthy." The leader asked, "Who made that judgment?" He responded, "I did." The leader also asked a mother if she would attend her daughter's wedding being held in the temple. She responded, "I would like to, but I am unworthy." He asked again, "Who made that judgment? She said, "I did."[1]

A majestic scene unfolds as John is ushered into heaven to view the throne of God. At the right hand of the throne is "a book written within and on the backside,...sealed with seven seals" (Revelation 5:1). "A strong angel" asks, "Who is worthy to open the book, and to loose the seals thereof"? (vs. 2). When no one is worthy to open the book, John weeps greatly because he longed to learn its contents. Then the elders tell John "the Lion of the tribe of Judah" has prevailed. The elders fall down before the "Lamb" saying, "Thou art worthy to take the book, and to open the seals thereof" (vss. 5-6, 9). Verse 12 repeats, "Worthy is the Lamb." *But why is the Lord Jesus Christ worthy of such praise?* His description as a Lion from Judah who descended from David all relate to His deity, identifying Him as the One promised by God the Father. But He is also called "a Lamb as it had been slain" (vs. 6). Isaiah 53 promised a divine Redeemer who would bear the sins of Israel so all Jews could be found acceptable to God the Father. Revelation 5:9 confirms, "for Thou wast slain, and hast redeemed us [Israel] to God by Thy blood out of every kindred, and tongue, and people, and nation." John witnesses the hosts of heaven, human and hundreds of thousands of angels, as a huge choir, worshipping the Savior by singing "a new song" (vs. 9). It gives praise and glory to the Lord Jesus Christ because He was worthy to open this mysterious book. He was, and is, worthy of all praise. Notice too, the focus is not on Christ in the manger, but as having died for mankind, yet triumphantly risen.

If the hosts of heaven exalt the Savior in songs of praise and worship, we should too! Go through today singing praises to your risen Savior for His payment for sins and majestic deity. He is worthy.

PLEASING WORSHIP TO GOD
Revelation 5:8

At the Christian university I attended to prepare for the ministry, the primary means of communication between the men and women was letters gathered from and delivered to each dorm every night. When a date was arranged on campus, it was common for the ladies to be dressed nicely and wear a tasteful amount of perfume. That evening, letters were exchanged thanking one another for the time together, and if the lady was particularly interested, she would often spray the envelope with perfume. The sweet smell of that fragrance was a pleasing sign that would linger and remind the men of the one who sent it.

When the Apostle John describes the worthiness of the Lord Jesus Christ on His throne in heaven in Revelation Chapter Five, praise and worship are given to Him. The twenty-four elders fall down before Him having "golden vials full of odours, which are the prayers of the saints" (vs. 8). This description has a connection to Israel's worship of the Lord in the tabernacle where they were to "make an altar to burn incense upon" (Exodus 30:1). "And Aaron shall burn thereon sweet incense every morning; when he dresseth the lamps" and likewise "at even[ing], he shall burn incense upon it, a perpetual incense before the Lord throughout your generations" (vss. 7-8). The chief ingredient of this incense was frankincense, which along with other spices, produced a perfume that was to accompany Israel when they came to meet with the Lord (Exodus 30:34-36). David gives us further insight into this practice when he writes, "Lord, I cry unto thee… let my prayer be set forth before Thee as incense" (Psalm 141:1-2). We see in these descriptions that God views the worship of His saints, through prayer, as a sweet-smelling incense, or perfume, that is to be offered every day, morning and evening, as a perpetual practice. It is noteworthy that the record of heavenly worship in Revelation 5:8 also includes the "prayers of the saints" being offered in golden vials, (gold always symbolizes great value), and that this is viewed by the Lord as a sweet odor.

The lesson to remember from these verses is that prayer is an important part of worship that pleases the Lord and is to be the constant practice of the saints. This basic principle is true even today. Make prayer a vital part of your daily walk with the Lord Jesus Christ. It will please the Lord like a sweet perfume.

MANY MARTYRS
Revelation 6:1-11

John and Betty Stam were missionaries to China who proclaimed eternal life by God's grace and faith in Christ Jesus. In 1934, they were arrested by the Communists and initially held for $20,000.00 ransom. They were marched 12 miles toward Miaoshou. While stopping for the night, Betty hid their baby, Helen, who was later rescued. The next day, John and Betty were both forced to kneel, and then they were beheaded. Their witness for Christ cost them their lives.[1]

As the worthy Lamb of God opens the book with seven seals, from which John desired to learn, a scene from the coming first half of the Tribulation is revealed. As each seal is opened, a horseman is released into the world. The first is on a white horse, but this is NOT Christ, though He too will return to the earth on a white horse (Revelation 19:11). The rider in Revelation 6:2 is the Anti-Christ, who is an imitator of the Messiah, and will actually claim to be the Christ. He will go forth methodically conquering with promises of peace until the world choses him as their leader, indicated by "a crown" (vs. 2). The riders of the other horses are his agents, demonic angels, likely indwelling human hosts. The red horse symbolizes activity causing bloodshed and death (vs. 4). Humans will be convinced to "kill one another" (vs. 4), implying authority to carry out murders while under demonic influence. The black horse (vs. 5-6) represents death for multitudes, this time through famine. The "pair of balances" indicates that evil men will control the food supply for great sums of money and deny food to those who proclaim Christ as Savior. He that rides the pale horse is called "Death, and Hell followed with him" (vs. 8). This agent of Anti-Christ will wreak havoc over a quarter of the world through the sword, hunger, and beasts. His actions will be savage, particularly as there will be growing persecution of Christians. Verse nine describes "the souls of them that were slain for the Word of God, and for the testimony which they held" (vs. 10). Note, the truth of God's Word, and faith in the Lord Jesus Christ, will be more important than anything, including their lives.

While not in the Tribulation, it is possible we in the Dispensation of Grace may one day face persecution, even unto death. If so, may we likewise hold Christ and His Word more important than our lives.

THE PROUD HUMBLED
Revelation 6:12-17

Saddam Hussein was a brutal dictator who believed he was destined to rule Iraq forever. He tortured and killed at will, including inflicting poisonous gases on his own countrymen. Defying warnings from the West, he continued atrocities, including invading neighboring countries. Ultimately, he was deposed by a worldwide coalition. Fleeing these troops and fellow Iraqis, he hid for eight months in tunnels until he was captured and executed by his own people. This once haughty and merciless man was humbled and then brought to justice by hanging.

John saw future martyrs from the Tribulation asking God to judge their persecutors, and "avenge our blood" (Revelation 6:10). As Christ opens the sixth seal of the book by His throne, it reveals divine cosmic judgments that will have a devastating impact on earth during the Tribulation. "A great earthquake" will be so profound, "every mountain and island were [or will be] moved out of their places" (vss. 12,14). The "sun became black as sackcloth" (vs. 12), indicating a darkness so intense day will be as dark as night. "And the moon [will become] as blood" (vs. 12). Beginning October 7-8, 2014, in separate six-month intervals, a phenomena occurred called "a blood moon," because each full moon appeared very red. In the Tribulation it will be God's warning to man that great loss of life lies ahead. Stars will fall from the sky and dynamic events occur in the heavens (vs. 14). No one, from kings to slaves will be able to escape (vs. 15). These catastrophes will be designed to draw men to faith in the Lord Jesus Christ. Stubbornly, rather than call on the Savior in faith, most will run from Him. They will call on the mountains to hide them "from the face of him that sitteth on the throne, and from the wrath of the Lamb" (vs. 16). The unsaved, some who were previously cruel and violent persecutors, will be humbled in God's judgments upon the earth. But all will be given the opportunity to escape eternal judgment if they will turn in faith to the Lord Jesus. Many will not, but as we will later see, many will be saved during this time.

We today who know Christ as Savior are not to fear these future troubled times, because we have been "delivered from the wrath to come" (I Thessalonians 1:10). But we are to warn others so they can escape these future judgments on earth and eternal punishment by trusting now in the finished work of the Lord Jesus Christ. Warn someone today.

SAVED, SEALED, SUCCOURED
Revelation 7

For more than forty years, the *Berean Bible Fellowship* held a summer Bible conference at a campground in Indiana. This was a time for Christians to get away from the distractions and the oppositions of the world, to join with those of like precious faith in a time of encouragement, study, worship, and praise to the Lord Jesus Christ. Everyone who attended was asked to register and wear a nametag throughout the week so all instantly knew they belonged to our group and they could be easily identified by name.

Like the eye of a hurricane, Revelation Chapter Seven comes between the opening of the sixth and seventh seal. It serves as a calm before the worst of the Tribulation, the last three-and-one-half years. Four angels are told to hold the winds from "the four corners of the earth" (vs. 1), picturing the four directions on a compass. These winds are not to howl until "we have sealed the servants of our God in their foreheads" (vs. 3). This seal represents two things. It identifies the recipient as belonging to God, although it is noteworthy that these believers are not sealed at the moment of initial faith but prior to the most intense time of tribulation. It is also an indication of divine protection. We believe this is not from the persecution of men but from divine judgments that are about to fall. The winds being temporarily held back will "hurt the earth" (vs. 2), as God will smite the earth with the scorching of the sun, fires, hail, and more (Revelation 8). A seal will be given to 144,000 male virgin Jews from the tribes of Israel who will trust in the Lord Jesus as their Messiah. They will be protected from cataclysmic events so they can carry the revived Gospel of the Kingdom throughout the world. Revelation 7:9-10 describe "a great multitude" who will believe this gospel message, be given eternal salvation, and remain faithful. But they will be martyred for their faith (vs. 14). Their trials are pictured in references to hunger, thirst, and heat, But "God shall wipe away all tears from their eyes" (vs. 17). After being resurrected, they will be rewarded by being able to "serve" their Redeemer sitting on His throne in the heavenly temple as He "shall dwell among them" (vs. 15).

In eternity, believers from the Dispensation of Grace will also be blessed to serve the Savior and forever live in His presence. Any hardship we face now will be worth it all! Be faithful.

BITTER CONSEQUENCES
Revelation 8

In 1922, Benito Mussolini seized power in Italy, then created his dictatorship by destroying all political opposition through his secret police. What followed was a total lack of freedom, atrocities, and arrogant military decisions. After 21 years he was finally overthrown. When Mussolini tried to escape to the north, Italian Communists captured and executed him. His body was hung upside down, on public display, to confirm his demise.[1] Mussolini learned there are severe and bitter consequences to stubborn arrogance.

Just prior to the second half of the Tribulation, the seventh seal is opened in the book by the throne of the Lion of the Tribe of Judah. Thirty minutes of solemn silence in heaven follows. It is as if God's judgment that is about to fall takes the breath away from angels and martyred saints. In Scripture, trumpets were often used by God to announce significant events, such as the giving of the Law (Exodus 19:16-19), or the conquest of Jericho (Joshua 6:13-16). When the events described in Revelation begin four trumpets will blow in heaven, each announcing a new divine judgment. With the first trumpet, hail and fire mixed with blood will be cast to the earth (Revelation 8:7). Softball size hail can go through roofs, level crops, and kill people. It will be devastating. Billowing fire will also burn up one-third part of all vegetation. When the second trumpet sounds, a meteor, "burning with fire" is cast into the sea causing one-third of the sea to become blood. It kills the sea-life therein, destroying one-third of worldwide ships (vvs. 8-9). The stench and economic impact from lost ships will be catastrophic. The third trumpet will sound with "a great star," or angel, "called Wormwood" (vs. 10), falling from heaven. This will cause one-third of rivers and fresh water to become very bitter to the taste. With usable water scarce, many will drink from these waters, but any who do will die. When the fourth trumpet is sounded, one-third of the sun, moon, and stars, are "darkened" (vs. 12). This will create fear while impacting growing seasons and causing unsustainable demands for electricity.

These four trumpet judgments will fall because of man's stubborn arrogance in rejecting Christ as their Savior and to avenge God's Tribulation martyrs. You can help others avoid this bitter end by talking about these events and sharing the gospel with a lost soul today. You can start with, "Have you ever heard of the Tribulation? These are some of things that will happen...."

YOU HAVEN'T SEEN ANYTHING
Revelation 9

In 2016, wildfires destroyed over 100,000 acres in Alaska, 3,559 acres in California, 17,787 acres in Nevada, and 15,401 acres in New Mexico. That totals more than 100 square miles. Many governmental agencies warn this trend is going to get far worse. They are saying we haven't seen anything yet.[1]

As Chapter 8 closes, an angel is sent from God to announce that three more mind-boggling judgments are about to be released. He begins by saying, "Woe, woe, woe, to the inhabiters of the earth" (Revelation 8:13). Despite how horrible the first four trumpet judgments were, it's as if he is saying you haven't seen anything yet. When the fifth trumpet is sounded, an angel is sent from heaven to open the bottomless pit. So much smoke billows out that the sun and air "were darkened by reason of the smoke of the pit" (vs. 2). It will be far worse than decades of forest fires in America. Next, an army of demonic forces will be unleashed, serving as God's agents, to "hurt...only those men which have not the seal of God in their foreheads" (vs. 4). They are symbolically described "as the locusts" (vs. 3), who will torment, but not kill, the lost for five months. They will inflict so much pain that "men seek death" (vs. 6), but God will not allow them to find it. When the sixth trumpet is sounded, four demonic angels will be unleashed to lead an army of 200 million "to slay the third part of men" (vs. 15). One-fourth of humanity will have already tasted death (6:8). Now a third of those remaining will be killed. Yet for all this, "the rest of men... repented not of the works of their hands" (vs. 20). Instead, they cling to the worship of devils, idols of gold, and...murders, sorceries, and fornication. One would think that all this suffering, sorrow, and pain, would bring an end of man's stubborn refusal to turn to the Lord Jesus Christ as their Savior. However, sin will have a treacherous hold on these souls. Also, for those who previously understood, but rejected, the gospel during the Dispensation of Grace, a divine blindness will be imposed on them (II Thessalonians 2:11). Their earthly and eternal fate is sealed.

If you know someone who has heard the gospel but refused faith in the Savior, share with them that they will have no opportunity for salvation in the Tribulation. Now is the time to flee from God's wrath to come while they still can.

TO TELL THE TRUTH
Revelation 10

"*To Tell The Truth*" is an American game show. A panel of celebrities try to identify a contestant who has an unusual experience or occupation. This contestant is required to tell the truth when questioned, but he is flanked by two imposters who are permitted to lie.

Revelation 10 does not contain the seventh trumpet of judgment because there will be an interruption in the dispensing of these judgments until Revelation 11:15. However, there are three things of note in this chapter. First, "another mighty angel" (vs. 1) is sent from heaven. Some believe this is the Lord Jesus Christ because the angel is clothed with a cloud, has a rainbow on His head, and has feet as pillars of fire. He also has the book no man or angel was worthy to open. These are all things identified with God, representing majesty, mercy, judgment, or worthiness. Others point out he is called an "angel," linking him to the six angels with six trumpets. He swears an oath to the Lord Jesus, the creator of all things (vs. 6). We simply don't know who this angel is. Second, while others lie in the Tribulation, he has an announcement of solemn truth: "there should be time no longer" (vs. 6). The meaning here is that there will be no more delay in avenging the martyred saints or in pouring out God's wrath. The time for both has come. Third, this messenger takes "the little book," gives it the Apostle John, and tells him to eat it (vs. 9). While this book specifically contains previously unrevealed prophecy about the judgments of the Tribulation, it also represents the written Word of God as a whole. Jeremiah figuratively said he ate God's Word (Jeremiah 15:16), and the Lord told Ezekiel, "open thy mouth and eat what I give thee" (Ezekiel 2:8). John then sees a book written by God. It was important for the Apostle John to eat this book because he "must [continue to] prophecy again before many peoples, and nations, and tongues, and kings" (vs. 11). He would not be prepared to so minister until consuming the Word.

We are to tell the truth of God's Word to others, but we will be unprepared until we consume it only for ourselves. We are to figuratively eat it, and then we have a moral obligation to share It's truths with others who do not yet understand them. Look for someone in your path today with whom you can share divine truth you are learning from Scripture.

JAW DROPPING
Revelation 11:1-11

Under Hitler's reign in Germany, the Jews faced growing hatred. They were required to wear a yellow star. They were blamed for crime, disease, and the financial problems of the nation. They became so hated that even children threw rocks, and cheered when they were deported to concentration camps. Millions were starved, forced into slave labor, medically experimented on, or slaughtered. When liberated by the Allies, even battle-hardened soldiers wept at the jaw-dropping atrocities they discovered.

The events that will unfold during the second woe pronounced by an angel announcing the trumpet judgments will be jaw dropping (Revelation 11:1-11). The Apostle John was told to measure a Jewish temple in Jerusalem. The Anti-Christ, who will rise to power at the beginning of these seven years, will make it possible for Jews to rebuild their temple through a covenant of peace with Israel. This temple must be rebuilt to fulfill the prophecy of the Anti-Christ desecrating the temple and demanding he be worshipped (Daniel 9:26-27). Two witnesses for God, likely Elijah and Moses, will have supernatural "power" as they proclaim the Gospel of the Kingdom for forty-two months (Revelation 11:3). Hundreds of thousands will believe their message of the Lord Jesus being the Messiah of Israel, and Savior of the world (Revelation 7:1-10). However, the majority of the world will not believe. They will hate these witnesses, and try to kill them because they will also perform miracles to punish those who refuse to believe (vs. 6). But until bring their message of eternal life to all the world is complete (Matthew 24:14), they are supernaturally protected and remain undeterred in ministry (Revelation 11:6). Ultimately, the forces of Anti-Christ will slay them and leave their bodies to rot in the street for 3½ days (vss. 7-10). The world will respond to their death with joy and celebration. Then, "the Spirit of life from God" will enter the two witnesses (vs. 11). The Lord's audible voice will command they "come up hither" (vs. 12), and all the world will see them ascend into the heavens. This event will be so stunningly jaw-dropping that great fear will fall upon all the unsaved.

Throughout history, God has always maintained His testimony to lost souls through human servants. Today, we who have trusted in Christ alone for eternal life must fulfill our mission of sharing the message of eternal life to a lost world. Regardless of resistance, hatred, or persecution, this is our primary purpose for being here after salvation. Report for duty.

JUST REWARD
Revelation 11:14-19

In December 2013, off-duty LA policeman Donald Thompson saw a vehicle crash into the divider on the freeway and burst into flames. Disregarding his own welfare, Officer Thompson jumped barriers, cut the seatbelt from the unconscious driver, and pulled him to safety. On May 17, 2016, President Obama presented Officer Thompson the Medal of Valor, the highest award in America for public service officers who exhibit exceptional courage in an attempt to save or protect others from harm.[1]

The third "woe" pronounced with the seventh trumpet of judgment (Revelation 8:1-2,13) is being described in Revelation 11:14-19. In these verses, John summarized everything that will occur from the middle to the end of the Tribulation (Revelation 20:3). The evidence for this conclusion is the many "days" referred to in Revelation 10:7. Also, the description of events in Revelation 11:14-19 pictures the anger of the nations who will war against believers and the coming of Christ to reign on the earth (vs. 17). However, it is our purpose here to focus on the coming just reward for the saved and unsaved. John refers to "the time of the dead, that they should be judged, and that thou shouldest give reward unto thy servants…small and great…" (vs. 18). The written Word of God repeatedly reminds us that there will be a just eternal reward for all mankind. Daniel promised, "them that sleep in the dust of the earth shall awake, some to everlasting life, and some to shame and everlasting contempt" (Daniel 12:2). The Lord Jesus warned that the hour was coming when those in the grave will hear His voice, "And shall come forth; they that have done good, unto the resurrection of life; and they that have done evil, unto the resurrection of damnation" (John 5:29). There will be a payday someday. In our text, John is picturing this future event, focusing largely on reward for those, like the two witnesses, who will remain faithful throughout the Tribulation. The King of kings Himself will award them with eternal life and entrance into the Millennial Kingdom (Matthew 25:31-46). The reminder of these things is intended to inspire Tribulation saints to remain steadfast in the Lord.

Similarly, believers in the Dispensation of Grace are to be strengthened in faithfulness by remaining focused on "things above" (Colossians 3:1-2), and remembering "your labour is not in vain in the Lord" (I Corinthians 15:58). Remain steadfastly faithful to the Lord, believer. There will be a payday someday, and a just reward.

TERROR*LESS* REVELATION
Revelation 12:10-12

On February 15, 2015, a video was released showing 21 Christian men in orange jumpsuits paraded to a beach in Libya by armed and masked terrorists in black garb. A Muslim man explained these Christians, who would not renounce Christ, were being executed to retaliate for the death of Osama Bin Laden. Then they were gruesomely beheaded. But the video also reveals that while some of these men were being executed, they were speaking the name of Jesus.[1]

Present-day murders of Christians by Muslims is the very spirit of the Anti-Christ's terrorism that will take place during the seven years of Tribulation. Revelation 20:4 refers to future martyrs saying, "...and I saw the souls of them that were beheaded for the witness of Jesus, and for the Word of God." Revelation 12:11 tells us these martyrs will die at the hands of cruel terrorists, but in a remarkably terrorLESS state of mind: "they overcame him [Satan]." It is important for all who know the Lord Jesus Christ as Savior to embrace the three ways these martyrs will find victory in the face of death. First, they will remain victorious **"by the blood of the Lamb."** In order to truly be a Christian, one must trust in the shed blood of the Lord Jesus Christ as the payment for one's sins, apart from all religious or moral works. It is trusting in His blood that gives us a righteous standing with God and eternal life. Martyrs overcome Satan in the sense that they refuse to abandon this trust. Second, they overcome Satan **"by the word of their testimony,"** which is an unfaltering trust and reliance in the written Word of God. It gives strength, comfort, and confidence, no matter what a believer faces. Third, they overcome Satan because **"they loved not their lives unto the death."** This means they chose to believe eternal life is more important than continued days of earthly life, and that their responsibility was to live or die to the glory of the Lord Jesus Christ who died for them. Nothing else really matters.

While we believers today will never experience the specific tribulation persecution sent from Satan's Anti-Christ, II Timothy 3:12 tells us "...all who live godly in Christ Jesus shall suffer persecution." Whether suffering for our faith is great or small, we can triumphantly remain terrorLESS by living the same three principles tribulation martyrs will possess. *Why wait?* Begin living all three now!

ANTI-SEMITISM
Revelation 12

During the 2016 Olympics in Rio de Janeiro, Islam el-Shehaby, a competitor in judo, refused to shake the hand of his Israeli opponent. He was under pressure by Islamics, Egyptians, and family, to drop out of the match so he would not be viewed as "a traitor and a normalizer in the eyes of your people."[1] Similarly, Syrian boxer Ala Ghasoun refused to fight an Israeli athlete because "that would mean that I, as an athlete, and Syria, as a state, recognize the state of Israel."[2]

Anti-Semitism is a hostility, prejudice, or discrimination against Jews. It can be practiced by individuals, groups, or governments. In all forms, anti-Semitism has its origins in Satan. Revelation 12:3 refers to "a great red dragon," clearly identified in verse 9 as "Satan," who led one-third of the angelic host in rebellion (vs. 4). Satan has always had a special hatred for the Jews and has historically been the power behind anti-Sematic efforts to persecute and kill all of Israel. He used Haman to convince the king to issue an edict to slay all Jews (Esther 8-10). At one point, the royal line, through whom the Redeemer King was to come, was reduced to one singular boy (II Kings 11:1-3). Satan also used Herod to attempt to slay the Savior shortly after His birth (Matthew 2). From the middle to the end of the Tribulation, the red dragon, dripping with the blood of believing Jews, will turn an unprecedented wave of anti-Semitism to a new height. His intensified efforts will be his response after he will be cast down from his domain in the atmospheric heavens. He will know "that he hath but a short time" (Revelation 12:12). With "great wrath" he will persecute all Jews (vs. 12). Some of the redeemed in Israel will be supernaturally hidden in "the wilderness" for 3½ years (vss. 6,14). For those believing Jews who remain, Satan's forces will go forth with a vengeance to "make war" against them and put them to death (vs. 17). As a liar and accuser of the saints, Satan will deceive the world into thinking the true people of God are deluded and dangerous. This will bring waves of betrayals, tortures, and deaths (Matthew 24:9-10).

We today should be extremely thankful we experience little meaningful persecution for our faith, that we will be raptured before God's judgments fall on the world, and prior to Satan's wrath upon believers. We should also not fall into Satan's trap of racism of any kind.

THE WORST DICTATOR EVER
Revelation 13:1-10

Mao Zedong was the communist revolutionary of the People's Republic of China who ruled the country from 1949-1976. To secure his power, he instituted a series of reforms including execution quotas. When land was seized from owners, at least one landlord was selected in each village to be beaten to death. Many deemed as threats were sent to labor camps where they perished. Governmental and industrial officials were publicly shot. Some estimate nearly 40 million souls were killed or committed suicide during Mao's reign.[1] Only by relating how many died under his cruel reign of terror can we comprehend how evil Mao Zedong's dictatorship was.

Revelation 13 gives a word picture of the evil reign of the coming Anti-Christ, describing him as far worse than any ruthless dictator before him. Verse 2 describes him as "the beast" because of his cruel actions. He will have the cunning and speed of "a leopard," the savage power of a "bear," and the ferocity of a "lion" when it roars. His mouth will constantly be filled with "blasphemy" (vss. 1,5,6). "Blasphemy" means "vilification, evil speaking, or railings." These fierce words will be targeted "against God" (taking His name in vain and likely denying His existence), against "His tabernacle" (because Jews will seek to worship Jehovah there), and against "them that dwell in heaven" (vs. 6). We take this latter reference to mean he will vilify true believers in the Lord Jesus Christ, even those who have been martyred, convincing the world they are deluded, dangerous, and that they needed to die. He will have an irrational anti-Semitic rage that will infect all who follow him (Revelation 12). He will also be deceitful, convincing, and will have unusual oratory charisma. While the Anti-Christ will be given satanic power "over all kindreds, and tongues, and nations" (Revelation 13:7), the Anti-Christ will be "wounded to death" (vs. 3) but rise from the dead, therein solidifying his power and wonder over the majority of the world (vss. 3-5,14). In vile egocentricity, he will demand to be worshipped (vs. 8).

Would you volunteer to experience these events described in the Tribulation? Would you want any of your loved ones to experience the rampages of this vicious dictator, the Anti-Christ? The only way to be certain to escape this vicious dictator is to trust in the Lord Jesus Christ who now offers eternal life as a free gift of His grace. If you haven't already, trust in Christ now, and urge loved ones to trust Him while they still can.

PROPAGANDA MINISTER
Revelation 13:11-18

In October of 1962, the White House was caught in a direct lie telling the public that the Pentagon knew of no offensive weapons in Cuba. The truth was that Department of Defense officials were debating whether or not to invade the island to remove the weapons they knew to exist. Assistant Secretary of Defense, Arthur Sylvester, defended the falsehood of their statements saying, "It's inherent in [the] government's right, if necessary, to lie to save itself."[1] More recently, all of our presidents have had a White House Press Secretary to spin current events. Some consider them only Ministers of Propaganda.

The Anti-Christ will likewise have a minister of propaganda. He is referred to as "another beast" (Revelation 13:11), because he too will be ferocious. He is called the "false prophet" (16:13; 19:20; 20:10) because he will be a religious leader who powerfully endorses the Anti-Christ. There are several important things to remember about this human instrument of Satan. First, he will have a worldwide spiritual influence. We believe his seat of authority has already been established. Second, John described his oratorical ability as one who "spake as a dragon" (vs. 11), which indicates being bold, authoritative, and effective in his speeches. Second, the purpose and subject of his speeches will be to cause "...the earth and them that dwell therein to worship the first beast [or Anti-Christ] (vs. 12). Third, he will exercise "...all the power of the first beast" (vs. 12). Specifically, this means he will do "great wonders, so that he [literally] maketh fire come down from heaven on the earth in the sight of men" (vs. 13). Satan is the prince and power of the air, and this description seems to indicate the false prophet can call down lightening at will. Fourth, the motive in these miracles will be to deceive "...them that dwell on the earth by the means of those miracles" (vs. 14), so that they willingly worship the Anti-Christ. Fifth, this evil religious leader will ruthlessly cause "as many as would not worship the image of the beast should [to] be killed" (vs. 15). He will do so by outright executions, but also through denial of commerce to any who will not literally wear the mark, or number, of the Anti-Christ (vss. 16-18).

True men of God who proclaimed real truth, including the Lord Jesus, were never popular, nor were their followers highly loyal. These descriptions of Satan's false prophet remind us we must evaluate any spiritual leader, especially those with large followings, by the authority of Scripture.

FAITHFUL BELIEVERS
Revelation 14:1-5

Thank God for the faithful prophets of Israel: Isaiah, Jeremiah, Hosea, and others. Thank God for the Apostle Paul, who, in the face of constant persecution, beatings, imprisonment, and weariness, continued to faithfully minister for his Savior until death. Thank God for Martin Luther who, in the 1400's, braved threats and intimidation to boldly proclaim justification by faith. Thank God for John Bunyan who, in the 1600's, was imprisoned in England for twelve years for refusing to stop faithfully preaching for Christ. During this time he triumphantly wrote the classic "Pilgrims Progress." Thank God for Paul Sadler, who worked tirelessly as a writer, preacher, counselor, and encourager as President of the *Berean Bible Society* for almost thirty years. In every era, God has had servants who remained faithful to Him regardless of difficult circumstances.

The spiritually and circumstantially dark days of the Tribulation, as described in Revelation 13, are contrasted by the encouraging description of Revelation 14. The 144,000 male Jews who are "the firstfruits" of salvation during the Time of Jacob's Trouble (vs. 4), are seen standing with Christ on earthly "mount Sion" in the future Millennial Kingdom. They will be singing "a new song" (vs. 3) which only they know. No one fully understands the trials of another, nor do we fully comprehend the difficulties these Jews will face. "No man could learn that song," but they undoubtedly sing with joy and thanksgiving for the enablement of God. "In their mouth was no guile" (vs. 5). "Guile" means "deceit" or "craftiness." In contrast to the lies and deceits of the Anti-Christ and the false prophet, these servants of God will straightforwardly tell God's truth to a lost world. They will be undeterred by threats, angry responses, being in the righteous minority, fears, or fatigue. They will, as their Savior before them, faithfully "reprove the world of sin, and of righteousness, and judgment" (John 16:8). They will effectively choose to stand between sinners and eternal damnation, offering God's eternal life. These redeemed saints are described as "they which follow the Lamb whithersoever He goeth" (Revelation 14:4). These saints will be rewarded for their faithfulness with the special honor of forever being close by the side of their risen Savior.

Don't falter! May we who live in this present Dispensation of Grace purpose to likewise be faithful to our Savior until ushered into His presence. May we be found in that eternal number who are found faithful.

REST OR TORMENT?
Revelation 14:6-13

"Rest in peace" has become a common expression used when someone passes away. It was said of those who died in the 911 attack, after the Sandy Hook shootings, when celebrities die due to drugs or suicide, and countless times regarding less public figures. It has become ingrained in our culture to think of those who die as resting in peace. This concept is furthered suggested by coffins that look like a plush bed. *But do all who die rest in peace?*

The future scene the Apostle John witnesses in Revelation 14 spans the entire seven years of the Tribulation. Verse 6 refers to an angel proclaiming "the everlasting gospel" to all nations of the world. This is not our present Gospel of Grace. It is the revived Gospel of the Kingdom, which offers eternal life to those who trust in the Lord Jesus as the promised Messiah of Israel and Savior of the world. Verse 7 warns of coming judgment and to worship only the Lord Jesus who created the world. Verse 8 announces Babylon (which pictures the vile, worldly worship of Anti-Christ) as "fallen." This won't occur until the end of the Tribulation. With every soul in every land previously warned to only worship Christ, another angel announces that those who reject the Savior and worship the beast, including taking his mark, will be "tormented with fire and brimstone…for ever and ever: and they have no rest day or night…(vss. 10-11). Clearly, the lost who refuse eternal salvation through faith in Christ will not "rest in peace." To the contrary, they will have no rest in unending "torment." But we must remember, it will be their choice to not heed divine warnings and offers of eternal life. Contrast this with the promise given to the martyred saints who are told, "Blessed are the dead which die in the Lord…that they may rest from their labours, and their works do follow them" (vs. 13). These tribulation saints will be given "rest" from earthly persecution and torture. They will be able to wait in tranquility until they are resurrected into their promised Millennial Kingdom, where proportionate reward awaits them.

While these descriptions apply specifically to those in the Tribulation, there are parallel principles for those in every dispensation. All who reject Christ will suffer unending "torment" in the Lake of Fire. It will be their choice. Only those who trust in Christ are "blessed" with eternal life and rest. Ask someone today if they want to "rest in peace?"

THE VICTORS
Revelation 15

At the 2016 Olympics in Rio de Janeiro, the USA's women's gymnastics team won the all around gold medal. If you watched these games, you can close your eyes and still almost see Simone Biles and Aly Raisman doing summersaults and back flips. None of us should think that what these young women accomplished was easy. They sacrificed dates, going to prom, and endured many injuries. But they kept their focus on their goal of winning the gold medal. To reach this goal, they became examples of hard work, drive, dedication, and commitment. As a result, they can now joyously wear their gold medal as the victors in their sport.

Revelation 15 is a scene of victors in the spiritual arena from the seven years of Tribulation. They are described as, "them that had gotten victory over the beast [the Anti-Christ], and over his image, and over his mark" (vs. 2). The means of their victory was described in Revelation 12:11. Their power will come through the blood of the Lamb, the Word of God, and a perspective that faithfulness to Christ was more important than their earthly life. Their victory is not one apparent to those who will persecute them for their faith in Christ, for many will be martyred, but they are triumphant nonetheless. These victors sing two songs. One is "the song of Moses" (Revelation 15:3), which was a song of victory sung by Israel. As recorded in Deuteronomy 31:22-30, it looked back to their deliverance from Egypt and forward to "latter days" of the Millennial Kingdom with exultation for the salvation and power of Jehovah. Revelation 15:4 confirms these victorious tribulation saints are likewise singing of God's holiness and coming kingdom. The second song is "the song of the Lamb" (Revelation 15:3), where the Lord Jesus Christ is praised for His greatness, truth, reign as their King, and His wonderful salvation is also implied.

This information is included in the record of Revelation to be an encouragement for any who go through the Tribulation. It confirms that anyone can be victorious, regardless of his circumstance. In principle, the same is true for us today. While it won't be easy and will require commitment and endurance through our trying circumstances, we too can be victorious. Keep your focus on the "prize of the high calling in Christ Jesus." Maintain a dedicated commitment to Christ and His Word with other saints. Remember to also frequently sing praises to God for His salvation and coming victory over the world.

WHAT GOES AROUND
Revelation 16:1-13

After a lad was rescued from drowning in a muddy bog, a Scottish nobleman arrived to thank and reward the farmer for saving his son. When a reward was declined, the nobleman asked permission to take the farmer's boy and give him the finest education available. The farmer granted his request. His son went on to graduate medical school and later to become known as Sir Walter Fleming, the discoverer of Penicillin. Years later the nobleman's son was stricken with pneumonia, but Penicillin saved him. The name of the nobleman's son was Winston Churchill.[1] Many believe, "What goes around, comes around." By that they mean, "A person's actions, whether good or bad, will have consequences for that person."[2]

Revelation 16 describes seven vials of God's wrath that will be poured out in the last half of the Tribulation. These are clearly to be seen as just consequences for sins that the lost commit during these seven years of God's judgment. The first vile judgment will produce a "grievous sore" upon those who take the mark of the beast (vs. 2). This represents their spiritual disease of false worship that is putrid to the Lord. The second vile causes the sea to become "as the blood of a dead man" (vs. 3). Their purposeful waywardness will be a stench in the nostrils of God. Therefore, they will smell this stench in the sea. The third vile makes all the rivers and fountains of fresh water to become "blood" (vs. 3). The angel's unmistakable explanation is that this happens because they have "shed the blood of saints and prophets" (vs. 6). The fourth vile produces a scorching "great heat" from the sun that will burn mankind, food supplies, and homes. The response of those suffering this judgment will not be humble repentance, nor turning to God in faith. Instead, they "blasphemed the name of God" (vs. 9), which indicates this unprecedented heat from the sun is the consequence of the hot words of defiance and blasphemy against the only Savior, the Lord Jesus Christ. The fifth vial produces darkness and intense pain, indicating the pain inflicted on the heart of God by their worship in spiritual darkness. The sixth vial dries up the Euphrates, to prepare for more judgment to come.

God's Word teaches the principle that people reap what they sow, either in this life, or in eternity (please compare: Galatians 6:7; II Corinthians 5:10; Revelation 20:11-12). *What kind of seed are you planting for a future harvest?* Trust in Christ alone for eternal life.

AN EVIL COALITION
Revelation 16:13-16

On August 2, 1990, under the direction of Saddam Hussein, Iraqi forces invaded Kuwait to seize their oil fields and seaport. International condemnation followed along with concerns Saudi Arabia would be next. Led by the United States, the largest coalition of international troops since WWII was assembled to restore order to the region. On January 17, 1991, "Operation Desert Shield" began this coalition's successful campaign to drive Iraqi forces out of Kuwait. While the conflict lasted only 100 hours after coalition forces began their ground assault, Iraqi forces still fought by launching missiles into Israel and Saudi Arabia.[1]

While good coalitions have often been formed to repel evil aggressions, there have also been evil coalitions. The worst coalition in the history of mankind will be initiated by the dragon (Satan), the beast (or Anti-Christ), and the false prophet (the propaganda minister and enforcer for the Anti-Christ). The Apostle John sees this future event begin with "unclean spirits like frogs" come out of the mouths of this unholy trinity (Revelation 16:13). These demonic spirits will be like frogs in the sense that they will be cold-blooded, arrogantly puffed up like a frog filling his mouth with air, and loudly croaking their authority. Empowered by Satan, these will "go forth unto the kings of the earth and of the whole world, to gather them to the battle of that great day of God Almighty" (vs. 14). Their efforts to form an evil coalition will be energized by swelling speeches and fortified by "working miracles" (vs. 14). Both will convince lost leaders and lost masses, to gather as one imposing military force for the purpose of destroying Jerusalem and all Jews. While these evil forces will participate willingly, God is ultimately drawing them to this final battle to vanquish the rebellion of mankind and establish the worldwide rule of the Lord Jesus Christ as the King of kings (see Zephaniah 3:8; Zechariah 12:1-11). While this great battle of Armageddon literally looms on the horizon, the divine judge of man announces, "I come as a thief" in the sense the lost will be so deluded they will not expect our Savior's return (vs. 15). However, they should expect Christ's return because the two evangelistic witnesses from God will be predicting it, and God will send devastating earthquakes to humble their stubborn hearts (vss. 17-21).

We must not be surprised or discouraged by the rising tide of resistance to the cause of Christ. These will increase until Christ's Second Coming. God is still in charge. Just remain faithful!

THE GREAT WHORE
Revelation 17

Prostitution has become a worldwide plague of epic proportions. The average age is 14 when young women are drawn to this "trade." Many are lured into the U.S. and Canada on work visas, then forced into this criminal enterprise through violence and induced drug addition. In an article by LifeSiteNews, former "madam" Tania Fiolleau admits that pimps usually rule over their prostitutes with lies, intimidations, threats, and violence.[1] Drunk with power and money, madams are willing to do most anything to fortify their positions.

Revelation 17 gives us a very descriptive picture of the Anti-Christ's false prophet, who is also referred to as "the great whore" (vs. 1). She bears this name because of two things. First, this great whore is also a worldwide religious power. As such, she should conduct herself with the integrity of leading others to a higher moral standard by pointing everyone to Christ. Instead, this despicable individual, and religious organization, will sell themselves to the services of the Anti-Christ. Second, once entrenched in power by Satan, this whore will do anything, including lies, deception, miracles, and wide-scale murders of Christians to stay in power. This religious figure will array itself in "purple and scarlet colour, and [be] decked with gold and precious stones…having a golden cup in her hand" (vs. 4). Some conclude this will be the rising influence of Islam, while others think the Roman Catholic Church meets this description. Which ever it might be, all mankind should alertly look for a religious power with these characteristics. The description from the Apostle John continues, saying, "I saw the woman drunken with the blood of the saints, and with the blood of the martyrs of Jesus" (vs. 6). While there has been a long history of such atrocities in the past, this scene specifically pictures the bloodshed of true believers during the coming Tribulation. During these seven years, "the kings of the earth" (vs. 2) will align themselves with this false prophet because of her deceit, and her intimidation of threats and violence. However, eventually, the rulers of the world will come to "hate the whore, and shall make her desolate… and burn her with fire" (vs. 16).

While remembering the great whore is in the context of the Tribulation, we should remember it is an evil thing for us to sell ourselves on the bed of doctrinal compromise, lust for power, or popularity. May we purpose to remain true in these areas, and stand with a church that stands for God's truth for today.

A GREAT CITY FALLS

Revelation 18

In 79 A.D., Mt. Vesuvius had a catastrophic eruption that literally entombed much of the ancient city of Pompeii, Italy. Previously, this city had been a vacation town for the Roman elite. Archeologists have uncovered pornographic artwork, graffiti, and living arrangements unlike anything one would see in a modern city. In the years and days prior to this devastating volcanic eruption, there were a series of earthquakes. Ultimately, the residents of the city died as superheated ash rained a fiery death upon all who remained.[1]

In Revelation 18 an angel with bright illumination comes to announce, "Babylon the great is fallen" (vs. 1-2). While some believe this refers to the city of Bagdad, and others, Jerusalem, this writer believes it to be the city of Rome that will be destroyed during the Tribulation. We know with certainty that it refers to a "city" (vss. 10, 16, 18, 21). It represents the spiritual fornication associated with the false prophet, and it must be his headquarters since this city falls immediately following her death (Revelation 17:18). This city is known for great "merchandise," or commerce, in "gold, and silver, and precious stones…and pearls" (vs. 12). John saw it as being "clothed in fine linen, and purple, and scarlet, and decked with gold" (vs. 16). This description certainly sounds like the priests, and pope, of Rome. It will be a place of talented "musicians" with harps, wind instruments, and trumpets. It will have many "craftsmen" who are skilled (see vs. 22). The "candle" will also be identified with this city. All of this sounds like worship at the Vatican in Rome. At its height, under the false prophet, with all the expensive adornments, people will ask, "What city is like unto this great city" (vs. 18)? But like Pompeii, it will be destroyed "in one hour" (vs. 19) as God's wrath falls upon it with "death, and mourning, and famine; and she shall be utterly destroyed with fire" (vs. 8), and "with violence shall that great city Babylon be thrown down" (vs. 21). This sounds like a fierce earthquake, and will be the direct result of the judgment of God.

We live in a day when people are enamored with ornate churches, huge crowds, religious rituals, and entertaining music. What is preached from the pulpit seems secondary, or unimportant. However, what impresses God is an emphasis on the Word of God, with preaching that grounds the believer in sound doctrine, and transforms the life into greater godliness. Decide today that this will be what enamors you!

AN EXTRAVAGANT WEDDING
Revelation 19:1-9

According to *The Knot* 2015 Real Weddings Study, the average cost of a wedding in America (excluding the honeymoon) is $32,641. The median price of the world's most expensive weddings is millions, and in one recent example, a full billion. Many seek to perpetuate the idea of "a dream wedding" with limousines, designer dresses, elaborate floral displays, extensive meals, exotic destinations, fireworks, and much more. However, all these examples will pale in comparison to the coming "marriage of the Lamb" (Revelation 19:7).

In this chapter, John was looking forward in time to the end of the Millennial Kingdom, a thousand years after the end of the Tribulation. This will be a remarriage of saved Jews, or Israel, back to Jehovah. It has absolutely nothing to do with believers in the Body of Christ. In the Old Testament, Israel was seen as the spiritually adulterous wife of Jehovah (Jeremiah 3:6-8; Hosea 2:2), whom He consequentially divorced (Isaiah 50:1). In eternity, the Lord will remarry Israel after taking her through the trials of the Tribulation and the final rebellion at the end of the Millennium. Their faithfulness in Tribulation persecutions is described as, "His wife hath made herself ready" (vs. 7). Her adornment is described as, "she should be arrayed in fine linen, clean and white: for the fine linen is the righteousness of [the] saints" (vs. 8). An angel will announce, "Praise our God, all ye His servants" (vs. 5), and the voice of "a great multitude...(sings) saying Alleluia: for the Lord omnipotent reigneth" (vs. 6). While in our culture, a wedding is "the brides day" to receive the primary attention, at this wedding, those singing will "give honour to Him" [the Lord Jesus] (vs. 7). However, we should note that, technically, the bride is not even Israel. An angel identifies "the bride, the Lamb's wife" as "the holy Jerusalem descending out of heaven from God" (Revelation 21:10). This will be a magnificent sight and wondrous occasion. This city represents the redeemed of Israel, rejoined in a holy relationship with the Lord Jesus Christ in a future eternal state.

While this "marriage of the Lamb" specifically belongs to Israel, there is a parallel for us in the Body of Christ. In a purely spiritual sense, we too "should be...married to another, even to Him who is raised from the dead" (Romans 7:4). The Savior would have us know that His purpose for us now is to make ready for this eternal state. *How?* "We should bring forth [spiritual] fruit unto God" (Romans 7:4).

MEETING HIS WATERLOO
Revelation 19:10-21

In 1815, a coalition formed from the United Kingdom, Russia, Austria, and Prussia to resist the advancing armies of Napoleon Bonaparte of France. Critically outnumbered, Napoleon knew his only chance of staying in power was to attack near Waterloo, Belgium, before the coalition forces were fully mobilized. Under the command of Wellington, the strength of coalition forces were concealed behind a 2.5 mile ridge. When Napoleon advanced with his troops, he was outflanked on three fronts and soundly defeated. Losing the Battle of Waterloo resulted in Napoleon abdicating power over France.[1] He had "met his Waterloo."

During the middle of the seven years of Tribulation, Satan will be cast out of his heavenly atmospheric domain, as described in Revelation 12:9. At this point, "he knoweth that he hath but a short time" before his ultimate demise (vs. 12). As if in desperation, he will turn a frenzied campaign of slaughter upon all Jews. As the Tribulation draws to a close, he will assemble troops from the entire world to attack Jerusalem. In an instant, the heavens will open to reveal the Lord Jesus Christ coming in power and great glory (compare Revelation 19:11 and Matthew 24:30). No longer offering mercy and eternal life as the Savior of the world, Christ now comes as the conquering "King of kings, AND LORD OF LORDS" (Revelation 19:16). "Out of His mouth goeth a sharp sword, that with it He should smite the nations: and He shall rule them with a rod of iron" (vs. 15). We take this to mean that the opposing world armies of millions will literally be cut down on the battlefield by His spoken word, and their blood will flow deep (Revelation 14:20). Then the beast (or Anti-Christ), and the false prophet will be taken and, "these both were [or will be] cast alive into the lake of fire burning with brimstone" (Revelation 19:20). Their arrogant voices will be forever silenced on earth, and their reign of terror will be over forever. They will meet their Waterloo of defeat. Then, the angel of God will call the fowls of the air to come feast off the dead bodies of the slain (vss. 17-18). What remains will take seven years to bury once the Millennial Kingdom begins (Ezekiel 39:8-15).

We must begin conversations with lost souls by asking if they know about the Battle of Armageddon that is looming on earth's near horizon. After giving the above details, present the gospel and urge them to flee to the safety of eternal life.

REPEAT OFFENDER
Revelation 20:1-10

The Bureau of Justice statistic reports that 77 percent of federal inmates are rearrested within five years after being released on parole.[1] That means incarceration doesn't "rehabilitate" an alarming number. They are simply habitual repeat offenders. Terry Joe Windham is an example who, while out on parole, decided to commit murder to see what it felt like. He chose a 16-year-old victim, Jeremy Flachbart, who was physically and mentally disabled. Windham ambushed Jeremy from behind with a two-foot long 4x4 fence post, killing him with a total of 16 massive blows.[2] As heinous as this was, there is a far worse violent repeat offender.

At the conclusion of the seven years of Tribulation, an angel will be given power to lay "...hold on the dragon...Satan," bind him with a chain for "a thousand years," and "cast him into the bottomless pit" (Revelation 20:1-3). For the duration of our Savior's Millennial reign "with a rod of iron" (19:15), Satan will be unable to tempt, deceive, or influence those on earth. All who enter the Millennial Kingdom will be saved individuals who either survived the Tribulation or will be resurrected from the dead from all human history, except the current Dispensation of Grace. It will begin as a genuine utopia on earth. However, those who survive the Tribulation will be able to procreate, and those born during this time will not have eternal life unless genuinely trusting in Christ. "And when the thousand years are expired, Satan shall be loosed out of his prison, and shall go out to deceive the nations" for "a little season" (vss. 7-8,3). Clearly, Satan's incarceration will not rehabilitate him. God previously governed man under goodness, law, grace, and, finally under glory in Christ's kingdom.[3] The King of kings will permit one final failure of man to prove man's nature is corrupt, no matter what his circumstances. Satan will persuade an innumerable company of lost souls to join in one final assault on Jerusalem. However, God will intervene with fire coming down from heaven. This fire will devour the human armies, and Satan will be permanently cast into the Lake of Fire to never trouble the world again (vss. 9-10).

Lost souls can put on a veneer of holiness, but only those who trust in Christ can be rehabilitated into genuine righteousness. However, this only comes through a yielded will and time in God's Word. Choose to be rehabilitated, or transformed, with both today.

THE HANGING JUDGE
Revelation 20:11-15

Isaac Charles Parker was an American jurist who became known as "the Hanging Judge" of the American old west due to the large number of men he sentenced to death by hanging. In one instance, 8 men were hanged at the same time. Wrongdoers feared appearing before Judge Parker. Some called it "the Court of the Damned."[1] His court had final jurisdiction over the Indian Territory from 1875-1889. Initially, there was no court for appeals.

Revelation 20:11-15 describes the most frightening and somber scene in all Scripture. Before God closes the pages of time for all His creation to enter an eternal state, one event must take place. After the Tribulation, after the Millennial reign of Christ on the earth, and after the final rebellion of man, all the lost will be assembled before the Lord Jesus Christ at the Great White Throne of Judgment. No one who has eternal life will be present. Those who trusted in Christ Jesus for eternal life in our present Dispensation of Grace will already be raptured, judged for accountability and reward, and will be dwelling in the heavens. The righteous Jews, from before and after the Dispensation of Grace, will be resurrected into the Millennial Kingdom. But the lost will be kept in the heart of the earth, in fiery punishment, awaiting sentencing in "the day of judgment and perdition of ungodly men" (II Peter 3:7). Our text describes the wicked dead being judged out of two books. One will be "the book of life," where the names of all who have eternal life through faith are recorded (Revelation 20:12). When the names of the lost are not found here, it verifies their just coming judgment. The second book will be one that records every single sin of each individual. "And the dead were [will be] judged out of those things which were written in the books, according to their works." This means that there will be proportionate punishment, but all there will suffer eternal torment. No one who refused Christ on earth will escape (vs. 13).

There will be no raucous rebellious parties in the Lake of Fire, no second chances, no rest day or night forever, and no court of appeals. There will only be regret for refusing eternal life through Jesus Christ, and eternal "torment" (Revelation 14:11), with the vilest of fallen angels and fallen mankind. Armed with this information, urge a lost soul to accept forgiveness while it is now available.

IS IT REALLY THAT BAD?
Revelation 20:11-15

Scores of websites try to rationalize the use of Methamphetamine, but the consequences are severe and undeniable. One of the most striking effects is in physical appearance. It causes destruction of tissue, loss of elasticity, rotting and broken teeth, acne, all of which causes the user to appear decades older. It eventually robs the user of cognitive abilities, libido, and often causes psychotic behavior.[1] It is also highly addictive. One user who lost his family and ended up homeless admitted, "I tried it once, and BOOM! I was addicted."[2]

Lost souls often try to rationalize their rejection of Christ by trying to minimize the severity of eternal punishment. So-called jokes, jeers about partying with friends, or even denying the existence of Hell are attempts to sooth inner fears about what they innately know awaits them. Some even ask, "Is it really that bad?" The answer is, "Yes." It is hundreds of times beyond our ability to fully comprehend. However, the Scriptures give us ample insight to be highly motivated to avoid this dreadful place. The final residence of all who reject eternal life through faith in the Lord Jesus Christ is called "the Lake of Fire" (Revelation 20:15). It is a place where one is bound "hand and foot" (Matthew 22:13) and kept in the fearfulness of literal "outer darkness" (Matthew 8:12; II Peter 2:4). "Soul and body" (Matthew 10:28) will experience unending pain where "their worm dieth not" (Mark 9:44). Great sorrow is evident through weeping and "wailing, and gnashing of teeth" (Matthew 13:42). Regret for having refused eternal life, and possibly for hindering others from trusting in Christ, is implied in the account of the rich man and Lazarus (Luke 16). Perhaps worst of all, the duration of punishment here is for all eternity. "The fire is not quenched" (Mark 9:44), and there is "no rest day nor night" because "the smoke of their torment ascendeth up for ever, and ever" (Revelation 14:11).

We have taken the time to document some of the horrors of the coming Lake of Fire for three reasons. We want all to grasp the Lord's point that it really is that bad. We want to urge any who have yet to trust in Christ alone for eternal life, to do so immediately. We all essentially choose eternal life or eternal punishment. Choose life. We also want to remind forgiven ones how truly blessed they are because Christ has saved us from this dreadful place.

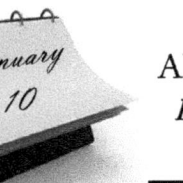

ALL THINGS NEW
Revelation 21

There is something very special and exciting about things that are new. When you get a car from the factory, it has that new car smell and everything is pristinely clean. When new carpet is installed, it has that new look, smell, and feel. Those who have been fortunate enough to buy a new home from a developer have experienced everything around them looking freshly new and (theoretically) working perfectly. Imagine being ushered into an eternity where everything is new and far exceeds any experience we can compare it to now.

As Revelation 21 opens, the Apostle John sees four new things: "a new heaven and a new earth...(a) new Jerusalem," and a new kind of life for the redeemed (21:1-4). There is no mystery as to the timing of this future scene. It will become a reality immediately after the Millennial Kingdom and the final rebellion of Satan and man. The events John witnessed will usher in a new eternal state. The first new thing in sequence will be a new heaven and a new earth. We must not mistakenly conclude earth will be destroyed and a new earth created. The covenants of Israel guarantee Israel will possess this present earth in perpetuity. Second Peter 3:5-12 explains that God will effectively renovate the earth with fire, destroying every remnant of man's sin, therein preparing a sinless earth and heavens for the redeemed to inhabit. John also saw a "new Jerusalem, coming down from God out of heaven" (Revelation 21:2). This will be a literal, walled city, described in detail as being greatly adorned and strictly Jewish in character and population (vss. 10-27). We must remember, the eternal home for believers today will be in the heavens. What John saw was what the redeemed of Israel were always promised, and righteous Jews desired and "looked for" (Hebrews 11:10). Revelation 21:4 also reveals a new condition for saints in the eternal state: "And God shall wipe away all tears...and there shall be no more death...sorrow...nor crying...neither...any more pain: for the former things are passed away." This will be so fantastic that it's hard to fully wrap our heads around such a blessed condition. But we believe it. We also believe that there will surely be a parallel condition for the Body of Christ in the heavens too.

When contemplating this magnificent future, it should make us want to sing the hymn: "How marvelous, how wonderful, and my song shall ever be." Rejoice believer. The best is yet to come.

I COME QUICKLY
Revelation 22

During the English Civil War in the 1650's, King Charles I was captured, imprisoned, and put to death. His son, Charles II, narrowly escaped his own capture and execution by disguising himself and fleeing to the European continent. While in Europe, Charles wandered from country to country. In 1660, Parliament restored the monarchy, and Charles returned to a jubilant reception by his countrymen.[1]

Long ago the King of Israel, the Lord Jesus Christ, was arrested, imprisoned, and put to death, essentially by His own countrymen. After His resurrection, His apostles had hoped He would establish His earthly reign immediately but were told at His ascension He would return in glory (Acts 1:6, 9-11). Three times in Revelation 22, the Savior assured the Apostle John that He will return to claim His reign on earth very soon. Christ tells him, "Behold, I come quickly, blessed is he that keepeth the sayings of the prophecy of this book" (vs. 7). John was to emphasize to his fellow Jews who were anticipating going through the Tribulation that faithfulness will be expected, no matter the circumstances. Their enablement will be rooted in God's Word. Next, the Savior says, "Behold, I come quickly; and My reward is with Me to give to every man according as his work shall be" (vs. 12). Those who face fierce hardships and brave persecution to preach the gospel in a very hostile world are to be encouraged with an assurance of reward proportionate to their faithfulness. By the time John records this revelation, there had been a delay in the Savior's return by nearly two decades. II Peter 3:3-9 explains to "scoffers," who were ridiculing an expectation that Christ would return, that "the Lord is not slack concerning His promise." His delay was to be seen as God's mercy in allowing additional time for lost souls to come to saving faith in Christ. The revelation to John closes with another comforting consolation, "Surely I come quickly" (Revelation 22:20). Believers were to continue to live in the confidence of His soon return, allowing this expectation to motivate them to greater faithfulness.

We now know the delay in Christ's return as the King of Israel is because a new Dispensation of Grace interrupted the fulfillment of prophecy. We also know we are to likewise live in anticipation of Christ's return to rapture us into the heavens, believe He will come soon, and expect proportionate reward for faithfulness. He will surely return soon. *Are you making yourself ready?*

WORSHIP CHRIST **ONLY**
Revelation 22:8-9

It has become commonplace for fans to scream and cry uncontrollably when meeting a celebrity or an accomplished athlete. It was true when the Beatles were at the height of their career. It has since only become more widespread and extreme. In 1992, late night talk show host Arsenio Hall introduced singing legend Diana Ross as a guest. When she entered for her segment of the show, Mr. Hall folded his hands and repeatedly bowed lowly, saying, "I am not worthy." While this may have been done in levity, it epitomizes a dangerous practice.

It seems to be inherent in humans to worship something or someone who they view to be greater than themselves. This isn't something new either. Twice in the book of Revelation, when the Apostle John encounters an angel of God, he seeks to give this heavenly messenger worship. After being instructed about the future "marriage supper of the Lamb," John says, "I fell at his feet to worship him. And he said unto me, See thou do it not: I am thy fellowservant, and...have the testimony of Jesus: **worship God**" (Revelation 19:10). The word "worship" means "to bow down, prostrate one's self, show adoration, or reverence." The quick response of the angel was to forbid such a practice and remind John that God is the only one who should be worshipped. John needed a second reminder after seeing the New Jerusalem. He admits, "And when I had heard and seen, I fell down to worship before the feet of the angel which shewed me these things. Then saith he unto me, See thou do it not: for I am thy fellowservant" (Revelation 22:8-9). In both instances, John should have known better. In Exodus 20:3-6, Israel was forbidden to worship any other gods (created objects, ascribed deity, or imagined concepts of deity), to make any images of them, or to "bow down thyself to them." Similarly, the Apostle Paul warned against "a voluntary... worshipping of angels, intruding into those things which he hath not seen, vainly puffed up by his fleshly mind" (Colossians 2:18). Such practices are gravely serious in the sight of God. They are wickedly sinful, detract from the glory of God, and often lead one to become entrenched in beliefs that ultimately lead to eternal punishment.

We do well to remember, and to remind others, that God the Father, Son, and Holy Spirit only are to be worshipped. Doing otherwise stirs the anger of God. "Worship God," and Him only.

FALSIFYING DOCUMENTS
Revelation 22:18-19

On December 2, 2002, Enron declared bankruptcy, plunging thousands of employees and investors into financial ruin. Enron was founded as a Houston pipeline company, but morphed into a brokerage that traded energy commodities. To hide an unhealthy debt ratio, the company created a complex scheme of inflating their net worth in relation to their debt. In so doing, they became this country's most glaring example of corporate crime and the falsification of corporate data. Perhaps most chilling, executives reaped millions in profits from Enron stocks while prohibiting employees from cashing in on their stocks while this investment still had value.[1]

As the book of Revelation given to John closes, a solemn warning is given about changing this sacred document in any way. The warning specifically says, "I testify unto every man that heareth the words of...this Book, If any man shall add unto these things, God shall add unto him the plagues...written in this Book: And if any man shall take away from the words of the Book...God shall take away his part out of the book of life" (Revelation 22:18-19). We realize believers today have absolute eternal security. This warning applied specifically to the book of Revelation, and the consequences solely to those of the Acts, or Tribulation era. Nonetheless, the gravity of changing God's Word is abundantly clear. Moreover, it is extremely noteworthy that God repeated this warning to Israel to not change His Word. In Deuteronomy 4:1-2, nearly the exact words were used to admonish Israel to obey God's statutes and never "add unto the Word... [or] diminish ought from it."

On the basis of these repeated warnings, Christians should consider every word in Scripture as highly sacred. It is a gravely serious matter to tamper with any of God's inspired Word. Therefore, it should be disturbing to us when modern translations change thousands of words and disparagingly suggest in their notes that Mark 16:9-20 should not be included in our Bible. It should be unacceptable to us when inaccurate translations falsify the document of Scripture. This writer believes the best and closest to a word for word translation of Scripture is the Old King James Version, based on the Majority Text. It is reportedly written on a fifth grade vocabulary level. Particularly with a dictionary or concordance in hand, nearly anyone can still easily understand it. May we all choose to revere God's Word as highly as He does and not embrace changing words in Scripture.

SUSTAINED BY GOD
Revelation 22:22-23

A man in his early 50's had worked for decades in New York City. His girlfriend had been killed on the streets, and he had been severely mugged several times. These events brought on a nervous breakdown. With little financial means he returned to Florida, where his brother and sister-in-law took him in. For nearly thirty years, he lived in an apartment they provided, used their laundry facility, and was even given a new car. In a very real sense, they sustained his needs when he was incapable of doing so on his own.

The two closing chapters of Revelation give us a further peek into an eternal state of existence for redeemed Jews. As we read these specifics, bear in mind that, in principle, there is likely some parallel for members of the Body of Christ who will occupy the heavens. In describing the New Jerusalem in eternity future, John described it as the dwelling place of "the Lord God Almighty and the Lamb" (Revelation 21:22). The obvious implication is that Jewish inhabitants will forever live in the presence of God. Verse 23 says that city will have "no need of the sun, neither of the moon, to shine in it, for the glory of the God did lighten it." It does not say there would be no sun or moon; only they are not needed for light because the glory of God will provide illumination. "A pure river of [the] water of life" (Revelation 22:1) will proceed "out of the throne of God and of the Lamb." There is no reason not to take this literally and to see it as sustaining life in eternity. John also saw "the tree of life, which bare twelve manner of fruit" (Revelation 22:2). We last read of the tree of life in the Garden of Eden. Adam and Eve were banned from eating from it so they would not have life without end before first having the righteousness of faith. Apparently, this tree will perpetually sustain life without end and pleasurable nourishment as well. The redeemed are also seen as reigning with Christ "for ever and ever" (vs. 5), which implies meaningful and fulfilling activity unto the glory of God.

These saints will literally be sustained by the power and provision of God. Until that eternal state, they were to constantly rely on God for their physical and spiritual wellbeing. May we today likewise rely on God for both.

HAVING COMPASSION
Romans 12:15

During my father's last days, many friends and family came to the hospital to comfort and encourage us. Wilber, a rugged man who had been a friend for decades came one afternoon. Realizing the end was near, he simply sat quietly beside my father's bed and held his hand in a long, loving embrace. After a short while, Wilber began to quietly shake as he silently wept over the thought of losing his friend. Among the many memorable things surrounding this time, this wordless love and compassion demonstrated by his friend ministered more to me than any of the kind efforts of many.

In Romans 12:15, we have important instruction that is often passed over or forgotten. It says: "Rejoice with them that do rejoice, and weep with them that weep." A demonstration of this is found in the shortest verse in the Bible. It simply says: "Jesus wept" (John 11:35). The context was when Lazarus had died. The hearts of his two sisters were broken over the prospect of losing the companionship of their beloved brother. They were weeping when the Lord Jesus came to comfort them. He reminded them that Lazarus would "rise again" (vs. 23) to everlasting life. While they believed this, their hearts still greatly grieved. The Lord did not rebuke them for their grief, nor did He continue to share biblical truth. Instead He did something amazing. He simply wept with them. This was not uncontrolled emotionalism, despair, confusion, nor helplessness. It was the outflowing of compassion. Mary, Martha, and Lazarus had been especially close to the Lord Jesus Christ. It was Mary who had wiped the feet of the Lord Jesus with her hair. It was Martha who had diligently attended to His need for food as the Savior taught in their home. All three had enjoyed multiple times of listening intently to our Lord's words, whole-heartedly trusted in Him, and opened their home for fellowship. During these times there had surely been joy and even laughter. But when Lazarus died, it was a natural time of sorrow. The Lord understood this and allowed His heart to grieve with them. What a powerful example for us to remember.

The experiences of life often leave us somewhat calloused to the needs and hurts of others. As a servant of Christ, we must learn to laugh with those who laugh, and demonstrate appropriate compassion by being able to "weep with them who weep." Doing so genuinely can be an effective means of ministry.

JUDGED ACCORDING TO OUR WORKS

I Corinthians 3:10-15

There is an ancient story about an owner of a vast empire with many servants. When he determined to go on a journey, the owner summoned several of his servants and entrusted much of his wealth to them. When the owner returned, he required his servants to report what kind of returns they gained. Several gained much and were duly praised and rewarded. But one had done nothing but secure the initial capital entrusted to him. The owner rebuked this servant for his sloth, seized his capital, and punished his servant. This illustration, based on the parable of the talents (Matthew 25:14-30), loosely parallels some aspects of the coming Bema Seat.

Unfortunately, some think of the Judgment Seat of Christ as little more than an awards ceremony with no mention of one's sins. Their premise is that only our "work" will be judged (I Corinthians 3:13-15), which they define as only inferior efforts, or workmanship, for Christ. But God defines "works" as any action, either good or bad. More often than not, God uses the word "work" as an obvious equivalent to sin. The "evil" Alexander the coppersmith did toward Paul was called "works" for which the Lord will reward him in eternity (II Timothy 4:14). The "works of the flesh" in Galatians 5:11 can only be categorized as sins, and not merely an inferior effort. Paul also told believers at Rome to "…cast off the works of darkness…" (Romans 13:12). While each of us may only want reward for faithful service for Christ and hope that our sinful choices after salvation will be absent, it simply will not work that way at the Bema Seat. Paul tells us that all our "good or bad" will be manifest and judged at the "Judgment Seat of Christ" (II Corinthians 5:10). We will each "give account of himself to God" (Romans 14:12), and the gravity of this reality is intended to motivate us to greater responsibility now on this side of eternity (II Corinthians 5:11). To be perfectly clear, this biblical description is NOT about punishment for sinful conduct after salvation. It is about responsibility and accountability for one's actions when standing before the Savior.

God provides this sober picture of the Bema Seat to convince us to not take a flippant attitude toward sinful actions after salvation. Instead, with carefulness and a grateful heart, we are to build a life of "good works" (Ephesians 2:10) that glorify the Savior. *How can you do so today?*

A SPECTACLE TO THE WORLD
I Corinthians 4:9-14

*W*ould *you want to be the President of the United States?* Those who assume this office do so knowing they will become a spectacle to the world. Every word and every decision will be scrutinized. Even their family members will be targets for criticism. The schedule is taxing, and the responsibilities so grave, that stress causes each president to age prematurely. Presidents Clinton, Bush, and Obama are examples. Yet despite the toll of the office, many seek this position out of love for our country and willingness to serve.

Those who purposely serve the Lord also do so knowing they too will become a spectacle to the world. It has always been this way. God instructed the prophet Hosea to "...go take unto thee a wife of whoredoms and children of whoredoms: for the land [the nation of Israel] hath committed great whoredom, departing from the Lord" (Hosea 1:2). Everyone would know the heartache and scandal in the life of this servant of God. The Lord instructed Isaiah to disrobe, "And he did so, walking naked and barefoot... three years for a sign and wonder upon Egypt and upon Ethiopia" (Isaiah 20:2-3). As embarrassing as it was, no one who saw this prophet of God could miss his message from the Lord. Similarly, the Apostle Paul described his life by saying, "For I think that God hath set forth us the apostles last...for we are made a spectacle unto the world, and to angels, and to men" (I Corinthians 4:9). The apostles were willing to look like "fools," be "weak" (vs. 10), to "hunger" (vs. 11), to be "reviled" (vs. 12) and "defamed" (vs. 13), for the cause of Christ. We should not think that putting themselves in these positions was any easier than it would be for us. But these men of God willingly embraced their scrutiny, criticism, humiliation, and stress out of love for the Lord Jesus Christ, and a firm commitment to further His cause.

How about you? Are you willing to become a spectacle for Christ? The Apostle Paul told the believers at Corinth that they were an "...epistle written in our hearts, known and read of all men" (II Corinthians 3:2). God has called every Christian to share the Gospel of Grace with lost souls and warn them about eternal punishment. Then we are to live a consistent godly life, knowing those we seek to reach will be watching us. We must not shrink from being a spectacle for Christ. We must willingly embrace it.

REJOICING IN THE RIGHT THINGS
II Corinthians 1:12-14

The 2016 College Football National Championship was won in dramatic fashion by the Clemson Tigers. As time ran out on the clock, jubilant pandemonium broke out among Clemson coaches, players, and fans. When interviewed by television crews immediately after the game, Clemson coach, Dabo Swinney, said he simply had no words to describe his joy over the win.

The books of Psalms and Philippians emphasize that the believer should remain in a constant state of rejoicing. Our joy should be rooted in things far more lasting and important than any athletic championship. The Apostle Paul's letters reveal what Christians should be focusing on as their source of joy. Paul told the saints at Corinth, "For our rejoicing is this, the testimony of our conscience, that in simplicity and godly sincerity…we have had our conversation in the world…" (II Corinthians 1:12). A clean conscience about living a godly life before others brought him joy. Paul also told them, "…we are your rejoicing, even as ye also are ours in the day of the Lord Jesus" (II Corinthians 1:14). At this time, the Corinthians found joy in their relationship with Paul who had ministered God's Word to them. These believers, who Paul led to the Lord, were a great source of joy because they represented great eternal reward. Paul said he chose to "…rejoice in hope of the glory of God" (Romans 5:2). His assurance of one day beholding the glory of God, and also being glorified with Christ, as is further explained in Romans 8:17 and Colossians 3:4, brought him great rejoicing. Paul had learned to "rejoice with them that do rejoice…" (Romans 12:15). When other saints rejoiced over victories or blessings in their lives, he allowed it to likewise bring him satisfying joy. Paul wrote that his response was that: "…if I be offered upon the sacrifice and service of your faith, I joy, and rejoice with you all" (Philippians 2:17). It was no drudgery for him to sacrificially serve the needs of other believers; it was a deep-seated pleasure. Perhaps most importantly, Paul learned to "…rejoice in Christ Jesus…" (Philippians 3:3). This implies he found joy in the Savior's holiness, humility in coming as the Son of Man, loving sacrifice for our sins, continuous longsuffering grace, and much more.

Likewise, may we choose to rejoice in these eternally-important things and place them in higher esteem than the fleeting things that captivate the hearts of many.

IMPUTING SIN
II Corinthians 5:19

The *"United States v. Wilson*, <u>32 U.S. 150</u> (1833), was a case in...which...George Wilson, was convicted of robbing the <u>US Mail</u>...and sentenced to death."[1] Due to his friends' influence, Wilson was pardoned by Andrew Jackson. Wilson, however, refused the pardon. The Supreme Court was thus asked to rule on the case.[2] The decision was that if the prisoner does not accept the pardon, it is not in effect: "A pardon... may then be rejected by the person to whom it is tendered; and if it is rejected, we have discovered no power in this court to force it upon him." Therefore, Wilson was hanged.

When the Scripture says that, "...God was in Christ, reconciling the world unto Himself, not imputing their trespasses unto them..." (II Corinthians 5:19), He is informing us of two things. He is telling us that Christ's wonderful payment for sin, or provision for eternal salvation, has been made and is now offered to all mankind. God is not saying that all the sins of all mankind, including the lost, are already forgiven. Long after the Cross, the Apostle Paul describes the natural state of all mankind as "dead in trespasses and sins" (Ephesians 2:1), "under sin" (Romans 3:9; Galatians 3:22), and "dead in your sins" (Colossians 2:13). He goes on to say the natural man is "inexcusable" (Romans 2:1), and warns unbelievers that "the wages of sin is death; but the gift of God is eternal life through Jesus Christ our Lord" (Romans 6:23). Before God will pardon one's sins, the sinner must see himself as "guilty before God" (Romans 3:19) and believe that he can only be "justified freely...through the redemption that is in Christ Jesus" (Romans 3:24). *How is a sinner redeemed from the eternal consequence of his sin?* It was not applied, or imputed, to all at the Cross, even though the payment for sin was made by the Savior at Calvary. The imputing of each individual's sins to the Savior is only "...upon all them that believe" (Romans 3:22), or trust, in Christ alone as the payment for their sins. Christ died corporately "for the sins of the whole world" (I John 2:2), but His payment is only applied individually to them "that believeth [or trust] in Jesus" (Romans 3:26). But, like George Wilson, if the pardon offered by Christ is rejected, it is a pardon not received.

Make your presentation of the gospel clear. Show lost souls that God offers them forgiveness of their sins if they will trust in Christ.

FICKLE AFFECTIONS
Galatians 4:8-16

One of our relatives had a cat that ran away when you tried to pet her. But before long she would crawl on your lap, purr, and give every indication she now wanted you to pet her. Yet, if you reached out to pet her, the cat would hiss at you and often bite quite hard. It was a confusing and frustrating mix of fickle affection and hostile reactions.

The saints at Galatia acted no better. When the Apostle Paul came and "preached the gospel" (Galatians 4:13) to these believers, he did so "through infirmity of the flesh." We assume Paul came to minister to them after enduring either the stripes, stoning, or beatings he described in II Corinthians 11:23-25, which he often suffered while being persecuted for preaching Christ. Though he came to them in weakness, he said they did not despise or reject him. He said, they "received me as an angel of God, even as Christ Jesus" (Galatians 4:14). In other words, their response was overwhelmingly receptive. In fact, they were so appreciative of his ministry to them, "if it had been possible, ye would have plucked out your own eyes, and have given them to me" (vs. 15). But their affections changed. When false teachers came into their midst seeking to place them under the bondage of the Mosaic Law, they embraced this false teaching. Paul sought to reason with them. He explained that the Law was a burdensome curse if one did not keep "all things...written in...the law..." (Galatians 3:10). He further explained that God only intended the Law to serve as a "schoolmaster to bring us unto Christ [in saving faith]" (Galatians 3:24). But when Paul explained this good news that Christ had liberated all saints in the Dispensation of Grace from the Law of Moses, he had to ask them, "Am I...become your enemy, because I tell you the truth?" (Galatians 4:16). Those who had once loved him with such sweet affection had now turned on him in hostility. The believers in Corinth were no better. Even though Paul had led them to faith in Christ, they later questioned his apostleship and became fickle in their affection toward him. With sorrow he told them, "...the more abundantly I love you, the less I be loved" (II Corinthians 12:15).

Have you also become fickle in your affection and appreciation for someone who shared the gospel or right division with you? Choose to let God change that pattern beginning now.

HEALING BITTERNESS
Ephesians 4:31-32

In the book *The Telling Room* author Michael Peteniti shares the true story of a very old woman who walked from her home to the cemetery and back every day. Rain or shine, she walked up the hillside every day to spit on her archenemy's grave.[1]

Christians can be just as eaten up with bitterness, but we must not be. Ephesians 4:31 urges believers to "Let all bitterness, and wrath, and anger...be put away from you, with all malice." When bitterness has grown in our souls, we need to allow the Lord to produce the acronym of H-E-A-L-I-N-G within us. **H**ealing begins by **H**anding over the offender to the Lord. Romans 12:17 tells us, "Recompense to no man evil for evil." It may not be what our flesh wants to hear, but only the Lord has the right to take action against the wrong doer. H**e**aling continues when **E**motions are given to God. Philippians 4:6-7 promises that when you let your "...requests be made known unto God...the peace of God, shall keep your hearts and minds through Christ Jesus." Regardless of our circumstances, when we pray, God can heal our hurting emotions. He**a**ling comes by **A**ccepting the consequence of our hurt. Romans 8:28 promises, "And we know that all things work together for good to them that love God...." Our omnipotent God is able to take the worst of circumstances and bring good to our lives as an end result. So, trust Him. Hea**l**ing comes by **L**ooking for God's **L**esson in our trial. Paul tells us while in his worst persecution, he learned,"...that we should not trust in ourselves, but in God..." (II Corinthians 1:9). When trials come, look for a spiritual life lesson. Heal**i**ng can be achieved by **I**nvesting in the wrongdoer. Admittedly, this is a hard one. Romans 12:21 tells us to "be not overcome of evil, but overcome evil with good." It helps you refocus and helps soften the wrongdoer. Heali**n**g is improved when we **N**ote our responsibility to forgive the offender. Colossians 3:12-13 urges believers to "put on...mercies, kindness...longsuffering...even as Christ forgave you, so also do ye." Healin**g** is complete when we choose to **G**o on with life without remaining paralyzed. Reliving hurtful events, or refusing to move forward with life, only deepens the wound in our spirit. Therefore, Colossians 3:15 counsels us to "let the peace of God rule in your hearts, to which also ye are called...."

Let the Great Physician heal your heart by applying these principles.

STAND FAST
Philippians 1:27

At Gettysburg, on July 1, 1863, the 16th Regiment of Maine held off repeated assaults by the Confederates. General Robinson ordered the 16th of Maine to remain behind to allow the rest of the division to escape. Colonel Tilden of the 16th protested because he knew his men would be slaughtered. But General Robinson persisted ordering the men of the 16th to "hold at all costs." Colonel Tilden told his men, "You all know what that means."[1] By the next morning, the regiment of over two hundred men had suffered an eighty-three percent casualty rate. But they followed their orders to stand fast.

To "stand fast" means to "hold something unyieldingly, or to refuse to budge." It is noteworthy how many times the Apostle Paul instructed the saints to "stand fast" and in what ways they were to do so. The Philippians were told to "stand fast in one spirit...striving together for the faith of the gospel; and in nothing terrified by your adversaries..." (Philippians 1:27-28). Strong opposition arose nearly everywhere Paul went to preach the good news of eternal life through faith in Christ. It was true for his converts too. These believers needed to band together and stand uncompromisingly for the clarity of the gospel without being intimidated by persecution. These same believers were urged to "stand fast in the Lord" (4:1). Internal strife within the church had produced self-conceited attitudes that had damaged their unity (2:2-4; 4:3). They were to keep their eyes on the Lord and strive to reestablish harmony by embracing the kind of humility the Savior demonstrated by dying for our sins. The believers at Thessalonica had suffered severe persecution for their faith (I Thessalonians 2:14-15), and Paul feared their "afflictions" (3:3) might cause their walk with Christ to wane. He told them, "For now we live, if ye stand fast in the Lord" (3:8). He would be encouraged and they would persevere if they remained unmovable in a close relationship with the Savior. Paul wrote these same saints saying, "...brethren, stand fast, and hold the traditions which ye have been taught, whether by word, or our epistle" (II Thessalonians 2:15). As it is today, a danger persisted for these believers that they might drift from the exclusive doctrines of grace given from the Lord and through the Apostle Paul. But they must not. They must stand fast!

In our daily battle against Satan, these are still our commands from our Supreme Leader, the Lord Jesus Christ. Stand fast at all costs.

A SINGULAR FOCUS
Philippians 3:13-14

A Russian proverb says, "If you chase two rabbits you will not catch either one."[1] There has been a growing business trend moving away from multitasking and toward becoming singularly focused. Many say that multitasking keeps one so distracted that it takes up to 100% longer to finish tasks, and it prevents you from becoming really good at anything. Bill Gates and Steve Jobs are used as examples of success because they developed a laser-type focus on one thing: Gates on software, and Jobs on design. They chose to become like a dog chasing only one rabbit. Consequently they achieved great success.

In the realm of spiritual things, it is likewise essential to be singularly focused. This was true of one of the most successful soldiers for Christ, the Apostle Paul. He was able to present the gospel to multitudes, to see perhaps thousands trust in Christ, to plant many churches around the Mediterranean, to write thirteen books of the Bible, to mentor a band of men to carry on in ministry, and to remain both faithful and productive until death. His testimony was "Brethren, I count not myself to have apprehended: but **this one thing** I do, forgetting those things which are behind, and reaching forth unto those things which are before, I press toward the mark for the prize of the high calling of God in Christ Jesus" (Philippians 3:13-14). Notice, after Paul trusted in Christ, he did not languish over the loss of friends and family, his promising future among the Pharisees, nor financial security and safety. He was able to say, "But what things were gain to me, those I counted loss for Christ...and I count all things loss...for the excellency of the knowledge of Christ...and do count them but dung, that I may win Christ" (3:7-8). Instead of focusing on these things that could have dragged him into self-pity and depression, he chose to concentrate on something different. He kept his eye on "the mark" (which describes a focal point on a target) "for the prize" (referring to a reward), "of the high calling of God" (vs. 14). Paul's laser-type focus was on living so faithfully for Christ that he was confident that meaningful eternal reward awaited him (I Thessalonians 2:19 and II Timothy 4:7-8).

What are your goals in life? The most important goal every Christian must choose is the singular focus of living so faithfully for the Lord that eternal rewards await. Nothing else really matters. Choose wisely.

PRAYER FOR EVERYTHING
Philippians 4:6-7

A Christian man who's wife was hospitalized with a life-threatening ailment posted on Facebook that he could not pray for these physical needs because the Pauline pattern was to only pray about spiritual things. Moreover, he did not believe God intervenes for physical needs today. Similarly, a Christian friend related to us that when his favorite Bible teacher was diagnosed with cancer, he said, "I knew I shouldn't pray for his physical well-being, but I did anyway. I just couldn't help myself."

In the minds of many there is confusion about what is acceptable before the Lord to be included in our prayers. Fortunately, God's Word gives us an abundant testimony. Philippians 4:6 encourages us to "Be careful for nothing; but in every thing by prayer and supplication with thanksgiving let your requests be made known unto God." Here we are instructed to pray for everything, including physical needs. When Epaphroditus was "sick nigh unto death" (Philippians 2:27), God certainly intervened because Paul stated, "but God had mercy on him," and raised him up in health so he could resume ministry (vs. 28). The Word of God indicates it is proper to pray for circumstantial things and that the Lord also frequently answers these requests. Paul said he prayed that "I might have a prosperous journey" to Rome (Romans 1:10). He also requested that others would pray for him "that I might be delivered from them that do not believe" (Romans 15:31), "that God would open unto us a door of utterance to speak the mystery" (Colossians 4:3), and "that we may be delivered from unreasonable and wicked men" (II Thessalonians 3:2). The Apostle Paul further clearly confirmed that God had answered the prayers of the saints for physical or circumstantial needs. When he described his persecution as being so severe that "we despaired even of life" (II Corinthians 1:8), he assured the saints "Ye also [were] helping together by prayer for us" (vs. 11). Second Timothy 3:10-11 is even clearer, saying, "But thou hast fully know my...persecutions...I endured; but out of them all the Lord delivered me." These patterns in prayer continued in Paul's teaching through the end of his life. When he referred to himself as "Paul the aged" (Philemon 9) he told the saints "...for I trust that through your prayers I shall be given unto you" (vs. 22).

Hold fast to the practice of praying about everything. Don't rob yourself of the divine comfort and intervention the Lord would give you. Pray about everything!

BEGUILED OF REWARDS
Colossians 2:18

On May 24, 2016, the Stock Exchange Commission filed a complaint revealing that a number of professional athletes had been scammed out of great sums of money by Ash Narayan. Reportedly, San Francisco Giants pitcher Jake Peavy lost $15.1 million, and Denver Broncos quarterback Mark Sanchez lost $7.8 million. Narayan secretly siphoned funds "using forged or unauthorized signatures." He then invested those funds in a failing online ticket company in which he had a stake. "Peavy, [and] Sanchez…said "…they trusted Narayan because he was a Christian and represented several other pro athletes…"[1]

There has been a persistent need in every age for true children of God to be very wary of the influence others have upon them. The Apostle Paul warned the saints at Colossae, "Let no man beguile you of your [eternal] reward in a voluntary humility and worshipping of angels, intruding into those things which he hath not seen, vainly puffed up by his fleshly mind" (Colossians 2:18). This chapter actually reveals several ways in which false religious teachers were robbing believers of future eternal rewards. Verse 18 specifies it was through the worship of angels. The Scriptures are very clear that angels are created beings and never to be worshipped under any circumstance. When the Apostle John sought to worship an angelic messenger from God, he was immediately stopped twice (Revelation 19:10; 22:9). The saints at Colossae were also being convinced to observe Jewish dietary restrictions and holy days, which have nothing to do with our present Dispensation of Grace (Colossians 2:16). These same false teachers, who appeared to be Christian, sought to impose the keeping of all the Mosaic Law, therein making Paul's converts "subject to ordinances" (2:20). But Paul warned these members of the Body of Christ that following these doctrines intended only for Israel would beguile, or rob, them of future eternal reward. At the Judgment Seat of Christ, the Savior will reward all who have trusted in Him alone for their faithful service to His name and obedience to His Word. But reward will be lost by many who have foolishly chosen to follow things the Scriptures teach us are inappropriate for believers today. This warning implies an urgent need for us to be knowledgeable about accurate doctrinal practices and obedient to what Scripture tells us pleases God.

Are you following religious, or even sinful, practices that will one day rob you of eternal reward? Don't let this happen. Chose wisely now. You will be glad you did in eternity.

EMBRACING THE TRUTH
I Thessalonians 1:13

We have a friend who began a Bible study in her community. A woman we'll call "JoAnn," heard a clear gospel for the first time and was wondrously saved. She was overjoyed and continued to grow through these studies. One day JoAnn asked twice if it was wrong to pray to Mary. Several grounded believers shared with her Scriptures that demonstrated Mary was only human and needed a "Savior" (Luke 1:47), that the Lord Jesus taught the principle that prayer was only to be directed to God the Father (Matthew 6:9), and that the Lord describes Himself as a jealous God (Exodus 34:14) who will not share His glory with another (Isaiah 42:8; 48:11). But JoAnn ignored these truths and clung to her practice of praying to Mary saying, "It makes me feel so good."

How do you respond to truth from the Scripture that may conflict with established practices in your life? The marvelous testimony of the believers at Thessalonica was, "...when ye received the Word of God which ye heard of us, ye received it not as the word of men, but as it is in truth, the Word of God, which effectually worketh also in you that believe" (I Thessalonians 2:13). You might say these sincere believers were on a journey searching for God's truth and were ready to obey whatever instructions the Lord gave them. It produced great changes in their lives too. They had previously worshipped false gods but had "...turned to God from idols to serve the living and true God" (I Thessalonians 1:9). They had come to embrace the concept that the Scriptures were "the Word of truth" (Psalm 119:43; II Corinthians 6:7; Ephesians 1:13; II Timothy 2:15). That meant any practices that conflicted with God's Word were error and to be immediately abandoned. These believers at Thessalonica were searching for the truth, the whole truth, and nothing but the truth from God's Word. Other Christians had joined them on this journey. The believers at Berea were called "noble" because "...they received the Word with all readiness of mind, and searched the Scriptures daily, [to see] whether those things [they were learning] were so" (Acts 17:11). The obvious implication is that they were not just searching for information in the Scriptures to inflate their egos with mere knowledge. They were searching for truth from God to transform their lives.

How will you respond to Scriptural truth that conflicts with something in your life? Let it be with immediate obedience.

DISCIPLING NEW CONVERTS
I Thessalonians 2:1-11

It was this author's privilege to be saved through the ministry of a vibrant and growing church. This church had what they called a "Timothy Program." Whenever someone was led to Christ, a seasoned Christian was assigned to the new believer. They attempted to meet weekly with the new convert over a meal to establish a relationship, and then to guide this new Christian through an organized Bible Study program that covered all the fundamentals of the faith. These new believers were invited to sit with other believers in church services, attend mid-week Bible studies, and invited into the homes of mature believers. Not surprisingly, the results were phenomenal.

Quite often when Christians lead a lost soul to a saving knowledge of Christ, we simply cease ministering to them. But we must not forget to genuinely attempt to continue ministering to them in an effective way that will ground them in truth, establish them in the faith, and encourage them to grow in Christ. The ministry of the Apostle Paul with those at Thessalonica is a shining example of effective follow-up and discipleship. Paul told them he had been "gentle among you" (I Thessalonians 2:7). Just as one would be gentle with a newborn, we must be gentle with babes in Christ. It doesn't work to try to force spiritual food down their throat or be demanding with requirements. Instead, Paul slayed his converts with love. He could tell those at Thessalonica he was "affectionately desirous of you" (vs. 8). Most people can tell when you genuinely love them, and they will usually respond well. Paul also was willingly sacrificial, or giving, to his converts. He told them "we were willing to have imparted unto you...also our own souls, because ye were dear unto us" (vs. 8). Caring enough to buy a meal or a Bible can have a great impact. Paul also provided a good example in his work ethic (vs. 9) and in godliness. He could tell them to remember his "laboring night and day...and...how holily and justly and unblameably we behaved ourselves among you that believe" (vss. 9-10). People will be turned off by a phony Christian, but everyone appreciates and respects a genuine Christ-like example that they can emulate. Finally, Paul encouraged his converts with exhortation, comfort, firm instruction, and pleas to truly walk worthy of the Savior who died for them (vss. 11-12).

Seize the opportunity to mentor a new believer whenever possible. Do so by practicing the principles for follow-up seen in Paul.

GROWING WEARY
II Thessalonians 3:13

Chesley Christian wrote on Facebook about a Christian friend who we will call Dan. Dan is considered a solid Christian who has been abstinent for years and is ready for a wife. However, he has become impatient in waiting for God to send him "the one." When an attractive co-worker approached Dan requesting a short fling, he consented. Dan knew it was wrong and that the relationship wouldn't last long, but he said he was "tired of doing the right thing" and he had "needs." Deeply saddened, Chesley wrote, "Too many times I have encountered Christian singles who are sexually tempted, because they were tired of doing the right thing for so long."[1]

It is a reality that many Christians become tired of doing the right thing. Even after years of physical purity, Bible reading, maintaining sound doctrine, church attendance, and actively serving the Savior, Christ's blood bought-believers are prone to waver. Too many simply stop doing the right thing. The same was true in the days of the Apostle Paul. He pled with the saints "But ye, brethren, be not weary in well doing" (II Thessalonians 3:13). Elsewhere he explained how and why Christians must remain faithful. In Galatians 6:9, Paul's encouragement was, "And let us not be weary in well doing; for in due season we shall reap, if we faint not" (Galatians 6:9). While we Christians often reap satisfying spiritual blessing from doing right in this life, we will receive bountiful eternal reward if we keep our eyes fixed on the prize of the high calling in Christ. As someone once said, "We must not sacrifice the permanent on the altar of the immediate." Paul also pointed out the motivation of opportunity and responsibility in ministry. He told the Corinthians, "Therefore, seeing we have this ministry... we faint not" (II Corinthians 4:1). We must remain faithful because others are counting on our faithfulness. Additionally, sometimes when we falter we never return to a proper walk, nor do opportunities to effectively serve Christ as before. Paul also reminded the saints of their source of strength by saying, "...though our outward man perish, yet the inward man is renewed day by day" (II Corinthians 4:16). God does not expect us to continue to do the right thing in our own strength. He provides the spiritual strength needed when we stay in His Word daily.

Have you grown weary in well doing? The stakes are too high to shrink from the ranks of the faithful. Keep doing the right thing.

CLOTHING BEFITTING GODLINESS
I Timothy 2:8-9

Courtney was a young mother who wore an extremely short miniskirt to church and unquestionably exposed entirely too much of herself. A deacon's wife called her to confront her about wearing immodest clothing in a place of worship. To her credit, Courtney took the conversation well. She appreciated being spoken to directly rather than being complained about to others, and she realized her clothing was an immature uncaring act to brothers in Christ. From that day forward she threw immodest clothing away and diligently tried to dress modestly.[1]

From the beginning of human history, both nature and God have taught that clothing sufficient to cover the body should be worn. As soon as Adam and Eve committed sin, they sewed fig leaves together to cover their nakedness (Genesis 3:7), which God replaced with animal skins (vs. 21). Ever since, it seems like Satan has been trying to unclothe us. When any stage of immodesty takes place, it is a sign of ungodliness. When Israel worshipped a molten calf, "Moses saw that the people were naked...naked unto their shame" (Exodus 32:25). We must realize that sinful actions often follow immodesty. When David saw Bathsheba "washing herself" (II Samuel 11:2), adultery, deceit, and murder soon followed. Similarly, when the stepdaughter of King Herod seductively danced before him, he succumbed to her request to murder John the Baptist (Matthew 14:1-10). It is indisputable that women have great seductive power over men, and, especially for Christian women, with that power comes a great responsibility. Therefore, the Apostle Paul gave instruction that "...women adorn themselves in modest apparel" (I Timothy 2:9). It has become commonplace for women and girls to wear plunging necklines, transparent fabrics, extremely short tight shorts or dresses, and even far worse. The world finds this acceptable, but it certainly is not for Christian women. Paul tells us the standard should be "modest apparel" (vs. 9) and only that "...which becometh women professing godliness" (vs. 10). That means that if a woman is exposed when bending or sitting, if her clothing would entice impure thoughts, or if she would cover up if suddenly in the presence of the Savior, then her clothing is unacceptably immodest. This by no means absolves men from thinking and acting in pure moral ways, but women must be careful not to dress in a way "...whereby thy brother stumbleth, or is offended, or is made weak" (Romans 14:21).

Ladies, choose today to become a real model, one of exemplary modesty! Your Savior will be therein glorified.

FIGHTING WORDS
II Timothy 2:14

Americans cherish the right we have to freedom of speech. *But did you know there are limits to this freedom?* When the police arrested a street preacher, he called them "racketeers" and "facists." S ubsequently, in 1942, the Supreme Court handed down the Chaplinsky Decision upholding the arrest. The court said that certain categories of speech fall outside the limits of constitutional protection: These include "the lewd, the profane, the libelous, and the insulting or 'fighting' words...which by their very utterance inflict injury or tend to incite an immediate breach of the peace."[1]

The Apostle Paul sought to spare believers from experiences where their peace would be stolen through needless bickering and debates. Therefore, he told Timothy, "Of these things put them in remembrance, charging them before the Lord that they strive not about words to no profit, but to the subverting of the hearers" (II Timothy 2:14). This in no way implies that Christians are not to speak out when very important truths are attacked. Paul told Timothy it was "a faithful saying" that Christ came "to save sinners" (I Timothy 1:15), then he went on to specify that God "...will have all men to be saved..." (I Timothy 2:4). When false teachers were compromising the clarity of the Gospel of Grace, Paul emphatically told the saints not to listen to them but "let him be accursed" (Galatians 1:8). When Jews sought to place Gentile converts under the Mosaic Law, Paul said, "...to whom we gave... subjection, no, not for an hour; that the truth of the gospel might continue with you" (Galatians 2:5). When Peter withdrew from Gentile converts, therein implying they could not be saved, Paul "withstood him to the face, because he was to be blamed" (Galatians 2:11). However, Paul specified that there are discussions Christians should avoid. He tells Timothy to "shun profane and vain [empty] babblings: for they will increase unto more ungodliness" (II Timothy 2:16). When more heat than light is being shed on a subject, it will only lead to sinful words and attitudes. In fact, "their word will eat as doth a canker...[and can] overthrow the faith of some" (II Timothy 2:17-18). This is particularly true when fundamental doctrines of our faith are questioned, such as the proven resurrection of the dead. Such truths as these are the very "foundation of God" (II Timothy 2:19) for our faith.

Some are just looking for an argument, and others seek to destroy the faith of Christians. When this is apparent, just walk away.

GOD IS TRUE
Titus 1:2

The world is increasingly becoming more belligerent toward Christianity and blasphemous toward God Himself. One example is found in an article by Dr. Michael Cohen. He wrote, "Are you aware that the greatest truth in your life that you can trust is not God, images, love, honesty, nature, or spirit? Your most trustable truth is what you experience in this moment, or at any moment."[1] Nonsensical statements such as this remind us of a statement made in the movie *A Few Good Men* by Colonel Nathan R. Jessep. While being asked for a truthful account while under oath, he blurted out, "You can't handle the truth."

Spiritual rebellion in man often makes him unable to handle real truth. The greatest truth that you can trust is not your perceived experiences or emotions. Our greatest truth that we can trust in is God and His Word! Paul assures Titus that we can confidently rest "In hope of eternal life [based on faith in the Lord Jesus Christ] which God, that cannot lie, promised before the world began" (Titus 1:2). Our apostle of grace was basically reiterating a concept the Holy Spirit repeated over and over throughout God's Word. In the Song of Moses, Moses wrote of Jehovah saying, "He is the Rock [of power and truth], His work is perfect...a God of truth and without iniquity, just and right is He" (Deuteronomy 32:4). King David wrote, "And now, O Lord God, Thou art that God, and Thy words be true..." (II Samuel 7:28). David continued in the Psalms saying that He "which made heaven, and earth, the sea, and all that therein is [He] which keepeth truth forever" (Psalm 146:6). Almost as if addressing the detractors of our faith today, Paul wrote, "For what if some did not believe? Shall their unbelief make the faith [faithfulness] of God without effect? God forbid: yea, let God be true [in your conclusions], but every man a liar" (Romans 3:3-4). We should maintain our confidence in everything God tells us in His written Word because "...it was impossible for God [in His holiness] to lie, [therefore] we might have a strong consolation, who have fled for refuge to lay hold upon the hope [of eternal life] set before us" (Hebrews 6:18).

The unchangeable truth about our unchangeable God is that He cannot lie. That makes absolutely everything recorded in Scripture absolute truth. Rest and rejoice in this today.

ENDNOTES

JANUARY 2

1. *Strong's Exhaustive Concordance of the Bible,* Hebrew Dictionary, #6662.

2. *Strong's Exhaustive Concordance of the Bible,* Hebrew Dictionary, #8549.

JANUARY 3

1. *Selecting the Right People is the Key to Successful Leadership,*
www.christianitytoday.com/pastors/2007/july-online

JANUARY 4

1. *Crime in Saudi Arabia,* http://en.wikipedia.org/wiki/Crime in Saudi Arabia

2. *The Awful Seriousness of Sin,* https://www.cmalliance.org/devotionals/
tozer?id

JANUARY 6

1. 7 Awesome Dog Videos in Honor of National Dog Day, ABC7.com/
pets7-awesome dog videos

JANUARY 9

1. https://en.wikipedia.org/wiki/Art_Schlichter

JANUARY 13

1. *Windtalkers,* https://en.wikipedia.org/walki/Windtalkers

JANUARY 15

1. *Praises,* Frank Garlock and Ron Hamilton, Musical Ministries,
PO Box 6524, Greenville, SC 29606.

JANUARY 16

1. https://familyshare.com/.../JustLetGo-8-incredible-stories-of-forgiveness-
that-will-touch-your-heart, August 20, 2015.

JANUARY 18

1. modernsurvivalblog.com.../why you should not blindly follow the rules
during disaster, September 10, 2015.

JANUARY 21

1. Stephanie Decker, www.dailymail.co.uk/.../Stephanie-Decker-Brave-
mother-lost-legs-saving-her children

JANUARY 22

1. A quick glimpse into what to expect from your 40s, brunch$columns...
www.hindustantimes.com/...quick-glimpse.../story-1msPVLnS0Szch

JANUARY 23

1. *Living Life With a Purpose*, Frank Sonnenberg,
   www.franksonnenbergonline.com/Blog
2. *Life Purpose, The Perfect Job*, theperfectjob.org/life-purpose
3. *Living on Purpose, The New York Times*,
   newelgege.blogs.mytimes.com/2014/06/03/living on purpose

JANUARY 24

1. *Royal Etiquette: Do's and Don'ts When Meeting Her Majesty*,
   Abcnews.go.com/Politics/international/story? Id-7228105.

JANUARY 25

1. *The Generation That Won't Grow Up*, AlbertMohler.com
   www.albertmohler.com/2005/04/.../the-generation-that-wont-grow-up
2. *Will You Grow Up?*, David Dykes, Discover Life Ministries,
   PO Box 131678, Tyler, Texas 75713.

JANUARY 26

1. *Scared Straight!*, https://en.wikipedia.org/wiki/Scared_Straight!

FEBRUARY 2

1. *Thanksgiving Day Race Organizer: I Can't Sleep*,
   www.Cincinnati.com

FEBRUARY 6

1. *In God We Trust*, en.wikipedia.org/in_God_We_Trust

FEBRUARY 12

1. *Wise and Foolish Leaders,* Psychology Today,
   https://www.pshychologytoday.com/blog/imcompetence/
   wise-and-foolish-leaders-Nove 30,2010-Stephen Greenspan Ph.D.

FEBRUARY 19

1. www.nationaljournal.com May12, 2014

FEBRUARY 21

1. Charles R. Swindoll, thinkexist.com

FEBRUARY 22

1. *How Do You Respond When Someone Has Offended You?*, youthspecialties.com

FEBRUARY 25

1. *Brilliance By Design*, Vicki Halsey, blog on 11-26-2014@
   www.vickihalsey.com

MARCH 19

1. *New York Daily News*, August 29, 2013.

MARCH 20

1. *Classic Sermon Manuscripts by Great Preachers*,
   Library of Classic Sermons, www.newsforchristians.com/classic.html

MARCH 23

1. Wikipedia, *High School Dropouts*, July 20, 2016.

2. *Bill and Melinda Gates Foundation*, Retrieved 2013-2014.

MARCH 28

1. www.biblearchaeology.org/post/.../He-Began-to-Send-Them-Out-
   Two-by-Two.aspx, Gordon Franz.

APRIL 24

1. *Strong's Exhaustive Concordance*, Abingdon Press, New York,
   Greek Dictionary #4103.

MAY 4

1. *The Hidden Cost of Heroism*, Christopher McDougall, Men's
   Health, 11-26-07.

JULY 6

1. *One Strike, You're Out*, https://en.wikipedia.org

JULY 7

1. The emphasis in bold is the author's.

JULY 13

1. *Burning Your Bridges Behind You*, Sermon by Johnny Carver,
   www.sermoncentral.com

JULY 16

1. *The Priority of Praying Together*, Lloyd Sulley, www.lifeway.com

OCTOBER 1

1. *The Washington Post and a Higher Military Standard*,
   http://isme.tamu.edu/JSCOPE02/Hedahl02.html

DECEMBER 9

1. Dr. Allen Barber, www.thebiblicalworldview.org/is-joel-osteen-
   a-false-prophet.

2. *The Bible Expository Commentary, Ephesians-Revelation*, Warren Wiersbe.

DECEMBER 10

1. *6 Reasons You Should Stop Listening to Joyce Meyer*,
   longfortruth.blogspot.com

DECEMBER 11

1. *The Bible Expository Commentary, Ephesians-Revelation*,
   Warren Wiersbe, p. 576.

DECEMBER 12

1. *Revelation*, Vol. 1, Paul M. Sadler, Berean Bible Society,
   p. 111.

DECEMBER 14

1. *What We Know About Heaven (and Hell)*, Mark Moring,
   www.christianitytoday.com

DECEMBER 15

1. *Being Worthy*, Marvin J. Ashton,
   www.lds.org/.../on-being-worthy?lagn

DECEMBER 17

1. *Murders of John and Betty Stam*,
   https://en.wikipedia.org/wiki/Murders_of_John_and_Betty_Stam

DECEMBER 20

1. https://en.wikipedia.org/wiki/Benito_Mussolini

DECEMBER 21

1. www.businessinsider.com/climate-change-out-of-control-wildfires

DECEMBER 23

1. LAPD Officer Donald Thompson Awarded the Medal of Freedom,
   www.lapdonline.org/home/news_view/60711

DECEMBER 24

1. LAPD Officer Donald Thompson Awarded the Medal of Valor by
   President Obama, https:..//wwwlapdonline.org/home/news_view/60711

DECEMBER 25

1. www.christianpost.com › world The Christian Post/Egyptian
   Christians Were Calling For Jesus

DECEMBER 26

1. thefederalist.com/.../anti-semitism-at-the-2016-olympics-is-
   completely-out-of-control/

DECEMBER 27

1. https://en.wikipedia.org/wiki/Mao_Zedong/Wikipedia

DECEMBER 28

1. www.cbsnews.com/news/white-house-lies-a-history

DECEMBER 29

1. https://en.wikipedia.org/wiki/Gulf_War

JANUARY 1

1. www.redbubble.com/.../2722449-what-goes-around-comes-around-a-true
2. https://en.wiktionary.org/wiki/what_goes_around_comes_around/Wiktionary

JANUARY 3

1. https//www.lifesitenews.com/...as-a-former-prostitute-and-madam-I-know

JANUARY 4

1. io9.gizmodo.com/9-ruined-cities-that-remain-a-mystery-to-this-day-1239294825

JANUARY 6

1. https://en.wikipedia.org/wiki/Battle_of_Waterloo

JANUARY 7

1. https://www.themarshallproject.org/.../seven-things-to-know-about-repeat-offenders
2. *Repeat Offenders, Parents of Murdered Children*, www.pomc.com/repeat.html
3. *Things To Come*, J. Dwight Pentecost, p. 548.

JANUARY 8

1. *Judge Isaac Parker, the Hanging Judge of Indian Territory*, http://www.legendsof america.com/ar-isaacparker.html

JANUARY 9

1. Adapted from Michael Paterniti, *The Telling Room* (The Dial Press, 2013), p. 175, Taken from *Preaching Today.*

JANUARY 11

1. *A King Returns to the Throne*, www.schools.ccps.k12.va.us/sites/tp/.../king%20returns%20to%20the%20throne.pp

JANUARY 12

1. *White-Collar Crime*, Falsifying Corporate Data, Enron Fraud, www.libraryindex.com/.../White-Collar-Crime-FALSIFYING-CORPORATE-DATA.html

JANUARY 19

1. *DeathQuest: An Introduction to the Theory and Practice of Capital Punishment in the United States,* Robert M. Bohm, p. 25.
2. http://press-pubs.uchicago.edu/founders/documents/a2_2_1s29. html *United States vs. Wilson*, wikipedia.org/wiki/United_ States_v_Wilson

JANUARY 21

1. *The Telling Room*, Michael Peteniti.

JANUARY 22

1. *At All Costs: The Stand of the 16th Maine at Gettysburg*, https://gettysburgcompiler.org/uncategorized/at-all-costs-the-stand-of-the-16th-maine-at-gettysburg/

JANUARY 23

1. *Success Requires a Singular Focus*, Inman News, http://www.inman.com/2013/02/04/success-requires-a-singular-focus/

JANUARY 25

1. Jake Peavy and Mark Sanchez ripped off in $33 million scheme, Jun...money.cnn.com/2016/06/22/news/ponzi-scheme-ash-naray an-sanchez-peavy/

JANUARY 28

1. *For Christian Singles Who Are TIRED of Doing the Right Thing*, https.//www.facebook.com/...tired-of-doing-the-right-thing/10151673598540446/

JANUARY 29

1. *I Was Confronted For Being Immodest*, Women Living Well, womenlivingwell.or/2012/06/i-was-confronted-for-being-immodest/

JANUARY 31

1. *The Greatest Truth You Can Trust is Not God Images, Love, Honesty, Nature or Spirit*, www.ecopsych.com/coretruth.html

The **BEREAN SEARCHLIGHT**
Studying God's Word, Rightly Divided

The *Berean Searchlight* is the outgrowth of a small church bulletin containing brief weekly Bible lessons by Pastor Cornelius R. Stam in 1940. Its publication has become the largest and most important function of the *Berean Bible Society*, reaching monthly into every state of the Union and more than 60 foreign countries.

The *Searchlight* includes in its mailing list thousands of ministers, missionaries and other Christian workers. Also, it is on display in the libraries of hundreds of Christian Colleges and Bible Institutes. The purpose of the *Berean Searchlight* is to help believers understand and enjoy the Bible.

**Send for our FREE Bible
Study Magazine today!**

BEREAN BIBLE SOCIETY
PO Box 756
Germantown, WI 53022

www.bereanbiblesociety.org

Growing in God's Grace

By John Fredericksen

The studies found in this book are intended to help any believer grow in their knowledge of key subjects in the Scripture. More importantly, we desire that each reader be assisted in their spiritual growth, considering how the Saviour wants to transform their lives by their yielding to the will of God, as revealed in the Holy Bible. May we begin in earnest a life long journey of growing in God's grace, and growing up unto Him in all things.

Paperback   96 Pages

Berean Bible Society, PO Box 756, Germantown, WI 53022

www.bereanbiblesociety.org

God's Meaning in Matthew

By John Fredericksen

Finally, a verse-by-verse commentary on the Gospel of Mathew written from a mid-Acts dispensational viewpoint! If you've ever been reading Matthew and asked yourself, "What is the meaning of this?" *God's Meaning in Matthew* is just what you've been looking for!

Paperback   **528 Pages**

Berean Bible Society, PO Box 756, Germantown, WI 53022

www.bereanbiblesociety.org

BEREAN BIBLE SOCIETY

Germantown, Wisconsin

The **Purpose** of the *Berean Bible Society* is to help you understand and enjoy the Bible. The **Mission** of BBS is to exalt the Lord Jesus Christ by proclaiming the whole counsel of God according to the revelation of the Mystery. Our **Goals** are to *evangelize* the lost, to *educate* the saved in "rightly dividing the Word of truth" (2 Tim. 2:15), to *energize* their Christian lives, and to *encourage* the local church.

- The Society publishes the ***Berean Searchlight***, a Bible study magazine that is sent out monthly free of charge.

- BBS offers a wide selection of **literature**, CDs, and DVDs, on various subjects to help believers grow in grace.

- BBS arranges **Bible Conferences** for the study of God's Word, rightly divided and to evangelize the lost.

- The BBS website offers free **MP3 messages** that can be downloaded for personal study or to share with others.

- ***"Two Minutes with the Bible,"*** is featured in newspapers across the country and is sent out as a daily email.

BEREAN BIBLE SOCIETY
N112 W17761 Mequon Rd., PO Box 756
Germantown, WI 53022

www.bereanbiblesociety.org